END OF THE FOURTH ACT

A Fancy Hornpipe by a Young Lady (her first Appearance)

END OF THE PLAY,

" *Bucks have 'at ye All," by Mr. Dalton.*

IN THE COURSE OF THE EVENING,

Mr. GROSSETE will sing a COMIC SONG.

After which, a PANTOMIME in One Act, (by Mr. DELPINI) called The

Life & Death of Pantaloon

Harlequin	Mr. AULD,
Pantaloon,	Mr. GROSSETE, (from the Theatre-Royal, Richmond)
And Columbine	Miss BRYSON.

To which will be added (compressed in one Act) the favourite Farce of

Lovers' Quarrels.

Don Carlos	Mr. WOULDSLEY,	Lorenzo	Mr. AULD,
Lopez	Mr. BARRE,	And Sancho	Mr. DALTON.
	Leonora	Miss BURTON,	
And Jacintha		Mrs. BARRE.	

BOXES 5s.—*PIT* 3s....*GALLERY* 2s.—*UPPER GALLERY* 1s.

Doors to be opened at Half-past Five o'Clock, and to begin at Half-past Six.

Tickets to be had of Mrs. BARRE, 5, Stafford-Street, Bond-Street, and of Mr. RICE, at the Theatre. where Places for the Boxes may be taken,

[W. Glindon,Printer. 48, Rupert-Street,Haymarket

HAYMARKET:
Theatre of Perfection

"The Little Theatre in the Hay": about 1768.

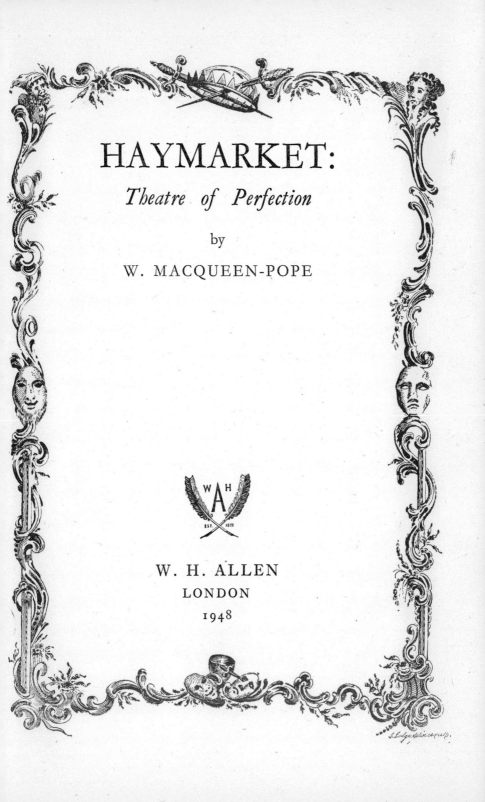

HAYMARKET:

Theatre of Perfection

by

W. MACQUEEN-POPE

W. H. ALLEN
LONDON
1948

Set in Imprint 10 pt. 1 pt. lead

Printed in Great Britain by The Camelot Press Ltd.,
London & Southampton.
Published by W. H. Allen & Co. Ltd., 43, Essex Street,
London, W.C.1

"To the WATSONS of the Haymarket, who keep
its traditions clear and bright."

CONTENTS

ILLUSTRATIONS

The author wishes to express his grateful thanks to A. V. Sutherland-Graeme, Esq., F.S.A., A.R.I.B.A., for the loan of valuable prints from his collection.

PRELUDE

(For Spinet, Harp and Violins)

IN the Haymarket, in the very centre of London's West End, stands the playhouse of perfection—the Haymarket Theatre—sometimes called Theatre Royal, Haymarket. That title it held, but only for the lifetime of one man, one of its most picturesque and exciting sons—and although his successor was allowed to carry on under an annual licence, the title died when he did. Nevertheless, the Haymarket is Royal —royal in age, royal in romance, royal in story and truly royal in atmosphere and charm. It is old, but it is ageless. It is the second oldest theatre in London; only to Theatre Royal, Drury Lane, does it accord pride of seniority. Otherwise the two march together as the twin theatres of glory in our great city.

It has not the vastness, the teeming throng of incomparable names, nor the Restoration glamour of Drury Lane. It has all else, however, that goes to make it a wonderful and fascinating playhouse, for it has much that is peculiarly its own, so much that is gracious and glorious that its story is as vivid, entrancing and curious as that of any place in London.

Theatre Royal, Drury Lane, was born great, but the Haymarket achieved greatness. It fought for its place in the sun, it set itself a standard of quality and a power of resistance which won that proud position it now holds. It was not the work of one man, or the result of some outstanding and electric events; rather was it the achievement of a never ceasing climb, often against what seemed insuperable difficulties, but always with a determination to give of the best, come what may. That is why its story is so fascinating, for it is pure "theatre." Its famous sons and daughters do not shine only in its glory, but add their own lustre to its tale.

The story of the Haymarket is typical of the true English tenacity of purpose.

If Drury Lane is the king of theatres, then the Haymarket is the queen. The two stand together in majesty of different kind. For the Haymarket is a place of fragrance, of silks and satins, of lavender and old lace, which has emerged from a stormy youth, as riotous and rakish as the times into which it was born, into a delightful, restful palace of the drama, with an atmosphere unique in these days, perfectly preserved and apparent to the least imaginative as soon as its doors are entered.

Here the past still lives alongside the present. Here is an up-to-date, modern, go-ahead theatre which is at the same time a perfect drawing-room, a place where you surrender to the lure of the play and cease to be of the outside world. A place where tradition endures and where the best of the old things will never die away and which by sheer example gives a quality and a gloss to all that happens within its walls. There is a glitter of diamond buckles, a sheen of powdered hair, a shimmer of silk and a whisk of fans at every turn of the stairs, in every nook and corner. There is a dignity without pomp, a sense of well-being hardly to be matched—a glory of the playhouse which nothing but tradition can give. The Haymarket has it all.

It is hard to imagine now that for years it was a battle-ground, where the fight for the freedom of the theatre was fought. It is hard to realise that this place, so serene, so tranquil, so essentially well-bred, has known riots, persecution, fights, upheavals and personal violence, where the military have been called out and where Royal dukes have led infuriated mobs to revengeful destruction. But as this story will make clear, these things happened here. Yet it was here that the true home of English comedy was created. It was here that new stars made their first appearances; here that so many actors, actresses, dramatists, and actor-managers wrote pages in the brilliant history of our stage.

For 226 years it has stood in the Haymarket watching life change as it passed by, but remaining changeless itself. It has moved once only during that time, a move so small as to be almost unnoticed. It moved from its original small foundation to the site next door and that was over 100 years ago. But it lost nothing by that slight shift. Its roots were untouched; it retained everything.

Now it stands, a handsome spacious building redolent of a handsome, spacious age, having little to do with the machine era which dashes by it, secure in its foundation of centuries, an integral part of the theatre of London and of London itself.

It has watched the Haymarket grow from a country lane, infested by footpads at night, to a busy thoroughfare, with a torrent of traffic coursing down its little hill. It has watched the neighbourhood change, and another playhouse arise to face it—a playhouse to replace that erected by Sir John Vanbrugh, who built Blenheim House, which became an opera house, the King's House, then changed into the Royal Italian Opera House and was pulled down to make way for another beautiful theatre, built out of money earned in the Haymarket Theatre itself, and a famous and smart hotel. It watched the Georgian age fade into the Victorian, the Victorian into the Edwardian, and back again into the new Georgian. It saw sedan chairs, hackney coaches, linkmen and huge lumbering carriages give place to cabriolets, hansom cabs and broughams. It saw horseback riders change their mounts to bicycles, and it saw the taxi hustle the hansom off the street, the brougham bow to the electric version of itself, and then to the limousine. It saw the horse-bus surrender to the motor-bus—it saw the whole world change whilst it remained changeless in spirit. It suffered from blast of bombs, but it mercifully escaped serious damage. It began as "The Little Theatre in the Hay"—it remains the Haymarket Theatre —Theatre Royal, Haymarket if you like, for it deserves the title.

Like most great things in this country, its beginnings were humble. It was not sponsored by a King's Charter. Its progenitor was a working carpenter, John Potter, who got little good by it. But, nevertheless, his theatre endured, and endures to-day. It has a cavalcade of great names, names which grace its story in particular and that of our stage in general. It has so often been the home of the dramatist-manager, as well as of the actor-manager. For in the palmy days of the theatre, the men in control wrote the plays and, more often than not, acted in them too. And of both these the Haymarket has had its share.

Its first great name is Fielding, who later achieved fame as a classic novelist. Macklin shines here, and that firebrand Theophilus Cibber walks its stage, but they make room for that extraordinary character (one of the Haymarket's priceless possessions), the great mimic-actor-dramatist-manager, Samuel Foote. Surely a more colourful man never lived, in the theatre or out of it, than this impudent, fearless, unscrupulous jester, who mocked the world, but truly loved his theatre —the Haymarket Theatre. He never rested until it became the peer of the great Theatres Royal, and this he achieved, though it cost him a limb to win it. Laughing at life, hating many and hated by many more, fearless of any but feared by all, he joked his way through his mortal span, and died with a joke on his lips. He is perhaps the leading man of the Haymarket story, being to it what Garrick, Kean, and Siddons were to Drury Lane, what Quin and Kemble were to Covent Garden.

And following Foote came the two Colmans, father and son, dramatists both. Two great stars saw their first London footlights during that time, John Henderson, on whom Garrick's mantle fell, and Elliston the actor-manager, the Great Lessee as he loved to be called, the super-showman who could gull his public, but who also delivered the goods.

Also the Haymarket can boast the most curious Shakespearean player in stage history, the West Indian amateur, "Romeo" Coates, whose brief but arresting career added to the gaiety of the contemporary scene.

And always the Haymarket fought its battle, the struggle against the overpowering monopoly of the Patents of Drury Lane and Covent Garden, improvising shifts and stratagems in face of persecution, but keeping its doors open and steadily growing in popularity, until Foote had it made royal—and until the power of the Patents were removed by Parliament.

Then indeed, the Haymarket started to create a new tradition. It set forth upon its career as the home of English comedy, a title which it holds, unchallenged, to-day.

But other names intervene in the story. Vestris was here; Macready, Edmund Kean, Phelps, Creswick, Benjamin Webster, J. B. Buckstone, whose ghost remains in the theatre he loved; Woodward, Bannister the elder, also Baddeley of cake fame, all played at the Little Theatre in the Hay. There was Ned Shuter, too, declared by Garrick to be the greatest comedian he had ever beheld, an odd character who was a religious drunkard, faithfully following George Whitefield wherever that divine preached in London. There was Weston, another fine comedian, and Quick. Nor must Edwin, another comedian who loved his cups, be forgotten. And here also was Miss Farren, who became the Countess of Derby.

They make a colourful company, these great ones of the Haymarket. In their ranks, too, are John Emery, Charles Kemble, Fawcett, Suett, Farley, Barrymore, Johnstone, Mrs. Mountain, Mrs. Davenport, Mrs. Gibbs, Charles Mathews the elder and Liston—the extraordinary droll. Old Dowton, the actor who would not be starred, caused a riot there when the tailors of London assailed him; Charles Young made his mark there as Hamlet.

Names like Oxberry, Miss De Camp, Mrs. Wood, Mrs. Glover and Miss Kelly shine in the Haymarket story, and like a giant amongst them stands William Farren. Charles Dibdin, king of song, wrote for the theatre. Ellen Tree, Helen Faucit, and Mrs. Stirling wove their golden threads in its tapestry. Barry Sullivan, Mme. Celeste, Miss Featherstone, Mrs. Howard Paul, J. L. Toole—these are also of the Haymarket company. Compton, the great Shakespearean clown, and Amy Sedgwick cross its stage. And there dances, for a brief time, that Perea Nena of whom so little is known, but who did so much to revolutionise the ballet.

Here played Edwin Booth, and here Edward Sothern created that figure whom so many believe to have been a real live person, Lord Dundreary. That story is a romance in itself. And here too the same actor played David Garrick in the play which afterwards Sir Charles Wyndham made so much his own. When Walter Montgomery played Hamlet here he had as his Ophelia a young and unknown actress, Madge Robertson, who blossomed and bloomed at the Haymarket, in the plays of W. S. Gilbert. It was here she met her husband, and, as Mr. and Mrs. Kendal, they wrote a chapter of their own in the annals of the English stage.

Ira Aldridge, the negro Othello, played at the Haymarket; Adelaide Neilson and John S. Clarke. . . .

Then came the Bancrofts, at the height of their glory, to finish at the playhouse of perfection, the theatre of their choice, their great stage partnership.

And after them came a young actor-manager who was to reach the heights, and who, as a result of his Haymarket management, built his own beautiful theatre, His Majesty's, over the way. The seeds of Tree's great Shakespearean productions were sown at the Haymarket. It also saw the production of *Trilby*.

Cyril Maude, still happily with us, and Frederick Harrison held it next, and under them it became more than ever our home of comedy. So evolved the Haymarket of recent times, and still romance attended it.

A company of almost strolling players, a family affair in the main, unknown outside the small playhouses of their native Scotland, came to this premier theatre to present a play written by one of their number, a play performed in dialect, and without a known name in the cast. The Haymarket, knowing their worth, gave them its blessing, and they swept to success.

A man who was a great actor and son of our greatest actor here showed that in him his father's genius lived on. He presented a play which was a first night sensation. But the changing fortunes of the dramatic world were against this man, whose bad luck darkened his whole life, and although he stepped into the small, select front rank, within a few months Laurence Irving went to a death as heroic as any role he had ever played, comforting his actress wife and cheering by his example those around him.

A Belgian dramatist's masterpiece conquered London at the Haymarket, where Maeterlinck's *The Blue Bird* was staged to charm and delight a sophisticated West End audience and sweep them to enthusiasm.

And it was on the Haymarket stage that J. M. Barrie reached his zenith, enriching the British drama with one of its loveliest plays, when Fay Compton moved all hearts in *Mary Rose.* And an almost unknown dramatist supplied it with a drama unlike its usual fare but which it made its own when *Ten Minute Alibi* ran for so many months. But it has never staged a musical comedy, although it has housed light opera and ballet. Although it specialises in comedy, the Haymarket is above all a theatre—and theatres are adaptable. Like Drury Lane, if it approves of you, it helps you. If it does not, it is merciless. But if you are really of the theatre, then it is your friend.

It is one of the most sought after and coveted theatres of our city, controlled to-day by the second generation of the Watson family, under whose loving care it remains the playhouse of perfection.

Small wonder that its staff spend their entire lives there; small wonder that every manager wants to produce and every actor and actress to play there. For this is a theatre in every sense. In an age which lacks a standard, it maintains a dignity and an air which only long tradition, long service and ancient lineage can bequeath.

Look at it from which angle you may, it dominates the street, that street whose name is a survival of a smaller, more intimate London. But though there is no odour of new mown or fragrant dried hay in the Haymarket to-day, just a few steps round the corner you are back in the eighteenth century. Your way to the Haymarket stage door, tucked away in a backwater where time pauses, is through a London which is of the past as well as the present—a London which knew leisure, wit and beauty. A sedan chair would not be out of place if you met one. Into it might step a lady, in patch and powder, attended by a gentleman as gaily dressed as she. With three-cornered hat under his arm, his white-wigged-head bows as she takes her seat, and he regales himself with a pinch of snuff as the sedan is borne away. Or a figure on horseback, gallant in frilled shirt, tight pantaloons strapped under his boots, might sweep off his tall beaver in salutation to you as you stepped through that unobtrusive stage door into the Haymarket Theatre, into a playhouse whose atmosphere has not changed in 226 years of crowded life.

Gone is the noise, the strident sounds of mechanism; gone the cosmopolitan mob of the pavements, the modern misses in trousers and the modern men in pullovers and corduroys.

You are back in a place of calm, quiet dignity, whose delicate features wear a welcoming smile, a place of leisure and peace, where a play may be enjoyed. It gleams, but with the patina of taste, not the glare of chromium. There is no braying of saxophones here, no jungle noises; this is a place for spinets and harp, for the delicate throb of the violin, for this is an English theatre keeping its English atmosphere in an English city which has lost too much of its native breath and custom.

Here, in the Haymarket Theatre, tradition lives on, the tradition of that quiet, unostentatious England which demands the best, makes the best and supplies the best. It does not shout its wares, it does not proclaim the super-excellence of what it supplies. It knows it has the quality and—you know it too, as soon as you enter the playhouse of perfection.

CHAPTER I

A PLAYHOUSE IS BORN

NOBODY knows to-day what induced John Potter, a working carpenter, to erect a theatre in the Haymarket in the year 1720.

He must have been conversant with current theatrical affairs, or his mind would not have turned to building a playhouse. Even in modern times, people who built and opened new theatres have had a good deal of difficulty to contend with; it has always been troublesome to put a new one on the map. Contrary to what might be expected, the public do not flock to a new theatre; they are usually chary of going there at all; even their curiosity does not impel them. It needs a very successful play to draw them, for the playgoing public are conservative and like the places they are used to.

But John Potter had greater difficulties than these. And he must have been aware of them.

He must have known that the Royal Charter—the Patent—held by Theatre Royal, Drury Lane, would stand like a lion in his path. For the Patent gave Drury Lane the monopoly of the drama in London, save only in the case of Lincoln's Inn Theatre, which also had a licence to perform plays, and which was, strangely enough, backed up by the Drury Lane Charter too. So even if the lordly Lane had considered Potter too insignificant, there was still John Rich, at Lincoln's Inn, to stamp out unwanted competition.

Potter must have been a born gambler—in other words, a man of the theatre—he took that risk without a qualm. Perhaps he had looked around him and decided that it was time London had another playhouse, and that he would give it one. He did.

In his day London was a small but growing city. Theatrically, it was limited. Gone were the old Tudor playhouses on Bankside, gone also were the Cockpit (or Phœnix), the Red Bull, the Blackfriars, the Salisbury Square—and the great theatre in Dorset Gardens, conceived in the mind of Sir William Davenant and built by Sir Christopher Wren, was decayed, derelict, and out of action entirely. From having a number of theatres, London had come down to two, surely in itself an object lesson to any speculator on the power of the Patent.

There was, indeed, one other theatre, away in the East End of the town, in Goodman's Fields, Leman Street, but that was no criterion for him. This was not the theatre in which Garrick first played, but an older one. It is first mentioned in 1703, when the following appeared in the *Observator*:

B

"The Great Playhouse has calved a young one in Goodman's Fields, in the passage by the Ship Tavern, betwixt Prescott and Chambers Street. It is a very good place in Rosemary Lane precinct, and I know no reason why the quality at both ends of the town should not have the same diversions. This will be a great ease to the ladies of Rag Fair, who are now forced to trudge as far as Lincolns Inn Fields to mix themselves with quality. The mumpers of Knockvargis will now have the playhouse come to them who were not able to stump it to the other end of the town on their wooden legs; the Does in Tower Hill Park and Rosemary Lane purlieu will be foddered nearer home this winter, and the sailors will have better entertainment for their loose coin."

All of which speaks for itself. Little is known of that obscure playhouse, which was evidently of low standing and which doubtless offered a type of entertainment suited to its clientele and was probably beneath the Patent's notice. Another—indeed, two other theatres were to arise in that same district, and were to make history, and both of them owed their existence to the theatre which Potter built, as will appear in due course.

Otherwise the town was poorly provided for in entertainments. There were, it is true, puppet shows, and there appears to have been a species of theatre in Litchfield Street, but it was probably only a room in which unauthorised plays were given by out-of-work actors or amateurs.

Potter may have seen the good business being done at the Theatre Royal, now in the hands of the Triumvirate, Colley Cibber, Robert Wilkes and Barton Booth. Old Doggett had already gone, driven out by politics, but the three actor-managers were on top of the world, despite their difficulties with the brilliant, if erratic, Sir Richard Steele. John Rich was doing well, too, at Lincoln's Inn Fields with that new thing called pantomime, which had arisen at Drury Lane in 1702. None of these worthies wanted any opposition.

Apart from all other deterrents that may have discouraged Potter, his most formidable headache must have been the fact that there was already a playhouse in the Haymarket where he proposed to build. Right opposite his site stood the King's House, built by the great Sir John Vanbrugh, which had been a source of trouble and loss ever since it had been opened in 1705. It had been the Queen's House; now it was the King's. It had never succeeded. It had been subscribed to by the nobility and it had held famous players like Betterton, Oldfield, and the rest. Its acoustics had been bad, but they had been rectified. One of its managers had fled the country as a bankrupt. Now it had gone over entirely to opera. Handel wrote for it and the best Italian singers were imported. Still it remained a burden to all concerned. In the very year in which Potter built, a Royal Academy of Music was founded there, and Handel was engaged to write a series of operas. The whole thing failed lamentably and £15,000 was lost.

The root of the trouble, of course, was the situation of the Haymarket. It was little more than a country lane, infested by footpads at night. One night two gentlemen, tempted there by a performance of Congreve's *Love for Love* played entirely by women, were set upon by thieves on their way home, forced to draw their swords and fight it out. That was only one case of many.

It is true that London was spreading, that Hanover Square and Grosvenor Square were in the making, but they were still the times when you either walked to the play, went by sedan chair, or even by coach. And so far as the City was concerned, the Haymarket was too far off for the playgoing cits, who naturally would not take the additional risk of hold-ups and bad roads as well when Drury Lane and Lincoln's Inn were so much nearer. Vanbrugh had tried to make his playhouse a rich man's theatre—and he had failed. Was there much chance for John Potter?

And there was yet another thing without which, in those days, it was virtually impossible to succeed in theatreland, and that was Court influence. It was all-important. Royal favour had given Drury Lane and the Duke's Theatre their Charters. Court influence—the Stuart love of the play which Mary possessed had persuaded William III to allow Thomas Betterton to open at Lincoln's Inn against Drury Lane. It was Court influence which allowed Vanbrugh to build his theatre-cum-opera house. It was the Court influence possessed by William Collier, Member of Parliament for Truro, which had got the great Triumvirate into the saddle at "The Lane" and it was his Court influence which made them take Sir Richard Steele into partnership later. The Lord Chamberlain then, as now, controlled the playhouses. But at that time this august official was amenable to a whisper in the ear from a great noble, and far more likely to make grants so requested. Indeed, he often got direct instructions as regards the conduct of the theatres from the very Throne itself. A friend at Court was extremely necessary—indeed, imperative.

John Potter had no friend at Court and, so far as is known, had no influence whatever. Yet, in spite of all these difficulties and drawbacks, he decided to build, and build he did.

The world of the theatre is a very restricted cosmos. What is known therein is deemed common knowledge. Doubtless Potter said to himself, "Outlying and inconvenient the Haymarket may be, but the public will always come to a good show well played." Many others have said the same, and often they have been right. But they had not the same trouble as Potter. He must have known what he was up against, and yet he went ahead and built his theatre. He appears to have been one of those incurable optimists to which the theatre of this country owes so much, and without whom it could not have survived; one of those men who believe that something will always turn up, who disregard the thought of failure and dream only of success. He founded a theatre which lives to-day, a theatre which fought against odds, struggled with terrific adversity and powerful foes, which overcame them all and has outlived all but two of its contemporaries and rivals—two which had the protective armour of their Patents to shield them. He started a theatre which stands to-day and which, like Cap'n Cuttle's watch, is "ekalled by few and excelled by none."

So, in the year 1720, when George the First, over from Hanover, was firmly on the throne, when the rebellion of 1715 was still a topic of conversation, and when the South Sea Bubble was bursting in ruin for thousands, John Potter erected in the Hay Market, as it was then spelt, a small theatre, little more than a barn, at the cost of £1,500. This sum included not only the building, but the decorations, seating and scenery and wardrobe, for theatre builders in those days did the thing in its entirety. They fitted it up ready for action, complete. All this Potter did at the extremely reasonable figure of £1,500. Even in those times it was still a very moderate cost for a playhouse.

He got it finished and then his troubles really began. He built it on the site of an old tavern, called "The King's Head," and a gunsmith's shop, owned by one Isaac Bliburgh, with the fine, resounding sign of "The Cannon and Musket." The King's Head Tavern was in the Hay Market itself, and the gunsmith's was in Suffolk Street at the back, so it extended, as it does still, from one street to the other. Years afterwards that site was again used as a place for eating and drinking, but different from the tavern which Potter pulled down. There it stood, his little playhouse, and doubtless he regarded it with pride. But he very soon discovered that the way of a theatre proprietor is anything but a primrose path.

His first problem was to get a tenant to open his theatre. He had no licence, no Charter, no Patent. So promptly he went off to the Lord Chamberlain and petitioned for one. But being a plain, humble man of no rank at all and without any influential friends, he got no licence. It was curtly refused, so his playhouse remained empty. Little did Potter—or the Lord Chamberlain—at that time realise that this small building might become great and achieve royal rank.

A licence being unprocurable, Potter thus had his theatre on his hands, an apparently still-born enterprise. He had to do something with it, and the best he could do was to let it out to amateur actors to show off their talents on its stage, instead of in the tavern rooms which had previously been their venue. And that sort of business was neither lucrative nor continuous.

But Potter never gave up hope. He believed in his theatre and he left no stone unturned. The unquenchable optimism which had made him build never deserted him.

However humble, the house was gradually becoming known, and it

was spoken of as "The Little Theatre in the Hay." Troupes of actors
and actresses out of work when Drury Lane closed for the summer
opened it "on spec." A few people came . . . but that was not good
enough for Potter. Then a ray of hope shone. Potter found a noble
client, no less a personage than the Duke of Montagu. His Grace was
evidently interested in the theatre, like most of the nobles of his day.
Also he was evidently of the opinion that they did things much better
in France, for he had apparently been to Paris, seen a troupe of French
actors and decided that London should see them too. It was not the
first French theatrical invasion by any means. French players had
been here before and generally they had met with much opposition. A
company had appeared at the Blackfriars Theatre in 1629 and had made
history, for they had introduced women to the stage and been pelted
off it for their audacious temerity. In 1635 a French company had
appeared at the Palace of Whitehall, sponsored by Queen Henrietta
Maria. They also had aroused public indignation because they were
allowed to play publicly at the Cockpit Theatre in Drury Lane during
Lent, when English players were forbidden to appear. And, later,
Charles II had supported and encouraged another French company,
to the furious indignation of his own company of players at Drury Lane.

But His Grace of Montagu cared little about such happenings. He
was going to show the town the cultural value of French theatrical
art—and maybe he expected to make a little money. Drury Lane
and Lincoln's Inn were obviously not open to him, so he arranged
with Potter to bring his company to the Little Theatre in the Hay.
There was quite a stir in the coffee-houses around Covent Garden
when, on December 15th, 1720, the patrons read in their daily paper
the following announcement:

> "At the new Theatre in the Haymarket, between Little Suffolk
> Street and James Street, which is now completely finished, will be
> performed a French Comedy as soon as the rest of the actors arrive
> from Paris, who are duly expected. Boxes and pit, five shillings;
> gallery, two and sixpence."

This was enough to set the town talking. The gossips of the day
at once got busy collecting more news, and soon it was generally known
that the company was to be called "The French Comedians of His
Grace the Duke of Montagu." There was chatter and discussion, and
doubtless the high prices came in for some comment. They were
considerably higher than at Drury Lane, where you sat in the pit for
half a crown and in the gallery for one shilling, and where a box seat
could be obtained for four shillings as well as for five.

No doubt some of the John Bulls immediately complained about being
exploited by foreigners, and made up their minds to boycott the affair.
But very likely Montagu and Potter knew what they were about. It was
the élite of the town who would patronise them, not the ordinary rank

and file of playgoers—who could not speak French, anyway. They were after the fashionables, who could speak that language, or who could at any rate pretend they understood it, and who would pay a high price because it would seem exclusive and place them above the ruck of common humanity.

It is likely, too, that Cibber, Wilkes and Barton Booth went into committee about this. One can imagine them talking it over at Drury Lane. Wilkes would probably be furious, Barton Booth a bit indifferent, and Colley Cibber careful and judicious, weighing the value of the opposition very carefully in the light of his experience. He probably came to the conclusion that it would do them little harm at the moment, because of the foreign tongue in which the performances would be given, the bad situation of the Haymarket and the high prices which would make a limited appeal. But it is also likely that he talked it over with John Rich as well, in whose curious mind the idea of building a new theatre was also taking shape. For only two years later Lincoln's Inn and the Lane formed a defensive alliance against the Haymarket. They drew up an agreement that neither would lure a player away from the other's theatre. They presented a united front against the Haymarket, and lists of players were compiled, like an inventory, each one being labelled either Drury Lane or Lincoln's Inn, and it was agreed there should be no poaching and no desertions. Colley Cibber knew all about desertions. He had experienced that sort of thing and always come out on top. The agreement was made on April 18th, 1722, two years after the Haymarket opened, but it was essentially a defensive measure against the new playhouse. The two established theatres said, in effect, to the public: "You want the best players. We have them." Naturally, it was a setback for Potter.

Neither the Lane nor Lincoln's Inn were unduly alarmed about the proposed French season, but it was causing talk. As so naively forecast in the preliminary advertisement, the rest of the French company duly arrived from Paris, and on the night of December 29th, 1720—or probably in the early evening—the Little Theatre in the Hay opened its doors with its first real production.

There is no detailed record of what the interior decoration was like, but it is known to have been quite plain and very small. As to the exterior, it was a squat kind of building, very much like a private house. It was two stories high, with a row of five windows to each storey, quite insignificant and quite undistinguished. When the audience entered the doors they were immediately inside the auditorium; there was no lobby, vestibule, or crush room of any kind. And all the corridors were extremely narrow, so that it was almost impossible for two people to pass each other. The sort of place that the London County Council to-day would condemn out of hand—and very rightly.

Playgoers in those days were not so squeamish. They did not expect comfort in a playhouse. It was as important that they themselves should be seen, as that they should see the show. Therefore the line of sight did not matter very much either.

We can imagine the scene on that winter's night in 1720, in the midst of the Christmas season, when the Little Theatre in the Hay Market first opened. The sedan chairs would be setting down their loads of ladies and gentlemen, the lumbering coaches would be doing the same, and the gentry on foot, probably cursing the weather, would be crowding through the door. Then, there would be a raising of quizzing glasses and a rapid survey of the new playhouse, with remarks varied according to taste, and a more leisurely and painstaking survey of the boxes, to see who of the smart world was present. That was the all important thing. The fops and the regular playgoers would be occupying the pit, the latter crushing into the middle, for they wanted to see and hear the play. The outsides were left to the ogling and perambulating young men about town, who came merely to show themselves off and to quiz the other playgoers.

The Duke of Montagu would be there, casting an air of dignity around him from his box, and receiving guests, whilst Potter and his family were probably in a state of considerable tension, for it meant much to them.

As regards the playhouse itself, what they saw was a plain building, with an apron stage, a ground floor all pit with plain backless benches running right up to the row of boxes at the rear. There were boxes at each side, and two tiers above the ground floor of boxes, but the topmost tier had boxes at the side, the back part being the gallery. The side boxes were actually on the apron stage itself, real stage boxes, and most of the action took place on that part of the "boards." The players liked to be on intimate terms with their audiences, and it was probable that if they played too far back stage they would not be heard above the din which obtained in the auditorium. There would be proscenium doors at the Haymarket, probably only one each side, which were used by the players for entrances and exits when the curtain which cut the apron from the main stage was down—and also for the purposes of taking calls. The curtain itself was not used to mark the end of acts, but only to hide changes of scene, and thus the action was quick and almost continuous. For if they started a scene behind the curtain line they practically always worked "down front" as soon as they could. The curtain was only used to mark definition after the epilogue had been spoken—between acts the stage was left empty—the characters got themselves off by means of "exit lines" or "tags."

Back stage the French players would be very excited. They were playing in a new theatre—and probably complaining of its inconveniences and the barbaric behaviour of the audience. The whole scene would be one of animation, bustle and excitement. And then, at length, the play would begin.

We do not know what was the size of the audience—there was no Samual Pepys or other diarist to give us a first hand account. Colley Cibber, who would have been so graphic and particular, never mentions this playhouse at all in his magnificent autobiography, though he has lots to say about its neighbour over the way. Perhaps he did not intend to give it publicity in any manner or kind.

The play was *La Fille a la Mode, ou le Badeau de Paris*, and the players were described as "The French Comedians of His Grace the Duke of Montagu."

But this first venture was not a success. Potter and his patron had counted on the support of the big people, the aristocracy and the cultured. They had expected to give four performances a week. But so poor was the support that soon they only played twice a week. The prices were obviously too high and the fare not attractive enough. So the prices were reduced. They came down to four-shilling box seats, half a crown for the pit and eighteenpence for the gallery. It probably cost His Grace of Montagu a pretty penny if he financed the French company. It must have reduced the unfortunate players to a state of penury if they were fending for themselves. It was a very bitter and costly pill for Potter. The season dragged on until May, 1721, when the Little Theatre in the Hay closed its doors once again.

Because of the French occupancy, it had become known as "The New French Theatre," which probably didn't help it with the very insular London public, who had a very poor opinion of their Gallic neighbours.

The next few years were lean ones for the new theatre and for Potter, its proprietor. Now and again the place opened for concerts and for amateur performances. Aaron Hill presented *Henry V* entirely with amateur support. Sometimes a disappointed dramatist, whose play had been refused at Drury Lane or Lincoln's Inn, would take a plunge and exhibit his slighted masterpiece at the Haymarket to a supposedly clamouring public. One of these daring authors had reached the advanced age of fifteen years (or so he said). He presented his spurned opus, *The Female Fop*, in 1723, with an amateur company. The two great theatres survived the shock and the audience stayed away in their hundreds.

In 1726, some venturesome spirit broke new ground by mixing up Italian opera with tumbling and rope-walking, the famous tight-rope exponent of her age, Signora Violante herself being the star. This lady did the stage a great service. She discovered a little Dublin slum girl who became the flaming genius, Peg Woffington. But her own evolutions on the rope did little good at the unfortunate new theatre.

In the year 1729, after the theatre had dragged along, unnoticed by the critics, by contemporary writers and historians of the time for nine solid years, success looked in.

It came, not in the form of a great actor or actress, nor in the shape

of a compelling new play, but in the person of a man called Johnson,
a dancing master from Chester. He took the little theatre and there
he staged an entertainment called *Hurlothrumbo, or the Supernatural*.
It was an extraordinary sort of show, with Johnson himself, who had
written it, playing the lead, a character called Lord Flame. Apparently
he supplied most of the action as well. We are told by a contemporary
that he did a great deal, "sometimes speaking in one key, sometimes in
another; sometimes dancing, sometimes fiddling, sometimes walking
upon stilts." But Mr. Johnson of Chester, although he did not know it,
was making history. He was progenitor of a line of actor-manager-
dramatists which was to exist at the Haymarket for a great number of
years—down to our own times indeed.

He did more than create a precedent with his oddly named and
curious production. He gave the Little Theatre in the Hay its first
success. For *Hurlothrumbo* and his own antics were evidently to the
taste of the town. The show ran for thirty performances, a very remarkable thing in those days.

Congreve's first success, *The Old Bachelor*, ran for fourteen nights,
Love for Love had run for thirteen, Addison's *Cato* only ran a month.
These were great plays with magnificent casts at the Patent Theatres.
Hurlothrumbo was a modest affair at a little, disregarded theatre in an
inconvenient part of the town. Yet it ran, without a star, without a
great name, for thirty performances. It goes to show that the playgoing
public of our Metropolis has not changed a bit. The bulls and bears
drew more on Bankside than Shakespeare, and now *Hurlothrumbo* was
to outrun Congreve and Addison. So much for art in the theatre. It
is the same old story that proves entertainment and not education is
what the masses wants.

Hurlothrumbo and Johnson must have gladdened Potter's heart,
who surely rubbed his hands and swelled with pride. Here was his
foresight justified. "Out of the way, are we? Inconveniently placed and
patentless, eh? A small plain barn of a theatre? My friend, it's all the
matter of the show. Give them what they want and they'll come along."
One can imagine him saying this to a crony—and of course, he was
right.

Few theatres have started on the path to success with such a strange
attraction as this *Hurlothrumbo*. The worthy Samuel Johnson from
Cheshire was perhaps a little mad, most certainly he was a charlatan.
It was the sorriest nonsense that he, dressed in black velvet and white
periwig, declaimed, and which his company ranted. A lot of it was quite
unintelligible, and when twitted with this Johnson had an answer. He
said he had written it himself with a violin in his hand and that no
person who could not play the violin could properly understand it. It
had an epilogue, as most plays had in those days, and this was written
by a John Byron, who had invented a system of shorthand and who was
also a rhymester—poet would be a misnomer.

The play was actually printed and the announcement reads: *Hurlothrumbo, The Super-Natural*. Written by Mr. Samuel Johnson from Cheshire."

> *"Ye sons of fire, read my 'Hurlothrumbo,'*
> *Turn it betwixt your finger and your thumbo,*
> *And being quite undone, be quite struck dumbo."*

Amongst the characters we find the following names: Scarethereal, Dologodelmo, Lomperhomock, Cademore, Sermentory, Lusingo and Cuzzonida. Yet it filled the Haymarket for a month and, what is more, a club was formed, "The Hurlothrumbo Society," with a members' list bearing on the front a picture of the monster described by Horace in his *Art of Poetry*.

The sort of play it was and its type of dialogue can be judged by such lines as "Pride is the serpent's egg, laid in the hearts of all, but hatched by none but fools," and "Conscience is an intellectual caul that covers the heart, upon which all the faculties sport in terror, like boys that dance on the ice."

Byron, who wrote the epilogue, evidently did not believe in the play, for in his private journal, which was published a long time afterwards, he leaves the following statement:

"As for Mr. Johnson, he is at present one of the chief topics of talk in London. Dick's Coffee House resounds *Hurlothrumbo* from one end to the other. He had a full house and much good company on Saturday night, the first time of acting, and report says all the boxes are taken for next Monday. . . . We had seven or eight Garters, they say, in the pit; I saw Lord Oxford and one or two more there, but was so intent upon the farce that I did not observe many quality that were there. We agreed to laugh and clap beforehand and kept our word from beginning to end. . . . For my part, who think all stage entertainment stuff and nonsense, I consider this as a joke upon 'em all."

So it seems likely that *Hurlothrumbo*, which filled the little theatre in the Hay and put it on the map, was something in the nature of an ancestor to *Young England*, that extraordinary drama which, a few years ago, drew all London to theatre after theatre (for it went from one to the other, packing them all) to laugh, jeer and join in the action. This extraordinary play was written in all sincerity by its author, who could never understand the reaction of the audience, but who kept it on and made a lot of money, as did the proprietors of the theatres in which it was played. It was only withdrawn when the audience at Daly's Theatre, its last home, got too unruly and invaded the stage, causing almost a riot and endangering the very licence of the house. There was, with *Young England* also, an informal Club, which attended performances, knew all the lines, joined in with the actors, called their attention to various parts of the plot and generally enjoyed themselves at the expense of the players.

And this strange play's forebear, *Hurlothrumbo*, was the means by which the Haymarket first began to take its position in the ranks of London theatres, an odd reflection when one thinks of the stately playhouse of to-day. It also goes to show that there is nothing new in the world of the theatre.

But, whether the public jeered or not, they came in crowds, the publicity was astounding, and Potter had every reason to be glad. As long as his theatre was open and talked about, it is unlikely that he troubled very much about the artistic side.

To him, a full house was the thing—just as it is to his successors in the theatre of to-day. But that March evening in 1729, when Samuel Johnson startled—and amused—London, was the beginning of the Haymarket's greatness.

Samuel Johnson of Chester did not stop at *Hurlothrumbo*. He continued a spasmodic career as a dramatist, and wrote other plays, which were performed at the Haymarket. One was obviously a sequel to *Hurlothrumbo*, for it was called *The Cheshire Comics, or the Amours of Lord Flame*. His Lordship had been the hero of the first epic. Produced at the Haymarket in 1730, it was only played four times. Johnson was at it again the following year, with another burlesque, *The Blazing Comets; The Mad Lovers, or the Beauty of the Poets*. This only survived one performance, in March, but under a new title *The Dramatic Everything*, they tried it again and it played three times. A new scene was tagged on and it lingered for a further three performances. Despite the madness of its title, the inspired insanity of *Hurlothrumbo* was not there. Or perhaps the management of the Haymarket—and the Cheshire dramatist—were learning the basic theatrical lesson: that you cannot do the same thing twice in the theatre and succeed. When Johnson crops up again, it is with a very different sort of thing and a very different sort of title—*The Fool Made Wise*—which had three performances in 1741, and was heard no more. Maybe Johnson himself was growing wiser, for his next contribution was a farce, *Sir John Falstaff in Masquerade* at the Haymarket in 1741, with which he scored only four performances. After that he disappeared from theatrical annals. Perhaps he went back to Chester and his dancing lessons again, to boast of his London successes and experiences.

We do not know to-day on what terms he had the theatre: whether it was his own venture, or whether Potter was footing the bill. It may have been a "commonwealth," where all shared the risks and the profits.

But at any rate, the Haymarket was striking a note of its own. It was staging, in the main, comedies (the basis of most comedies in those days was satire), either burlesques or comedies of manners which held to ridicule the morals and methods of the day.

Johnson's company played other things besides his plays—proved successes like *The Unhappy Favourite, The Orphan, Don Carlos,*

Venice Preserv'd, and *Oronoko*—in direct opposition to the Patent
Theatres, which had the monopoly of this sort of thing. Yet no action
appears to have been taken. It may have been that the shows were too
bad and the players too indifferent and undistinguished, or it may have
been that these plays were done in the summer, when the two great
playhouses closed down. At all events, there was no direct opposition
to the Haymarket as a theatre.*

But we know that Colley Cibber had his eye on it. There has already
been placed on record that agreement with Rich, of Lincoln's Inn
Fields. The Great Triumvirate—now nearing its end—and Master
John Rich were just watching points. The time had not yet come for
Theatre Royal, Drury Lane, to launch its thunderbolt at the humble
little playhouse—and not get too much good by it at first.

And the two men who were to begin the fight between the theatres,
the long fight which culminated in breaking the monopoly of the
Patents, are already upon the scene in London and already active in the
theatre. One of them is the son of Colley Cibber himself, the reprobate
Theophilus Cibber, about whom there is very little that is good to
chronicle, except perhaps a certain swashbuckling courage in respect
of the Haymarket—and even that had a selfish motive. He will soon
appear and his story unfold.

But there is another man as well, watching all this business at the
Haymarket, watching the success of *Hurlothrumbo* and the doings of
Johnson and his company; a young man destined to be the first great
name in the little theatre's annals, and to bring to it the first touch of
genuine fame.

He is a young man who has already won his spurs as a dramatist.
He has a brain seething with ideas, a facile pen with which to express
them, and a truly great gift of satire. Also, he has an empty pocket,
and the only means he knows of filling it is by writing plays. Here is the
Haymarket, a theatre which might be glad of him, for he is as yet not
famous enough to command a ready market at Drury Lane, or even
Lincoln's Inn. But the name he bears now shines with lustre in the
history of English literature, for it is—Henry Fielding.

* AUTHOR'S NOTE. Close to the village of Gawsworth, near Macclesfield, is a
wood, known to the local inhabitants as Maggoty Johnson's Wood. It is, despite its name, a charming place and in Spring a mass of bluebells. But in that
wood is a grave and in the grave lie the remains of one Johnson. On the tomb-
stone in still decipherable letters is recorded the fact that this Johnson was an
actor and that he was known as Lord Flame. It is doubtless the last resting
place of the man who popularised the Haymarket—and his odd behaviour is
enshrined by local lore in the description of the wood as 'Maggoty Johnson.'
How he came to be buried there must remain a mystery. The information
comes from the well-known dramatist Philip Johnson, who does not claim descent however from the Maggoty one. Incidentally Gawsworth was the birthplace of Lady Mary Pitton (or Fytton), the Dark Lady of the Sonnets.

CHAPTER II

THE CHALLENGE

HENRY FIELDING comes into the Haymarket story when he was only twenty-three years old, but already an acted dramatist. He was born at Sharpham Park, near Glastonbury, in the county of Somerset, on April 22nd, 1707. He came of good parentage, his father had achieved the rank of general under Marlborough, and his mother was the daughter of Sir Henry Gould, a judge of the King's Bench.

Fielding's early education was obtained at home. Then he went to Eton and later to the University of Leyden, in Holland, a famous centre of learning. He appears to have been a good student, and he stayed at Leyden for two years. Then his father married again and could no longer afford to keep young Henry in Holland. So Fielding came to London, where he had to shift for himself.

The change from the cloistral calm of the Dutch University to the crowded pleasures of London life naturally affected Fielding. Whilst at Leyden he had shown a love of the theatre and had even started to write a play.

Now, in Town, he went to Drury Lane, and to Lincoln's Inn. He met the fops and he met the players. He made up his mind. The theatre was to be his career. Its careless, easy, Bohemian way of life, its air of outlawry, its give and take, were all to the taste of a wild young man alone in London, free from trammels and control of all kind, and with the urge of his future greatness pulsing in his mind. He would be a dramatist; that must be his vehicle of expression.

The drama was, at that moment, in a pretty poor way. Congreve, Farquhar, Vanbrugh, Wycherley and the rest had deluged the Town with their wit and had used up, it seemed, almost every situation which could exploit immorality, faithlessness and profligacy on the stage. Fielding was no tragedian, and knew it. His gift was comedy—satiric comedy. It was therefore not a very bright outlook. Indecent thoughts, actions and words were the regular ingredient in the plays of the time, and they were wearing a little thin by constant repetition. But the young man was not dismayed. Few young men starting a theatrical career are ever dismayed by the thought of hardship, failure and heartbreak.

Fielding wrote his play and had beginner's luck. Young, unknown and inexperienced, he could not hope for much at first, yet he succeeded in getting his trifle—it was little more—produced at Theatre Royal, Drury Lane itself. That august playhouse had just staged *The Provok'd Husband*, Vanbrugh's unfinished play, completed by Colley Cibber. It had run with great success for twenty-eight nights. Wilks, the great

actor, had played Lord Townly and Anne Oldfield had scored a
tremendous hit as Lady Townly. This magnificent actress had moved
surly, fierce old Charles Macklin to say of her that "she appeared to
rush upon the stage in the full consciousness of beauty, youth and
talent"—surely one of the most vivid word pictures ever painted of
any player.

And this matchless daughter of Old Drury actually consented to
play in *Love in Several Masques*, Fielding's first dramatic effort,
thereby assuring it of a degree of success when it appeared at Drury
Lane in February, 1728. Fielding was grateful, and when the play was
published he paid tribute to the "civil and kind behaviour of Wilks and
Cibber." His luck was with him, indeed, for Colley Cibber, the great
actor-manager, was by no means tolerant of or helpful to most young
playwrights, promising or otherwise. But then, of course, he was also
a dramatist himself.

Fielding's second play was produced at Goodman's Fields Theatre,
in Leman Street, in January, 1730. This theatre, the second in that
district, had been opened by Thomas Odell, only a short time before.
He converted a shop into a theatre and engaged Henry Giffard, a good
actor and honest man, as his manager. Giffard afterwards got entire
control (when Odell was made Deputy Licensor of Plays, as will be
seen hereafter), and rebuilt or created another Goodman's Fields
Theatre, at which Garrick made his debut.

The second play of Fielding's was not a resounding success, but it
contained a plot which has been used many times since by successive
dramatists down the years. The play was called *The Temple Beau*.
A good, respectable country gentleman sends his son to study law in the
Temple. The young man studies Life instead, with loose companions.
His father arrives in Town and all the situations which have since
become familiar in farce are employed to throw dust in the old gentleman's eyes. But it added to Fielding's experience and standing,
although he was still too prone to write carelessly and not take pains,
on account of the facility of his wit and ideas.

No other opportunity was at hand, and Fielding, his appetite whetted
and with a sure knowledge now that he had a gift of satire at his disposal,
resumed his favourite pastime of knocking about Town, living as best
he could.

He had been lucky so far, but the big success of *The Beggar's Opera*
at Lincoln's Inn Fields, and the almost unbroken success of the
Triumvirate of Cibber, Wilks and Booth at Drury Lane, made it very
difficult for a young playwright to get a proper hearing, even with two
produced plays to his name. So he continued his Bohemian life, fre-
quenting the taverns, hanging around the theatres and visiting the green-
rooms, there meeting other of his kidney, dining with anyone who invited
him, drinking at the expense of gay young blades, existing in squalid
garrets, and always wondering from whence his next guinea would come.

It was not a good existence, but it was teaching him life, it was making him observant, giving him a chance to study characters which he was afterwards to draw for the stage. It made him fierce, reckless and not a little bitter, but it was breeding in him that gift of satire he was to use so brilliantly. He, a poor, needy author with a fire of genius burning in him, grew restive and angry at the poverty and injustice of the rough side of life, as he observed to his own cost how brains and intellect were at the mercy of mere purse-strings. But these things were to inspire him, did inspire him, and made him all the more anxious to get his plays produced—plays in which he might show the world the corruptness of the times. But plays need a theatre—and at the moment the Patent theatres had not the slightest use for him.

But it was never easy to keep Henry Fielding down for long. He cast his eyes on the little theatre in the Hay. There might be a chance there—he was already sufficiently of the theatre to believe that, if the play was right, the public would come, even to such an outlying and insignificant place as this neglected, struggling playhouse. He knew that it was monopoly that kept the Haymarket in subjection, just as it confined him. Perhaps a combination of struggling theatre and struggling author might succeed.

So to the Haymarket Theatre he went, armed with a play. It was *The Author's Farce; And the Pleasures of the Town*, and he got it produced at the Haymarket Theatre in March, 1730. Who was in control of the theatre we do not know—people did not bill themselves as presenters of plays in those days. Nor do we know where the money came from. It may have been Potter, it may have been a "commonwealth" or maybe Fielding scratched up some money from friends and influential relatives—he certainly paid much civil attention to Lady Mary Wortley Montagu, a kinswoman and perhaps a patroness. But whoever was in charge, Fielding would be sure to have the last word and the direction of his own play. Whether actors got paid in those days was a matter of little concern to anyone but themselves, and the small field of choice made the players take any risk.

Fielding was in the Haymarket and his play upon its boards. It was a farce, but a farce with a sting. He had begun to show his mettle, he had begun his self-appointed crusade on behalf of brains *versus* moneybags. He had commenced war upon privilege and vested interest, and was championing the under-dogs. In *The Author's Farce* he castigated the follies of the day. He denounced the craze for opera from overseas, which had become such a formidable rival to the English theatre. He poked fun at the way people ran after new acrobats and tumblers and puppet shows, at the expense of the drama proper. And, just to keep things fair with no favour, he turned his satire on the drama itself, ridiculing without mercy the flamboyant nonsense which held the stage all too often. Nor did Colley Cibber and his son escape the lash. Fielding saw things clearly and was not afraid to speak out. Here is a

sample of what he said in *The Author's Farce*, through the mouth of the
character Witmore, his *raissoneur*:

> " 'Sdeath, in an age of learning and true politeness, where a
> man might succeed by his merit, there would be some encourage-
> ment. But now, when party and prejudice carry all before them;
> when learning is decried, wit not understood; when the theatres are
> puppet shows and the comedians ballad singers; when fools lead the
> town, would a man think to thrive by his wit? If you must write,
> write nonsense, write *Hurlothrumbo*, set up an oratory and preach
> nonsense, and you may meet with encouragement enough. Be
> profane, be scurrilous, be immodest; if you would receive applause,
> deserve to receive sentence at the Old Bailey; and if you would ride
> in a coach, deserve to ride in a cart."

Plain speaking this, and pretty daring, seeing that it was spoken
from the stage of an unlicensed theatre, which existed simply because
the Patent theatres were ignoring it. But Fielding had no fear.

The play got talked about; people came to the theatre; it was a
success. This sort of stuff was new, it had a tang, and it was scandalous
as well. It could be chattered about in the coffee-houses. The beaux
went to the Haymarket.

In the second half of his play Fielding gave what he described as a
"Puppet Show"—there was a craze for them and he derided it. He
brought on the stage "The Goddess of Nonsense," who had with her an
"Orator on a Tub," who preached or spoke a ridiculous sermon or
oration all about a violin. This was a direct hit at a man called Henley,
who had set up what he called an Oratory in Lincoln's Inn Fields, where
he preached sermons of the most obvious kind on everyday subjects,
such as fish—proving to his own satisfaction that all mankind are fish
and live like fishes—and yet gulling his audiences into believing him to
be a man of wisdom. He was evidently the forerunner of Dickens'
immortal Chadband. But the smart young men now going to the
Haymarket recognised the hit and were delighted.

In the same "Puppet Show" Fielding scarified the usages of the
publishers and booksellers of his day, showing how they forced their
hacks to work for them. He showed how these unfortunate men were
treated, and how they were paid less than common labourers. He showed
also the shifts to which they resorted.

Fielding knew the state of things amongst the hacks and their
employers. He had not sunk to it himself, but he knew that sometimes
these poor slaves were better off than the struggling dramatist. He
despised them for their tricks and servility as much as he despised the
men who ground them down. Yet his own associates were men who
lived entirely by their wits, scheming where to obtain free meals, free
drinks and the loan of a few guineas. He knew all about living in garrets
and low lodgings. But he had independence of spirit and genius to lift

Above
Mr. Edmund Kean.

Above
Mr. Samuel Phelps.

Centre
Mr. Robert Coates.

Below
Mr. Farren.

Below
Mr. Henry Fielding.

Top right
Mr. C. Kemble as Romeo.

Above
Mr. William Dowton.

Above
Mr. Samuel Foote.

Left
Mr. Mathews as Gold-
finch.

him from the ruck. What he wanted at that time was the gift of concentration and the real desire to work, which the people around him made light of.

But be that as it may, he was bringing the people to the little Theatre in the Hay to hear his invective. And *The Author's Farce* was even played at Drury Lane, after he had touched it up and improved it. With Fielding as its playwright, the Haymarket was becoming quite a strong youth. For *The Author's Farce* was a success.

Now Fielding had found his feet. He had become the satirist of his time, the burlesquer of his day. Success, if not fortune, was flowing his way. He can only have made a bare living by his plays at the Haymarket, but his name was in everyone's mouth and he felt the reaction of fame. Success inspired him and he gave to the Haymarket a play which was its first resounding triumph and which was to hold the stage for generations, its topical humour being altered to suit the times. Indeed, this play was still being performed less than one hundred years ago, and there have been performances almost within living memory. If *Hurlothrumbo* had told the people where the Haymarket Theatre was, this play of Fielding's drew them there in crowds. Its title was *Tom Thumb*.

Produced at first in one act, Fielding saw its opportunities and lengthened it. He also lengthened the title until it became *The Tragedy of Tragedies, or the Life and Death of Tom Thumb the Great*.

As Vanbrugh before him had done in *The Rehearsal*, so did Fielding in *Tom Thumb* ridicule the stage and its ways. Sheridan did it in *The Critic*. If done brilliantly, as in these three examples, this theme seldom fails. And Fielding went for the stage bald-headed. He had much to satirise. He found easy targets in the stiff, formal, ranting, mouthing acting of the day, in the highfalutin and often meaningless repetition of lines which might at first seem resounding, but did not bear dissection. On the stage, they got as far from Nature and being natural as possible. The public was ripe for an upheaval. It was already showing signs of arrival, for to Lincoln's Inn Theatre a few years before had come an actor from the country, a grim, gaunt-looking, bad-tempered man with great ability, who dared to speak much more naturally on the stage than any actor of his time, or before him. His name was Charles Macklin, and the management told him he had better go away and learn a bit more about his job. For what the public wanted, they said, was the method of Booth and Quin, the latter perhaps the greatest of the old school of studied, slow, super-elocutionary and unnatural tragedians of the stage—yet its leading and most popular figure. It was what the public wanted—or had wanted. But Macklin thought a change was due, and so too thought Fielding. Both of these men were right, and were paving the way for the natural acting of great little David Garrick. Macklin and Fielding were to come together; that was natural. Meanwhile in *The Tragedy of Tragedies*, Fielding piled it on thickly. He burlesqued Dryden, Lee, Rowe, Thompson, all the great

C

tragedians. Nothing was sacred to him. And the public laughed and
applauded to the echo. The Haymarket was packed to hear the fun.
His parodies were magnificent, his mock heroics superb. Listen to the
fierce King's declaration:

> *"Let nothing but a face of joy appear*
> *The man that frowns this day shall lose his head*
> *That he may have no face to frown withal."*

And this further mandate:

> *"Petition me no petitions, sir, to-day*
> *Let other hours be set apart for business*
> *To-day it is our pleasure to be drunk*
> *And this our Queen shall be as drunk as we."*

There was a play by Thompson, *Sophonisba*, which, although a
pretty bad specimen of its kind, had nevertheless served Anne Oldfield
well. It contained a line which was probably a test one—it must have
needed good enunciation to put it over with effect. It was "O Sophonisba, Sophonisba O." Too good a chance for Fielding to miss. The
name of Tom Thumb's Queen in Fielding's play was Huncamunca.
That famous line became, therefore, 'O Huncamunca, Huncamunca
O." And it brought down the house.

Those who have applauded the original will laugh their heads off
at the parody of the same thing. That was as true in Fielding's day as it
is now.

The allusions were too easily recognisable for any mistake to be
made. All the town went to see the show and to laugh and applaud.
Fielding was now a name to reckon with. And *Tom Thumb*, by the
way, was the only one of his plays which survived for posterity.

Although he was packing the Haymarket and earning fame for himself, he did not settle down. He still frequented the green-rooms and the
taverns. He still turned night into day and took few pains over his work.

When he had to deliver a play he would stop up as late as possible
with friends, then go home and in the morning a scene would be ready,
written on the paper which had wrapped up his beloved tobacco (he
was a great smoker), and he would hand it to the players in that rough
style. He seemed to be more interested in good fellowship than in
literary fame, yet at the same time he knew what he was doing, and his
sense of justice spurred him on to expose public grievances and wrongs
he thought capable of redress. He might be pursued by creditors, he
might still be penniless and sleep where he could, but nothing daunted
him, nothing subdued his fierce spirit, and nothing dimmed his observation of the life around him. He had no money sense at all, a failing not
unique amongst literary men. But he was doing fine work, and he was
putting a struggling theatre on a firm foundation.

And still the two Patent theatres took no action.

In that same year of 1730—it was during April that *Tom Thumb* was produced—Fielding did yet another play at the Haymarket. It had at first the title of *Rape upon Rape; or The Justice Caught in His Own Trap.* This was produced in June, at first anonymously but afterwards under his name as *The Coffee House Politician; or The Justice Caught in His Own Trap.* This time he lampooned well-known figures in real life.

His central character was "Mr. Justice Squeezum," a clearly-drawn picture of the incompetent and ignorant justices of his day. And the day was to come when Fielding himself was to be a justice!

He must have known what pitfalls to evade. At this time, the magistrates got their income from convictions and committals. So, in his play, Fielding makes his justice say: "It is better for the public that ten innocent people should suffer than that one guilty should escape; and it becomes every good person to sacrifice their conscience to the benefit of the public."

Fielding was certain that, in his time at least, there was one law for the rich and another for the poor, and he said so in this play by putting these lines into the mouth of Squeezum: "Well, sir, if you cannot pay for your transgressions like the rich, you must suffer for them like the poor." That was the sort of thing which went down well at the Haymarket.

The actor who played this part was Hippesly, who was the original Peachum in *The Beggar's Opera.* He had no equal when it came to the delineation of knavishness or cunning, and in Squeezum he had a part after his own heart.

Much of the dialogue of this play cannot be reprinted. It was of a grossly indecent kind, designed, no doubt, to draw the attention of the Town to what depths the stage in general had descended. But it contained some gems as well. Fielding poked his fun at those politicians of the coffee-houses who always knew better than anyone else how the government of the country and the world in general should be run. Such know-alls still exist.

It is generally believed that Charles Macklin made his first London success in *The Coffee-House Politician.* He was cast only for a very small part, that of Poser, one of the friends of the Coffee-House Politician himself. Macklin played the part when the play was done at Lincoln's Inn Fields in December, 1730. The part of Poser was so short that he "doubled" and appeared as Brazencort, in the last act; another tiny role. But here he had the lines: "I was forced to turn her off for stealing four of my shirts, two pair of stockings and my Common Prayer Book." In the hands of a lesser actor these lines would have amounted to nothing. But Macklin did it so well that he made a great impression and got much applause. His name appeared on the bills as Maclean. Nobody worried very much about "billing" in those days, so far as the smaller fry were concerned, and the smaller fry themselves were much more concerned with getting their salaries paid than by seeing their names correctly spelt. Macklin used to boast that he made this play of Fielding's by his performance of this tiny part. But Macklin's later statements are not to be relied on. Actually, it had been a big success at the Haymarket long before it went to Lincoln's Inn Fields. But it is a link between old Charles, Fielding and the Haymarket, with which they were both to be identified in theatre history.

In 1731 Fielding supplied the Haymarket with *The Grub Street Opera*. This was a strange, jumbled show which had originally been called *The Welsh Opera, or The Grey Mare the Better Horse*. The action was mostly in Wales. It was one of those careless things which Fielding staged, with little trouble taken over it, and he laughed at the public for applauding it. He also did *The Letter Writers, or A New Way to Keep a Wife at Home*, which was only a trifle.

But now Drury Lane took a hand. It accepted a play from Fielding —*The Lottery*—and Fielding went to the great Patent theatre. The little Haymarket had served him well, and he in turn had served it well. That chapter came to an end.

But the Haymarket was now alive and kicking. It could, however, ill afford to lose its dramatist, but that is the way things go in the world theatrical—a season of up and a season of down. The Haymarket had been through what was, for it, a prosperous time. It had kept open its unlicensed doors without let or hindrance. A stormier time was ahead of it.

To understand the condition in which the Haymarket now found itself it is necessary to examine what was happening at the other theatres, and especially at Drury Lane. The great Triumvirate—that management of three which had brought such splendid times to the famous theatre—was disintegrating. Barton Booth, stricken in health, had retired in 1728. Robert Wilks died in September, 1732. Old Colley Cibber was left alone to bear the burden. He had had enough, he wanted to take his ease and rest—and enjoy the honour of being Poet Laureate during his last years. That was how Fielding got in; new blood was wanted. During the years 1731, 1732, 1733, and 1734 he was quite a regular Drury Lane dramatist. And other things were happening.

Booth had sold his share of the Drury Lane Patent to one John Highmore, in 1732. Mr. Highmore, of Hampton Court, had an income of £800 a year, considerable in those days, and fancied himself as an actor. He persuaded Wilks and Cibber to let him play Lothario for one night. His friends packed the house, and he presented the management with the elaborate suit he had worn on the occasion. He played, so he said, to win a bet which he had made with Lord Limerick, at White's Club, for £100. If the bet concerned his ability as an actor, he must have lost it, for he was a shocking performer. But if it simply concerned his playing—or perhaps going through—the part, then he won. It was this performance which led him to buy Booth's share in the Drury Lane Patent.

When Wilks died on September 27th, 1732, the stage lost its best comedy actor. His widow deputed an entirely inexperienced man to administer her share in the Patent. It was a sad day for old Cibber, who had really been the brains behind the concern. Now, tired and elderly, he was badgered by two amateurs. It was beneath his dignity. For once in his long and careful life, he made a mistake. He deputed his son, Theophilus, to be his representative and manage for him, whilst he himself withdrew from active participation in the theatre which he loved and for which he had done so much.

Now, Theophilus Cibber is the next figure on the stage of the Haymarket Theatre, and it is as well to have a good look at him at this juncture, as he makes his entrance into the story.

He was his father's eldest son, and if ever natal conditions were a presage of what was to follow, it was so in his case. For Theophilus Cibber was born in the great storm of November 26th, 1703, which ravaged all England. Throughout his whole life he was a storm centre and a maker of strife and trouble. He was to die in another storm, for he was drowned whilst crossing to Ireland to fulfil an engagement when the ship in which he and the rest of the company were sailing was wrecked in 1758. He came in storm, he lived in storm, and he died in storm. There is no good to be said of him whatever.

A contemporary described him thus: "His person was far from pleasing; the features of his face were rather disgusting. His voice had the same shrill treble but without that musical harmony which Mr. Colley Cibber was master of. Yet still an apparent good understanding and quickness of parts; a perfect knowledge of what he ought to represent, together with a vivacity in his manner and a kind of effrontery which was well adapted to the characters he was to represent, pretty amply counterbalanced these deficiencies."

Chetwode, the stage historian, tells us that Theophilus was educated at Winchester School, and that his strong genius for the stage brought him early upon it "where he appeared in full lustre in the various branches of Comedy, and though he has performed several parts in Tragedy with success, in my opinion the Sock fits easier upon him than the Buskin." During his career he wrote, or altered, some plays. The first was his own version of Shakespeare's *Henry VI* produced at Drury Lane in 1723, which attracted little notice. He did a ballad opera called *Pattie and Peggie, or The Fair Foundling* at Drury Lane in 1730. His comedy, *The Lover*, was well damned by the critics at the Lane in the same year. They were always laying in wait for Colley Cibber and they believed he, and not his son, had written this play, and treated it accordingly. But the old man had not done so—indeed, he had refused to see even a rehearsal, in case the rumour of his authorship should get about, which it did. But he wrote an epilogue, spoken by Theophilus and his first wife, Miss Johnson, a pretty good actress.

The Lover ran for six performances, four at its first production and two more the following year. So probably the third day of the run —the author's benefit—did not produce much, and it is likely that old Cibber kept it on to annoy the critics.

Theophilus had two children by his first wife, the Miss Johnson aforesaid—both daughters. He married again, Susanna Maria Arne, sister of the great Dr. Arne, who under the name of Cibber rose to be the greatest tragedienne of her time. When she died, Garrick said of her: "Then Tragedy died with her," but was careful to add: "On the one side." Cautious Davy excluded himself. Of all the tragedies in which Susanna appeared, her own life was one of the most tragic. She should never have married the flashy, braggart Theophilus. His own father opposed it, but when it was done he gave his daughter-in-law the training in the art she subsequently adorned so greatly. Her horrible husband, when they had been married for four years, threw her much in the company of a gentleman named Sloper. Then he brought an action against Sloper for having seduced his wife. It was pure blackmail. He asked for £5,000 damages, and was glad to take £10. He had another try in 1739, this time claiming £10,000 damages. For reasons which cannot possibly be understood, he was awarded £500, despite Theophilus's known character and the fact that his own father gave evidence against him. Perhaps, however, that was why he got so much. This thing alone is enough to show what sort of a man Theo was. But through all his life he was malevolent, nasty and mischief-making. His wife lived on with Mr. Sloper, greatly respected and at the top of her profession, and when she died she was buried in the cloisters of Westminster Abbey. Theo found his grave in the turmoil of the Irish Sea.

Young Cibber wrote a pantomime for Drury Lane in 1733, called *The Harlot's Progress; or The Ridotto Al Fresco*. He played in pantomime too. He leaves his own record of it. "I remember that, for want of a better performer, I undertook to be the Harlequin and, as few knew who it really was, I was received with more applause than I could have imagined. Nor was this my only success in pantomime; everyone who remembers *Dr. Faustus* at Drury Lane must remember the statue. All the pantomimical pantomimes of this magic statue had a good effect in that scene; they surprised, they elevated, they pleased and were applauded." Master Theo had a pretty good conceit of himself, and it is not surprising that his greatest success was Shakespeare's Pistol. He was a flamboyant, dashing actor, but not a bad one. And it must always be remembered that he was the creator of the immortal "George Barnwell" when Lillo's melodrama was first produced at Drury Lane in 1731. He fought a duel with the great Quin, who had spoken no more than the truth about his treatment of his gentle wife. They drew their swords under the Piazza in Covent Garden and were slashing at each other when they were parted by those standing by. Had Quin been left alone, he would probably have slain Cibber, for he was a noted swordsman and duellist. Not a soul liked the wretched man, whose dishonesty and shiftiness was always too apparent. His father had little time for him, but did not always get the better of the exchanges. He met his son once when that worthy was out of work and was issuing impertinent challenges to Garrick to play alternate parts with him, if he dared. Theophilus was arrayed in a marvellous suit of clothes. Old Colley eyed him over, and remarked superciliously: "I pity you." "You had better pity my tailor," replied the scapegrace son, who had some of his father's vitriol in his composition.

Theophilus got his entrée into Drury Lane management, as stated, because Colley Cibber would not argue with amateurs. At once he began to misuse his powers. He did understand the theatrical profession; the others did not. So he began to have his fling. He put on his own pantomime, *The Harlot's Progress*—based upon Hogarth's great contemporary success. The public liked it and it made money. But Theo was getting overbearing, farming out his father's shares to his own advantage, and already the amateur Highmore smelt a rat. Rather than put up with the son, Highmore decided to buy the rest of the Patent from the father. He got it, but at the cost of 3,000 guineas, an expenditure which lay like a millstone round his neck. And even then he found young Theo a very difficult gentleman to unhorse. Using his superior knowledge, he thwarted Highmore at every turn.

Highmore had been his own master for a bare two weeks when he found himself confronted with mutiny. His own company had been stirred into revolt against him, and as the rebels were led by Theophilus Cibber—as might have been expected. It was a real *coup d'état*.

The line he seems to have taken was to harangue the company on the disgrace of their being transferred from manager to manager like a lot of slaves, and to exhort them to make a stand in their own interests and for their own individual freedom. This was pretty good from a Cibber, whose father had just made 3,000 guineas out of the sale of the Patent, and whose proudest boast it was—and true at that—that he never had a written contract with any artist or tradesman, his word being good enough.

But Theo warned the players of the unqualified state of the new management and taunted that they would be at the beck and call of the man Ellis (or Ellys) deputed to look after Mrs. Wilks's share, but now made chief of staff by Highmore. Was a man like that, an outsider, not even a professional, to lord it over them, the players of the Lane— His Majesty's servants? Had they, the finest company in London, sunk to that? No, perish the thought. Let them rather refuse to serve, let them set up on their own, let them be their own masters. Actors then —and often now—were easily swayed, and they listened to Theo. The wily intriguer then put forward an idea. There must be a leader, there must be a captain—one who must do the thinking, take the decisions, and also take the blame. Well, he did not want to overpersuade them, but he was his father's son. They had known, trusted and respected his father, whose advancing years had caused him to leave them. If they so desired, but only if they so desired, he would take over the reins his father had laid down. For, he told them, he had a scheme, he had an idea, but before going further—had anyone else of the company a better suggestion to put forward? Of course, nobody had, and well he knew it. Actors have always had grievances, and until they formed a trade union recently were never able to get them redressed. They acclaimed young Cibber and listened eagerly to his idea. And it was—the Haymarket Theatre!

Said Cibber: "Let us fling off this foreign yoke and manage ourselves. We cannot at this moment take over Theatre Royal, for this Highmore and the rest have the Patent. But let us leave Highmore to sink or swim—I need not tell you which he will do—and let us walk out and encamp ourselves at the Little Theatre in the Hay. There we will stage plays, there we will show the public the best acting—for when we are gone whom can he get?—and when he is down and broken and eager to surrender, then we will walk back and take possession of Theatre Royal, Drury Lane."

Theophilus Cibber got his way. He and most of the principals walked out of Drury Lane, leaving behind only two players of note—Mrs. Clive and Mrs. Horton. The rest followed the Cibber banner and the battle which had been brewing for some time, Drury Lane *versus* the Haymarket, was joined at last.

CHAPTER III

INTO BATTLE

THE fight between the great Patent theatres and the little Haymarket, which hadn't a licence, was long overdue. The Haymarket had broken the law for some time, but the two other theatres had ignored it. It was doing them no harm. Probably they were wise enough to wish to avoid legislation, and here one sees the hand of Colley Cibber. He had ignored it, too, even in his wonderful Apology for his life—making only a passing reference to a "broken wit," by which he meant Henry Fielding, who had assailed him. Cibber was used to abuse, and big enough to ignore it.

But now lesser people were in the saddle and the Drury Lane players themselves had revolted against their own house. They chose as their headquarters of assault that same little theatre in the Hay which had for so long existed on sufferance. The tables were turned and the Haymarket was now the attacker.

The revolt of the players was the chief topic of town talk, and town talk was all important in those days of few newspapers. Sides were taken. Those who sympathised with the actors pointed out that they were free people, not to be sold with the Patent like so many black slaves. That was true enough, but they had no contracts at all. There was only the word of the Triumvirate as to their employment. That had always been good enough. The revolt was entirely fostered by Theophilus Cibber, and was to serve his own ends. The players would never have acted without him. But having taken the step, the battle was well and truly joined. Thus in 1733 the town buzzed with the affair. A print was issued by Laguerre (a most appropriate name) which showed Theo Cibber as Pistol posturing and gesticulating, as was his wont, at the head of his army of players. There is a waving banner inscribed "Liberty and Property." Highmore of Drury Lane exhibits a scroll on which is written, "It cost £8,000," and he is supported by a tough-looking customer in his shirt-sleeves, armed with a single stick, symbolic, no doubt, of Highmore's determination to fight it out. It is probably meant for Ellis (or Ellys), the obnoxious general manager. Behind Highmore stands Mrs. Wilks, in her widow's weeds, with her daughter, and carrying a banner, on which is the legend, "We'll starve 'em out." And in the rear is a crowd of people with donkeys' ears, representing, no doubt, the many shareholders (or renters, as they were called) in the Patent. Aloft, and godlike, pointing at Highmore, Colley Cibber surveys the scene, with his lap full of money bags. This print enjoyed much popularity.

Meanwhile both parties were busy, but Theo was the busiest of the lot. He sent to Potter at the Haymarket a proposition. Things had not been too prosperous with Potter since Fielding left. There is no record of how he carried on, but it was doubtless in a very hand-to-mouth fashion, with long closures and short seasons with very in-different, otherwise unemployed actors. Here was a chance. Here was Theophilus Cibber, at the head of the best of the company from Drury Lane. Here was the town agog over the revolt and likely to support the rebels—at any rate to crowd in for a time. Here was a chance not to be missed. Potter doubtless knew all about Theo Cibber, but he had also by this time learned a good deal about theatrical management too, and had gathered the truth of Shakespeare's dictum about the tide in the affairs of men. It has special application to those who run playhouses.

He soon came to agreement with the revolters, although on what terms is not known. The Haymarket was now to be a real battleground.

Cibber and his company got together their productions, their wardrobe and all the things they wanted. But they did a bit of publicity too. They took a booth at Bartholomew Fair to air their grievances further, to let the public have a taste of their quality now they were free, and possibly to get some new recruits. They succeeded in all these things. They now protested that they had taken a lease of Drury Lane, but had been excluded by the sharp practice of Highmore, who was out for nothing but money. Thus the old bogy of commercialism in the theatre raised its head.

It may be thought strange that players of such standing should perform at Bartholomew Fair, which was as tough and rough as it was popular, and that prestige would be lost thereby. But it was the custom of all prominent actors and managers to take a pitch and give per-formances there. Colley Cibber had done it; they had all done it. The first stage celebrity not to do so was David Garrick, who was regarded as a snob for his abstention. But David was wise out of his generation.

Anyway, at the booth at Bartholomew Fair Cibber Junior began the fight. He tells us that he gained some recruits. He states that he appeared in person, to throw defiance in the teeth of Drury Lane, and he hung out, as his banner, a print of "The Stage Mutiny," adding to it the slogan, "We Eat." This was obviously in reply to Mrs. Wilks's "We'll Starve 'Em out."

The chief recruit that Theo gained was Milward, a good actor, who came to him from Lincoln's Inn, having quarrelled with Rich.

But the Patentees had not been idle. Highmore had staged *Æsop*, with an extra scene by Vanbrugh which dealt with a former stage mutiny. It was felt that this would discredit the rebels, but the rebels laughed. Next Drury Lane staged *An Author's Farce*. This was Fielding's play from the Haymarket itself, so Highmore was trying to turn the tables. But Theo remarked on this: "They next attacked us by another old, worn-out, rhapsodical affair of one Fielding, called *The Author's Farce*, in which I and my father were daily ridiculed. But all this I laughed at in my sleeve, well considering that joking on the Cibbers could not hurt us." Theo knew a good deal about publicity. In September, however, Cibber returned the fire and unmasked his guns at the Haymarket. His comment is: "We opened with *Love for Love*, and got up all the strongest plays with a diligent expedition. Our company consisted of the old veterans, who were allowed by the town to be greatly superior to our antagonists; for, excepting Mrs. Clive and Mrs. Horton, there was not one of their company but was the contemptible refuse of the theatre. We had also received an additional force by receiving Mr. Milward, who, having left Mr. Rich in some disgust, joined our forces."

Theophilus Cibber does well in excluding Mrs. Clive and Mrs. Horton from what he so tersely describes as "the refuse of the theatre." For Mrs. Clive was Kitty Clive herself, and Mrs. Horton was the successor to the great Nance Oldfield. She was chosen for this by Wilks himself, who suffered much when Oldfield died, as they had played together so often. Mrs. Horton was best in Millamant and Estifania; it was said, indeed, that she was the only copy that could remain of that excellent original. She had a plain face and a bad voice, but she overcame these drawbacks by her acting, and was justly a great favourite. It is remarkable, too, that in this licentious period she had a spotless reputation.

Piquancy is provided in this theatre battle by Fielding, who is now on the side of Drury Lane as against the Haymarket, which had brought him fame. In a Prologue he wrote for his *Intriguing Chambermaid* at Drury Lane in 1733, he pays Kitty Clive a very high tribute, and strikes a blow for the Patentees against the players:

"In the present dispute between the players and the Patentees, 1733, the part you have maintained is so full of honour that had it been in higher life, it would have given you the reputation of the greatest heroine of the age. You looked on the case of Mr. Highmore and Mrs. Wilks with compassion; nor would any promise or views of interest sway you to desert them; nor have you scrupled any fatigue (particularly the part which, at so short warning you undertook in this farce) to support the cause of those whom you imagined injured and distressed; and for this you have been so far from endeavouring to exact an exorbitant reward from persons little able to afford it, that I have known you offer to act for nothing rather than the patentees should be injured by the dismission of the audience. In short, if honour, good gratitude and good sense, joined with the utmost entertaining humour, wherever they are found, are titles to public esteem, I think you may be sure of it."

These words give an insight into the straits to which Theo and his deserting company had reduced the great Theatre Royal. Fielding speaks of Kitty Clive's actions saving "the dismission of an audience."

That meant that so few people had paid for admission that it was cheaper for the management to return the money, send the audience away and close down for the night. To such a pass had things come at Old Drury owing to the rebels at the little, despised Haymarket.

Now to examine the opposing forces at that theatre. Cibber had with him, amongst others, Mills, Johnson, Miller, Griffin, Harper, and Milward with Mrs. Heron as leading lady.

Of Mills, old Victor, the prompter, spoke highly.

Johnson was a first-class, all-round comedian of the Noakes school.

Miller was a more high-spirited comedian, who could assume a strong Irish brogue, more to the liking of an English audience than the real thing.

Griffin was Benjamin Griffin, a good, all-round actor.

Harper was the low comedian, and a famous Falstaff at Drury Lane. When they played *Henry IV* there, with Booth as Hotspur, Wilks as the Prince, Cibber as Glendower and Harper as Falstaff, they always packed the place. Harper played the part more frequently than Quin, one of the great Falstaffs of all time, but never made quite such a deep impression.

Mrs. Heron was a fine actress who, with Mrs. Horton, had shared the Oldfield roles when that great woman passed on.

Milward was at this time at the beginning of his career. Born in 1703, he was like Garrick, a native of Lichfield. He was educated at Uttoxeter, and his great grandfather, Sir Thomas Milward, had raised a troop of horse for Charles I. At fifteen his father brought him to London and apprenticed him to an apothecary in Norfolk Street, Strand. Later he reached great heights as an actor; he was the Bassanio to Macklin's Shylock, and the Lusignan in *Zara*. He died at the early age of forty.

John Potter must have been rubbing his hands over all this theatrical strife. He could see good coming to himself. For the first time his little theatre housed a company of stars, some of the most distinguished in Town. The Haymarket was redecorated as much as possible and made smart for the large audiences who were attracted by "The Company of the Revels," as Theo Cibber called his troupe. Potter doubtless smelt success; he saw his theatre the equal of the Patent Theatres and probably had a rosy vision of a Patent for himself. And these things he might have obtained had anyone but Theophilus been in charge. Where that young man had power, there could be no good, no stability, no cohesion and precious little honesty.

Meanwhile the battle raged. Pamphlets and counter-pamphlets were issued, arguments ran high in the coffee-houses, but on the whole there was more sympathy for the players than the Patentees at Drury Lane.

Theophilus Cibber delivered addresses from the stage of the little Haymarket, a thing to which he was prone, and pleaded his cause. He placed a scroll with the word "Conabimur" upon it over the stage. He set up in its walls, he said, the "Standard of Liberty." Cibber crusaded better than he knew. This fight, which he was waging from purely selfish reasons, was the first of a long series of blows that eventually led to the breaking of the power of the Patents.

For a hundred nights did this battle rage, and success lay mostly with the Haymarket. It was a battle, not only between privilege and free enterprise, but also a contest between actor-manager and a purely commercial manager. Had that actor-manager been any other than Theophilus Cibber, there is no knowing what might have happened. Drury Lane had declined under Christopher Rich, an attorney; Lincoln's Inn had ascended under Betterton and young Rich, both born to the stage. Drury Lane had reached to its great heights under the control of Cibber, Wilks, Doggett and Booth, actor-managers all, and now it was failing miserably under Highmore, an amateur who looked upon it as a business. It took Garrick, another actor-manager, to put it on its feet again.

Despite the fact that the Haymarket was crowded, there was always trouble. Theophilus's mischievous and malicious mind provoked strife. They played *The Fall of Mortimer*, a great satire against Court favourites. They probably overplayed it, for constables came down with warrants for the arrest of the actors, which somehow they managed to evade. They staged a pantomime called *Love Runs All Dangers*. In this they made pointed references to the Excise Act, which the Prime Minister, Sir Robert Walpole, was bringing before Parliament. They libelled Walpole openly. He went down to the theatre himself, heard the words spoken, and dashed back stage, demanding of the prompter to know if the words were really in the script. On being assured they were not, but that the actor had "gagged" them, he gave the player a sound drubbing with his cane. The beaten actor's name is not on record, but it was undoubtedly Theo who should have received the thrashing. What a situation! What a picture of the times! A Prime Minister of England going back stage and beating up an actor for cracking jokes about him. That was the sort of thing which occurred whilst Cibber Junior was in command at the Haymarket.

He did one grand thing, however. He gave Mrs. Pritchard, the finest Lady Macbeth until Sarah Siddons arose, her first West End chance. She graduated to the Haymarket from booths such as those at Bartholomew Fair.

Business continued good at the Haymarket, but internal dissension was creeping in, as might be expected under such leadership, and Theatre Royal, Drury Lane, was preparing its long-delayed thunderbolt—the legal aspect of its Royal Patent.

The Patentees tried gentle means at first—just a threat of action to come if their warning was neglected. In this action, Highmore was joined by Rich of Covent Garden, which he had recently opened, for the warning letter was signed by Mrs. Wilks, John Highmore, John

Ellys and John Rich. It was sent to Mills—Cibber was ignored—
and the company at the Haymarket, and it read:

"We have been daily in hopes that the mediation of friends would
have put an end to the differences, and we are unwilling to take such
methods as the law prescribes, assuring you we are willing to do
whatever is reasonable. But if you persevere we shall proceed, as the
law directs, to support the Patents."

There was nobody in authority at the theatre when this letter was
delivered by hand, so it was taken to Mills's house. It was obvious that
the move had been foreseen, for in two hours the letter was returned to
Drury Lane unopened.

It was readdressed, this time to Theophilus Cibber, no doubt on a
lawyer's advice. This time an answer came. Theophilus meant to draw
the fire on himself and get all the glory: he would take evasive action if
it got too hot, as he well knew how. But in this instance his attitude
was calm strength and defiance. He replied that he was advised that
what he was doing was perfectly legal, and he knew that it was reasonable and that therefore he would not dream of changing his position for
servitude.

The Patentees of Drury Lane and Covent Garden now had no
option but to press their case legally. Rich would be as anxious as
Highmore, for he had only just got his new playhouse in Bow Street
open, and he wanted as little competition as possible. He knew, as
Highmore knew, that he and Drury Lane must now be rivals to each
other, but in this instance they must stand together to crush the
Haymarket. So they issued a summons against the Company of the
Revels to appear before a bench of justices and answer as to why they
dared give performances of plays in public in defiance of the Royal
Patents held by the two great theatres, who by virtue of those patents
had the sole rights for London for the playing of the drama.

They included the management of Goodman's Fields Theatre, in
far-off Leman Street, in the summons as well, just to show their
power and prove they meant no nonsense.

Now this business of a Royal Patent is a very complicated affair.
There had been so many transferences, so much trouble, so much
sub-division of rights and part rights, that the case was a very nice one
for a cunning lawyer. So much dust was thrown, such legal arguments
were raised, that it is not surprising the justices could come to no
decision. They fell back on questioning the validity of the summons, and
dismissed the case. Round 1 to Cibber and the Haymarket—and the
unexpected ally in Goodman's Fields.

The publicity gained filled the Haymarket at every performance and
emptied Drury Lane. Cibber went a step further. By some means, he
actually obtained a licence to perform at the Haymarket.

This was a blow to Highmore, who was already in deep water. It was pretty serious for Rich as well. If such things could be, then the value of their Patents was at an end. They took a desperate step in a desperate moment. They actually challenged the Crown itself as to its right to issue a playing licence in opposition to a Patent. And, to precipitate matters, they made a false move.

Their course of action was to arrest the Haymarket Company as a vagrant for acting without a Patent. They selected one player as a test.

The victim was Harper, the fat jolly actor and splendid portrayer of Falstaff. A worse choice could not have been made, although at first it succeeded.

Harper was haled before Sir T. Clarges at St. George's Vestry, where the previous case had been heard. No counsel were present that day, which was November 12th. The magistrate took it upon himself to commit Harper to Bridewell as a vagrant and to give him hard labour, mentioning that his bulk seemed to fit him as little for this as it did his vagrancy.

Even the vicious mind of Cibber revolted against this stupid sentence. Harper a vagrant? He was a most respectable man, with a house in Westminster (actually in the parish of St. Paul, Covent Garden), valued at £50, and was a freeholder in Surrey. A vagrant was someone who wandered about to do his playing. Harper did no wandering. Why, he even had a vote. Yet he lost the case. The sentence gave rise to the greatest public indignation. It was openly asked why Harper had been singled out when there were plenty of the other members of the company who were not of his substance and standing, and who might well have been legally described as vagrants. The idea got abroad that wires were being pulled and that Harper was chosen to give weight to a cooked-up verdict.

It was not allowed to rest there. Trust Cibber for that. The case went before the Lord Chief Justice Yorke on November 20th, 1733, and was argued by six counsel on either side. The Lord Chief Justice listened to the arguments, granted Harper bail in his own recognisances and ordered a feigned issue to try the validity of the commitment. The result was awaited with avidity, and crowds congregated to hear the judgment. The Court found in Harper's favour. Amidst cheering and shouting, the actor was escorted home in triumph by his friends. The Haymarket had won all along the line.

The trial broke Highmore. Never a man of much wealth, bad business and costly legal proceedings had straitened him financially. He was, however, a man of his word, and kept it, no matter what it cost him.

All this while he was fighting another lawsuit. For when Cibber and his company left Drury Lane they laid a suit against Highmore for ejection and this came up for trial the same day as Harper was acquitted. To everyone's surprise, and probably their own as well, Cibber and

Company won that too. But there was a legal catch in it. They could
have a lease of Drury Lane, but Highmore must hold the Patent.
Consequently, neither could move without the other. It was stalemate
for all except Highmore's pocket.

It was a hollow victory too, for on November 28th the Company of
the Revels at the Haymarket Theatre were ordered by His Majesty's
Court of Justice to return to Drury Lane.

Here was a fine state into which Cibber had led them. They were
to go back to the Lane, still under Highmore, after all their trouble.
Thus they were no better off than if they had never revolted at all.

Mills, Harper and some of the others, no longer young, were tired
of all these alarums and excursions. Although they had filled the
Haymarket, the house was too small to bring salaries up to their
expectations or to the fine promises of Master Theo. They began to
realise he had used them for his own purpose—to upset the Drury Lane
management so that he himself would finally have to be called back
and put in charge once more. They were a bit ashamed of themselves.

But the artful Cibber was fully aware of what was passing in their
minds. He had wit enough to keep his head and to get them to agree
to his being their representative to fix the new terms with Drury Lane.
He persuaded them that he was much more used to this sort of thing
than they were, and had a more astute mind, which was true. And they
agreed.

So Cibber had the supreme glory of meeting Highmore alone as
the plenipotentiary for signing peace. It must be admitted he did
a good job—for himself as well as the players. And back to the Lane
they all went.

The chief sufferer, of course, was the Little Theatre in the Hay.
Potter, who had cherished such high hopes, whose house had been
filled and whose stage had been graced by fine actors, was back where he
started. Indeed, he was worse off. Up to the Cibber interlude, the
Patent theatres had ignored him. Now they had shown their teeth,
and he knew they would watch him like a cat watching a mouse.
What was he going to do for the Haymarket, which had won battles,
but lost the war?

Fortunately, a change in the management at Drury Lane once again
helped the Haymarket. Highmore had given up, defeated and ruined.
He had sold out to one Fleetwood, a man about town, who got Highmore's share for half-price. He knew as little about running the theatre
as did his predecessor and he made the initial mistake of appointing the
glib, rascally Theophilus Cibber his stage manager. That way ruin
lay, as later he was to find out.

But the change of management also disturbed an old friend of the
Haymarket who had left it for Drury Lane and who had stood by
Highmore. It disturbed Henry Fielding. There was no room for him
and for Cibber in the same theatre. Cibber had left the Haymarket

INTERIOR *OF THE* LITTLE THEATRE. *HAYMARKET.*

FRONT *OF THE* ABOVE.

The interior and exterior of the Little Theatre in the Haymarket as they
appeared about 1815.

Right
Mr. Vanderhoff as
Coriolanus.

Below
Mr. Ira Aldridge as
Mungo.

Mr. Macklin as Shylock in
The Merchant of Venice.

for the Lane? Right, Fielding would leave the Lane for the Haymarket. And he did.

This time Fielding came to the Haymarket, not simply as dramatist, but as manager too. He had found backing, he had gathered together some "adventurers," as theatrical speculators were so rightly called in those days, and he assumed entire control.

He knew what he was up against. He had watched the scales being weighted on the side of vested interest all through the Haymarket's recent battle with Drury Lane. Fielding was on the side of the under-dog; he had been one himself. He was now an established dramatist. He knew he could draw the town. He decided he would draw it to the Haymarket and he would do so by burlesques and satires of such virulence that those he had done before at the little Theatre would seem pale by comparison. He had his knife in Sir Robert Walpole, the Prime Minister. This statesman would seem to have been the target for all the mud which could be thrown at a politician. He was always being denigrated on the stage; he was ever a subject for lampoons and innuen-does elsewhere. Fielding had a personal grudge against him too. He had solicited the patronage of the great man and it had not been forthcoming. This rankled.

Fielding had married during his absence from the Haymarket, and had squandered his wife's fortune. So when he took over the place, it was as much a fresh start in life for him as it was for the theatre. Both were very hopeful.

During the interval between Cibber's departure and Fielding's return, a company of actors without any managerial status had per-formed his comedy, *Don Quixote in England*, at the Haymarket. They had met with some success. The election scenes in the comedy had been much applauded. It gave Fielding an idea for another and an al-together more violent outburst of vitriolic satire. He got hold of this com-pany, who had not a well-known name amongst them, and engaged them for his venture at the Haymarket. They were only too glad to serve him.

He now threw his bombshell at the public. There was even satire in his first announcement. He remembered how the little theatre had been opened by the Duke of Montagu's French company under the pompous title of "The French Comedians of His Grace the Duke of Montagu." He knew how the snobs always considered anything foreign so much better than anything English. So he announced his opening by bills which stated:

"March 5th, 1735. The Great Mogul's Company of English Comedians, who have dropped from the Clouds. Newly imported at the New Theatre in the Haymarket. Sealed tickets for Monday, March 8th, being the third day of the play, may be had at The Two Blue Posts, Bow Street, Covent Garden, and at the Bedford Coffee House, in the Great Piazza."

D

This question of sealed tickets may have had one of two meanings. Either Fielding was trying to evade the Patent law by not taking money at the doors of the theatres—an evasion tried later by another celebrated figure in the Haymarket annals, or else that third day was, as customary, the author's own benefit, and he wanted to get the full amount of money into his own hands. The latter seems the more probable, for Fielding does not appear to have tried to obtain a licence. He just opened in defiance of everyone, despite the recent lawsuits and findings, and determined to carry on until an attempt was made to stop him. He was always a law unto himself and cared little for restrictions, legal or otherwise.

His company was a scratch one, but some authorities include Macklin in it.

But whether he was there or not, Henry Fielding was installed and on the advertised date he presented his play, "*Pasquin, a Drumstick Satire on the Times, Being the rehearsal of Two Plays viz: A Comedy called The Election and a Tragedy called The Life and Death of Common-Sense.*

In this, one of his most successful efforts, Fielding returned to the method employed by Vanbrugh in *The Rehearsal* and to some extent in his own previous success in *The Tragedy of Tragedies*. Sheridan employed it in *The Critic* some time later.

It showed the supposed rehearsal of two plays, one dealing with country elections, with all their bribery and corruption, and the other dealing with the gross blundering of the law and the offences committed in its name against ordinary common sense. Both gave the author great scope for his mordant wit. *Pasquin* has been described as a "bold and unwarrantable satire." It is bold, but hardly unwarrantable. For it let the light in on the corrupt politics and the prevailing nepotism, and it turned the spotlight on the devious and wilfully complicated methods of the law of the time, by which it was quite possible to prove that white was really black.

Pasquin ran for fifty performances, a marvellous run. It brought Fielding added fame and, what he wanted just as much, some ready money. It filled once more the Haymarket Theatre with excited audiences, and the heart of its owner once more rejoiced.

Potter had gone through a rough time. Doors were always opening for him and his beloved playhouse, only to slam in his face. But at any rate, the Haymarket was open again and for the moment flourishing. Good times were sure to come if one waited.

It looked like it indeed. The satire of *Pasquin* was much to the fancy of the public. Fielding spared nobody. He called a spade a spade. He accused Members of Parliament of bribing voters. In a scene quoted, this can be seen quite clearly:

Trapwit. (the author). You mister, that act my lord, bribe a little more

openly if you please, or the audience will lose the joke, and it is
one of the strongest in my whole play.

Lord Place. Sir, I cannot possibly do it better at the table.

Trapwit. Then get all up and come forward to the front of the stage.
Now, you gentlemen that act the mayor and alderman, range
yourself in a line; and you my lord and the colonel, come to one
end and bribe away with right and left.

Fustian. (*the tragic author*). Is this wit, Mr. Trapwit?

Trapwit. Yes, sir, it is wit; and such wit as will run all over the
kingdom.

Fustian. But methinks Colonel Promise, as you call him, is but ill
named; for he is a man of very few words.

Trapwit. You'll be of another opinion before the play is over; at
present his hands are too full for business; and you may remember, sir, I before told you this is none of your plays wherein
much is said and nothing done. Gentlemen, are you bribed?

Omnes. Yes, sir.

Trapwit. Then, my lord and colonel, you must go off, and make
room for the other candidates to come and bribe too.

Pretty straightforward stuff this, which was coming from the Haymarket stage.

Fielding made personal attacks too. He had a nasty dig at Colley
Cibber, of whom he had no opinion, and who was now Poet Laureate.
It was generally held that Cibber's politics, and not his poetry, got him
this post, and indeed his verse confirmed that suspicion

Fielding made his opinion quite clear in a scene in *Pasquin* where a
voter, who admits to not being a poet, and who does not know what an
ode is, is nevertheless promised the Court post in return for support at
the poll.

The mud was flying at the Haymarket. Fielding, flushed with
success, was casting it about with both hands. Some of it was to stick
and bring forth consequences. And, as usual, those consequences
would not help the Little Theatre in the Hay.

CHAPTER IV

RIOTOUS TIMES

THE year 1737 saw Fielding, now a successful dramatist-manager, unleashing his most acid satire. He had flouted the Patent theatres, probably too busy with their internal affairs to worry about him, and smarting from the rebuff they had received over the Cibber affray. He had exposed in his plays scandals and chicanery in high places; he had attacked the law and politics. He had got away with it, and filled his little theatre with people who liked spice in their coffee-house gossip and who also enjoyed a good laugh. It will be observed that the Haymarket is treading the path of its destiny as the home of English comedy. Fielding seemed able to write what he liked, to say whatever he chose from the stage without let or hindrance. So he made up his mind to fly at bigger game—indeed, to tilt at the biggest personage in the country —Sir Robert Walpole, the Prime Minister.

But before he did so, he staged another burlesque which had a long and very involved title—*Tumble Down Dick, or Phaeton in the Suds*. A Dramatick Entertainment of Walking, in Serious and Foolish Characters; Interlarded with Burlesque, Grotesque, Comick Interludes, call'd Harlequin a Pickpocket . . . Being ('tis hoped) the last entertainment that will ever be exhibited on any stage. Invented by the Ingenious Monsieur Sans Esprit. The Musick Composed by the Harmonious Signor Warblerini. And the scenes painted by the Prodigious Mynheer van Bottom-Flat."

This was only marking time for something over which he had taken much more care and trouble, something which he hoped would put the cat amongst the pigeons with a vengeance, something which would advance his self-chosen crusade of reform more than anything he had done before. That something was the production of his new play, *The Historical Register for the Year 1736; to which is added a Very Merry Tragedy, called Eurydice Hiss'd or a Word to the Wise.* If it was an impact he wanted, he most certainly got it, but not in the way he expected. For the production of this play and its undoubted success was the cause of a revolution in the whole control of the theatres by the passing of the Licensing Act of 1737. This Act came about through Fielding's play at the Haymarket, and it is the first imperishable footprint the little theatre left in the sands of time.

The Historical Register was far more daring and outspoken than had been *Pasquin*. It bristled with libels. Fielding went beyond all bounds. He libelled old Colley Cibber, presented on the stage as a character called Ground Ivy, whom he castigated for daring to mutilate the works of Shakespeare. Old Cibber took no notice; he was used to it. His rewriting of Shakespeare was nothing new and it had been accepted by the public, whose taste was such that they seemed to prefer old Cibber's *Richard III* and Nahum Tate's garbled *Lear* to the method of the Master himself. But one admires Fielding for knowing better and for taking up the cudgels, even if he has a self-interest in so doing. All Colley did was to leave his reference to Fielding as "a broken wit" in his *Apology* for his life.

Fielding chose, in this play, to bring on to the stage a perfectly recognisable impersonation of a living and well-known man, one Mr. Cock, the leading auctioneer of the day. All he did was to alter the name to Mr. Hen. He had this part, probably to draw more attention to it, played by a woman in male attire, and the actress who played it was Charlotte Charke, the extraordinary daughter of Colley Cibber. Charlotte Charke had already played a man's part (Lord Place) in Fielding's *Pasquin*. She was quite at home in male attire, which she wore for years in ordinary life. Her own strange story will be told later.

But at the time of *The Historical Register* she was married to Richard Charke, also a member of the Great Mogul Fielding's company. He was a well-known violinist, but a man of most disgraceful and dissolute habits.

To Charlotte Charke, as Mr. Hen, fell not only the burlesquing of the celebrated Mr. Cock, but also a scene which plunged the spear of irony and satire deep into the political life of the day.

Hen, as might be expected, conducts an auction:

"Gentlemen and ladies, this is Lot 1. A most curious remnant of Political Honesty. Who puts it up, gentlemen? It will make you a very good cloak. You see it is both sides alike, so you may turn it as often as you will. Come, five pounds for this curious remnant. I assure you, several great men have made their birthday suits out of the same piece. It will wear for ever and never be the worse for wearing. Five pounds is bid; nobody more than five pounds for this curious piece of Political Honesty? Five pounds, no more. (*Knocks.*) Lord Bothsides."

The scene continues with other lots being put up; the tirade against all forms of political dishonesty mounts. So-called patriots who serve their own purpose, and judges and bishops whose consciences are so capacious that they will hold everything, are in turn excoriated. But the main attack is reserved for Sir Robert Walpole. This statesman seems to have laboured all his life under constant accusations of political and personal dishonesty. Nothing was too bad to say about him in the current gossip, and the paragraphs in the prints and newspapers were always hinting, sneering, and suggesting that he carried through his measures by a system of wholesale bribery and recouped himself for money thus expended out of the public funds. But so far nothing direct had been said on the stage.

Fielding remedied this omission. Into *The Historical Register* he put the character of Quidam, a fiddler, who made people dance to his tune by means of bribes. There was not the slightest doubt who was meant; there was practically no attempt at concealment. Everyone, even those of the meanest intelligence, must recognise Quidam as the Prime Minister. There was not a shadow of doubt at whom Fielding was aiming his shafts. There was personal spite in the attack, as well as the zeal for reform.

Fielding had a scene in his play which showed a whole lot of politicians sitting round a table. It probably represented a Cabinet Meeting. The character of Medley, who is a kind of compère, is exhibiting them to an interested onlooker:

> *2nd Politician.* These mighty preparations of the Turks are certainly designed against some place or other. Now the question is, what place are they designed against? And that is a question which I cannot answer.
>
> *3rd Politician.* But it behoves us to be upon our guard.
>
> *4th Politician.* It does, and the reason is, because we know nothing about the matter.
>
> *2nd Politician.* You say right, it is easy for a man to be on his guard against dangers which he knows of, but to guard against dangers which nobody knows of, requires a very great politician.
>
> *5th Politician.* Hang foreign affairs. Let us apply ourselves to Money.
>
> *All (eagerly).* Ay, ay, ay—money, money, money.
>
> > [Enter the character of QUIDAM, the fiddler, who has a cue in a question asked by the—
>
> *1st Politician.* I desire to ask you all one question. Are we not a set of miserable poor dogs?
>
> *Omnes.* Ay, ay.
>
> *3rd Politician.* That we are, sure enough, that nobody can deny.
>
> *Quidam.* Yes sir, I deny it. (*Sensation.*) Nay, gentlemen, let me not disturb you. I beg you all to sit down. I am come to drink a glass with you. Can Corsica be poor whilst *this* is in it?
>
> > [*He lays a purse upon the table as a bribe and the faces of the Politicians light up. Quidam plays his violin, the orchestra strikes up a gay country dance and everyone dances.*
>
> *Medley.* Sir, every one of these patriots have a hole in their pockets, as Mr. Quidam the fiddler there knows, so that he intends to make them dance until the money is fallen through, which he will pick up again and so not lose one halfpenny by his generosity; so far from it, that he will get his wine for nothing and the poor

people, alas, out of their own pockets pay the whole reckoning. This, sir, I think is a very pretty pantomime trick and an ingenious burlesque on all the Fourberies which the great Lun has exhibited in all his entertainments.

The great Lun referred to is John Rich, of Covent Garden, who played Harlequin under that name.

The Historical Register drew the town. It convulsed the audiences and it was loudly applauded.

The wits quoted it in the coffee-houses, and very speedily it came to the knowledge of Sir Robert Walpole himself.

The affair could not be passed over. Gossip was one thing, lampoons were another, but the direct word of the dramatist to an audience was a different matter.

Walpole decided to take action. No chastisement of actors this time; something far more salutary. These little theatres were getting too cheeky. One could rely on the Patent theatres, but these upstarts required a sharp lesson. They should have it.

Walpole decided to bring before Parliament a new Licensing Bill for the better conduct of theatres and the better supervision of the plays they produced. He knew this would be unpopular, because it would be considered an infringement on the people's liberty, and also because he introduced it. So he trod warily, but with determination.

It might, or it might not, have been a coincidence that just at this time a play was submitted to Giffard for production at Goodman's Fields Theatre called *The Golden Rump*. This was a dramatised version of a libellous article which had appeared in a paper called *Common Sense*. This article had amused the mob of the Town, always ready and willing to believe the worst of their governors and government. It should be remembered that elections were not so free as now and that the majority had little say in who was to represent them in Parliament.

The piece was so blatant, so obviously libellous and dangerous that the worthy Mr. Giffard took it along himself and laid it before the Prime Minister. He read it, and it went the rounds of the Government, being universally condemned. Now, there was no question about it at all: an Act of Parliament there must be and that quickly.

This incident, coming so fortuitously on the top of Fielding's play, may have been just one of those strange coincidences which occur at times. Or it may have been inspired by a clever and wily man who wanted clear and independent proof of the necessity of an Act of Parliament. It is strange, indeed, and beyond ordinary understanding, how these events crop up when power wishes to exert itself.

Anyway, all the bigwigs were convinced that the nebulous power of the Lord Chamberlain, who was in charge of theatrical affairs, needed clarifying and strengthening, and here was the opportunity. The situation had been brought about entirely by the persistent opening of two unchartered theatres, the Haymarket and Goodman's Fields. Both were villainous in the eyes of authority, but maybe the Haymarket was worse, because it was nearer the centre of things—and it had Fielding in it.

There had been trouble before concerning Goodman's Fields. When it was first built there was a howl of protest against Odell, its founder. The City Fathers, always anti-theatre, claimed that the houses near the new theatre, previously offices and warehouses, now became taverns resorted to by all sorts of lewd people. They claimed that a play had been presented there called *King Charles the First* which was nothing but sedition, appealing to republicans, sectarians and the like by exhibiting the worst features of that unlucky time. Sir John Barnard, a magistrate, kept his eyes open for the chance of laying the actors by the heels as vagrants, but they gave him no opportunity.

Then Fielding dropped the lighted match of *Pasquin* near the powder magazine.

When Giffard took control of the old Goodman's Fields and built the new theatre, there were constant reports of disorders, which were all remembered and brought up by Walpole. In March, 1735, two years prior to the now contemplated Act, that same watchful Sir John Barnard asked leave to bring in a Bill to "restrain the number and the scandalous abuses of the playhouses."

He particularly represented the mischief done by them in the City of London, in corrupting youth, encouraging vice and prejudicing trade. This would be greatly increased if another theatre was built, as projected, at St. Martin's-le-Grand. He did not get much support, although Walpole was a seconder. Walpole doubtless remembered that, too. A Mr. James Erskine spoke for the proposed Bill. He counted up the playhouses: the Opera House—Vanbrugh's old house in the Haymarket—Drury Lane, Covent Garden, the Haymarket, Lincoln's Inn Fields and Goodman's Fields. There were twice as many as in Paris! He spoke with contempt of the French as being degenerate. But he mentioned the astounding salaries the Italian opera singers received, which was equal to Lords of the Treasury and judges! This caused a bit of interest. He was careful not to mention the salaries of the ordinary actors, it should be observed.

The mover and seconders of the proposed Bill did a bit of general lobbying and petitions began to come in.

In the April, Sir John Barnard returned to the attack, opposing the suggestion that the powers given to the Lord Chamberlain should be increased. He was told the King would not pass the Act without this amendment, and the proroguing of Parliament ended the matter for the time being.

But the anti-theatre gang were not idle. Petitions continued to pour in, chiefly directed against Goodman's Fields. They came from justices of the peace, deputy lieutenants and important residents in the

Tower Hill district, all urging that the theatre was a "great nuisance."

The theatre itself now took a hand and rallied its supporters. Counter-petitions appeared; one from those who had taken shares in it (and were therefore hardly disinterested). They disclosed that they received 17s. 6d. for every night the theatre was open. The capital involved was £2,300. What carried weight with the prejudiced Government was a petition from merchants, shopkeepers, weavers and dyers of the vicinity (it was near Spitalfields), who all praised its management and said it interfered in no way with their business. Odell, who then controlled the theatre, took counsels' opinion. They told him he had every legal right to carry on his business. He did so for some time, but sold to Giffard, who entered the lists, built his new theatre and complained that this was an attempt to deprive him of his livelihood. This is the same man who in 1737 carried the *Golden Rump* to Walpole.

The actors of Goodman's Fields put in their plea. They said it would deprive about three hundred people of the common necessities of life, for their sole dependence was on this theatre, and they had not been bred or taught any other business save that of acting. They pointed out their small chance of employment at the other playhouses, who were already overstaffed and more likely to discharge than employ fresh people.

There was a petition to the House of Commons appealing to the sense of justice and humanity of His Majesty's faithful Commons, the petitioners saying that "to render any man incapable of getting his bread in the business or occupation which he had been trained up to from his youth is depriving him of life in the most terrible manner." The answer of His Majesty's faithful Commons in Parliament assembled was to reject this petition completely. There was no doubt that the House had made up its mind two years before the thing actually happened; all that was necessary was a bombshell, and that bombshell Fielding provided in *The Historical Register*.

The strolling players of the fairs took a hand, with a Mrs. Lee, of Southwark Fair, as their mouthpiece. This good woman said she owned two booths there, which she opened each year for thirty years, and the booths and scenery had cost her £2,000. She was old now, and if the Bill became law she would be ruined. She pointed out that players at the Patent theatres had graduated in her booths, instancing Mrs. Boutel and Mr. Booth (Barton Booth).

The Comptroller of the Revels himself, a Mr. Charles Lee (no relation of the lady of Southwark), complained that it would interfere with his privileges. And our John Potter came on the scene with his story. He also pleaded that it meant ruin for him.

A curious old fellow, Antony Aston, also pleaded ruin and said he was so poor that he wanted to address the House of Commons himself as and by way of evidence. He was an attorney who had taken to the stage. He had played in practically every theatre, but took to strolling

with a company composed almost entirely of his own family. He had a
weird show he called his "Medley," made up of songs and interludes of
his own writing, sandwiched between excerpts from popular plays. He
considered he had a right to play in every town, and an exclusive one
at that, and made it warm for any other company that opposed him. He
curried favour with the nobility living in the district in which he played
and managed to get them to give him enough cash to get him to his next
pitch. He was always either in a state of comfort or stark penury.

Such were his powers of persuasion, even in his old age, that his
plea to give personal evidence was granted—probably the Commons
scented some fun. He showed them how the Bill they proposed could
have coaches and horses driven through it galore—his legal knowledge
came to his aid there—and as a result the first proposed Act was
abandoned.

But now Walpole, in 1737, took it upon himself to get an Act on the
Statute Book. And when Walpole made up his mind to pass an Act, it
was as good as done.

Fielding was aware of the danger. He appealed to the public. An
article had appeared in the *Gazetteer*, a ministerial print, which
denounced his play as aiming at the overthrow of the Ministry. Fielding
wrote a witty and forceful answer, and begged the public, his great
patron, to stand by him in his fight for free speech and no favour. That
sort of thing was, of course, extremely popular and got him much
support. Tell the public that something they have is in danger, and
even though they are unaware of the possession, they will rally. As will
be seen, they rallied for Fielding.

That there was need for reform was only too apparent. It was within
the power of the Lord Chamberlain to prevent any performance being
given without his licence, or any play to be performed which had not
his approval. But there had been great laxity in this respect. All this
Walpole proposed to alter and he drafted his Bill. He made much of
The Golden Rump, but he did not mention that Giffard had received a
reward for bringing it to him. He implied that the play was written by
Fielding, but produced no proof of this. In theatre-land it was suspected
that the play never existed at all or else it had been inspired by Walpole
himself as a weapon to put down Fielding. Nobody knows the truth.
But it served its purpose.

Walpole went on steadily and introduced his Bill. He had the
support of the Patent theatres, who were servile in this matter and blind
to their own interests, for the Bill contained a clause which gave the
Lord Chamberlain power to issue licences, if he approved, for any
theatre, and that was certainly against their interest—and their Patents.

On Friday, May 20th, 1737, Sir Robert Walpole presented his Bill
to the House of Commons "to explain and amend so much of an act
made in the twelfth year of Queen Anne, entitled 'An Act for reducing
the laws relating to Rogues, Vagabonds, Sturdy Beggars and Vagrants,

and sending them whither they ought to be sent, as relates to Common
Players of Interludes.' "

The principal point about it, not mentioned at all in the preamble,
provided that every dramatic piece, previous to public performance,
should receive the licence of the Lord Chamberlain. That continues
to-day.

It was read for the first time on Tuesday, May 24th. In the Upper
House, Lord Chesterfield had denounced the Bill in a long and very
able speech, describing it as not only an attack on liberty, but on property
as well. It was resisted at every stage, but such was Walpole's power that
it went through both Houses and was ready for the Royal assent on
June 8th. Very commendable speed in legislation. It got that assent
on June 21st.

An official appointed under the new Act, to be responsible for the
reading and licensing of plays, was Odell, the identical gentleman who
had caused so much of the trouble by building the theatre at Goodman's
Fields. He had been hiding from his creditors, but he had written many
poems in praise of Walpole. Now he got his reward.

The moment the Act became law, Walpole struck. Goodman's
Fields (Giffard notwithstanding) was closed down. And so was the
Little Theatre in the Hay. Fielding was thrown out, the Great Mogul's
Company was dispersed and scattered, Potter was again without a
tenant.

But Fielding's appeal to the public was bearing fruit. They espoused
the cause of the Haymarket Theatre, its witty manager and its native
actors, whom they considered had been very badly treated. They
regarded the Act in the light presented to them by Fielding, and
supported by Lord Chesterfield, as an attempt to curb their liberty,
their right to free expression of opinion and speech, and their property
in respect of the right to attend entertainments of any kind they chose.
They were not so sure about this property business, but took it that way.
Here was the now popular Haymarket Theatre closed to them. So was
Goodman's Fields. Here were English actors and actresses thrown out
of work with little prospect of employment. This was an occasion for
Minister baiting, for riot and disturbance such as the mob and rabble—
and not only those—of the times thoroughly enjoyed.

The public—or the more noisy and vocal portion of it—were on
the side of Fielding and the Haymarket. Goodman's Fields had no such
mouthpiece or champion as the clever author and dramatist who had
been dispossessed by Walpole and his Act. He lost no chance of rubbing
it in. The Haymarket was again the battlefield. The Little Theatre in
the Hay was at war again, not this time against rival theatres, but
against the law of the land and the Prime Minister himself. Few, if
any, other theatres have ever played such a role.

Trust Fielding for fanning the flames. He had come out of the
Haymarket, despite his successes there, no better off than he went

in, richer only in a hatred of Walpole which he determined to avenge.

If he could no longer direct the plays in the Haymarket, well, he would do his best to direct the audiences and see what came of that. Before long, he had a chance.

The Lord Chamberlain's Department, working under the new order, made a most tactless move. They issued a licence permitting a French company of players to appear at the Haymarket Theatre, from whence the English players had been so recently evicted. Here was Fielding's chance to appeal to the mob. Here were Frenchies going to play in an English theatre at the expense of English actors.

The announcement declared that "a French Company was about to give a series of representations under distinguished patronage at the Little Theatre in the Hay." It did not, however, give details of that distinguished patronage.

The word went round, and threats as to what would happen were publicly made. Violence was openly preached and promised. The authorities became nervous. They made another false move. They sent down a detachment of soldiers to protect the French players— (they said to protect the theatre), and a Westminster magistrate, Mr. Justice Deveil, with a copy of the Riot Act in his pocket, was given a seat in the pit. He represented law and order.

But those two commodities were not in fashion on that particular evening. It promised to be a lively bit of playgoing for all concerned.

Nothing exasperated the public of that time so much as anything French. Towards that great nation the English bore a hearty contempt. They had defeated them in battle, thanks to the Duke of Marlborough, and held the poorest possible opinion of them. The Englishman then was a true Xenophobe. He despised foreigners of all kinds, but Frenchmen most of all. And here was a pack of "frog-eaters" daring to come to the Haymarket and play where English actors should be appearing.

It is not surprising, therefore, that there was a large, noisy, milling crowd outside the Haymarket before the doors opened for the first performance by the French players. Crowds in those days were much rougher and less good-natured than they are to-day. On this occasion they rushed into the theatre as soon as it opened and filled it to suffocation. From ceiling to floor stood a mass of English citizens, all determined to voice their grievance against the new Act in general and foreign players in particular.

Waiting for the rise of the curtain, they indulged in cheers and counter-cheers for their favourites, hoots for unpopular names, general uproar and the loud and lusty singing of patriotic songs, such as "The Roast Beef of Old England."

Mr. Justice Deveil took a dim view of the proceedings. He rose in his place and declared it was a riot. This was hotly disputed. The excited mob listened whilst various people in the house argued with the worthy magistrate.

Deveil informed the house that he had come there as a magistrate to maintain the King's authority; that Colonel Pulteney, with a full company of the Guards, was there to support him in the execution of his duty. He also informed them that it was the King's command that the play should be performed and any obstruction thereto was in direct opposition to the King's authority. If this was tried, then he would read the Riot Act, and all offenders would be arrested by the Guards.

It was now near the time of performance—six o'clock—and the distinguished members of the audience began to take their places in the boxes reserved for them. The French and Spanish Ambassadors came in, with their wives, as well as Lord and Lady Gage and Sir Thomas Robinson, the latter a Commissioner of the Excise and therefore not likely to be popular. All this array of power, influence and aristocracy appeared together in a stage box. It made no impression on the unruly audience.

Then something happened which had an electrical effect upon the audience of John Bulls. The authorities made another and even greater mistake. As soon as the party of V.I.Ps. was seated, the curtain went up. And with it, a howl of genuine and furious rage rose from the auditorium, for the stage disclosed the French actors standing between two files of British Grenadiers, with fixed bayonets. This was too much. British Grenadiers, as British as roast beef and beer and John Bull himself, being used to guard a lot of French play-actors who were usurping native talent! Things looked very ugly. The gallery bellowed with rage, the pit rose as one man and demanded of Justice Deveil what this meant? If he were there to represent justice, where was the justice in this? It was a perilous moment. Deveil knew it. It did not need the yelling of the mob nor the heated, angry and threatening attitude of the pit people around him to indicate things had gone too far.

He assured them he did not know that this step was to be—had been —taken. Whereupon the whole house demanded, in its loudest and fiercest tones, the withdrawal of the soldiery. He agreed, and sent word at once to Colonel Pulteney to withdraw his men. During the short time taken for the delivery of this message, the temper of the crowd was at fever heat. One false step now and destruction and bloodshed would have followed. The lives of those French actors hovered in the balance —and maybe the safety of Deveil also. It might have led to mutiny, for it is doubtful if the soldiers would have fired upon or beaten the crowd.

But Colonel Pulteney understood. A sharp order rang out and the Grenadiers wheeled and left the stage.

Instantly the humour of the mob turned. There were shouts of laughter. A voice cried, "The British Army is in retreat," and was answered by another who yelled, "Send for His Grace the Duke of Marlborough." There was more laughter at this. But the crisis was not over

One can imagine the feelings of those unfortunate French players. Whatever their rank in their profession, whatever their personal courage, or lack of it, they stuck to the player's creed that "The show must go on." Scared out of their wits, they nevertheless made an attempt to carry on. It was useless to try to sing in face of that pandemonium, futile to try to speak. So they fell back on another form of their art —they tried, poor souls, to dance!

But the crowd was prepared for that. With an angry shout at what they considered the impertinence of these foreigners for trying to continue in face of their very open show of hostility, they hurled an avalanche of peas upon the stage. That would stop these despicable French dancing-masters from trying to take the bread out of honest English actors' mouths under cover of an unjust Act of Parliament.

The poor players slid all over the place as the dried peas showered down. The Ambassadors of France and Spain hastily withdrew, taking their ladies with them, and the English quality followed amid the derisive hoots and boos of the audience. There was crisis in the air again. It could be felt. There was that sway and murmur in the crowd which precedes a mass rush, that swirl like a wave dashing at a rock, like the beginning of a tremendous roll of thunder.

Deveil had to do some quick thinking. He shouted loudly a demand for a candle; the mob paused a second. Was he going to read that Riot Act—for if so . . . ? Deveil seized the opportunity to appeal to them once more, whilst the French actors cowered on the stage, too afraid to move. He stood on his seat and waved his hand. The crowd quietened to hear what he was going to say.

English to the backbone, he was for compromise. If they would allow the play to proceed this one night, he begged, according to the King's command, then he would himself take their grievances against this Act and this use of the theatre to His Majesty, whom he doubted not would see justice done. . . .

But the crowd was not for compromise nor for temporising. It wanted a fight to a finish. "No Treaty! No Treaty!" it bellowed. Uproar broke out worse than before. Deveil ordered his candle to be lit. He ordered the military to stand by: he was desperate; he was going to read the Riot Act.

But a man of courage and sound judgment stepped forward. He begged Deveil to stop, he begged him for his own sake, for the sake of the public and for the sake of the King Himself. "You see the temper of the mob," he said. "The sound of the Riot Act and the sight of the troops to enforce it will drive them beyond all limits. What is merely a bad disturbance might turn into open revolt—and that revolt might spread to greater lengths if blood were shed, as it would assuredly be. I beg of you to think and to order the curtain to be rung down. Then the mob will disperse and no great harm will be done. Believe me, it is the only way."

Deveil thought for a moment. He was beaten and knew it. He blew
out the candle, he did not send for the soldiers and he ordered the curtain
to be rung down. It descended to the delighted cheers of that audience
of sturdy John Bulls, who had come there to see what they considered
justice done to their fellow countrymen. They had won, and they now
dispersed in good temper, but filling the Haymarket—both street and
theatre—with their triumphant cheers. They considered their victory
complete as the Battle of Blenheim.

The incident was over. The French company did not reappear.
Thus ended the first of the notable series of riots at the Haymarket
Theatre, that theatre which is now so placid, so calm and so restful in
its noble age. But at the time now dealt with it was a place of riot, of
dissension and battle, fighting, not only for freedom, but for its own
existence against great adversaries, and even the Government itself.

The curtain had come down at the Little Theatre in the Hay and
it was not to rise again easily.

CHAPTER V

A KILLER, A ROGUE AND A WOMAN

WHEN the curtain fell on the attempted performance of *L'Embarrass des Richesses* by the French players, it really looked as though it would stop down for good.

The Licensing Act was being enforced and was unpopular. Plays known to have been licensed under it were hissed when performed at the Patent theatres, and the public were indignant for some time. But, as usual, it died down and things became more normal.

The Haymarket was seventeen years old. It had started with the Duke of Montagu's French company, it had housed all sorts of indifferent shows until the sensational *Hurlothrumbo* brought the fashionable world to see it. Fielding's plays kept them coming, and then came the Company of the Revels, led by the odious Theophilus Cibber. Fielding had been a rebel against conditions; Cibber and company were rebels against Drury Lane. The Haymarket was becoming a rallying place for rebellion. Names to be notorious or famous were creeping in—Charlotte Charke, Charles Macklin and Mrs. Pritchard. Stars like Mills, Milward, Harper and Mrs. Horton had played there. It was assuming importance.

And, at odd times, dramatists had presented other plays than those already chronicled. The Little Theatre was staging comedy, burlesque, farce, and ballad-opera. Apart from some of the old classics played by the Revels, it staged only one tragedy. It was making its name as the home of comedy. There were more reasons for this than the fact that Fielding was a writer of satire. Tragedy was the top attraction, and too much of an incursion into that field would have brought about, all the sooner, the interference of the Patent Theatres. Covent Garden was now open and the old Lincoln's Inn Theatre was in decline.

Amongst those plays which first saw the light at the Haymarket through this period were a terrific mock tragedy with a terrific title, *The Tragedy of Chrononhotonthologos; Being the Most Tragical Tragedy that was ever Tragedyed by a Company of Comedians*. It was done in 1733, and although announced as by Benjamin Bounce, was written by Henry Carey. In 1729 there had been a ballad-opera by Charles Coffey called *The Beggar's Wedding*, which had also been performed in Dublin. Coffey provided *The Female Parson, or Beau in the Suds*, described as an opera and produced in 1730. The latter was, in the parlance of the times, "damned" at its first performance.

In 1730 there was a satire by Thomas Cooke, *The Battle of the Poets*, and in 1731 a comedy by Matthew Draper entitled *The Spend Thrift*. Its one and only original tragedy, *The Rival Father*, or *The Death of*

George Colman.
From an original picture by Sir Joshua Reynolds in the possession of the Earl of Mulgrave.

George Colman the younger.

Mr. Thomas Weston.

Middle
Mr. R. W. Elliston.

Mr. Aickin.
*An engraving from a
picture by A. Devis.*

Achilles, by William Hatchett, happened in 1730. It ran for only three performances.

A woman dramatist, Mrs. Eliza Maywood, was responsible for a burlesque in opera form of Fielding's famous *Tom Thumb*, which she called *The Opera of Operas, or Tom Thumb the Great*. The music was announced as composed by Arne, in the Italian manner. If this is so, then there is another fine name on the annals.

Alexander Gordon had supplied more comedy in 1731 with *Lupone or The Inquisitor* and in 1735 a show which appeared to run the whole gamut was put on. This had the remarkable title of *The Rival Milliners, or The Humours of Covent Garden. A Tragi-Comi-Operatic-Pastoral-Farce*. You could not wish more for your money. It was by Robert Drury. This by no means completes the list, but it shows what sort of fare the Haymarket was providing.

Then came the darkness. From 1737 until 1744, the Haymarket Theatre adds nothing to stage history. It is doubtful when it opened or for how long. Probably a few desperate out-of-work actors took a chance and lost their money.

One can imagine the optimistic Potter, still full of faith, having a drink with the manager of the great Opera House opposite, and discussing affairs with him. For Vanbrugh's theatre was now the home of opera and about this time was under the control of the Earl of Middlesex—so early did society espouse the opera. Handel had just retired, and things were not too happy for either of the Haymarket houses. Both would tell tales of past success and fabulous receipts, and both hint darkly at future arrangements which would surprise everyone—for theatre managers have changed very little down the years and still have a sublime belief in to-morrow and the play it is to bring forth.

But no figure of importance goes near the Little Theatre. Doubtless it was watched closely by the licensing authorities and by the Patent theatres. It was, to both of them, a dangerous place which had given them a lot of trouble. They did not want the playhouse—still sometimes referred to as New—to be a further thorn in their sides. The Patent theatres were having it all their own way. Rich was going along steadily at Covent Garden, but things were not so happy, from the managerial point of view, at Drury Lane, where Fleetwood was squandering money and getting into all kinds of scrapes. Macklin had startled the world as Shylock, and shown everyone that he was one of the finest actors our stage had ever possessed. He had persevered with his "natural" style of acting, despite the hostility of Quin, the exponent of the old ponderous, orating style. He had paved the way for the arrival and success of the great star which had only recently appeared in the theatrical firmament—the peerless, immortal David Garrick. Much had happened of a most exciting nature, but the poor little Haymarket was shut and dark.

Then rebellion broke out again. Once more, at Drury Lane, the

E

actors struck. They struck against Fleetwood, his methods and his unpaid salaries. Led by Garrick and Macklin—firm friends at that time —they petitioned the Lord Chamberlain to allow them to leave Theatre Royal and open in opposition at the Haymarket Theatre. Potter must have been on his toes with excitement and hope.

But the Lord Chamberlain turned them down. He sided with the vested interests of Drury Lane. The actors went back, beaten in the tussle, but the better by a new agreement and a stronger hold over Fleetwood. One man only of that company was expelled from Drury Lane—and that man was the fierce, implacable Charles Macklin— who had already killed a brother actor in Drury Lane's green-room, and although found guilty of manslaughter, had got away with it unmarked and unpunished. That sort of man is not lightly reckoned with.

He was accused of being the ringleader—which he was not. He had even opposed an application to the Lord Chamberlain until Fleetwood had been given one more chance. He had been Fleetwood's friend and manager; he had lent him money. Now he was cast out. Macklin was not the sort of man to take this lying down. Holding, with a good deal of reason, the view that Garrick had let him down and gone behind his back he broke the friendship and vowed revenge. Tough gentry, paid by Macklin, made Garrick's performances inaudible with their howls and rioting. Garrick offered to pay Macklin's salary from his own purse until the Irishman was reinstated at Old Drury, but Macklin refused with scorn. For two nights the row continued until Fleetwood engaged an overpowering number of thugs, pugilists and desperate men from Hockley-in-the-Hole and routed Macklin's small army by superior numbers.

But Charles Macklin was out of work. Now, Charles Macklin was an actor, and there is no harder thing in this world than to stop an actor from acting when he makes up his mind to do so.

Macklin, always independent, decided to set up on his own. He was in rebellion. Right, he would make his rebellion active by playing against Drury Lane. He was what we now call a star, he was very popular with audiences, so he would take a theatre himself.

He went to the Haymarket Theatre, which had now become the Cave of Adullam for theatrical rebels, and decided to open that theatre once again. It was not easy. He could obtain no licence. If he began acting without one, he would be arrested. But Macklin was never one to stop at trifles. He knew force was no good at the moment, so he resorted to strategy. He could not take money at the doors and run the Haymarket as an ordinary commercial theatre. But there was a way out, and he took it.

Prevented from taking money at the doors, he sold tickets privately in advance, away from the theatre. He advertised a concert, and actually always began his performances that way, and thus was the great Act of

Parliament, which had occasioned so much trouble, safely and securely evaded.

Macklin got together a company mostly, if not entirely, composed of the rawest of raw amateurs. He rehearsed them in his own way and he taught them their business very quickly. He compelled them to listen to him, he compelled them to follow his instructions and his guidance. He made them do it "his way." And Macklin knew all about it.

He was in all probability the first actor to really dissect the characters he had to play and then to integrate them with superb technique, into proper flesh and blood realities, expressing exactly what the author had intended, and not using the lines merely as an occasion for a display of elocution or rant.

The adventure at the Haymarket was, therefore, a thing which might have been of paramount importance to the theatrical profession. Here was a great actor who was also what would now be called a great producer, prepared to teach young aspirants all the mysteries of the art of acting. Here was a chance for new blood, for new talent. There was nothing like it to be had at the Patent theatres, either then or before. It was the first professional dramatic academy, with an eminent and practical professor at its head. The Haymarket was making more history.

Stage-struck young people flocked to Macklin and endured his ill temper, his rough rebuffs and his violence of treatment—that is, if they were keen enough on their calling—for the sake of what they were learning. If they were not real actors, they soon left.

But there was one amongst them who got his preliminary training under Macklin at the Haymarket at this time who was to make an enduring name for himself, and who was to raise the Little Theatre in the Hay to the rival of the Patent theatres.

This young man had knocked about the town for some time previously. He had won a good deal of notoriety by writing a pamphlet in which he described the crime and execution of an uncle of his who had murdered his brother (another uncle), giving all the gory details. The writer boldly put his name to it, and the thing sold for sixpence a copy.

The name of the author was Samuel Foote.

This young man, of good parentage and education, was making a reputation for his daring, his effrontery and his wit. He did not know what modesty meant; he would always be in the forefront of every gathering in which he found himself, or into which he forced himself. He was living, although not studying, in the Temple and, of course, he was in debt. It mattered not to him who might be holding forth in dispute or criticism in the Bedford Coffee House, the home of the wits; he would put his oar in and talk as brilliantly as any there. He became *persona grata* everywhere, he was free of the theatres and the green-rooms, and he began to show considerable powers of mimicry, which he had possessed even as a child. But money had to be earned. The stage was an obvious choice—here was Charles Macklin wanting recruits and willing to give training. So Samuel Foote, easy-going young man about town, enrolled himself in the scratch company at the Haymarket to learn what he could of his new job under the best master of the day. He was short and stout, he had a round and full face. He strolled in to the first rehearsal wearing, it is likely, a suit of green trimmed with silver lace, a smart wig, a sword and probably carrying a modish bouquet—the complete gallant of fashion—for was he not a gentleman, and was it not as well that the rest of the crew should know it at once? Not that he feared them—Samuel Foote feared no man, at any time, except perhaps Dr. Johnson, of whom he was very cautious and wary. But he considered it better to make his standing and position clear from the outset.

Macklin gave him the lead in the opening play. It is likely that the two already knew each other (it would have been strange indeed if they had not), and Macklin was therefore aware of Foote's clever mimicry. But a mimic is not of necessity a good actor, nor is a good actor always a good mimic. However, Macklin took the chance—most likely he had no option. The announcement went forth that the Haymarket Theatre was to reopen. It said:

"On February 6th, 1744. At the New Theatre in the Haymarket, a Concert, and after it, *Othello*. 'Othello'—a gentleman. 'Ludovico' —a gentleman. 'Iago'—Mr. Macklin. The character of Othello will be now dressed after the custom of his country. No money will be taken at the doors, nor any person admitted but by printed tickets, which will be delivered by Mr. Macklin."

This short concert followed by a play seems a very simple way of beating the hated Licensing Act, even with the device of tickets sold only in advance, but it appears to have satisfied the authorities, for no action was taken. Maybe they remembered the French riot; maybe they knew the fierce, indomitable fearlessness of Macklin and wanted no trouble with him. A man who had killed another, who had flouted the noted duellist-actor Quin and beaten him up, and who had had the temerity to have the already great Garrick booed and hooted was dangerous to meddle with. They decided to give him rope, in the hope of his hanging himself. For Macklin was a killer—he had no fear and no compunction.

Now, the "gentleman" who played Othello was Samuel Foote. a less suitable Moor could not have been found. He had not a single attribute for the part, except perhaps supreme self-confidence. Macklin was not one to make mistakes, and one imagines that it was his only choice. Probably no possible Othello existed amongst his players, but Foote had intelligence. It is noteworthy that Macklin dressed him as a Moor and not in the usual costume.

The "gentleman" who played Ludovico was John Hill. He had been keeping an apothecary's shop, but left it for the boards. He was not away for long. But he proved a remarkable character, this actor who made his debut at the Haymarket on this somewhat historic occasion. For he took leave to confer a knighthood on himself, and always called himself Sir John Hill.

Failing as an actor, he went back to the apothecary's shop and also to authorship. He wrote books—one of his works filled twenty-six gigantic volumes and had 1,600 illustrations. He wrote plays and they failed. But he always blamed the management. He met his match in Garrick, who had risked a farce of his, and when it failed, as usual was called over the coals by the irate author. But Garrick was more than equal to the attack. He penned a little epigram which settled the matter:

> *"For physic and farces,*
> *His equal there scarce is.*
> *His farces are physic,*
> *His physic a farce is."*

Master David could look after himself when it came to wit.

All three names on that bill for the Haymarket were of men who spent their whole lives in battle, in attacking the world and the people in it who incurred their dislike. Foote, Hill, and Macklin—seldom has such a trio been gathered together. This Haymarket reopening is an affair which has never had justice done to it—in stage annals it was a great occasion. For it saw the debut of Foote, and of Hill, and it saw also the Iago of Macklin.

Macklin had a good deal of temerity to start off his almost untrained company in such a test. But doubtless he wanted to play Iago. It was, of course, a good Iago, but did not reach the heights of his Shylock. But it set a precedent. He did not make the character the patent villain which actors had done up to then, and his example was followed by Garrick, when his turn came to play it.

The production of *Othello* failed. It failed largely because of Foote, who was shocking. His failure shook even his self-confidence. Macklin told him he was useless in tragedy and his friends seem to have also persuaded him of the fact. Nothing abashed, he turned to comedy.

To Hill, the Ludovico, historians are indebted for an extraordinary little book called *The Actor*, which he wrote and published in 1750, and in which he had a good deal to tell about Macklin's Haymarket season, which might have accomplished so much and actually accomplished very little, except his own return to Drury Lane and the all important introduction of Foote to the stage—and to the stage of the Haymarket.

In his book, Hill lays out the whole of the function of the actor's art as he sees it—and he probably saw it through the eyes of Macklin. He gives an extremely interesting picture of something which happened

when that ill-fated production of *Othello* took place and which shows
the excellence of Macklin's methods of teaching and the fact that there
was another actor in the cast who might have made a better Othello
than Samuel Foote.

"When Mr. Foote played Othello at the Haymarket, for the
benefit of the very ill-treated Mr. Macklin, there was a person among
the under-actors who had been instructed by that masterly judge of
speaking [Macklin], to pronounce about six lines sensibly, that never
had been pronounced so before; and who acquired more applause by
it than he had ever done in his whole life, though he had frequently
appeared at some of the motley theatres above-mentioned, in the
characters of King Richard, Bajazet, Torismond and Lord Townly.

"The person we hint at was one York; his part in Othello was
that of Montano, who engages with and is wounded by Cassio.
'Tis the great reproach of our managers that they esteem parts, not
from the nature of them, but their quantity; and a long part or a
short one are always understood as synonymous terms for a good and
a bad one. In consequence of this, Montano, whose part in the whole
does not much exceed a dozen lines had always used to be played at
the theatres by a person somewhat above the degree of a scene-
shifter, and what he spoke had been always laughed at accordingly;
the audience were on this occasion surprised, on Othello's asking this
person the cause of the quarrel, for which he very severely repri-
manded him, to hear him answer in an extremely forcible manner
and without anything of the cant of tragedy:

> " '*Worthy Othello, I am hurt to danger.*
> *Your officer Iago can inform you,*
> *While I spare speech (which something now offends me)*
> *Of all that I do know;—nor know I ought*
> *By me thats said or done amiss this night*
> *Unless self charity be sometimes sin*
> *And to defend ourselves it be a crime*
> *When violence assails us. . . .*'

"The audience looked with astonishment at one another, and gave
a thunder of applause; the young fellow was taken great notice
of, was soon afterwards promoted in one of the theatres, and put in
the way of arriving at all that perfection in the profession, the
presages of which the world thought they saw in him. He was not
sensible, any more than other people, that to keep up his credit he
must always act Montanos and that, though he did this very well,
he would have made a very miserable Othello. He obtained no more
applause in the higher characters he afterwards was thrown into,
than he had done before; and had not some good fortune carried him
off the stage in time, he would certainly have again been reduced the

next season to Montano, Rossano and the rest of the gentlemen of
that character."

It is not possible to agree with Hill completely. York would probably
have been a better Othello than Foote (although there is reason to be
grateful that Foote played it), and also, when he went to the other
theatres, he was no longer under the able production of Macklin, whose
instruction had obviously a great deal to do with his success. But maybe
that good fortune which carried him away from the stage was all for the
best. Hill, as becomes a brother Haymarketeer, let Foote down lightly
over his Othello and finds an opportunity of bestowing more praise on
Macklin. He says:

"It is not many years since Mr. Foote attempted the character
of Othello; he played it with much applause, and though not without
faults, yet perhaps with more beauties than have been seen in it
since; he owed much to the peculiar manner in which he spoke many
of the more pathetic speeches in this character to the instructions of
Mr. Macklin, who was then labouring at a scheme which our greatest
players have since very judiciously given into, though they have not
very gratefully acknowledged to whom they owed it; we mean, that of
bringing playing nearer to nature than it used to be.

"Some of the critics, as they esteem themselves, who were present
at the first night of Mr. Foote's appearance in the character we have
just mentioned, complained that although he was at least pompous
enough in the main, yet in some particular parts he fell down from
the dignity of tragedy, and gave into too plain a manner of speaking;
the instance is too much in everybody's memory to render it necessary
for us to quote the particular passages for which he was censured in
this manner; it is sufficient that we say in his vindication, that
the audience, or this part of the audience, very often condemned in
him those tones and gestures as too much approaching to familiarity,
which had no small share in the making of his performance more
natural and affecting than that of any man who had ever before been
seen in the same character."

This is indeed praise for a man who knew himself a failure as Othello.
But we must bear in mind that Hill was an idolater of Macklin's—
and it is very likely that he wrote this about Foote to spare himself the
agony of coming under the public flail of Foote's impersonations and
caricatures at that same theatre. For later Foote scared every character
in Town with the threat of mimicking him at the Haymarket.

Hill puts future generations of theatre lovers under a debt by the
insight he affords into Macklin's Iago. In speaking of what he calls
finesse and what is to-day called restraint, he speaks of his hero thus:

"An instance of the same kind we have in a soliloquy of Iago's in
Othello, in which, after an infinite deal of finesse on every occasion,

Mr. Macklin first set an example which has been followed by Mr. Garrick, of delivering plainly and without ornament, a speech in which we have been used to see a world of unnatural contortions of face and absurd by-play."

The speech he instances is Iago's:

> "*If I can fasten but one cup upon him,*
> *With that which he hath drunk to-night already,*
> *He'll be as full of quarrel and offence,*
> *As my young mistress' dog,*" etc.

That Haymarket first night of February 6th, 1744, was the first mass production of the natural school of acting, as understood then, as compared with the older form of bombast and over-theatricality. It was to have its effect. The Haymarket may claim, if not the inception of the natural school, at least its first big exploitation.

But Macklin's bold effort at creating a new school of acting at the Haymarket was not to be long-lived. He was wanted back at Drury Lane, from which his enemy Fleetwood had fled, disgraced, dishonoured and broken in fortune. The famous theatre had been acquired by two bankers, Messrs. Green and Amber—and Macklin went back.

He had done something at the Haymarket and something for which the little theatre was to be for ever his debtor. He had brought upon its stage the man who was to give it greatness.

This time the Haymarket was not closed for long. An old tenant, an old manager, came creeping back, rather the worse for wear, and again in revolt against authority. This was our old acquaintance, Theophilus Cibber. Nobody wanted him, nobody would employ him; he must perforce shift for himself. All knew him for a worthless rogue.

So once again he took the Haymarket and once again the rebel's banner flew. Cibber brought with him a very indifferent company, composed of people like himself who could not get work elsewhere. He also brought his young daughter Jane and his odd, extraordinary sister, Charlotte Charke. She had been at the Haymarket before, with Fielding.

Cibber made quite a to-do about coming back. He made speeches, he recalled his former successes—when he had had a fine company around him by the way—he promised wonderful things, and he made a general pest and nuisance of himself with his persistence and antics.

But he opened the little theatre once more on September 11th, 1744, with Shakespeare's *Romeo and Juliet* which he announced "was played for the first time for one hundred years." Master Cibber was wrong there, for Pepys records seeing it in 1662, less than a century before. But Cibber neither knew nor cared about that.

Since about 1680 it had been in the form of a tragedy by Otway, called *Caius Marius*. The star-crossed couple of Veronese lovers were depicted as noble ancient Romans, but that did not prevent a wholesale use of the story and of Shakespeare's lines—for the lady in the play breathed, "Oh Marius, Marius, wherefore art thou Marius?"—lines which later Fielding mimicked with "Oh, Tom Thumb, Tom Thumb, wherefore art thou Tom Thumb?" Most people thought he was making fun of Otway, so little was true Shakespeare known then and so much had he been despoiled by the vandals. Nor was Cibber's version pure Shakespeare; it was a bit of the Bard, a lot of Otway, and a little of his own.

But before he dared open, Theophilus had to fall back upon a device as well. He probably enjoyed this and was much more involved and artful about his method of selling tickets and taking money than downright Macklin had been.

He claimed to be opening an academy, no less. He announced in the daily Press—the *General Advertiser*—"At Mr. Cibber's Academy, in the Haymarket, will be a Concert; after which will be exhibited, gratis, a rehearsal in the form of a play, called *Romeo and Juliet*." He put back the old name, it will be observed.

Tickets were again sold outside the theatre in advance. The idea of the concert was kept, because it had succeeded with Macklin, but now the public were invited to see "a rehearsal" of a play, and for nothing. A very palpable shift, but it got by for a time.

Cibber cast his daughter Jane for Juliet, and Mr. Hill—Sir John as he called himself—late of the Haymarket, now of letters and medicine, has left a description of it:

"We remember a little Juliet of very considerable merit at the Haymarket; and nothing is more certain, than that she would have appeared, even with the same share of genius and accomplishments much more pleasing than she did, if there had been some gay young fellow for her lover, instead of a person whom we could not but remember, at every sentence she delivered concerning him, to be too old for her choice, too little handsome to be in love with, and into the bargain, her father."

This was, of course, Theo himself, and one recalls the description: "His person was far from pleasing; the features of his face were rather disgusting." What a set-up for Romeo!

But, of course, Cibber claimed it as a triumph and declared in the *General Advertiser* "that many persons of distinction were last night in the pit and gallery who could not get into the boxes." He also stated that it had been bespoke again, by some ladies of quality, for September 14th. Be that as it may, he was turned out by order of the Lord Chamberlain on October 22nd, and he goes out of the Haymarket story to find his death in the Irish Sea.

His sister, Charlotte Charke, made an attempt to keep the theatre open, but she too failed. The Haymarket was not lucky to the Cibbers, though perhaps they were lucky to it. So in this short period the Haymarket was run by Macklin the killer, Cibber the rogue, and Charlotte the woman.

This Charlotte Charke, who is already in the narrative, was the youngest child of old Colley Cibber, and by her father the least wanted, although beloved by her mother. Her father, however, gave her a good education. But she could never settle down to ladylike ways. The needle, then the hallmark of womanhood, was a useless implement in her fingers. Early on, she showed a spirit of impishness and mimicry. She adored periwigs, a weakness she inherited from her sire, and one morning when they lived at Twickenham, she got up very early, put on a most elaborate wig of her father's, and an equally elaborate waistcoat of her brother's, buckled, by some means, a belt and a sword around her diminutive person and paraded the garden, the whole surmounted by a large beaver laced hat of her father's too. She was quite convinced people would take her for him. The passing populace stayed to stare and to laugh. The parents laughed too, but although she had failed in this first impersonation, the spirit of the stage entered into Charlotte. When she grew older, she delighted in country life, and instead of the ladylike arts of music and embroidery, she became an expert rider, a fine shot and a groom who could hold her own with any professional. She suddenly evinced an interest in medicine and reading herbals, concocted brews of her own, which she administered to some aged invalids. Instead of dying of her doses, they came back for more.

She married Richard Charke, member of the Drury Lane orchestra and a thoroughly bad man. It was a good match for him to marry Colley Cibber's daughter. They had a child. His behaviour and pursuit of ladies of easy virtue made Charlotte leave him.

Eventually he died in Jamaica. Charlotte went on the stage, and made her first appearance at Drury Lane in 1730. She did very well as an actress, but never reached the front rank. She earned between twenty and thirty shillings a week. When her brother revolted against Highmore, she left the theatre too, but she was back again under Fleetwood, with whom she quarrelled. She played with Fielding at the Haymarket and with her little daughter lived in Oxendon Street nearby. Then she was with her brother again at the Haymarket and when he left she became its manageress. Failing completely, she went into trade. She knew nothing about it, but she ran an oil and colour and grocer shop in Long Acre. Of course, she failed. So she started a puppet show in James Street, Haymarket. And at this time a worthy widower paid attentions to her —she was very personable—and she married him secretly. So secret was it kept that people wondered if the ceremony had ever taken place at all, but she never disclosed his name and lived with him, or under his protection, until he died, when bad times hit her again. She fell into debt and was put in the Marshalsea Prison. Her good friends, the coffee-house keepers of Covent Garden, got her out.

On gaining her freedom, she adopted masculine attire altogether for everyday wear. It will be remembered she had played male parts for Fielding. She must have made a likely lad, for a young lady of fortune fell in love with her and there was a fine scene when she found out her mistake.

Cibber senior had now quarrelled with his daughter irrevocably. He never forgave her. She had appealed to him for help for her child and herself. He returned the letter unopened.

Charlotte now was reduced to straits. Still dressing as a man, she became a peddler, a valet to a nobleman—who never discovered she was a woman—an actor in booths at fairs, a waiter in a coffee-house, and always she struggled with courage to support herself and her child. She spent some time as a strolling player; she tried to keep pigs, but was swindled. She tried growing fruit, but thieves robbed her. She tried writing plays and writing novels. But she never had any luck at all and went down and down. When her father lay on his deathbed, she hastened to his house to attempt a reconciliation and get his blessing. He refused to see her, and died without saying a word to her.

Our last glimpse of her is in a hovel in Islington, amongst the heaps of refuse dumped by scavengers, trying to sell another novel to a publisher. She has practically no furniture, and is wearing old rags, but the hut is clean. There is a dog snuggled against her and she is using an old pair of bellows as a desk for writing on. She asks thirty guineas for her book. The publisher offers five. An old flash of the Cibber pride asserts itself, and, starving and needy as she is, it is refused. The publisher relents—and offers ten guineas. With a weary, hopeless smile, Charlotte accepts. And as she takes the last money she is to earn we leave her—daughter of a great actor-manager-playwright Poet Laureate, a clever brilliant woman, who was actress, beauty and authoress, but in whose nature a curious uneven streak had brought her to the depths of despair. She died in 1760, a woman of many parts— and not the least of them, the first manageress of the Haymarket Theatre.

CHAPTER VI

THE ENGLISH ARISTOPHANES

THE way in which greatness comes into the theatre and by means of which playhouses become great, is nearly always unexpected and curious. It is not always the fine, handsome actors, the beautiful actresses, the heroic figures, with "Hyperion's curls, the front of Jove himself," who do the trick. It is oftentimes men with apparently insuperable physical defects, which they conquer by their art, and by so conquering cover their careers and theatres with lustre. Betterton had a big head and short arms, and not too good a voice; Colley Cibber was short and had a high, squeaking voice. Macklin was frankly ugly. Garrick was small, yet could take on any role he chose and not only be it, but look it. Edmund Kean was shorter still—almost dwarfish. Irving had mannerisms over which his art conquered, but which would have slain a lesser man. Tree had curious qualities of voice, gait and other drawbacks. Yet all these became immortals in their calling and all added to the stature of the theatres in which they habitually played.

Samuel Foote, the man who was to bring the Haymarket Theatre to greatness, was just such another. He has made his entrance already, when playing for Macklin. He was both a great character and a great man of the theatre. His genius ran to mimicry. He was perhaps the greatest mimic who ever lived. His mimicry was more than mere impersonation; it was caricature in the highest degree; yet with all its elaborate malice, it never lost sight of its original. Samuel Foote was more than a mimic. He was a playwright as well. His plays are not great plays; they would not bear revival to-day. They were, however, brilliant commentaries on his time, designed to exploit his mimicry of living personalities. One or two of them held the stage for some years. And he was an expert manager; he knew how to run a theatre, he knew how to handle the public, he understood showmanship, he had his fingers on the pulse of the people, and above all he loved the theatre in which he worked. He took it from the depths and raised it to the heights. When he came it was an unlicensed place, the resort of those who could find no home elsewhere. When he left it, it was Theatre Royal.

Foote was in the true succession of the Haymarket dramatist-managers. Fielding, Macklin, Theophilus Cibber and even Charlotte Charke—all were playwrights as well. That line of managers who produced the goods they sold, who knew all about their craft as actors, managers and authors, continued at the Haymarket from 1720 until 1879—one hundred and fifty-nine years of unbroken tradition. No wonder the beautiful playhouse is so well rooted and stands so firmly. It has always been a house run by professionals, individual, distinct and distinctive, and it remains so to-day.

With theatres destined for greatness, as with nations, a man always arises in their hour of need. So it was with the Haymarket in the year 1747. Another three years of inactivity and depression had been suffered since its last burst of strife. Now it was fast becoming derelict; it might have suffered the fate of so many other places. But Destiny was on its side and did not mean that this brave, struggling house, which had endured so much, should suffer extinction. The hour was at hand, and with it the man. And the man was Samuel Foote. Let us make his acquaintance more fully and formally. He was a Cornishman, born at Truro in the year 1720, so he and his theatre were the same age when they came together in partnership. It was evidently in his stars. His father was a man of considerable importance locally, being a magistrate. His mother had been Eleanor, only daughter of Sir Edward Goodere. There was a strain of insanity in the family, which probably accounted for his erratic and extraordinary mind, but Samuel was sane enough. It accounted, however, without doubt, for the murder of one of his uncles by another, a deed which gave him his first boost into the town talk of London, when he wrote a pamphlet all about it and never tried to disguise the relationship between the murdered, the murderer and himself

Young Samuel Foote was sent to Worcester Grammar School, the Principal of which was a friend of his father's. The boy's impishness showed itself almost at once. He became the ringleader of all mischief: he led some other rebel boys in locking out the masters; he blacked another master's face whilst that worthy man was asleep; he undermined the chairs of his tutors so that they collapsed when sat upon, and showed at school all the devilry and disregard for other people's feelings which were to be his means of making a mark in life and history. He must have been a nice handful for the headmaster.

His gift of mimicry was discovered by his father when young Samuel gave him a perfect imitation of how a couple of justices of the peace were likely to behave at a local *cause célèbre* to be held on the following day. It showed itself at school as well. At the early age of ten he kept his schoolmates in a roar and became popular with those whom he amused by mimicry, even if it made him unpopular with those whom he mimicked. Popular or otherwise, it did not matter to Foote; he was indifferent to this all through his life. When invited to parties to amuse by mimicry of others, he turned the tables the next day by giving perfect imitations of his hosts, to the delight of the rest of the school. Foote's main idea in life was to be feared. In this he succeeded.

From Worcester Grammar School he went to Worcester College, Oxford, getting on the foundation through the influence of a relation. His behaviour at the University was what might be expected. He did things which entitled him to be "sent down." Yet he survived. He seems to have held the authorities there in awe of him, as he afterwards held all London. He went to Bath for a gay time. He returned, not surreptitiously, but seated on a coach, with a most undesirable acquaintance alongside him, a couple of footmen and dressed in extra fine clothes. Yet he had the gift of learning, for he acquired much knowledge of literature and of the classics, which stood him in good stead. He was always proud of his Latin and Greek.

His disregard for others showed itself when his old schoolmaster came to call upon him. His late pupil presented him with a very handsome piece of plate, which he selected from many such on his sideboard. The doctor, astonished at such generosity and knowing the young man's financial standing, asked what these things had cost. "I don't know what they cost," said Samuel, "but I shall soon know what they will fetch."

The whole of his career at Oxford is full of his pranks and his mischief. Yet he managed to stay there for three years. Then he tired of scholastic restraint, and the authorities were getting very tired of him too. So in January, 1740, he walked off without a word to anyone. He was in trouble at the time, of course. So he took the law into his own hands and vanished.

It was in the following year that the murder was committed in his family. And it was also that year in which Samuel Foote burst on the West End of London with his pamphlet, his impudence, his push and his wit. He was living upon expectations of his mother's money and, like all such cases, living well beyond his non-existent means. He had good rooms in the Temple, a well-stocked library, and was constant in his attendance at the Grecian and Bedford Coffee-houses, the smart resorts at that time. The men of the Temple went to the Grecian each morning in their elaborate dressing-gowns and slippers for their morning draughts, their scanning of the news and their conversation. It was a great place with Addison. The Bedford was the theatrical coffee-house. Here, by amateur critics, plays were made or broken, players condemned or extolled.

These were just the places for Samuel Foote. He went there unknown, but such was the force of his personality and such was his gift of wit and the quickness of his tongue that he took his place quite naturally amongst the greatest there.

There was only one end to that sort of thing, especially when gambling was joined to it. Debts grew and mounted, the situation became desperate. So Foote, as related, went on the stage. He went to the Haymarket, which thus became his first theatre and was fated to be his last. He made no great success there with Macklin, but he went to Drury Lane. There he made a hit in the part of Bayes in *The Rehearsal*. This was only natural. Part of the fun of the play is that the actor who performs Bayes should mimic the great players of his time. This Foote did to perfection. He was now being talked about, even if he was practically an amateur. But he never admitted his lack of knowledge. Foote was always sure he knew all about everything. He took no advice —unless he believed in it himself—he argued with experienced men, he made his own rules, he brooked no authority. That sort of thing does not go down in the theatre, where discipline must be maintained. And at Drury Lane there was David Garrick, also a famous Bayes. Foote never believed in playing second fiddle to anyone. But Garrick was a difficult nut to crack. Foote presumed on the fact that he was a "gentleman," which few of the players of those times could claim to be. But then, so was Garrick. Garrick had charm and polish in private life which Foote lacked. He got his effects by sarcasm, mimicry and fear. There was not room for the two of them in the same theatre, especially as Garrick was the unchallenged head of his profession and the greatest actor of his time.

All this rankled with Foote. He determined to be the equal of Garrick in position if not in talent. He knew in his heart of hearts that Garrick was the supreme actor; he knew he could never really challenge the versatility and power of that man. But he determined that he would himself control his own theatre, and that, in his own line, he would stand on a pinnacle too. It was his own jealous dislike of Garrick which made Foote take the step he did, and which spurred him on all his life to make a position for himself in which he should be as eminent as the great little David. And in this he succeeded. For, during a very considerable period, the two great contemporary forces of the English theatre were Garrick at Drury Lane and Foote at the Haymarket: entirely different in appeal and art, utterly unlike each other in their methods and performance, yet each supreme in his own domain.

Samuel Foote used David Garrick whenever he wanted to. He borrowed money from him; he demanded his help. Garrick, as mean a man as ever lived and as cautious with money as a miser, never refused a demand upon his purse by Foote, and always treated him with consideration. Foote was rude to him, lost no chance of flouting him, and yet always turned to him for assistance. It is probable that he knew he had Garrick on the run, and that he would never scruple to make use of the knowledge. Foote never respected anyone's feelings, never spared friend or foe. A thoroughly bad-natured man, he had courage and always fought for himself and for his theatre. To what lengths this went, this story will show. Foote, for all his talent, for all his undoubted greatness, was not a lovable character. He was a strong, resolute man, determined to achieve his destiny against any odds. He had the same tenacity which endowed the Haymarket Theatre. These two products of the year 1720 were made for each other, and made each other in turn.

That Garrick was nervous of Foote and that he permitted himself to be practically blackmailed by him is quite patent. For the great actor had the strongest dislike to being mimicked. It will be seen how another actor suffered for this, and at the Haymarket too. Foote was a supreme and ruthless mimic. No wonder he embarrassed and scared Garrick.

As regards the acting ability of these two contemporaries, there is no question at all. Garrick was equally great as tragedian or comedian. There has never been a greater or more versatile actor in history. Foote was a low comedian, by appearance and by nature. His face was round, his figure short and stout, he had none of the attributes of romance or the Tragic Muse. But he stood alone as a mimic. It was upon this and the droll ideas which seethed in his fertile brain that his fame depended.

A lesser man would have been horsewhipped and driven from the stage—indeed, from the town itself—for attempting a third of what Foote did. But Foote's supreme egotism, which clothed him in armour, his contempt for other people's opinions, and his utter fearlessness made even those he offended most leave him alone, lest he might do worse.

He was a shrewd man. He reckoned up his assets and he decided on comedy and mimicry. Nobody had exploited mimicry as an entertainment to the exclusion of all else. He would do so. He has had many successors. But he was the first to make mimicry a real basis for entertainment. And he did this at the Haymarket.

He could not get hold of Drury Lane or Covent Garden. Those places were beyond him. So for a while he played on in various roles, to get his name known. And almost at once, his personality, strong and arresting, got him into the limelight and the front rank. He played a wide range of parts (Fondlewife, Sir Paul Pliant, Bayes), etc. He had made his first appearance at Drury Lane on November 1st, 1745, as Sir Harry Wildair in *The Constant Couple*, with Peg Woffington playing opposite him. And his only previous experience had been his short season at the Haymarket with Macklin. He played Ben in *Love for Love*, and although the critics spoke badly of it, the public applauded him to the echo. He had been in Dublin, too, and made a success.

In the short space of three years he considered himself able to take a theatre for himself and to throw down the gauntlet to Drury Lane and Covent Garden. It was a considerable risk, but he never feared that. Nobody knew better than Foote that he would be watched, persecuted and even imprisoned if he put a foot wrong. But opposition only heartened him. He liked to be alone, to stand alone, and to fight alone. He would show them what could be done by a clever man, a man of birth and breeding, a man with brains and ability. Master Davy Garrick might think himself very grand; Master John Rich might think he was a great man. But he, Samuel Foote, was as great and maybe greater. They had Patents, had they? He hadn't. But he made up his mind that, before he died, he would stand the equal of any of them, and that the theatre he controlled should equal their playhouses as well.

The smart, social world of London was considerably startled on the morning of April 22nd, 1747, to read in the public prints an announcement which said:

The stage and interior of the New Theatre Royal, Haymarket, as seen on the opening
night, July 4th, 1821.

Top left
Mrs. Charles Kean.

Top right
Madame Vestris.

Middle
Mr. Charles Dibdin.

Right
Charlotte Cushman.

"At the Theatre in the Haymarket this day (April 22, 1747) will be performed a Concert of Musick, with which will be given gratis a new entertainment, called "The Diversions of the Morning, and a farce taken from The Old Bachelor, entitled 'The Credulous Husband'—Fondlewife—Mr. Foote. And an Epilogue by the B-d-d Coffee House."

It was an impertinent announcement, especially the reference to the Bedford Coffee-house, where, as Foote and all London knew, the show could be discussed and torn to pieces later in the day. But it had the desired effect. The town turned up in force to see this new thing. Foote had with him Shuter, an excellent comedian, Costello and one or two other first-class performers from Drury Lane.

What sort of a show did they see? First they heard a short and probably indifferent concert. Then came the *pièce de résistance*. It was practically a monologue by Foote, relieved by one or two other people whom he could use as stooges. He took the idea which Vanbrugh and Fielding had used, and under the pretence of conducting a rehearsal he exposed the failings and foibles of the principal actors and actresses of the day by superb and trenchant mimicry. He assigned them each a role in life which they could fulfil if (and when) acting failed them, and he showed by his impersonations how perfectly well fitted they were for it.

Quin, with his deep sonorous voice and weighty manner, he depicted as a watchman, and the house rocked when Foote concluded by shouting, "Past twelve o'clock and a cloudy morning." He was cruel to Delane, a good actor, but who was reputed to have only one eye, by impersonating him as a beggar in St. Paul's Churchyard, whining, "Would you bestow your pity on a poor blind man?"

He had the voice of Ryan, a shrill, rasping pipe, when he cried, "Razors to grind, scissors to grind, penknives to grind," at the same time imitating the exact sound of a grindstone at work. He greatly diverted all Peg Woffington's friends and admirers in the audience, by impersonating her as an orange girl, giving a faithful imitation of her voice, lovely at one moment and then running into a squeak, when he cried, "Would you have some oranges? Have some orange chips, ladies and gentlemen. Would you have some nonpareils? Would you have a bill of the play?" The fair and talented Peg was furious when she heard about it—and she heard fast enough.

There was also an actor called Woodward who came under his lash. This man also was a mimic, but he never mimicked unless someone imitated him first. Then he hit back shrewdly. He was a good harlequin, a fine comedian, a great Aguecheek in *Twelfth Night*, and a superb Bobadil. He was immensely funny, immensely popular, and extremely graceful.

Foote depicted him exactly as he was—despite the difference in their

F

appearance—but confessed it hard to discover what trade Woodward was fitted for. So, to sum up the character, he gave an impersonation of Woodward playing "Sir Fopling Flutter"—"Wherever I go, there goes a gentleman, and when you have said Gentleman why, Oh, you have said more than is true." Woodward, it may be mentioned, was the son of a tallow-chandler.

But his final imitation, and the one for which they were all waiting, was that of David Garrick. It was a masterpiece; it was Garrick to the life. It portrayed the man and the method, and the highlight came when Foote played, as Garrick, the death scene of *Lothario*. Here he introduced the hesitancies with which Garrick played this sort of scene. Foote played around with this mannerism, but kept the picture clear as he gasped, "Adorns my fall and che-che-che-che-cheers my heart in dy-dy-dy-dying." It brought down the house. Nothing pleases the public more than to see a great figure, especially a great actor, ridiculed. It is not so funny for the victim. Garrick had done his share of mimicry, but he never liked others to mimic him. The only person who did so and got away with it was the very Woodward whom Foote had mocked that same day. Garrick probably forgave this because he knew there was no malice in it. But although in his heart he hated Foote's imitations of him, he always pretended to be vastly amused. Foote was a big man now, and powerful. It did not do to fall out with him, So Garrick put up with it, and was always careful to keep on the right side of Foote. Probably he knew that his forbearance annoyed Foote. He did not lose his temper or show resentment, which was exactly what Foote was trying to make him do.

Foote followed *The Diversions of the Morning* with the excerpt from *The Old Bachelor*, playing Fondlewife, in which part he fancied himself. But it was a mistake, for by so doing he had broken the law. He had performed a play without licence in an unlicensed theatre.

However, the success was enormous and a tremendous epilogue was spoken in the Bedford Coffee-house that night, as Foote had intended. He performed it again the next day to a packed house— and then the blow fell. The Patent theatres took immediate action— those imitations may have swayed Garrick—and constables burst into the theatre, dismissed the audience, and left Foote high and dry. Round 1 had gone against him.

But the man who ranges himself against his whole profession and the laws which govern it, and who does so with his eyes open, is not easily put down. Foote knew the reason for the closing as well as anyone. But he also knew that he had invited it. He had taken money at the doors; he had performed a short play. But he had learned his lesson. He got to work once again, and the town was tickled by his ingenuity. For the very next day they read in their *General Advertiser*:

"On Saturday afternoon, exactly at twelve o'clock, at the new

Theatre in the Haymarket, Mr. Foote begs the favour of his friends to come and drink a dish of chocolate with him, and 'tis hoped there will be a great deal of company and some joyous spirits. He will endeavour to make the morning as diverting as possible. Tickets to be had for this entertainment at George's Coffee House, Temple Bar, without which no one will be admitted. N.B. Sir Dilbury Diddle will be there and Lady Betty Frisk has absolutely promised. . . ."

There was a rush on George's Coffee House. Sir Dilbury Diddle? . . . Lady Betty Frisk? . . . To make the morning as diverting as possible? Foote was at it again. Those who had seen the *Diversions* and those who had missed them crowded to get tickets. There was the additional spice, too, of breaking the law, always an inducement if it can be done without personal risk. Foote was always worth-while.

A large and distinguished number of "guests" assembled in the Haymarket Theatre to meet their host and to drink his chocolate. There was a hum of suppressed excitement. What had this joker got up his sleeve? Where was the chocolate? Why had they been invited to drink it?

The curtain rose and mine host Foote came forward amidst great applause. He welcomed them all and told them that he was then engaged in training some young people to be actors. With their permission, whilst the chocolate was being prepared, he would continue with the work of putting the youngsters through their paces. He called on the "beginners," all specially engaged for the purpose, and under the pretence of rehearsing them gave a long programme of his inimitable imitations. It was a tremendous, resounding success.

The law could not touch him. He was not charging people to see a play, he was not even performing a play; he was conducting a rehearsal. All that he was selling was cups of chocolate, and there was no law against that. Nor was there any restriction on the price. He could charge what he liked, if people were willing to pay it.

No action was taken against him. He had won the battle. He was an actor-manager in his own theatre. There was little likelihood, unless he lost his head completely, of that theatre ever being closed again so long as Samuel Foote had the wit and ingenuity to please the town. Foote and the Haymarket had triumphed.

Some authorities give the date of the opening as Friday, April 24th. It matters little. What matters is the success. It became the rage of the town, this performance by Foote, who entertained in his theatre as if he were in his own drawing-room. There was so much to enjoy, so much to laugh at, so much to discuss afterwards. Nobody escaped his lash. All the actors and actresses trembled—those who were being pilloried and those who knew their turn would come. Even the fierce Macklin did not escape—and for once he does not seem to have taken any reprisal. Perhaps he knew that, unless he killed Foote, that individual would only turn his own action against him. And he had got away with murder once; he dare not risk it a second time. Meanwhile, the Haymarket was full and Foote's treasury was full as well. Only one thing was dubious—the hour of the show. Midday was a little early for some of the brighter spirits, who kept it up late, and certainly a little early for the fine ladies, whose elaborate toilette required time. Nor were they eager to expose their charms to the bright midday sun.

So, on June 1st, 1747, came a further announcement. It stated:

"At the request of several persons who are desirous of spending an hour with Mr. Foote, but find the time inconvenient, instead of chocolate in the morning, Mr. Foote's friends are desired to drink a dish of tea with him at half past six this day, to-morrow and Wednesday, at which time they are obliged to give over, most of the company being engaged to set out on Thursday for country expeditions. N.B. Doors open at half after four."

This caused a bigger rush than ever, which was just what Foote desired. The ladies and gentlemen of fashion fought to get in, hoping to see their friends lampooned by Foote and praying that they themselves might escape his lash. Such was his success that Foote employed the old, worn-out trick of "positively the last performance." On June 6th out came the notice: "June 6th. The 35th and positively the last, at the desire of several persons of quality, Mr. Foote will give tea this day at half after six, having persuaded all the performers to postpone their journey until Monday." Again a house packed to suffocation.

It will be observed that Foote, by his *Diversions of the Morning*, had been the true inventor of the *matinée*. The hours of playgoing had been getting later and later. In Restoration times it was three o'clock, but by now playgoing was an evening affair. Foote got an audience at midday and was the first actor-manager to do so.

The name and fame of Foote and his Haymarket increased. The Little Theatre in the Hay had found its champion at last—a very strange and curious one, but a champion who was afraid of nothing. All opposition went down before his lance and those who might have given him pause were afraid to do so. Foote was now known as the English Aristophanes, and the title has always remained his.

There was resentment, of course; there were curses low and bitter. If a tenth of the wishes for bad luck had assailed him, Foote would have been ruined. But because of this bold impertinence and his fearless aggressiveness, those curses, those ill wishes, were muttered in vain.

Lacy, David Garrick's partner, who had been a victim of Foote's imitations, was furious. He threatened to break Foote's neck, and complained to the Licenser of Plays. But the clever Garrick sent a private note to that official, stating that he did not object and that Mr. Foote was quite welcome to deal with him. He did not want it said that the step had been taken at his instigation. He trusted he was too courteous for that. . . . So nothing was done by the Lord Chamberlain's Department.

Samuel Foote was soon at it again. In 1748 he presented a new show called *An Auction of Pictures*. The pictures were, of course, his imitation of celebrities, and the same marvellous likenesses they were, too. It was as big a success as his "Tea." It went on and on. He now included imitations of other people besides those of the profession. The net was spreading, and it was all fish that came into it, so far as Foote was concerned. It was necessary to broaden the scope, or the repetition would become tiresome. Besides, it kept people on their toes with expectation and with fear. London was now divided into new sections, those who had been imitated by Foote and those who had not. These were again sub-divided into those who had suffered and resented it, but kept on going to see their friends suffer too; those who had suffered, but did not mind because they thought it gave them social standing ("You must be somebody, my dear, if Mr. Foote picks upon you. He does not deal in anyone but celebrities"); and those who went in deadly fear that they might find themselves, in Foote's phrase, "brought upon the stage" and held up to ridicule. The whole thing was exciting, anyway. And Foote reaped a fine harvest.

But one person he never attempted to imitate. It must have irked him, for the subject was one which lent itself admirably to mimicry and characterisation. It was that great, bear-like, odd, shambling, untidy mass of brain and body called Dr. Samuel Johnson.

Samuel Foote and Dr. Johnson knew each other well. They were both great figures of their time. They had something in common too. Neither of them had any fear of public opinion; both spoke their minds freely. Neither minced words or cared twopence about other people's feelings. Dr. Johnson had a very high opinion of Foote's talent and wit. He would praise him loudly in public—it is probable that this galled Garrick, too—but he did not approve of Foote's basic character. How could he? Nevertheless, when Boswell decried Foote's habit of making fun of his guests and audiences, Johnson spoke up. Boswell had said that Foote's action was "making fools of his company." "Why, sir," came the reply, "when you go to see Foote you do not go to see a saint; you go to see a man who will be entertained at your house and then bring you on a public stage. Sir, he does not *make* fools of his company; they whom he exposes are fools already; he only brings them into action."

On another occasion Boswell said that Foote had a great deal of humour and a singular talent for exhibiting character. "Sir," replied Johnson, "it is not a talent—it is a vice; it is what others abstain from. It is not comedy, which exhibits the character of a species, as that of a miser gathered from many misers; it is a farce which exhibits individuals."

Foote probably had a pretty high respect for Johnson and what

he said of him, for the greater Samuel had a way of going right to
the root of things. And he never lost a chance of making a good remark
on the subject of Foote. A bit later, when Foote had gone to Dublin,
a report came to London that he had been kicked. This gave great joy
to most of his victims. But Dr. Johnson had the last, and best, word.
Said he: "I am glad of it. He is rising in the world. When he was in
England, no one thought it worth-while to kick him." Johnson at his
best.

Johnson on Foote is the best guide to that extraordinary fellow's
character: "The first time I was in company with Foote was at Fitz-
herberts'. Having no good opinion of the fellow, I was resolved not to be
pleased—and it is very difficult to please a man against his will. I went
on eating my dinner pretty sullenly, affecting not to mind him. But
the dog was so very comical, that I was obliged to throw down my
knife and fork, throw myself back in my chair and fairly laugh it out.
No, sir, he was irresistible."

But Johnson knew him and never paid the slightest attention to
anything Foote told him as gossip or news. "He is quite impartial,"
he said, "for he tells lies of everyone."

Later Foote was tempted at last to bring Dr. Johnson "upon the
stage." Probably the supply of celebrities was running short. The
temptation was great. It would make such an impact, it would draw
such crowded houses. He put the story round; of course, Dr. Johnson
soon heard it. He and Foote met at dinner at Thomas Davies's, the
bookseller. Looking very hard at Foote, he inquired of Davies what was
the price of an oak stick? He was told, "Sixpence." "Why then, sir,"
said the doctor to Davies, with a full stare at Foote, "give me leave to
send your servant to purchase me a shilling one. I'll have a double
quantity." It was enough. Foote never mimicked Dr. Samuel Johnson.

But very few others escaped. The *Auction of Pictures* was quite an
institution at the Haymarket, and everybody went repeatedly to see it.
The Haymarket, for the purpose of this entertainment, became known
as Foote's Auction Rooms, a pretty obvious bit of dust thrown in the
eyes of the Licensing authorities, who, wise in their generation, let
Foote severely alone after they closed his *Diversions of the Morning.*
He was getting more and more independent and caring less and less
about them, but he still kept up this device, although the sale of tea and
chocolate had gone. It is noteworthy that when the Entertainment Tax
had been increased and was being resisted by West End of London
managements between the two World Wars, it occurred to one smart
firm to sell a box of chocolates at the box office instead of a seat for the
show—the box by a coincidence being the same price. This attempt to
evade taxation did not succeed. But that manager probably thought he
had struck a brilliant and new idea. Really old Samuel Foote had
forestalled him nearly two centuries before.

Foote's seasons were not long, the public was too small for continued runs, but he always did a lot of advertising, and found reasons for performances, such as being "for the sufferers in the late calamity, when Mr. Foote will exhibit a choice collection of pictures." On June 11th, *The Auction* was performed for the thirty-fifth time. On the 14th and 16th June, he revived his "Tea."

The next season he revived *The Auction* with as great success as before, and a new lot of pictures. He opened that season on January 2nd, and with considerable impudence announced that the performance would be in aid of the Lock Hospital.

Another announcement of his that season read:

"At the forty-ninth day's sale at his auction room at the Haymarket, Mr. Foote will exhibit a nice collection of pictures—some entirely new lots, consisting of a poet, a beau, a Frenchman, a miser, a tailor, a sot, two young gentlemen, and a ghost; two of which are originals, the rest copies from the best masters."

He also added to his attractions what he called a "Cat Concert" which was a burlesque imitation of the popular Italian opera which was the drawing card at the Opera House across the way from him. Society rolled up as usual to see itself and its tastes turned to ridicule.

For this Cat Concert he engaged a man who, because of his mastery in animal—and especially cat—imitations, was called "Cat" Harris. The whole thing was a furore. Foote was getting prosperous, and so was the Haymarket.

But running the Haymarket was not yet a full-time job for Foote. He did not consider the time was ripe. He still appeared at the other theatres, and it was strange that they engaged him. He got engagements from Garrick at Drury Lane, who had never ceased to show him friendliness and never ceased to suffer for it. That Foote hated him, he knew. Whenever he told a story about Foote in company, he would always preface it by saying, "You know that Mr. Foote hates me. . . ." He hoped that, by his own good deeds to Foote and Foote's churlish treatment of him, to win and keep the public sympathy. He need not have troubled about public opinion. Nobody liked Foote; nobody could like him. Garrick was universally popular, despite his besetting vice of meanness, which he kept to himself as much as possible. But Foote exulted in the insults he poured upon Garrick and bled him whenever he could. By 1748 he was a successful actor-manager. He was not Mr. Foote the mimic or Mr. Foote, the actor. He was Mr. Foote of the Haymarket Theatre.

And that playhouse was now on the verge of fresh success, fresh excitements and strange happenings. Its days of uncertainty and difficulty were over and done with. It was now quite definitely an important London theatre. It was London's home of comedy.

CHAPTER VII

FOOTE RULE OF JOY AND TERROR

FOOTE disliked a victim retaliating as much as he enjoyed making that victim wince. Woodward, the actor who had imitated Garrick, decided that Foote should be checked. He wrote and performed, at Drury Lane, a little play called *Tit for Tat*, in which he in turn ridiculed Foote's performances and Foote himself. One of his "hits" at Foote ran:

> *"But when I play'd Othello, thousands swore*
> *They never saw such tragedy before."*

Foote was furious. He wrote to Garrick, demanding that this should be stopped. He said that he appreciated the actor's attempts to ridicule him as little as he did the manager's "passive wit" for allowing him to do so. And he made grim threats of reprisals. He warned that he had a farce which would be very bitter to some, amusing to many and very profitable to himself. And, as a gesture of disapproval, he removed himself from the Free List at Drury Lane. He had a sneer for Garrick in this, for he wrote: "If the book-keeper returns this, he will be cheating you of five shillings—a sum not very contemptible to you." This was not only a dig at Garrick's parsimony: it was also a declaration of war on Garrick. But Garrick, although he wrote a mild letter and tried to return good for evil, could not prevent the production of the little farce, *Tit for Tat*.

It led to a most childish display of bad temper all round, and the production of farce and counter-farce in which personalities were indulged freely, but honours remained even. It is typical of Foote that he should, thus early in his career, dream of trying to give orders to Garrick as to how he should run his theatre. But there was no limit to his effrontery.

Foote had a hearty contempt for his public, and for mankind in general. He did things which would have ruined those of lesser insolence or smaller courage, and he always got away with it. Once, however, the public turned on him—but even then they soon forgot and forgave.

Foote was a real showman. He knew how to attract the masses. He knew that curiosity is an overweaning human trait. He knew that there were thousands who would pay good money to see something which they did not believe possible. He worked a hoax on London which was so successful that it caused another riot at the Haymarket—a riot led by a Royal Duke. And although this aroused great anger at the time, he was to profit by it in the end, for it got him and his theatre more talked about than ever. Those who had not been made fools of crowed over those that had, and the name of Foote and the Haymarket was on every one's lips.

In 1749 an announcement in the Press caused great excitement. Foote understood advertising. This is what the public read:

"At the New Theatre in the Haymarket, this present day, to be seen a person who performs the several most surprising things following, viz.: First, he takes a common walking cane from any of the spectators, and thereon he plays the music of every instrument now in use, and likewise sings to surprising perfection. Secondly, he presents you with a common wine bottle, which any of the spectators may first examine; this bottle is placed on a table in the middle of the stage, and he (without any equivocation) goes into it, in the sight of all the spectators, and sings in it; during his stay in the bottle any person may handle it, and see plainly that it does not exceed a common tavern bottle. Those on the stage or in the boxes may come in masked habits (if agreeable to them) and the performer (if desired) will inform them who they are.

"Stage 7/6d. Boxes 5/-; Pit 3/-; Gallery, 2/-.

"To begin half-an-hour after six o-clock."

This announcement had a startling effect. On the night of January 16th, 1749, the Haymarket was besieged by a mass of people, all eager to pay their money to witness something which their senses told them was quite impossible. There was a wild rush when the doors opened and the theatre was packed to its utmost limits. Foote had increased the prices and the takings were a record. But the public paid without a murmur. His Royal Highness the Duke of Cumberland—"Butcher" Cumberland, whose purple visage made children scream when they saw him—was an early comer and paid his money like everybody else. There was a hubbub of excitement as the audience waited for the marvels.

And it soon became obvious that they were being hoaxed. For half-past six came and went, and there was no sign of the conjuror or his bottle. At seven o'clock the house became restive. Shouts and cat-calls were heard. The audience was clearly getting out of hand, but still there was nothing doing on the stage. The uproar grew every moment. Suddenly, Foote's prompter appeared on the stage, looking pale and nervous, and took off his hat, as a signal that he wished to address the house. The audience quietened to hear what he had to say.

With a glance at the wings, to make sure of his retreat, the prompter told them that the management regretted deeply that the Great Bottle Conjuror was indisposed and could not appear that evening. Those who so desired could have their money returned, but if they would come the next evening, and pay double, the Great Bottle Conjuror, to make up for his non-appearance—would get into a pint bottle instead of a quart bottle. . . .

This was too much. The audience now realised they had been hoaxed, and they made the response usual in those days. A lighted candle was thrown on the stage—the prompter fled hastily. The Duke of Cumberland drew his sword and shouting to the audience to follow him, leapt on the stage and began to hack at the hangings and scenery. The audience followed with a will. In the mêlée Cumberland dropped his sword—a diamond-hilted one—and it vanished for ever. He yelled with rage and cursed heartily, and the crowd, never a respectful one in those times—raised the cry that "Billy the Butcher had lost his knife." Everyone, except the Duke, was delighted. It added zest to the chase. Curtains, scenery, hangings were torn down, seats and boxes kicked to pieces, and the debris was carried from the theatre and made into a huge bonfire outside the entrance. Despite their having been fooled, the audience thoroughly enjoyed themselves. It is a marvel that the theatre escaped complete destruction by fire. And the mob were in the mood for a general riot, a very popular pastime then, and this might have had serious and far-reaching consequences.

Samuel Foote, true to his nature, made pretence of being very aggrieved—in public. He wrote to the papers complaining of the damage done and the loss which he had suffered, because he, like the public, had been gulled. But to himself and his staff, he chuckled with glee. He had wanted new scenery and hangings—and the money he had taken would buy them for him.

The story went round later that he had done this trick as a result of a wager with the Duke of Montagu, who laid odds against the public being hoaxed by so transparent a joke. But it is more than likely that the whole idea was Foote's.

Despite Foote's complaint, the damage was soon repaired, and the theatre opened again ten days later.

Foote was now to blossom forth as a dramatist and actor-manager-dramatist in the true Haymarket manner. He began to write his own plays and to stage them. The first was called *The Knights*. Probably he knew that the one-man mimicry would begin to pall—and there must have been few new subjects for his shafts—so he decided that the time had come for more substantial fare. *The Knights* had curious construction. One of the chief characters, Sir Penurious Trifle, never appeared at all. He was talked about and described, and then Foote, in the character of Hartop imitated the unseen knight. No doubt it was founded on a well-known personality. The other knight rejoiced in the name of Sir Gregory Gazette because of his fondness for reading newspapers. That descriptive form of nomenclature was a stage and novelists' tradition for centuries—down to living memory, in fact. Foote tacked on his *Cats' Opera* to this work, so as to have plenty of buffoonery. He had Shuter and Harris in this, and at the last rehearsal Harris, the king of cat imitators, was missing.

This was a disaster. Nobody knew where he lived, other than that he had lodgings somewhere in the Minories. Foote sent off Shuter to find Harris. Shuter, a good animal mimic himself, was told to go down to the Minories and explore it and its courts whilst he made cat noises. Very soon, as he catawauled in a nearby alley, he had his answer. Harris, who had overslept (he was probably sleeping off "the night before") heard the familiar sound and answered in like manner. This is probably the most extraordinary "call" to rehearsal in stage history.

Just after the run of *The Knights*, Foote vanished from the scene. He went to France; nobody knew why. He had been doing well at the Haymarket, and should have been in funds. Some said he had scuttled to dodge his creditors; others said he had inherited another fortune and gone off to spend it. At any rate, he is missing for two years—from 1750 to 1752—and he came back to do a play of his own at Drury Lane.

It is not possible in these pages to register all the amazing sayings and doings of this remarkable man and great figure of the Haymarket Theatre. His jokes and jeers, his rude, insolent comments on all and sundry, and on Garrick in particular, were repeated daily in the coffee-houses. Only once did Foote meet his match, and this was in a protégé of his own, the wily, acute-minded Tate Wilkinson, who imitated him so well on the stage that the delighted audience yelled, "Foote outdone." There was continual war between Wilkinson and Foote—and if the former is to be believed in his most entertaining and instructive *Memoirs*, Foote served him some pretty dirty tricks.

But Foote, despite his malice and ill humour, never succeeded in harming him—and much less did he harm Garrick. He had a satellite in one Arthur Murphy, a brilliant but unscrupulous dramatist and journalist, who helped Foote in his attacks. But David Garrick was too great for them.

In the early 1750's John Potter, creator of the Haymarket Theatre, died. He had lived to see his theatre famous—even if the fame was spasmodic; he had lived to see it become a regular theatre of repute in London, so he had at least realised part of his original ambition and proved his early judgment to be right.

He was succeeded by a man called John Whitehead, about whom little is known. There is not much of note at the Haymarket during Whitehead's reign. Things were to be hand to mouth until Foote returned to his spiritual home. This he did in 1758. According to the records, he treated for a licence for the theatre. His name is coupled with Theophilus Cibber's in this matter, but it is difficult to understand how anything in the nature of a partnership could have existed between these two men. Theophilus was just the sort of man to arouse the contempt of Foote. On the other hand, his unpopularity may have inclined Foote's perverse mind towards him. What is most likely, however, is that Theophilus, now totally discredited and nearing the end of his career, may have approached Foote whilst that worthy was away on his travels and during his Dublin season, with an idea of getting the theatre between them, and to have held out all sorts of inducements in connection therewith. He had a glib and persuasive tongue. At all events, there was a lease of the theatre to the pair of them. As it dates from 1758, when Foote was in Dublin, Cibber may have done plays at the Haymarket of which we have no trace nowadays, and it may have suited Foote to have the theatre kept warm for him. A strange fact is that Theophilus Cibber was drowned in 1758, when he was on his way to Ireland.

Anyhow, in 1760 Samuel Foote re-entered the Haymarket as lessee. And for the first time in its forty years of existence the Haymarket assumed its place as a stable and established theatre. The periods of long closing and of haphazard openings were nearing an end. Foote was there, and he made it secure. Unstable and unreliable himself, he created the Haymarket as a home of drama; its theatrical vagabondage was over. It was now to enter the lists seriously against the two Patent theatres.

Foote started off with a play which he had already produced in Dublin with success. It was called *The Minor*. For London, he rewrote, enlarged it and gave it much polish. It is perhaps his best play. It was a very daring one, for it satirised religion, or at least the preaching and teaching of Whitefield, then at the height of his power. Foote had been to hear him preach. He regarded him as fair game. He may also have regarded him as a rival in attracting audiences. But he put him in *The Minor* and the portrait was unmistakable.

It is characteristic of the man that he seized upon the most notice-able defect of the great preacher and, in the play, called him "Dr. Squintum." One character was a disreputable, immoral and dissolute woman, called Mrs. Cole, which Foote played himself. She is converted by and becomes an adherent of the preacher. Whitefield had a fanatical manner, which Foote mimicked. To those who complained, Foote could plead self-defence, for Whitefield was constantly attacking the theatre from the pulpit.

Foote knew he was sailing close to the wind in lampooning a popular preacher at a time when religion was becoming fashionable, and he took every precaution to protect himself and prevent his satire being blunted. Also it should be remembered that all plays now had to be submitted to the Licenser of Plays before they were performed. It is said that Foote, to make doubly sure, had submitted the play to no less a person than the Archbishop of Canterbury himself for his approval. His Grace was not to be caught, and returned the play, asking to be excused. He realised that Foote would have exploited the Arch-bishop's comments. That he read it there is little doubt, for he tried to prevent it from being licensed, and it is quite likely that he struck out certain passages which were disallowed.

Foote was not only content with a smack at the great Whitefield, but he also had a cut in this play at that Tate Wilkinson who was fast becoming a thorn in his side. In the play he libelled him atrociously. But Wilkinson said nothing and eventually had his revenge. He and Shuter were regular in their attendance at Whitefield's Tabernacle, for the purpose of taking notes. Shuter may have been really touched by Whitefield's eloquence, for he seems to have made liberal contributions to the collections, so much so that Whitefield approved of him, despite his being an actor, and actually advised his congregation to support Shuter's benefit. Which may have been what Shuter was aiming at.

Foote produced *The Minor* at the Haymarket in 1760. Once again he relied upon his own powers, for he had an unknown company. It was an immediate success. It ran for thirty-eight consecutive nights and was put into the regular bill at intervals for years afterwards. It became also a regular piece in all stock companies. It owed a great deal to the tremendous controversy which it aroused. Foote did not mind what people said of him or his works, so long as they paid to see them. *The Minor* has little or no plot—just enough to string the scenes together—but it is a gem of characterisation. Some of its scenes are so brilliant that there is little doubt they inspired Sheridan's *School for Scandal*.

As letters and protests from Whitefield's admirers poured in, Foote answered them all, scoring all along the line. It was just the sort of publicity he wanted. And his own performance of the iniquitous Mrs. Cole was a masterpiece of comic acting.

The Minor was such a success that it was done at Drury Lane as well. Wilkinson, the libelled, had gone to Covent Garden. He persuaded Rich to do the play, and get it out before they could produce it at Drury Lane. He would, he said, play Mrs. Cole and mimic and ridicule Foote himself. It was this news which made Foote issue his famous threat to Rich. He had rushed to Covent Garden and bounced unbidden into Rich's office. And thus he addressed him:

"Damn it, you old hound, if you dare to allow Wilkinson, that pug-nosed son of a —— to take such a liberty with me as to mimicry, I will bring yourself, Rich, on the stage. If you want to engage that pug, black his face and let him bring the tea kettle in a pantomime; for, damn the fellow, he is as ignorant as a whore's maid. And if he dares to appear in my characters in *The Minor* I will instantly produce your old and ridiculous self, with your three cats, and that hound of a mimic, all together, next week at Drury Lane, for the general diversion of the pit, boxes and galleryes, and that will be paying you, you squinting old Hecate, too great a compliment." And he slammed his way out.

It frightened Rich, who counselled delay, but Wilkinson and his friend Sparks, another actor, egged him on. Rich argued the point with them, calling them all out of their names, as was his habit—Sparkish, Williamskin, and referring to Mr. Footseye—but at length gave way.

Meanwhile, Foote and the company at Drury Lane, to which he had transferred himself, pushed ahead. Foote got advance puffs in all the papers, and the bills went up on the walls, when the sudden death of King George II on Saturday, October 25th, 1760, put an end to all rivalries. The theatres were closed for a fortnight. Then they both opened, and at Covent Garden Wilkinson mimicked Foote mimicking Whitefield. The battle between the theatres raged for a while and occupied so much of Foote's time that he missed the chance of opening the Haymarket that next summer of 1761, when the other two theatres were closed. Instead, he stopped at Drury Lane and ran the place himself.

He was on top of the world. Everyone paid him court out of fear and he had a ready reply for all occasions. At a nobleman's house, a footman drew his attention to the fact that his handkerchief was hanging out of his pocket. "I thank you, my good man," said the wit. "You know your company better than I do." When established at the Haymarket, the Duke of Cumberland, once wickedly hoaxed there, came round to the green-room. "Well, Foote," said he, "here I am, ready as usual to swallow all your good things." "Really," replied Foote, "Your Royal Highness must have a good digestion, for you never bring any up again."

A friend of his was constantly humming an air. Foote asked him why he did so. "Because it haunts me," was the unsuspecting reply. "No wonder," retorted Foote. "You are continually murdering it." A very dull and extremely eminent physician who had written some poems bored him on the subject. He told Foote that he had a mind to publish them, but he was so busy; he had so many irons in the fire! "Take my advice, Doctor, and put your poems where your irons are," was Foote's quick retort. He could never let Garrick alone, even in private. He had a small bust of the great actor on his desk. He would say to people who admired it, "Ah, I expect you wonder why I keep him so near my money. But you see, he has no arms." He never lost a chance to expose the parsimony of Garrick.

Once when they were together at the Bedford Head, David dropped a guinea. Both men searched for it without success. "I wonder where it has gone," remarked Foote. "Gone? Gone to the devil, I should think," said Garrick impatiently. It was Foote's chance. "Trust you to make a guinea go further than anyone else," he snapped.

Even the angry, dangerous Macklin was not immune from Foote's sarcasm. That fine, though fire-eating, actor set up a room in a Covent Garden tavern wherein he lectured. It was an ill-fated venture which brought ruin upon Macklin. Foote, instead of helping the ageing man, used to stand at the end of the room and interject rude remarks. Macklin remonstrated with Foote.

"Sir," said he, "do you understand what you are talking about?"

"No, sir," said the imperturbable Foote. "Do you?"

Once Macklin was lecturing on memory, how to train it and how to master any speech instantly on the spot. He asked anyone to write down, or recite a speech, which he said he would repeat word for word. Foote instantly supplied this bit of nonsense which has become a classic: "So she went into the garden to cut a cabbage leaf to make an apple pie, and at the same time, a great she-bear, coming up the street, pops its head into the shop—'What, no soap?' So he died, and she very imprudently married the barber, and there were present the Picninnies and the Jobillies and Garolillies and the Great Panjandrum himself, with the little round button at top, and they all fell to playing the game of catch-as-catch-can till the gunpowder ran out at the heels of their boots."

It beat Macklin.

Foote was by now the unchallenged English Aristophanes. A fine performer, a great mimic, a good playwright and a consummate showman, his supreme achievement was the creation of a theatre royal— the Haymarket. All his life he encountered confusion and trouble, but still he pursued his way. His dislike and jealousy of Garrick spurred him on, and the heritage of that one-sided feud is the Haymarket Theatre we know to-day. Foote was, despite his acid tongue, a good mixer. He had the entrée everywhere, and his wit would keep the table in a roar. All this added to his reputation, gave him support and patronage for his theatre.

In 1762 Foote produced a play at the Haymarket called *The Orators*. Again it was a rambling affair, but he had a rather better cast than usual. It included Shuter, Weston, Palmer, Quick, Bannister and himself— a company of stars, indeed, for the little theatre to house. It was a free-and-easy show, with Foote as a lecturer. Two of the characters make their first appearance in a stage box and have a chat with a candle-snuffer (an important functionary in those days of stage lighting by candle). They then demand that Foote shall come and talk to them. When he arrives, he is interrupted by another character called Suds from another box, who wants lessons in lecturing, which Foote proceeds to give, with backchat from the boxes—much as pantomime and revue comedians do to-day. He gave peeps of life behind the scenes, he pretended to show them how he ran his theatre.

The chief object of his wit in this play was a character called Peter Paragraph, whom he intended for George Faulkner, the well-known publisher of Dean Swift's works, famous for his books, his newspaper called the *Journal*, his two wives, his wooden leg and his limp. Most of these things came under the merciless lash of Foote's wit and tongue —and acting. For he played Paragraph himself, and even simulated the limp, hobbling grotesquely about the stage and getting roars of laughter. Little did he realise that in a short time he would himself be hobbling about that stage, the possessor of a wooden leg. Faulkner, who lived in Dublin, took no notice, but Lord Chesterfield wrote and told him he was being injured by Foote's burlesque. His lordship advised Faulkner to prosecute and Faulkner brought an action in the Dublin courts.

Foote went over to answer it, and to play there as well to earn his expenses. The Judge did not like Foote and made him find bail. He had difficulty about this and when he found the case going against him he left the country and the bail was estreated, but later Foote paid this back. Damages were awarded against him.

Action of any kind against Foote always brought its recoil. It did so in this case. He wrote a travesty on Irish courts of law and produced it at the Haymarket. He had the whole of London laughing at Irish justice. And the next time he visited Dublin, he actually produced *The Orators* there. No action was taken. He was thus amply requited for the loss of his case.

In 1763 he went back to the Haymarket. He was now taking life— managerial life—seriously. For five years he had carried on a feud against his one-time protégé, Tate Wilkinson, who had out-mimicked him. Now he wanted that accomplished gentleman on his side. Foote was not one to let any pride stand in his way. He had another play in preparation, *The Mayor of Garratt*, and he wanted Wilkinson for a principal part. He was an excellent foil as well as an excellent actor. Foote sent for Wilkinson, who was playing at Norwich. He offered the most generous terms. He told his ambassador, one Kennedy, to inform Wilkinson that he thought people might be growing tired of seeing only Foote in the plays, so he had written a good part for his friend Tate, which, if not accepted, he would cut out rather than let anyone else try it. He promised Wilkinson benefits, a fair share of leading roles with himself, his personal friendship and the extra inducement of welcome guest at his home. Wilkinson, no fool, accepted. He made all haste to the Haymarket and found Foote rehearsing his company, as usual a very indifferent one. Foote welcomed him profusely, took him home to dinner, and introduced him to a lot of people of quality. Wilkinson was flattered.

His part was that of Peter Primmer, a burlesque on Thomas Sheridan, the Dublin actor-manager, and father of Richard Brinsley Sheridan. Wilkinson could play it "on his head." Everything was nicely arranged. The two rivals were again friends.

Tate Wilkinson was the son of a Chaplain of the Chapel Royal, Savoy, who had been imprisoned and transported for a breach— quite innocent—of the new marriage laws. He had been educated at Harrow, but the change in the family fortunes enabled him to go on the stage, where his real ambition lay. He had been a mimic from his youth, and he made great strides. Frequently in trouble, frequently at logger- heads with the great ones of his profession—especially Peg Woffington —he had been befriended by Foote, who had cast him out when the audience acclaimed the pupil above the master. Later he became a manager on his own account and ran the Northern Circuit—based on York—sending many stars to Town. Now, in this story, he becomes another star at the Haymarket. He was a broad-faced man with turned-up nose, which accounts for Foote nick-naming him Pug or Puggy.

So far, the Haymarket has been a man's theatre. Mrs. Pritchard has appeared, although humbly, and Charlotte Charke has played there, and managed—but even she affected male attire. Whilst women played important parts in the early story of all other theatres, the males completely ruled the roost at the Little Theatre in the Hay.

Foote began the season at the Haymarket in June, 1763. He opened with *The Minor*. Wilkinson played Shift (the part satirising himself) and Dr. Squintum. Foote played Mrs. Cole and Smirk. It was a great success once again and ran for several nights. Then came *The Mayor of Garratt*. Foote again played two parts, Major Sturgeon and Matthew Mugg, and Wilkinson played Peter Primmer. It also was a great success, and it played for the rest of the season. It was a brilliant satire on the airs and graces of the officers of the Volunteers and the Militia. But it also burlesqued the well-known Thomas Sheridan. He it was, as Primmer, who was elected "Mayor of Garratt," and Wilkinson gives a description of his make-up and business:

> "Peter Primmer I dressed with an old tie-wig, like the barber's in *The Upholsterer*, a long band neckcloth, a large rod in my right hand and a Scotch plaid nightgown and had six boys with primers and rods, and six girls with horn-books, as my attendants in procession as the candidate for being chosen Mayor of Garratt. My likeness was well taken."

But he admits his appearance was too farcical and he modified it until he was the very image of the man he mimicked.

It was in this play that Foote had intended to ridicule Dr. Johnson concerning his serious inquiries into the matter of the Cock Lane Ghost, but it has been shown how he changed his mind.

It was a short piece, and they played others with it, but it was immensely popular. Again, it had practically no plot, relying on dialogue and satire for its appeal.

All was now prospering at the Haymarket, where the union of Foote and Wilkinson seemed well set. Then Master Tate had to overdo it at his benefit on August 20th. He chose to play Bayes in *The Rehearsal*, which had not been seen recently and which Garrick, then in Italy, had put aside for some years. It filled the house to overflowing. The redoubtable Churchill was so pleased with Wilkinson's mimicry of other actors, including Holland, that he led the cheers and gave Wilkinson an encore which he promptly took. He was delighted with his success. But not so Mr. Samuel Foote. He was not at all pleased. Here was his old rival scoring again and in his own theatre. Foote wanted Wilkinson as second string, despite his promise to him. He did not relish a rival scoring a success and an ovation such as he—the first mimic—has seldom received.

G

Tate Wilkinson repeated his success when the treasurer of the theatre, one Mendez, had his benefit. There had been an incident at Wilkinson's own benefit which is worthy of note for many reasons. It shed a light on theatre management of those times and the Haymarket in particular. It clearly resulted in another of those disorderly scenes which had occurred at the Haymarket under the French players and under Foote with his Bottle Conjuror. It is an episode of interest to all who are playgoers or who are closely connected with the theatre.

CHAPTER VIII

"ROYAL" AT THE COST OF A LEG

TATE WILKINSON tells this story himself. He was as much an imp of mischief as his present friend and late opponent, Samuel Foote himself. His style of writing cannot be improved upon for the telling of this Haymarket story, so he shall, from the pages of his *Memoirs*, tell it again himself:

"Mr. Mendez, a Jew and an appraiser in Bow Street, was treasurer that season: On his benefit he requested me to repeat the character of Bayes, which entreaty I granted; he had a full house and the comedy received additional credit. I had very near been deprived of the play, as Mr. Foote's Theatre at that time, merely consisted of a few trumpery scenes, no wardrobe but such as was hired from Mr. Barber's in Monmouth Street; and as to stage properties, they were less known there than in the most distant rustic company that scoured the country round. I was quite out of favour at Drury Lane, so had no hopes of assistance from that quarter; but Mrs. Rich, on application being made to her, supplied me with thunder, lightning, earth, moon and sun, also sent to my aid a full troop of horse; they had been well trained, were very quiet, and of a great age; were never turbulent, though sometimes troubled with headstrong wanton riders. It was a custom for the gentleman and his lady, who were proprietors of the Haymarket Theatre, to reserve a box for themselves, of which they kept the key. I sent a card the week of my benefit requesting the favour of that box, as all the others were disposed of; A very rude refusal was sent back; at which time Mr. Ruspini, now of Pall Mall, and some gentlemen were with me and complained of not being able to procure any box whatever. On my receiving an uncivil answer, I said, 'Damn this Mrs. Proprietor, it would serve her ill-natured spleen right to break open the door and fill the box.' This hint was no sooner given than seriously taken and put into practice; for as soon as the doors were opened a large party paid and finding every place was taken except the proprietors, which the box-keeper assured them could not be opened on any pretext whatever, they unanimously burst the old lock and filled the whole box nor had the turnkey of the Recess rhetoric sufficient to have the least effect, for expostulations did not signify; so they remained sole masters and sat in triumph until near seven, when the play was going to begin; at which instant up came a limb of the law, no less a personage than Mr. George Garrick, escorting the Lady Proprietress, with a large party gratis, who summoned the garrison to surrender

and be treated as prisoners of war; but they were as obstinate as
Turks, and determined to defend the citadel sword in hand. The
Lady Proprietress was astonished at the rudeness committed and
insisted on her privileged right; then tried angry and soothing words;
but neither her persuasive eloquence, nor the authority of Mr.
George Garrick, aided by John Doe and Richard Roe, of Westminster Hall, with all their united prowess, could by any means
avail. The possessors of the inside works defended their entrench-
ments from any breach, and they only in exultation laughed, and
told Gen. Garrick if himself and party would pay a crown per head
they should be admitted, not otherwise. It cannot be imagined that
it was an easy matter to extract coin from a lawyer's pocket, consequently the Lady, George Garrick and party, finding it ineffectual
staying in the box passage, retreated in disgrace, but denounced
vengeance on Wilkinson. For my own part, I chuckled at the adventure, not so much for the trifling pecuniary advantage I had gained,
but at that time I should have disliked the curious Garrick's party
gratis over my head than any other. Next day the enraged lady waited
on Mr. Foote (who loved mischief and despised his landlady) where
she gave an ample scope to her anger, and repeated her wrongs;
but Mr. Foote told her it was impossible to prevent what had
happened; as to the improper conduct respecting the box, he could
only say he was sorry for her disappointment; and as to Mr.
Wilkinson's rudeness, he wished to excuse it, but he had not sufficient
authority to whip him for his fault, and there the matter rested,
ending evidently to my advantage; for I must mention that the year
following the lady herself sent me permission to let her box to any
particular friend of mine, if the boxes were so taken as to make such
permission necessary on my benefit night."

That is a very illuminating picture of the Haymarket Theatre in
the year of grace 1763. It shows the willingness of Mrs. Rich (John
Rich's wife) to help another member of the profession and the amount
of "props" thus lent. The troop of horse refers to the hobby horses
used in the burlesque battle scene in *The Rehearsal*—and apparently,
from Wilkinson's joking description, they were fairly old props, even
for Covent Garden. The Lady Proprietress is probably John Potter's
widow. Although the name of John Whitehead crops up in the records,
it is probable that he was only acting on behalf of John Potter's heirs,
and may have been an executor himself. The episode throws a nice
light on the antiquity of what are called "proprietary seats" and which
still exist in the theatre to-day, to the great annoyance of those who
rent playhouses and are thereby deprived of some portion of takings.
Where proprietary seats exist, they are held by an agency on behalf
of the proprietor and sold for him. But sometimes they are empty,
often in the case of a box, and show a gaping, unsightly void in an

otherwise packed house—as would have happened at the Haymarket on this occasion.

The George Garrick referred to is David Garrick's lawyer brother, who was his devoted slave.

There is a nice touch by Wilkinson in his statement that Foote loved mischief and also that he despised his landlady. Foote despised everyone, and landlords and landladies have been fair butts for lesser wits than he. It is certain he treated the proprietress with terrific mock courtesy and had a fine time. He was not afraid of her, nor of losing his theatre. There were few clients in the field for the Haymarket, and none of his standing.

If Wilkinson was a good manager, Foote was a bad one, and a slack one. But he had that quality which means so much in the theatre —he often did the unexpected. Thus he engaged the great Spranger Barry and his wife to appear at the Haymarket. Barry was Garrick's rival; they had fought it out in the theatre when they played Romeo and Lear against each other, Garrick at the Lane and Barry at the Garden. Garrick won as Romeo by a short head, but he won by many lengths and to spare as Lear. But Barry was a fine actor, nevertheless. He is always called "silver-voiced" and he was a very handsome man. Yet he and his wife played for Foote at the tiny Haymarket Theatre. It shows the power of the man. His reason for the engagement was typical of him. "Why, to tell you the truth, I have no great occasion for them, but they were such bad neighbours last year that I find it cheaper to give them board and lodging for nothing than to have them any longer opposite to me." He was referring to a season they had played at the Opera House across the Hay.

Foote went on at the Haymarket, writing and producing his plays, but using it as a summer theatre, and leaving the field clear for the two royal playhouses during the winter season. How he managed to get his plays licensed by the Lord Chamberlain is a mystery. Maybe he sometimes omitted this formality and was let alone, on account of his acid pen and still more acid tongue. Except for some excisions in *The Mayor of Garratt*, he does not seem to have been troubled.

Plays came steadily from his pen. There had been *The Lyar* in 1762, *The Orators* in 1762, *The Mayor of Garratt* in 1763. And before that he had written, apart from his mimicry shows, *The Knights* (1749), *Taste* (1752), *The Englishman in Paris* (1753), *The Englishman Returned from Paris* (1756), *The Author* (1757), *The Minor* (1760), and he had turned his *Diversions of the Morning* into a farce.

Taste had been performed at Drury Lane; *The Lyar* at Covent Garden; *The Orator*, of course, at the Haymarket, as was also *The Mayor of Garratt*.

At that little theatre, in 1763, he also presented his skit on the trial he had undergone in Dublin, which he called *The Tryall of Samuel Foote Esq. for a Libel on Peter Paragraph*. There were only four characters and two actors, for Foote played two of them, himself and Counsellor Demur, the prosecuting attorney. The Judge was played by a Mr. Lewis, Sen., and Counsellor Quirk by a Mr. Kennedy. In 1764 he produced at the Haymarket *The Patron*, and in 1765 *The Commissary*.

From now on it is his home and his sole theatre. He is the Haymarket and the Haymarket is Foote. They may not be great works, those Foote comedies, but they are the finest of running commentaries on the life and habits of his day. They would not hold the stage nowadays, but to read them is quite a joy and often a revelation of the man's power.

Foote was doing well in 1766. His insolence and his violence increased with his success. He still jeered at the world and he still pursued the patient, smiling Garrick with ridicule, jokes and sneers. Foote's great ambition was to be a Patentee himself, to obtain a charter for his theatre. He had tried many ways to obtain a Patent. Only the King had the right to grant a Patent, and the King did not see fit to do so. No doubt Foote made up his mind that he would find a way of making the monarch take notice of him and his little theatre.

And that way he found—by accident—and an accident of so dramatic a kind that his own fertile brain could not have invented the tale. He got his Royal Charter, he became a Patentee, and the price he paid for it was his own leg!

It came about in this way. Foote was snobbish. He loved the company of the great ones; lords were much to his liking. In their turn, they encouraged him; they liked to listen to his malice, his jokes and his witty sallies. Although of decent birth and education, he was, in their eyes, only an actor—and they invited him to their houses, to their feasts, in his capacity of clown. If Foote realised this, he did not care. He was among the great, and he could use them in his turn as characters in his plays. He was the gainer in every way. He joked to them and about them. But on one occasion they had a joke at his expense—and a very dangerous and terrible joke it was.

He was invited to the seat of Lord Mexborough at Methley, near Leeds. It was a very distinguished house party indeed, for it included the Duke of York (the brother of the King), Lord Delaval, Sir Francis Delaval and many others. It was Foote's ideal—good company, a good house, good food and drink and a chance to show off and gain applause and patronage. But this time the nobility had determined to play a joke on the joker, for the amusement of the Duke of York. They wanted an opportunity and Foote supplied it himself. The talk turned on horsemanship. Foote immediately began boasting. He told wonderful stories of his equestrian feats, and his covering joke was that "he could ride as well as most men he knew, though indeed he preferred a post-chaise." He was actually speaking the truth then, if they had realised it. But they hatched their joke. They would put Master Foote for the next day's hunting, on a horse which happened to be in the stables. It was a horse which so far nobody had been able to master, let alone ride.

So, the next morning, as they prepared to follow hounds, the horse was brought round as Foote's mount. He knew nothing of its reputation, and the company all kept their faces straight and waited to see the English Aristophanes fly through the air.

Unsuspicious, Foote mounted the horse and flamboyantly gave it a touch of the spur to make it show its paces. Immediately the horse reared and threw him. Foote, not a light man by any means, fell heavily and fractured his leg in two places.

The roars of laughter were stifled as the company dismounted and rushed to his aid. He was carried indoors obviously in the greatest pain. He bore his injury stoically enough and even made jokes about it. Two of the best doctors procurable tended him, but his life began to be endangered. His host was beside himself with remorse. The doctors gave their decision. Foote's leg must be amputated or he would die.

Here was tragedy displacing comedy. Here was an actor, whose livelihood depended largely on his ability to move about the stage, on the point of losing a leg, and thus shattering his career at the height of his success.

The news was broken to Foote. Whatever his feelings may have been, he took it well. He kept up his reputation as a jester, he showed his courage at this moment of trial. If it must come off, well, then, take it off, he said. "No matter, I still would not change my one good leg for Lord ——'s pair of drumsticks," he jested, "and as for acting, well, a one-legged actor will be a novelty. If I cannot walk, I can hop."

The outlook for a crippled actor was bleak. Audiences then were not so tolerant or so well-behaved as now. Physical infirmities gave rise to ridicule. Foote himself had joked about such things and got roars of laughter for his sallies. Actors with odd appearances were often hooted from the scene. But Foote would risk it—he would have to risk it. His busy brain was active, even in his pain and affliction. He planned his course of action then and there.

His noble friends of the house-party were deeply moved and truly sorry. Nobody was more contrite than the Duke of York himself. He felt a double guilt, for he knew the joke which had ended so tragically had been hatched for his particular enjoyment. He paid a special visit to Foote's bedside. He expressed the deepest sorrow and was very kind. Was there anything he could do? he inquired.

Here was Foote's chance, and he seized it instantly. Yes, he replied, there was something His Royal Highness could do. Something which would be of the greatest service to a poor, stricken, one-legged actor, something which might put him on his feet—he begged pardon, foot—

again. Would the Duke beg his royal brother, the gracious King George III, to grant him, Samuel Foote, a Patent for his humble playhouse, the Haymarket Theatre? He knew he was of no great standing—of still less standing than heretofore, because he would be but a peg-leg actor, even if the public would allow him to exhibit his infirmity. But his way would be simpler, his chance of livelihood easier, if His Majesty could see his way to grant this plea and make him in fact what he was in spirit, the King's most obedient, humble and loyal servant.

Naturally, the Duke promised. He may not have had much hope, for the granting of such a Patent was no easy matter, even for the King. There were the vested interests of the two other theatres to consider; there was such a thing as precedent to be considered also. But the Duke knew he must do something about it and, to his credit, he bestirred himself.

He saw his brother and put the case. He argued the point, stressed the special circumstances and the worthiness of the matter. And although he did not get all he asked for, he got a compromise in the true British way. The King granted Samuel Foote a Patent for the Haymarket—with restrictions. It was to apply only to the summer season, from May 14th to September 14th of each year, and it was to be active only for the duration of Samuel Foote's life. It was a half-hearted concession, and less than Foote had hoped for—less by many degrees. But one thing he had accomplished. He had got the Haymarket Theatre a Royal Patent. There was something else too, even better. He himself was now a Patentee, the equal of Rich and the equal of his self-conceived rival, David Garrick. He would ruffle it on equal terms with them now—even though he was minus a leg. He was Mr. Samuel Foote, Patentee of the Theatre Royal, Haymarket.

When at last he got back to Town, he was a person of some consequence in the theatre world. If he had not a title at least his Theatre had one. Immediately he put a long cherished scheme into operation. He had simply rented the Haymarket, now he would acquire it outright. He soon completed the purchase. The theatre passed from the estate of the late John Potter, its builder and creator, into the hands of the man who had made it Theatre Royal—Samuel Foote.

He was not content with the mere purchase however: he mus tdo more. A theatre royal must assume a dignified appearance, must increase its stature. So he rebuilt. He added the house in Suffolk Street to the theatre. He removed two shops which abutted on the front. He built a portico—which it had always lacked—and thereby gave the exterior more dignity. He added a second gallery and he increased the number of gangways and passages. It was still a small, a very small theatre, but it had more of the appearance of a playhouse than ever it had before.

Foote's physical handicap might easily have ruined a less courageous person. In those crude, unfeeling, ill-mannered days, a cripple was a joke. Right, he would make the jokes; he would lead the laughter. He would make capital of his infirmity. That was the way to disarm his enemies.

His so-called chief enemy turned up trumps. David Garrick, the mean, the scrape-halfpenny man, sent him a delightful letter, expressing the grief all his friends felt (Foote's snorts can be imagined, but he read on). Garrick went on to say: "If I could convince you of my regard by any other proof than that of mere words, I should be proud and happy to show it on this occasion. All I shall say at present is that, should you be prevented from pursuing any plan for the theatre, I am wholly at your service, and will labour in your vineyard for you in any capacity, till you are able to do much better for yourself."

It was a gallant and generous offer, and it took a great man to make it. Garrick offering to leave Drury Lane and play at the Haymarket? Wonder of wonders!

It seems to have touched even Samuel Foote, for he sent a reply in terms very different from his usual vein. It was a very much changed Foote who wrote: "I thank you very warmly for your offer as to my hovel in the Haymarket; but the stage to me at present is a very distant object, for notwithstanding all the flattery of appearances, I look upon my hold in life to depend on a very slender tenure; and, besides, admitting the best that can happen is a mutilated man, a miserable instance of the weakness and frailty of human nature. It has been my misfortune not to know Mrs. Garrick much, but from what I have seen and all that I have heard, you will have more to regret when either you or she die than any man in the kingdom. As to my present condition, I wish I could meet you with a more favourable account, but I am in truth very weak, in pain, and can procure no sleep but by the aid of opiates. Oh, sir, it is incredible all that I have suffered. And you will believe me when I assure you that the amputation was the least painful part of the whole. . . ."

For once, Samuel Foote is human and understanding; for once he responds to kindness, even from a man whom he dislikes and envies. But it did not last long, that temperate mood induced by suffering. As soon as he recovered, he was after Garrick again. The old insults were pouring out upon the man who had been the first to offer a helping hand. It is again to Garrick's credit that he took no notice and bore no malice. Probably he expected nothing better.

Foote got himself a wooden leg. It was just one of those rough affairs such as old sailors who had lost a limb wore. But Foote dressed it up in a silk stocking and a shoe with a gold buckle and hobbled about as best he could, making jokes about his name and his missing leg every time anyone looked at him.

It took the best part of three months for him to get the repairs and rebuilding of his theatre done to his liking. Then he got a shock. It was not to be called Theatre Royal, despite the Patent. That did not suit him, so he conferred the title on it himself, and by dint of constant endeavours had it confirmed the next year.

In 1768, in his new theatre—his Theatre Royal—he presented his new play, *The Devil on Two Sticks*. He had some trouble over this because his old crony-antagonist Tate Wilkinson had stolen a copy of the manuscript and tried to produce it in advance. Authors had no protection then. But Foote out-manœuvred him. The same wily Wilkinson was to break his leg and go lame, like Foote. But he left the stage and kept to management.

The Devil on Two Sticks was a success. It jeered at the doctors, the chief object of ridicule being Sir William Browne, President of the College of Surgeons. Foote impersonated this man to the life.

Instead of invoking the law against him, the doctor complimented Foote on his skill of mimicry. Foote was disarmed for the moment. As usual, the plot was of the slightest. Two lovers elope and find a devil imprisoned in a bottle. They set him free. He in turn warns them against all doctors and physicians. Some of Foote's wittiest work is shown here. It is, in some ways, a precursor of *The Doctor's Dilemma*.

The Devil on Two Sticks became a most popular play, however, and remained in use for years.

He followed this, in 1770, with *The Lame Lover*. Here he ridiculed his own single leg. In this he played Sir Luke Limp, a one-legged knight. One of the characters said he was none the worse for his loss. Sir Luke replies: "The worse? Much the better, my dear. Consider, I can have neither strain, splint, spavin or gout; have no fear of corns, kibes, or that another man shall kick my shins or tread on my toes. . . ."

He made them laugh as much as ever. He was still Foote the irrepressible, Foote who loved to make personal jokes, even against himself.

Now came another landmark in the progress of the Haymarket. As it now was Royal, it could be noticed by Majesty. And duly King George III paid it a visit.

That night Foote was starting the evening bill with *The Mayor of Garratt*. It will be remembered that this poked fun at the Volunteer forces and the Militia, and Foote played the part of a comic major.

It was, it still is, the honour and privilege of the Manager of the theatre visited by Royalty to receive the monarch and usher him into the Royal Box. It is a much easier task to-day than it was in the time of Foote. For then it was *de rigeur* to wear court dress for this job, and to light the King to his place by walking backwards before him with the lighted candles, one in each hand.

On the occasion of the first royal visit to the Haymarket, Foote broke all the rules. He hobbled to meet the King in his stage attire, for he was already dressed and made up. He wore an immense cocked hat, enormous boots and a very grotesque military uniform, as befitted the comic major he played in the farce. Thus he appeared before King George III. The monarch, a very simple-minded man, gazed at the extraordinary figure before him, which bowed as profoundly as it could and waved its wooden leg in the air in so doing, and started back in astonishment. "What is that man? What regiment does he belong to?" he demanded brusquely. It took him some time to realise that it was Samuel Foote, the Patentee of the theatre, who was humbly bidding him welcome. He had never seen Foote before. But later he laughed heartily.

In 1771 Foote produced *The Maid of Bath*, based on Miss Linley's elopement with the young, brilliant and dashing Richard Brinsley Sheridan. Again it was a success. One never knew, when he went to Foote's Haymarket, what might happen. Foote put in all sorts of gags, he commented on his audience, he made full use of any celebrities who might be in the house. In this he ante-dated current American night-club practice by a couple of centuries.

One night Foote gave the beautiful Mrs. Baddeley (wife of the pastry-cook-actor who left Drury Lane its famous Twelfth Night Cake) a box which was so situated that everyone in the house could see the occupants, which was just what box folk liked in those days. There came a scene where Foote enlarged upon the beauty of the "Maid of Bath" and he put in a gag. Quoth he: "Not even the beauty of the Nine Muses, not even that of the divine Baddeley herself, who there sits [and he pointed straight at the lady] could exceed that of the Maid of Bath." There were thunders of applause. Foote took an encore, and pointed to the box again. He did it a third time, and every eye was on Mrs. Baddeley. She rose, curtsied to her audience, and it was some fifteen minutes before she could cease doing so to resume her seat. This was stopping the show with a vengeance. An eyewitness who records the story says that he had never seen Mrs. Baddeley so confused. "This trick of Foote's put her so much to the blush, that the colour did not leave her face the whole evening," he relates.

Well, it must have been the exception that proves the rule. For it took a great deal to make the fair, frail and wayward Mrs. Baddeley blush, even if one-third of the accounts of her goings-on are true.

Foote was never at a loss for a joke or a situation. He turned everything to account. Even when cornered, he turned the tables on his opponents. His next Haymarket play, *The Nabob*, in 1772, nearly got him into trouble. It made riotous fun of the gentry who returned from India with enlarged livers and very greatly enlarged bank balances. They were very prevalent at the time. Foote presented a typical specimen in the person of Sir Matthew Mite—a character study of General Richard Smith, whose father had been a cheesemonger. The Anglo-Indians in town went to the Haymarket to see the show and were very much annoyed. They swore revenge. A party of them went to Foote's house to beat him up. They were let in, and Foote met them, all smiles. He showed no fear and no resentment. He spoke them fairly and he reasoned with them. He was sorry they should be so mistaken.

He confused them with his glibness and his quick wit. He read them portions of the play, with his own emphasis, to show them that Richard Smith had never been in his mind for a moment. No, no, it was the Indians, the naughty Indians he was getting at, not the Nabobs, whom he admired and respected. The irate, livery, hot-tempered gentlemen who had come to whip, stopped to dine. They made a night of it, and left in the small hours, to stagger home and swear that such a good fellow as Foote never existed before.

He did very well with *The Nabob*, for the respectable people who believed all the tales of the licentious and luxurious life in India came to see it and to applaud the satire.

In the year 1773, Foote produced, not a play, but a puppet show called *Piety in Pattens*. He spoke a prologue and said he had been forced to employ puppets because all the actors of the day were so incompetent and second-rate. He then proceeded to deride a sentimental comedy in which virtue is triumphant and vice defeated, by means of making fun of a housemaid who refuses the diamonds offered for "something worse than death" and by her virtue conquers the lust of the villain. But the public did not think this was funny. They liked to see virtue triumphant. They thought it should be, even if they did not practise it. On the first night there was some rioting, but Foote was able to quieten things down. He turned the show into a meeting and demanded a show of hands for "Aye" or "No." He declared the "Ayes" to have it, but the puppets soon made their final bow.

He did better in 1774 with *The Bankrupt*. Here the central figure was a bold, bad baronet who speculated and then tried to get out of his liabilities. But Foote was also tilting at all who tried to get out of paying their debts. He knew something about that himself.

A change was now coming over him. The wit was still there, but it was not so care-free. He had always been biting, but now he was mordant. He had always been caustic but now he was bitter. The long struggle to keep going in spite of his infirmity was telling upon him. He was wearing himself out in body and spirit. However much he smiled and laughed in public, he brooded when he was alone. The physical effort of keeping up constant activity handicapped by a wooden leg was beginning to take its toll. Those old wooden pegs were fatiguing for a physically strong man. Foote was not a very muscular person and had not led a careful life. The old flame was dimming, the old glitter and brilliance were losing lustre, the acid of bitterness was seeping through. He was a Patentee, it is true, his theatre was royal, but he was infirm and could not enjoy it. But he kept on.

Another new play saw the light of the "floats" at the Haymarket in 1774 beside *The Bankrupt*. This bore the title of *The Cozeners*. It was Foote's bitterest yet, and he sailed very near the wind. His character of Mrs. Fleecem was a very transparent image of Mrs. Grieve, who got money by promising to procure Government sinecures, and who

lent money to Charles James Fox so that his carriage might be seen
standing at her door. This was thin ice for Foote, for he was suspect of
having taken money himself in the form of an annuity for arranging a
marriage between Sir Francis Delaval and a Lady Nassau Powlett,
who had, if report were true, been Foote's own mistress. He also
ridiculed Lord Chesterfield and his famous advice to his son, and a
preacher who had been recently hanged.

Then the end began. He wrote a play called *A Trip to Calais*. Here
he pilloried the notorious Duchess of Kingston, who was a complete
adventuress. Her career of amorous intrigue had begun when she was
young. She was of good birth, but had no moral sense at all. Yet she
had been Maid of Honour to Princess Augusta of Wales. There was
little honour and precious little of the maid about her even then. The
Duke of Hamilton fell deeply in love with her, but, fortunately for him,
his family got him away. She, however, met and married secretly a
young man called Augustus Hervey. A child was born and was got rid of
to foster-parents. They quarrelled, and Hervey, who was in the Navy,
went off to sea. But his brother became the Earl of Bristol and he was
heir presumptive.

Then came on the scene the old Duke of Kingston. He fell a victim to
Mrs. Hervey's charms, and she passed herself off under her maiden
name of Chudleigh, not disclosing her wedding. She was determined to
become a duchess. She was by now living with the Duke, and she felt
sure of him. She brought an action against her real husband, accusing
him of representing himself falsely as her husband and swearing they
had never been married. What is more, she won. There was now little
doubt that Hervey would become Earl of Bristol. He wanted to find
out how he stood. He could not bring a divorce against her, because the
courts had decided, in face of false evidence, that he was not married.
He—and she—knew very well that he was. It was a pretty situation.
He took the chance and brought the action. The lady faced him out
in the most audacious way. She had destroyed every particle of evidence
of the wedding. She swore on oath she was single. Again she won. In
a few weeks after this judgment, she married her Duke.

For five years she was received everywhere as the Duchess, even at
Court. In 1773 the Duke died and she inherited all his property on the
condition that she did not marry again. That was a fresh complication
indeed. The Duke's relatives, who had always had their doubts, now
took a hand. They managed to suborn a confidential maid of hers and
got sufficient evidence for a prosecution for bigamy. Then Hervey
succeeded to the Earldom of Bristol. So she was now legally the
Countess. She was forced to appear before Lord Mansfield, who bound
her over to stand a trial before her peers. This time the tables were
turned. She was found guilty and fled the country.

This was the woman with whom the tiring, failing Foote now chose to
cross swords. Even in the days of his prime she would have been a redoubt-

able opponent. Now she was to be his last adversary and was to be the means of bringing him down. He was worthy of something better than that.

The Duchess had two protectors, a couple of the biggest rogues unhung. They were clerics as well, the Reverend Dr. Jackson and the Rev. Mr. Foster. They took up the fight for her, and immediately the battle was joined.

CHAPTER IX

EXIT ARISTOPHANES—ENTER COLMAN

THESE two champions of evil were men who knew the ropes. They were arch-crooks of their day, sheltering behind their clerical clothes and behind the voluminous skirts of their disreputable client. From that cover they shot their poisoned darts.

The obnoxious Jackson ran a paper—he ran several—and the object of these sheets was—blackmail. Unless the victim disgorged, he would be pilloried in these journals. It was Jackson who entered the lists against Foote. He wrote a letter to the actor, as coming from the Duchess, which brought matters to a head, and it was he who fought the whole fight, with her in the background.

He is worthy of a little attention, therefore, this man who dared what all London feared to do, attempt to overthrow the English Aristophanes. He was reckless by nature, was Jackson; he was extravagant either in or out of funds; he had to keep the purse replenished and he did not care how he did it. But he had talent, he had courage, and but for the streak of evil might have been a worthy man. He had been parson and tutor, and he was an excellent preacher. A Republican, he was a violent opponent of constituted authority, yet he believed quite sincerely that his views were in the best interests of his country. He went in for journalism of the most sensational and personal nature. His invective was wonderful.

Then he published his own paper the *Public Ledger*, a journal entirely composed of short paragraphs—all libellous, all vindictive and all well aimed if seldom true. This paper he used for blackmail. Yet he was selected to write pamphlets to counter some written by Dr. Johnson himself, and he put up a good show. In many ways he was like Foote. He turned withering flame of satire upon his victims in print, as Foote did in the spoken word and action of the stage. And their satiric gift was to bring a tragic end to both, though Jackson's was the more dramatic and violent. He committed suicide in the dock when standing his trial for high treason.

This was Foote's opponent in his last great duel, a fitting foe, one as well equipped as himself, but a much greater rascal. From the moment their swords crossed, it was a duel *à outrance*—seconds out and to the death.

The first move was with the Duchess. Hearing the gossip from friends that Foote intended to show her up on the stage in *A Trip to Calais*, she knew what it would mean to her in the forthcoming trial she had to face. Representations were made to Foote to the effect that his ridicule would probably ruin her. Foote had no finer feelings on this score at all. He was thinking how busy the box-office at the Haymarket would be. So, at the instigation of the Duchess, the Lord Chamberlain was informed. Very naturally his Lordship refused to issue a licence for the play. He was a friend of Foote's, but he did his duty.

This round went to the Duchess. But she was artful; she knew it would rankle with Foote and that he would find some way of getting his own back. She wanted to cover her tracks.

So she sent a friend of hers to invite Foote to call upon her. This friend was Lord Mountstuart, who does not come out of the affair too well. He appears to have run with the hare and hunted with the hounds. He had read the play with Foote—probably Foote had asked him to look it through and see if he could recognise the central figure and the allusions. Mountstuart appears to have told Foote he thought it was all right, and he even took it to the Duchess for her to read. When the row blew up, he declared that the Duchess herself had read it and had seen no likeness to herself therein. Lord Mountstuart evidently wanted to keep out of trouble—or else was doing a bit of covering up himself. Anyway, Foote went to see the Duchess, and she received him most politely. When he came away his mind was clear. Everything was going to be all right. It was obvious to him that, as she had made no objections, he could approach the Lord Chamberlain again for a licence for the play. He did so.

So the Duchess, and her Jackson, moved again. A weird announcement appeared in the Press, curious, involved, and indeterminate in many ways, but more than enough to set tongues wagging in those gossiping days. It was to the effect that for once an item of gossip was true and that the Lord Chamberlain had forbidden Mr. Foote's play, *A Trip to Calais*. It went on to print Foote's letter to the Chamberlain, and stated that Foote intended to publish those portions of the play said to be a libel on the Duchess of Kingston, with a dedication to Her Grace.

That letter had been a typical Footean missive. He had told the Lord Chamberlain that Lord Mountstuart had read the play and so far had he been from recognising the character of Lady Kitty Crocodile as a picture of the Duchess, that he had taken the play to that lady to read. And the Duchess had also said she saw no sort of resemblance. That being so, said Foote, he was emboldened to ask the Chamberlain to reconsider the matter and let him enjoy the reward to which his work entitled him. If not, he said, he must bid farewell to the stage and to the service of his public, whom he had never flattered, whose faults he had pointed out, but who had, nevertheless, supported him. Furthermore, he himself had called on the Duchess at her own invitation, and had been told that she considered there was no offence. But if his Lordship continued to take the contrary view then there was nothing left for him but to retire.

It was a good, well-written, well-reasoned letter. He may have had his tongue in his cheek when he made references in it to the high principles which had always inspired him in his work, but it was a perfectly balanced and reasonable appeal for justice.

It did not move the Lord Chamberlain (Lord Hertford), and Foote's indignation got the better of him. He determined to lay his case before the public. He never had any intention of retiring. It would not have hurt him to put the play in the waste-paper basket, if he had such a thing, and write another. It was easy for Foote to write plays. But he had lost his temper. He announced he would print his play. Now this was almost the same as performing it, so far as the Duchess was concerned. The publicity which had arisen would make everyone buy it and in all probability read far more into it than Foote could have put into the stage play.

Now the gloves were off. The Duchess took no further direct part, she turned the matter over to her two assassins of the pen, Jackson and Foster. And it was Jackson who drew the knife to do the deed.

Public interest ran high. Gossip buzzed. Lord Hertford, although a friend of Foote's outside his official capacity, was not to be won over. The proposed publication was a blow at his authority.

The rumour went round—from Foote's friends—that the Duchess had tried to bribe Foote into tearing up the play, but that Foote had refused with scorn. Jackson and partner made capital out of this. They swore an affidavit before Sir John Fielding that the boot was on the other leg. They deposed that Foote had demanded £2,000 hush money. They followed it up with paragraphs in Jackson's papers to the effect that Foote, not able to frighten the Duchess into agreement that the play should be performed or published, was now doing his best to libel her in rival newspapers. They represented him as a very incarnation of malignity. They kept it up. Each day brought a fresh attack on Foote, and everyone was talking. Foote knew he must rebut these things. And he made a bad mistake. He wrote a very ill-advised letter to the Duchess:

"Madam, A member of the Privy Council and a friend of Your Grace's (he has begged me not to mention his name, but I suppose your Grace will easily guess who) has just left me. He has explained to me, what I did not conceive, that the publication of the scenes in the *Trip to Calais* at this juncture, with the dedication and preface, might be of infinite ill-consequence to your affairs.

"I really, madam, wish you no ill, and should be sorry to do you an injury. I therefore give up to that consideration what neither Your Grace's offers nor the threats of your agents could obtain; the scenes shall not be published, nor shall anything appear at my theatre or from me that can hurt you, provided the attacks made on me in the newspapers do not make it necessary for me to act in defence of myself. Your Grace will therefore see the necessity of giving proper instructions."

H

Foote thought he had been very clever. His idea was to get the whole matter dropped and to appear to have acted in a most courteous, merciful and magnanimous fashion. But he had written a bit too much. He had more than implied that the attacks on him were coming directly from the Duchess. And nobody would have been fool enough to believe that he did not know of her impending trial, and that his action, if he produced or published the play, was bound to hurt her. But he tried to carry it off with a high hand and by the use of big names, such as Privy Councillors, etc. He had laid himself open both to the Duchess and the unscrupulous Jackson.

The mud began to fly and splash around. The Haymarket was once more a battlefield. It had seen fights against the Patent theatres, fights against foreign actors, and fights against Acts of Parliament. Now it was the cockpit wherein the man who had made it royal was battling for his professional existence, if not for his very life.

It is certain that, Foote's letter in her hands, the Duchess lost no time in getting Jackson to take action. Foote had made a mistake, he should make others; they would goad him into them—and then he was at their mercy as a target for public attacks which should drive him from the stage or for a nice bleeding by blackmail which would equally ruin him.

To Foote went the Duchess's reply, which is worth giving *in extenso*:

"SIR, I was at dinner when I received your ill-judged letter; as there is little consideration required I shall sacrifice a few moments to answer it.

"A member of *your* Privy Council could never hope to be of a Lady's Cabinet. I know too well what is due to my own dignity to enter into a compromise with an extortionable assassin of private reputation.

"If I before abhorred you for your slander, I now despise you for your concessions. It is a proof of the illiberality of your satire, when you can publish or suppress it as best suits the needy convenience of your purse. You first had the cowardly baseness to draw the sword; and if I sheathe it until I make you crouch like the subservient vassal as you are, then there is no spirit in an injured woman nor meanness in a slanderous buffoon.

"To a man, my sex alone would have screened me from attacks, but I am writing to the descendant of a merry-andrew and prostitute the term of manhood by applying it to Mr. Foote.

"Clothed in my innocence as in a coat of mail, I am proof against a host of foes; and, conscious of never having intentionally offended a single individual, I doubt not that a brave and generous public will protect me from the malevolence of a theatrical assassin. You shall have cause to remember that, though I would have given liberally to the relief of your necessities, I scorn to be bullied into a purchase of your silence. There is something, however, in your *pity* at which my nature revolts. To make an offer of pity at once betrays your insolence and your vanity. I will keep the pity you send until the morning before you are turned off, when I will return it by a Cupid, with a box of lip-salve, and a choir of choristers shall chant a stave to your requiem.

E. KINGSTON."

The letter infuriated Foote. He sent a characteristic reply, which was just what the other side wanted. It was a much better letter than the one from the Duchess, but it only made things blacker all round. It also is worth recounting:

"MADAM, Though I have neither the time nor the inclination to answer the illiberal attacks of your agents, yet a public correspondence with Your Grace is too great an honour for me to decline.

"I cannot help thinking that it would have been prudent in Your Grace to have answered my letter *before dinner* or at least postponed it to the cool hour of the morning; you would then have found that I had voluntarily granted the request which you had endeavoured by so many different ways to obtain.

"Lord Mountstuart (for whose amiable qualities I have the highest respect, and whose name your agents very unnecessarily produced to the public) must recollect that, when I had the honour to meet him at Kingston House by Your Grace's appointment, instead of begging relief from your charity, I rejected your *splendid offers* to suppress the *Trip to Calais* with the contempt they deserved. Indeed, madam, the humanity of my royal and benevolent master, and the public protection, have placed me much above the reach of your bounty.

"But why, madam, put on your coat of mail against me? I have no hostile intentions. Folly, not vice, is the game I pursue. In those scenes which you so unaccountably apply to yourself, you must observe that there is not the slightest hint at the little incidents in your life which have excited the curiosity of the grand inquest for the county of Middlesex. I am happy, however, madam, to hear that your robe of innocence is in such perfect repair; I was afraid it might be a little the worse for wearing. May it hold out to keep your Grace warm the next winter.

"The progenitors your Grace has done me the honour to give me are, I presume, merely metaphorical persons, and to be considered as the authors of my muse and not of my manhood. A merry andrew and a prostitute are no bad poetical parents, especially for a writer of plays—the first to give the humour and mirth; the last to furnish the graces and powers of attraction. Prostitutes and players too must live by pleasing the public; not but your Grace may have heard of ladies who by *private practice* have accumulated great fortunes.

"If you mean that I really owe my birth to that pleasant connection, your Grace is grossly deceived. My father was, in truth, a very useful magistrate and respectable country gentleman, as the whole county of Cornwall will tell you; my mother the daughter of Sir Edward Goodere, baronet, who represented the County of Hereford. Her fortune was large and her morals irreproachable till your Grace condescended to stain them. She was upwards of four score years old when she died, and, what will surprise your Grace, *was never married but once* in her life.

"I am obliged to your Grace for your intended presence on the day (as you politely express it) when I am to be turned off. But where will your Grace get the Cupid to bring me the lip-salve? That family, I am afraid, has long quitted your service.

"Pray, madam, is not J——n the name of your *female* confidential secretary? and is not *she* generally clothed in black petticoats made of your weeds?

" '*So mourned the dame of Ephesus her love.*'

"I fancy your Grace took the hint when you last resided at Rome. You heard then, I suppose, of a certain Pope, and in humble imitation have converted a *pious parson* into a *chambermaid*. The scheme is new in this country and has doubtless its particular pleasures.

"That you may never want the benefit of clergy in every emergence in the sincere wish of

"Your Grace's most devoted
"Most obliged humble servant
"SAM. FOOTE."

The battle was rising to a peak. All forms of pretence were thrown to the winds. These letters were published in the papers, and Foote made it clear that it was Jackson who was his chief opponent—the Duchess being merely the cloak behind which this gentleman was working. Jackson, and doubtless Foster as well, saw a chance of making money. They would, they hoped, get it from both sides. They were being paid by the Duchess, and if Foote had offered them money to withdraw opposition and let him perform *A Trip to Calais* without further trouble, they would have taken it without a word. Foote had no intention of being blackmailed. He was not the sort; they mistook their man there. But it is certain that he had been offered money by the Duchess to scrap the play—and may be did not think it enough. That would have been between the Duchess and himself, but he was not having any dealings, save hard words, with the two clerical rogues. Meanwhile, the affair was doing nobody any good, and the harmful publicity grew apace.

Jackson kept up a constant barrage of scandalous attacks on Foote. Foote determined to bring up new guns to silence him. He had thrown over the *Trip to Calais*—he had no option, with the Lord Chamberlain's refusal of a licence. But his agile brain and quick pen were at work on another. This was aimed directly and point-blank against Jackson and Foster. Nor did he rely on his usual satire and ridicule. He dipped his pen in undiluted venom as he drew them in pictures which nobody could mistake. He called the play *The Capucin* and the two chief characters were Dr. Viper who was Jackson to the life, and "Father Dominic," who was the image of Foster. As he saw them, so he wrote them, excusing nothing, omitting nothing—it was a frontal attack with horse, foot and artillery.

The marvel is that he got it past the Lord Chamberlain. Perhaps that high official did not think much of them either and, at any rate, wanted to avoid getting involved any further in this unsavoury affray.

But the time for the production was not yet. It took even Foote a little while to get ready. Meanwhile, the attacks against him increased, assuming a more menacing and a far more sinister tone. Covert suggestions of a foul nature began to creep in. But Foote went on, and paid far less attention to them than he should have done. He felt secure in his own theatre. He felt that he, as Patentee of Theatre Royal, Haymarket, would have the public on his side. A Patentee must be above reproach (which was sheer nonsense), and that on the Haymarket stage he would influence public opinion, turn it to his way and use it finally to defeat and pulverise his foes.

Strange that such an astute man should forget that it was possible, for money, to hire roughs to make continual disturbance. He seems to have underrated the lengths to which Jackson would go. Everything published about him was read with avidity. The man who had so long terrorised the society of his day was now getting a taste of his own medicine. A thing said often enough, without a crushing and final reply, gets believed. The clever, ceaseless and insidious attacks of Jackson were bearing fruit. And not even the Haymarket could shield Foote, as later he was to discover.

That theatre had been closed during the winter months, according to the terms of the Patent. All that time the steady undermining of Foote's reputation had gone on—as a contemporary "Life" of him says: "to the no small entertainment of the town." Now he appeared again on the stage. In May, 1776, he reopened the Haymarket with a perfor mance of *The Bankrupt*. He knew there might be trouble, he knew his enemies, and he knew how many people would also be glad to see him fall. But Foote was no coward, he was not one to show the white feather.

On that May evening the Haymarket was packed to the doors. All the smart people were there, and all the intelligentsia too. Everyone who was anyone did their best to get in. And a crowd of people who, from Foote's point of view, would have been better outside got in as well. The curtain rose, Foote walked on the stage. Instantly there was pandemonium. Jackson's men were there in force and there were boos, hisses, catcalls, yells and imprecations. The very air was thick with menace—this was no ordinary disturbance. The ladies in the boxes, knowing what such noises portended, got out as fast as they could. For there was more in it than met the eye. And Foote was to tell them the news. That very morning he had brought his enemy before the court and the court had given judgment for Foote. He faced that raging, yelling mob, amongst whom were those demonstrating in his favour and making confusion worse confused. He stood alone before them and asked for a hearing. There, with his wooden leg, but his courage high, his hat in his hand to show his desire to speak, he pleaded for a hearing. He got it, too. Courage in face of a mob, especially an organised one, always counts.

Then he said:

"Gentlemen, it was not my intention after the charge that has been made against me, to appear before the public until I had an opportunity of proving my innocence; but as this charge was made at this critical point of time when I usually opened my theatre, and having engaged as good a set of performers for your amusement as I could procure, it was the unanimous advice of my friends that I should open my house, in confidence that the public were too noble and too just to discard an old servant for a mere accusation.

"I am ready to answer every charge that can be brought against me and have pursued such legal steps to clear my reputation from the virulent attacks of a public paper as will speedily bring the writer to an issue in the Court of King's Bench, which has this day made the rule absolute against the publisher. I beg leave to return my thanks for the marks you have now given me of your humanity and justice; permit me to promise that I will never disgrace your protection."

His friends rejoiced, but his enemies were furious. However he got his hearing and the play was allowed to proceed.

But the victory was only for the moment. Now a really revolting whisper went round the town, and it also appeared in print. Foote was to fall at last. This time it was certain. He had played his *Capucin*, his last new play at the Haymarket, and the dastardly Jackson was implacable. There were no lengths now to which he would not go, no means too vile to attain his ends.

And then the sensation broke. It went around the town like wild-fire. On July 8th, 1776, a coachman who had been in Foote's employ and whom he had discharged, went before the magistrates and indicted Foote on a charge of sodomy. A true bill was found—although Foote was given no chance of answering—and a warrant for his arrest was issued. It was noticed that the coachman had Jackson as a sponsor. Someone rushed to Foote and told him. He dashed to the court as quickly as he could, and thereby escaped the supreme indignity of arrest, for the officers with the warrant crossed him on his journey. He took some friends with him, and was granted bail.

The town was agog. Whilst the case was preparing, up came Jackson again to the court with another man to depose a similar complaint. But this time Foote had counsel. He got the charge removed to the Court of King's Bench, where there was a guarantee of a fair trial.

Foote now stood in the centre of as pretty a scandal as London had ever seen. But, despite it all, he was true to his calling and true to his theatre. His foes wanted the Haymarket closed, to spike his guns. Foote did the wisest, the only thing a man in his position could do. The guilty man runs away; the innocent man stands his ground. Foote appeared at the Haymarket on the night of his arrest. It must have cost him dear; it must have been a terrible ordeal, but he went through with it. From that beloved stage of his he had roasted so many people and had laughed at their squirmings. Now he in his turn would have to bear the brunt.

He knew his enemies would be there. But he faced it out. Many women had come to the play and the unruly element took the opportunity of calling them very rude names. So they walked out—and got a round of applause. To face a house at the fever heat of excitement, and brimful of mischief and malice, Foote hobbled on to the stage. His courage was rewarded. A great burst of applause greeted him, though there were hoots and hisses from the organised opposition. He faced the demonstration and was cheered to the echo.

Now that he was in real danger, old feuds against him were forgotten. The public rallied to him, and he found out who were his friends. The staunchest he had was the man he had most attacked—David Garrick. He stood by his old detractor nobly and cheered him up by every means in his power. To Foote's credit, he appreciated this friendship. He wrote to Garrick:

"MY DEAR SIR, I am exceedingly obliged to you for the kind conclusion of your letter. I promise I would not have hinted it to you, but in the confidence of your friendship and if at the same time I could not, with the greatest truth, say that I am most sincerely and affectionately yours. I have been cruelly used but I have thank God got to the bottom of the infernal contrivance. God for ever bless you."

And Foote meant it, too. There is small doubt that the "hint" was for a loan, which he got.

A great many others stood by him. Whilst the trial was pending the King himself showed his sympathy by coming to the Haymarket— some authorities say he "commanded" a performance, but in view of what was to happen later on that is hardly likely—but he certainly came to see Foote act. And, of course, in his capacity as Patentee, Foote himself received the King. He was as irrepressible as ever. He told the King that the play he was to see was written by one of his chaplains and added: "And dull enough to be by a bishop."

Foote, in his hour of need, had no lack of friends.

In due course, he stood his trial. He who had put so many people in the pillory of his satire, now stood in the dock himself. But he conquered. He was acquitted, without a stain on his character, of the vilest charge that can be brought against a man. It was utterly baseless, totally without a shred of foundation. Foote was no homosexual; quite the contrary. He had many love affairs. And he had a wife, a daughter and an illegitimate son. He had, after his own way, cared for his wife, and when she died his countenance was rueful. Even then he could not keep his sense of humour under control. A friend asked him what was the matter? Foote said he had been searching the town to find a second-hand coffin for his spouse! His daughter Maria had a story of her own. She was a bit of a storm-centre too. The trial had been attended by royal personages and all the notables. Some might have gone out of morbid curiosity. Garrick, however, was a true friend all through this time.

Why no action was taken against Jackson for perjury is inexplicable, but Foote did what he could. He laid a further action for libel against him—but Jackson died before it came to trial.

The strain on Foote, however, was too much. His constitution, undermined by his mode of life—and he had never fully recovered from the amputation—caused him to have a seizure. He had been stricken down just when the future was rosy, just when he might have expected a quiet life and a successful one, with his hold on the public, his own theatre and his Royal Warrant.

He had made money, but he had spent it. He was a poor man, and a sick one. He knew in his heart he was a beaten one, too. He knew that he could not carry on. One thing only remained to him—his theatre. That must provide for his old age—if indeed he was to have an old age. So he decided to sell it. What this resolve cost him we can imagine. He had built up the Haymarket—he was the Haymarket. He and his theatre were on top of the wave. Then had come his play—*A Trip to Calais* and the trouble with the Duchess of Kingston. That he may have overcome but for his unfortunate letter and his wicked, unscrupulous foes, the gangsters set on him by the guilty Duchess. He had fought them—and, indeed, now he knew that it had been a fight for his life. And he had won. But at what cost! His health was gone, his money was gone. His only asset was the Haymarket. It was like a child to him, but he must sell it—or he must starve. Nobody could employ a one-legged actor. And he knew, too, that he could only work for himself.

He could not face London as a broken man. So with what he could get for his theatre he would go abroad in search of the sun and so end his days. He called on Garrick, but David was ill with the gout. Foote would not have him disturbed. So he wrote him a letter, saying he was going abroad. He tried to laugh things off, but no doubt Garrick read between the lines:

"There is more of prudence than of pleasure in my trip to the Continent. To tell you the truth, I am tired of racking my brain, toiling like a horse, and crossing seas and mountains in the most dreary season merely to pay servants' wages and tradesmen's bills. I have therefore directed my friend Jewel to discharge the lazy vermin at my hall and let my hall too (hell it would seem is the correct word) if he can meet with a proper tenant. Help me to one if you can. . . ."

There is a wealth of pity in that last phrase. The hall is, of course, the Haymarket and the lazy vermin the actors. It was Foote's way. What he loved he still made fun of.

He put it about that he would sell the Haymarket. But he wanted a good tenant and he had ideas. In a short while he got a nibble. A man called John Colborne came along, and treated with him. They fenced, and Foote formed the opinion that Colborne was really negotiating for someone else. Who it was he could not imagine. But he laughed with his friends over the poor fool who wanted to risk and certainly lose his money.

At dinner with another theatrical manager, George Colman, he waxed very facetious about it when the question of the sale cropped up. He said to the company: "Now here is Mr. Colman, an experienced manager. He will tell you that nobody can conduct so peculiar a theatrical concern as mine but myself. But there is a fat-headed fellow of an agent who has been boring me every morning at breakfast with terms for some blockhead who knows nothing about the stage, but whose money burns in his pocket." "Playhouse mad, I presume?" said Colman. "Right," replied Foote; "and if bleeding will bring him to his senses, he'll find me a devilish good doctor. . . ." Nobody laughed louder than Colman. But the fat-headed agent did his work well and finally terms were agreed. The parties met at an appointed time to settle the matter, sign and hand over the money. If Foote could ever have looked foolish, he might have done so then, for the blockhead was none other than George Colman. . . .

But Foote had kept his word about being a good doctor. The terms of the agreement looked all on his side. Colman was to take over the theatre and all expenses and responsibility. He was to pay Foote an annuity of £1,600 a year, payable half yearly. Foote was also to be employed as an actor, when he felt so disposed, at a good salary, and Colman was to take over his plays, at an agreed sum of £500, for Foote's lifetime, after which they were to go to his son. The £1,600 yearly was not in purchase of the Patent, but as an annuity for Foote. It came to the same thing, as the Patent was for Foote's lifetime only.

It looked a bargain for Foote; actually, as will transpire, it was a bargain for Colman. The deal was done. On October 18th, 1776, the Haymarket control passed from Foote to Colman, but Foote was still Patentee. He still had his one sound leg in the theatre. And well

Colman knew it. For that good man got to work at once and was much hindered by Foote, who came down to the theatre and, as was to be expected, interfered and found fault with everything. Colman, who was a man who believed in quality and good productions—not personal, haphazard affairs like Foote—wanted to do things well.

The tired and aged cripple continued to put in his oar. He would come to the Haymarket, lean against the wall, or stand in a corner, half sagging down with weakness and fatigue, and watch what was going on, from time to time interjecting a caustic remark. He played for Colman three times only, his last appearance being in his own play, either *The Maid of Bath* or *The Mayor of Garratt*, on July, 30th, 1777. His power seemed to have left him and he was hissed. This pulled him together and he played finely and drew much applause—for the last time! He had a stroke as the last words were spoken. And then he could bear it no longer. It was not his Haymarket; he was not wanted there now. He was wanted nowhere. He would go away. His spirit was dying within him. He went to Brighton—Brighthelmstone then— but it did him no good. He decided to go abroad.

He went to his theatre, where he had done so much, and bade it a quiet farewell. He may have had a presentiment that he would never see it again. Then he went to his house in Suffolk Place and wandered round the rooms, touching his favourite possessions with loving fingers and gazing at the portraits with which he had surrounded himself. He paused long before a picture of Weston—a man he had liked and who had played with him, a man of talent, a great comedian, but always without a penny. "Poor Weston," he murmured, shaking his head. Then he turned to Jewel, his treasurer, who was with him. "It will very soon be poor Foote," he said, "or the intelligence of my spirits deceive me." He had glimpsed the future.

He could find no rest. He closed the door of his house, where he had lived so well, eaten so well, drunk so well, and entertained so royally, where he had, indeed, run through two fortunes and squandered another of his own making. He got into a coach and he left London. He was going in search of the sun, to brighten his remaining days.

He never found the sun. He got as far as Dover. He put up at the Ship Inn, on the harbour-side. But he joked to the last. He cracked his last gag to the cooks and scullions of the little Inn. That night he slept badly. The next day he was seized by a fit of shivering. His breathing got weaker and weaker and at last there was a long sigh—and silence. Samuel Foote, the English Aristophanes, had breathed his last, at the age of fifty-seven, on October 21st, 1777.

The strange, complex character, the great wit, the clever dramatist and supreme mimic—the man who feared nobody and who finally defeated himself—had gone to his rest. He had accomplished much. He was proudest of two things, his title of "the English Aristophanes," which was justly his, and the royal title he had gained for his theatre, the Haymarket. He did indeed resemble Aristophanes in his satiric genius, and he made the resemblance clearer by naming his first play *The Knights*, as his great Greek prototype had done also. And he had made a new and famous theatre for London out of a desolate, barn-like occasional playhouse. He had, by his own endeavours and his own sacrifice, made it Theatre Royal, Haymarket.

He was buried by torchlight in the cloisters of Westminster Abbey. All the great players walked in procession behind him.

The place where he lies is unmarked, for no memorial was ever erected. He needed none. His monument is still there—in the Haymarket —the Little Theatre in the Hay which he had made Royal.

Let Dr. Johnson speak his epitaph—it never went on his grave:

"Did you think he would be so soon gone? 'Life,' says Falstaff, 'is like a shuttle.' "

"He was a fine fellow in his way and the world is really impoverished by his sinking glories. I would have his life written with diligence. . . ."

An epitaph by Dr. Johnson and a theatre which stands, second to none, to-day—what more could life give at parting to Samuel Foote?

CHAPTER X

GREATNESS COMES TO THE HAYMARKET

THEATRE ROYAL, HAYMARKET, was fifty-seven years old when it passed under the management of George Colman. Once again a dramatist-manager had control.

In that short space of time it had risen from the lowest rank to the highest—from an unlicensed booth to a Theatre Royal. That title it lost when Samuel Foote died, so the Haymarket was only actually a Theatre Royal for eleven years, the Patent dying with Foote. But still it is called Theatre Royal, and well it deserves its title.

Besides achieving this rank, it had most definitely become the home of English comedy. From the very beginning of its career, comedy had been its metier. As it matured under Colman, and as the star actors came to grace his stage—for there had been few of them as yet—so it was to widen its horizon. But always comedy had suited it better than tragedy. Smaller than Drury Lane and Covent Garden, its grace, its intimacy and its greater delicacy is more befitting the sock than the buskin. It seemed destined for comedy from the very beginning.

Before taking leave of Samuel Foote, there must be a backward glance or two to pick up threads that make the pattern of this story.

Foote was a great man within his own limitations, and a fine actor in parts which he wrote to suit himself. A master of monologue, he would hold the stage by himself for half an hour on end. Otherwise he was a very indifferent performer. He was a modern, and had no use for the classics. He was of his day and cared little about posterity. His great hold on the public was his personality, his power of observation and topicality and his incredible, daring mimicry. His plays are not so much plays as running commentaries—but as such they are magnificent. There was no other writer of comedy in his day who could hold a candle to him.

His death coincided with the year in which London saw its classic English comedy, *The School for Scandal*, produced at Drury Lane. It is as well for Richard Brinsley Sheridan that Samuel Foote died when he did. What a burlesque he would have made of the brilliant, improvident, unbusinesslike Irishman. But Sheridan owed something to Foote. The inspirations of many of his most brilliant scenes are in those careless patchworks of our Aristophanes.

The two men had much in common. They were both careless in money matters and both slovenly theatre managers. But Sheridan had the charm which Foote lacked entirely. However much one may admire Foote's courage, wit and genius, one finds little to admire in the man himself. Yet he was a pioneer. He started the light and airy entertainment like *The Diversions* at the Haymarket, he was the first London actor of eminence to play in Edinburgh, and there was a time when he contemplated making the puppet show a much more elaborate and grand affair than it has ever become. He saw a chance for more impudent burlesque. The puppets were becoming popular; there was a puppet show in Panton Street, near his theatre, and he went to see them. They amused him, but he saw their limitations. What, however, if he could make them life-size, dressed and painted in exact resemblance of people he wanted to insult and burlesque? It was a great idea. And he carried it out, although he did not insult so many celebrities as he had first intended. There were too many threats of bodily reprisals when the news went round. But he did bring his puppets on the stage of the Haymarket in his own way and in an entertainment which he called *Piety in Patterns, or The Handsome Housemaid.* It was a burlesque of the current craze for sentimental novels of the "Pamela" type. It was not a success, although ingenious and, so far as the technical side was concerned, very well done. He announced it for the next night, which led to disapproval and the breaking of a bench or two, as and by way of protest. So he left it alone and kept to ordinary plays—although he said he thought he might do better if he got actors to play the puppets—their woodenness would be most natural. And it gave him a chance for a "crack" at his favourite butt at that time. A lady asked him if the puppets were to be life-sized. "Oh dear, no, madam," replied Foote. "Not much above the size of Garrick."

The other threat concerns the play called *The Tailors. A Tragedy for Warm Weather.* This will have another entrance in the Haymarket's story—and a most important one. But did Foote write it? It is often attributed to him, but there is a grave doubt. He played in it—the part of Francisco—he spoke an excellent prologue written by Garrick, and he had a good cast, including Weston, Bannister, Palmer and Shuter, with Mrs. Jefferies as his leading lady.

He disowned the play himself—but that proves little. It is in blank verse of a kind, which was by no means his method. Foote mentions it in a letter to Tate Wilkinson, whom he wanted for a part in it. The letter is typical of the man and his methods:

"DEAR SIR, If I had not a pretty shrewd knack of guessing, it would not be quite so easy a matter to answer your favour from Hull. You desire to know if I had commissioned Giordini to give a particular sum for this or the next summer. . . .

"Your old friend Shuter is locked up in the playhouse and is soliciting a licence from his creditors, in which number I find Jewel is included for ten guineas borrowed during the last season. Fie upon him! I am glad to hear that your affairs prosper. I have a piece of three acts, not my own, which I shall give in the month of May, called *The Tailors*. The subject is a rich one—the dispute between the masters and the journeymen of that respectable profession—and I think the author has done it exquisite justice. It is a parody of the best passages in the most favourable plays, conveyed with great gravity in blank verse. I think you will appear in it to advantage, and I shall be glad of your assistance. I cannot say I am quite so well as I had reason to expect; I thought myself obliged to give Barry a lift on two critical nights which injured me extremely; but I am now better, and, except the trifle of a leg, as much yours as ever.

"SAM FOOTE."

In that letter he definitely disowns it,—but no author's name appears on copies of the play which are extant,—and it may be that despite all he said, the work was Foote's, who desired on this occasion to remain anonymous. That greatest authority, Professor Allardyce Nicoll, does not, however, include it amongst the plays of Foote. It was, however, to work as much mischief as ever Foote worked—and at the Haymarket.

With Foote dead in 1777, it was clear who had got the best of the bargain over the theatre—and that was Colman. Foote died after drawing the first half-yearly payment of his annuity, so Colman got the Haymarket almost for nothing.

It must be remembered that it was still a summer theatre, only able to open between May 15th and September 15th, inclusive, each year. Colman, on the death of Foote, stood possessed of the whole thing. He had taken over the wardrobe. It was not a very grand affair, for Foote ran his theatre on what he considered cheap and clever lines, but which actually landed him into more expense than a proper capital outlay would have done. Young George Colman states:

"With the Theatre, certain decayed and moth eaten articles, which Foote dignified by the collective name of a wardrobe, and which might have produced altogether at a sale, if well puffed by a knowing auctioneer, about twenty pounds at the utmost, were made over to the lessee. The fading gaiety of Major Sturgeon's regimentals, trimmed with tarnished copper-lace, was splendour itself, compared with the other threadbare rubbish of this repository.

"Foote's stock plays were in fact chiefly of his own writing, and his dramatis personæ required little more than a few common coats and waistcoats; when he wanted more habiliments than he possessed, he resorted to a friperie in Monmouth Street, not to purchase but to job them by the night; and so vilely did some of the apparel fit the actors that he was often obliged to make a joke of the disgrace, and get the start of the audience if he could, in a laugh against his own troop of tatterdemalions. There was a skeleton of a man belonging to his company who performed a minor part in the scene of a debating club, in which Foote acted the president; this anatomic vivant was provided with a coat which would not have been too big even for the late Stephen Kemble; the arms were particularly wide and the cuffs covered his hands. Foote, during the debate, always addressed this personage as the 'much respected gentleman in the sleeves.' So improvident was he, that he even hired most of the printed music which was played between the acts, whereby he had given its original price ten times over, and in the end, not a scrap of it was his property!"

Stephen Kemble, by the way, was the only actor who could play Falstaff without any padding. He was brother of John Philip Kemble and Mrs. Siddons, and for a short time manager of Drury Lane Theatre. As regards Colman junior's sneer at Foote's improvidence, this does not come too well from a man who, later, was to try and run the Haymarket Theatre from a debtor's prison. Whatever else may be said about Foote, he did make a success of the Haymarket by his own acting in his own plays and, for a considerable time, against the handicap of a wooden leg.

George Colman senior, who now stood possessed of the Haymarket, was a man of a very different type from Samuel Foote and even from his own son, who was to inherit the theatre from him. He was of good birth. He had the Countess of Bath for an aunt and a duke for a patron. He was well educated and had been destined for the law. But the theatre called him too loudly and too insistently. When he should have been away on circuit, he was haunting the playhouses and scribbling plays. He became a friend of Garrick's, and that astute man thought so much of Colman's judgment in theatrical affairs that when he went abroad he laid it down that Colman was to be consulted over anything which might happen at Drury Lane.

Colman's attempts at playwriting when he should have been brief-studying bore fruit. He became a successful dramatist. He was part author, with David Garrick, of *The Clandestine Marriage*. They had a dispute about this—quite the usual thing for collaborators—and Garrick would not play in it when it was presented at Drury Lane. So his part —Lord Ogleby—gave that fine actor, King, one of his biggest successes. Garrick knew he was wrong.

Colman came into an inheritance. John Rich, of Covent Garden Theatre, had died and the Patent was in the market. Colman joined with three others, Harris, Rutherford and Powell, and bought the Patent and the theatre. This dismayed Garrick, who scented strong and knowledgeable opposition.

Colman became Stage Manager—he would be called General Manager to-day. He did fine work there. He started Oliver Goldsmith on his dramatic career when he produced *The Good Natured Man*. But things are never easy in theatrical partnerships, and Colman quarrelled with his co-directors. They went to law, and Colman won He carried on, and presented Macklin; he staged Bickerstaffe and Dibdin's opera, *Lionel and Clarissa*, and much fine work. But he, the practical man, was beset by the others of his partnership. They carried on eternal strife. They locked him out of the theatre, they took away the wardrobe, the prompt-books and the music. This led to more legal troubles, and Colman won, but at a shattering cost. He made one mistake in judgment. He did not believe that Goldsmith's *She Stoops to Conquer* was any good and he was so antagonistic towards it that the play nearly succumbed during rehearsals. The result of its production everybody knows. Colman was entitled to a mistake. It was not his bad judgment, but his partners and legal troubles arising from their ignorance which drove him from the great theatre, where his record is clean, honest and excellent.

Colman, when he took over the Haymarket, had quite as many troubles to face as when he was in charge at Covent Garden. Samuel Foote was not the least of them. But he was a man of vision and determination, and now he had no partners to hinder him. Like a true man of the theatre, he saw troubles as simply so many obstacles to be overcome. He was determined to make the Haymarket into a real playhouse, to advance it from the one-man dominance and one-track productions of Foote, to produce new and old classics and favourites, and to give it what it had never yet had—first-class casts and companies, and a regular succession of stars.

He worked quickly. The summer was upon him, the season in which he was allowed to play. He had to get a good company, and Bath and other centres of fashion would be competing too. But he succeeded, and for the first time the Haymarket stood possessed of a company of which it might be proud. When George Colman opened the Haymarket under his management he had the following players with him who might well be called the original Haymarket company:

Actors

Aickin	Edwin	Kenney
Bannister, C.	Egan	Massey
Bedford	Fearon	Palmer
Bissett	Foote	Palmer, R.
Bransby	Francis	Parsons
Davies	Griffiths	Pierce
Davies, J.	Henderson	Stevens
Digges	Hitchcock	Walker
Dubellamy	Jackson	

Actresses

Miss Barsanti	Miss Hall	Miss Morris
Mrs. Colls	Mrs. Hitchcock	Mrs. W. Palmer
Mrs. Davis	Mrs. Hunter	Miss Platt
Miss Farren	Mrs. Jewell	Mrs. Poussin
Mrs. Fearon	Mrs. Love	Miss Twist
Mrs. Gardner	Mrs. Massey	

Mr. Younger was his deputy manager and Mr. Brownsmith the prompter. He had Monsieur Georgi's pupils, who were children, as dancers. The number of "joint engagements" of husbands and wives will be noted. And it did not stop there. The second generation got in, too. For when he produced Garrick's pantomime entertainment called *Lilliput*, a children's play, parts were performed by Master Edwin and Misses Bedford, P. Farren, Francis and Hitchcock. There were really theatrical families in those days and the Haymarket must have been indeed a family house.

It is worth while taking a closer look at some of these members of the Haymarket Company; they repay inspection. As it is the Haymarket, comedy takes preference. John Palmer must come first. He was one of the best comedians of his day. He was the original Joseph Surface in *The School for Scandal*. Yet he had suffered much in his endeavour to be an actor—his career is one of which the despondent stage aspirant should take note. Garrick would not look at him at first, and told him to go for a soldier. He became a strolling player and endured all the worst hardships of that life. Then he applied again to Garrick, who gave him some work. Foote then employed him, but only as a man who had to play anything he was ordered to undertake: Foote said he was bad in tragedy—not surprising, since he was a comedian.

He starved on the salary he got from Foote, but he kept on. Then he married a girl who had expectations of a fortune. Because of that marriage, she was cut off with, or without, the proverbial shilling. So Palmer struggled on. He had a chance of playing Iago to the Othello of Spranger Barry, but his nerve failed him. Then he went with Garrick again, who rated him a bad "study," but found out his mistake. Palmer now made progress, only to be checked by being accidentally stabbed by Mrs. Spranger Barry (he had been frightened of her husband) in a play called *The Grecian Daughter*. He got to the top, and here he made many successes, helped by his fine figure and his handsome face. He excelled in hypocritical parts like Joseph Surface and he was indeed something in that way himself. One of his exploits was to build a theatre—the Royalty in Wellclose Street, E., but, as it was not licensed, he was always in trouble. The debts he incurred pursued him perpetually in the form of bailiffs, and sometimes he had to live in the theatre for a week at a time, getting out finally hidden amongst a bundle of "properties." It was thus he travelled to the Haymarket, from Drury Lane, to start his engagement with Colman.

Robert Palmer, his brother, was also an excellent comedian, but of a much more robust type than John.

In Parsons, Colman had another fine performer. Again, this was a comedian. He had begun as an apothecary and was also an excellent artist, but preferred acting to either calling. He made the right choice, for he was one of the best low comedians of his day. He played many parts which Shuter had made famous before him, and always said the

I

credit was due to Shuter, for he was modest about his own achievements. He need not have been, for the town loved him. He was the original Sir Fretful Plagiary in *The Critic*. His greatest exploit was, however, not at Drury Lane, but at the Haymarket. Under Colman he was appearing there when King George III paid the theatre a visit to see *The Siege of Calais*. Parsons played a carpenter who is also a hangman. He and another carpenter are erecting a scaffold on which the patriotic burghers are to be hanged. There is a line in the play which says, "So, the King is coming; an the King like not my scaffold, I am no true man." On the night of the King's visit, Parsons, who had got much applause, was a bit carried away and "gagged." When this line arrived, he went right down to the Royal box and said, "An the King were here and did not admire my scaffold, I would say, 'Damn him, he has no taste.'" Nobody laughed more heartily than old Farmer George.

Old Parsons died, worn out by asthma, in 1795. Before he was buried, whilst he still lay in his coffin upstairs, the widow married his son's tutor. The dead husband had left her a hard-earned fortune. The new husband spent it and left her and her boy destitute. How Parsons' shade must have laughed—except perhaps for his son.

Parsons' chief rival was Edwin, who was in the same company. This was another supreme comedian who was also the best comic singer in the light operas and burlesques of his period. He began his career at Dublin and ended it at the Haymarket. He lost his job in the Pensions Office because he would act. Old Ned Shuter had a discerning eye and said to him, "You will be a great actor when I am laid low." At first playgoers did not take to his style of humour at all. But he won them round, and finally they were his complete slaves. He took immense liberties, for he was a heavy drinker. He would be driven up to the stage door dead drunk at the bottom of a chaise. His brother actors would carry him in, put him in a chair, dress him somehow, drag him down to the wings and push him on. He would stagger across the stage to the centre and then stop. He would gaze at the audience, who knew quite well what was the matter, rub his eyes a time or two, and then give them a grin. They would give him a round of applause and then he would make them laugh—and keep them laughing. The more drunk he had been— and still must have been—the better he played. He was immense in scenes which consisted of "business" and required no words. Henderson, who was to play Falstaff at the Haymarket, said that when Edwin played Sir Hugh he had seen the audience rock with laughter for minutes on end at this dumb show whilst preparing for the duel. Edwin was an actor who was always topsyturvy. He played old men when he was young and young men when he was old.

He always played to his audience—he was fully aware of them, there was no highfalutin artistry about Edwin. He formed an alliance with the friends in front from his first entrance and would play with them more than with his brother actors. Most inartistic, of course, and right out of the picture. But the audiences of those days adored it. Sometimes he must have overdone it. It is recorded that on one occasion he was playing Bowkit in *Son-in-Law*. He was not a very handsome man and there was some reason, it seemed, when in the course of the play Old Cranky declined to accept him as son-in-law because of his ugliness. Edwin stared at him and repeated the word "Ugly" in an amazed, wondering tone. Then he advanced to the footlights and looked round the house. He pointed of a sudden to a gentleman sitting in a balcony box. "Now," said Edwin, "now I submit to the decision of an enlightened British public, which is the ugliest fellow of us three? I, or Old Cranky, or that gentleman in the front row of the balcony box?"

The audience followed the lead of his pointing finger and the gentleman thus singled out was treated to loud hoots of derision and fled from the theatre. It may have pleased the house, but it certainly meant that one member of the public would never enter the Haymarket again. Or probably any of the other theatres where Edwin might play.

He had a curious, dry and characteristic smile which pleased everyone, and when his enemy the brandy bottle laid him low and his friends and brother actors gazed on his dead face for the last time, that smile was still there. . . .

In Aickin, George Colman had another fine actor. He was the original Rowley of *The School for Scandal*, and a very sound performer indeed. There were two Aickins, "Tyrant Aickin" and "Belly Aickin."

Charles Bannister was the father of the more famous Jack Bannister. Charles, the father, had a marvellous bass voice of such depth and power that it was said to be able to crack a window pane by its low vibrations.

Of the ladies the chief is Miss Barsanti. She was the original Lydia Languish. Shortly after the opening of the Haymarket, she went to Ireland, where she remained. She was a good, honest woman and a good actress, who married a man called Lesley, of some family, and that family forbade her ever to use his name. Being a peaceable soul, she agreed. Her second husband was Daly, an important Irish manager of his time. She swore never to wear male attire on the stage—"breeches parts" were very popular with actresses and audiences alike—and only once did she do so. Then she compromised by wearing very wide Turkish trousers and a veil.

Most of the others had been with Foote. Mrs. Jewel was the wife of the treasurer.

Such, then, was the team that George Colman senior had got together, and it was good. Colman opened his theatre with a flourish on May 15th, 1777, with his own comedy of *The English Merchant* and Garrick's *Lilliput*. He closed down again at once. He had been a bit too quick. The two Patent theatres had not yet shut up for the summer season, and at Drury Lane the just-produced *School for Scandal* was playing to immense business.

It was bad luck for Colman, for as a rule his two competitors would
have been shut, but just to spite him, it seems, they ran on and on. The
state of theatrical affairs was that Garrick had retired, Sheridan was in
command at Drury Lane and Harris was running Covent Garden,
which had, for the moment, gone all musical.

So Colman had to shut up, in view of a practically empty theatre on
his opening night, and bide his time. Foote probably laughed at him.
However, he rehearsed his company in various plays, got on with
business, and perhaps a young girl in his company caught his eye. Her
name was Farren: she was destined for greatness.

He had not made an auspicious beginning. His little comedy was ten
years old and no great attraction, whilst Garrick's *Lilliput* was even
older and had become outworn. Monsieur Georgi's children did not
help much either. They were not efficient, poor little things, and were
probably indifferently trained. They were pushed on and capered about,
kicking up their heels and losing their shoes, whilst Georgi cursed them
audibly from the wings. One or two were overgrown and the rest were
so small that it seemed a shame to keep them out of their little beds.
The audience laughed at them good-naturedly and gave them sympathetic applause. Stage children have to be excellent if they are to be
endured—and these poor little wretches were very far from excellent.

The Haymarket remained closed until May 28th, and then re-opened
to give three performances a week. People began to come along. On
June 11th—the two big theatres having at last shut up—Colman was
able to announce that he would now play every night in the week,
Sundays excepted. This was an improvement on Foote, who had only
played every alternate night. The Haymarket was gathering momentum.

But the bad opening had taught Colman a lesson. He saw it was no
good relying, as they mostly did in those days, on old successes with an
occasional new play. He had a good enough company, but he must do
something sensational. He must find new actors, new actresses, to make
an impression on the town, for the public will always run after a new
thing

He cast his eyes around the dramatic world. He searched the theatrical
firmament, and he fixed them finally on Bath; and upon a young actor
there called Henderson. He would bring the new actor to Town. He
surveyed his own company, and he observed Miss Farren, still only in
her teens. He would try her out. And he bethought himself also of
Digges, of his company, who had an immense reputation in the North
of England and in Edinburgh.

Colman decided that his line should be novelty.

He had, of course, to put up with Foote. That eccentric genius was
still there, watching the iconoclasm (from his point of view), which was
happening in what he still regarded as his theatre. Probably he had
expected Colman to run it as he had done, with himself still the central
figure and with his own plays. He made himself a confounded nuisance.

He would come pegging down to rehearsals and hop on the stage, making a great noise with his wooden leg. They were rehearsing *The Spanish Barber*. Colman was having trouble with the company, who could not get the "business" of a scene right, wherein one servant is supposed to be suffering from a sleeping-draught and another from sneezing-powder instead of snuff. "Well," growled Foote to the harassed Colman, "how do you get on?" "Oh, pretty well," said Colman, "but I cannot teach one of these fellows to gape as he should do." "Can't you?" sneered Foote. "Then read him your last comedy, *The Man of Business*, and he'll yawn for a month."

He was even worse behaved when Digges made his London debut a few days afterwards. This actor was of the old school and had elected to appear in *Cato*, playing the name part made famous by Barton Booth, and playing it just as Booth had done. He dressed the part in the same way, too. He wore a "shape," as costumes of the classic type were called, of black, decorated with gilt leather, black stockings, black gloves and a powdered periwig. Even for those days it was hopelessly *vieux jeu*. Foote went into the pit to see this performance. Digges stalked on in the pompous old style, and got the usual round of applause always accorded to the leading performers, especially newcomers, in those days.

As soon as this had subsided, Foote's voice was heard by all in the loudest possible stage whisper, saying, "A Roman chimney sweep on May Day, by God." It got a laugh, but Foote should have been thrown out. Digges, however, was not put off; he played the part well and, although old-fashioned, he succeeded, and even repeated it. He played Cardinal Wolsey too, and was very good indeed. His playing of the scene of the great Cardinal's fall drew genuine tears and applause from even the most seasoned playgoers and critics present. How cross Foote must have been.

There had been another big success, too, before the season was more than a few days old. That was Miss Elizabeth Farren. She had come from the North; she had been a Columbine at Wakefield, and she had played at Liverpool, where all the young men had fallen in love with her. Her father had been a surgeon who left Cork to go on the stage, and got himself locked up in Salisbury. She struggled on, and beauty and talent told. She could act, she could dance, she could sing. Colman gave her a chance in his Haymarket company. He gave her a big chance. He let her play Kate Hardcastle in *She Stoops to Conquer*—the play he had disliked—at the Haymarket on June 9th, 1777. Edwin was playing Old Hardcastle, and what a performance that must have been. Miss Farren swept to success. She was acclaimed and feted. Colman was delighted. Things were going well at the Little Theatre. His policy was right; give them something new, and they would come in. The time was ripe for a new actress—there had been nobody great since Mrs. Abington. And this little girl would fill the breach, the Haymarket

Theatre, and Colman's pockets too. To see her, the town flocked to the Haymarket. Colman therefore gave her other parts. She was Maria in *The Citizen*, and a huge success again. He put her into the lead in *The Spanish Barber*, and he got Garrick to write her an epilogue, which she spoke beautifully. She was the town's darling. This young star had, as other young stars have had since, a "mother." By that is meant a "theatrical mother," who accompanied her carefully guarded daughter to and from the theatre, and through the long hours whilst the girl rehearsed, sat watching every point, argued with the management and looked after her precious daughter's every want. But this mother did more marvels than that. She saw to to it that, no matter how long the rehearsal, how skimpy the time for food, her Elizabeth always got a hot dinner. Meat, gravy and vegetables appeared as if by magic, and the young actress ate heartily and kept her strength and her looks. This intrigued the younger Colman very much, for he was always hanging around his father's theatre when his studies allowed—and often when they did not—and he was of a very inquiring turn of mind. He could not make it out. Here was the pretty young thing, eating a square meal and enjoying it, yet, watch as he might, he never saw the mother bring the food into the theatre. Nor did anyone else bring it to her. He determined to find out, and, by careful hiding and watching her, he did. Mrs. Farren senior had a pocket made under a full skirt of most voluminous proportions, and she had it specially lined as well. That was the travelling kitchen, and the mystery was solved!

Miss Farren's success was too great for her to remain at the Haymarket for long. Covent Garden lured her away, and then Drury Lane, on Mrs. Abington's retirement, captured her from Covent Garden. Good as she was, she was never Abington's equal. But she was not only a leading actress, she was to be more. A vast crowd of lovers was sighing at her feet, but she remained immaculate. Probably the inventive chaperone saw to that. But one of the lovers was more determined than the rest. He followed her wherever she went, even home after the theatre, though she took not the slightest notice of him beyond a polite bow. No guilty splendour for her—she would be no man's mistress. For that young man—he was the Earl of Derby—had a wife.

For eighteen years he paid his devoted court to Miss Farren. For eighteen years she kept him at a distance. Then the Countess died. To do him justice, it must be chronicled that the Earl had long been separated from her. At once, he laid himself and his coronet at the Farren's feet. She accepted both, and retired from the stage.

It was starting from the Haymarket that she rose to such heights, for at the Little Theatre in the Hay, honest, discerning George Colman had given her a chance. She is the first famous woman in the Haymarket saga.

But the stage is set for the coming of someone even greater—someone who was to ascend the topmost pinnacle of dramatic fame, upon whom the mantle of David Garrick was to descend, and between whom, even though Garrick had retired, bad feelings were to exist to the end. A man who had started in poverty and bad health, but who by courage, resolution and grim determination was to survive blows which would have felled a lesser man, and was to go from triumph to triumph, until at last he reposed beside his great rival, in Westminster Abbey itself.

It was Colman who gave this man his chance, and it was at the Haymarket that he took it. That theatre was the London cradle of his fame; it was from there he was to reach the pinnacle on which had stood Garrick. He came to the Haymarket from Bath, where he was known as the Bath Roscius—no very great compliment to be called after a clown. His story is so remarkable that it must be told in some detail. He comes into the Haymarket actively on the night of June 11th, 1777 —a hot, sweltering summer night which should have emptied the theatre, a contrast to the bitter winter's night of Edmund Kean's debut at Drury Lane. He is the next novelty which Colman, only open a very few days, is to spring on the public at the Haymarket Theatre. And his name is John Henderson.

CHAPTER XI

THE CAVALCADE BEGINS

JOHN HENDERSON, the first of the great actors to win fame at the Haymarket Theatre, was born in Goldsmith Street, London, of Scottish ancestry. He was a descendant of Dr. Alexander Henderson, who had the famous conference with Charles I when that Monarch was imprisoned in Corfe Castle. Henderson's grandfather was a Quaker and his father a merchant who traded with Ireland. There was no theatrical background to this man at all.

A year after John's birth, his father died, leaving the mother and two sons, with means so slender as to be almost invisible. But the mother had the pluck and resolution which John Henderson was to inherit. She brought the children up well and tended them with care. All through his life Henderson revered his mother.

When he was only two years of age, the family moved to Newport Pagnell, in Buckinghamshire. There they resided for ten years, Mrs. Henderson making great sacrifices to educate them. She gave young John a volume of Shakespeare, and as soon as he could read he devoured its contents. He learned great masses of it by heart, which he would recite.

The boy also showed a taste and an ability for drawing, and he was later apprenticed to an artist named Fournier, who was eminent at this time. Henderson worked hard, and one of his drawings was exhibited by the Society of Arts and Sciences. It won him a small premium. Then a relation, one Cripps, who was a silversmith in St. James's Street, gave him a job, but shortly afterwards Cripps died.

Wherever Henderson went, his volume of Shakespeare went with him. He now knew most of it by heart. He had studied all the parts, he had visualised them, he knew all about them. So when Cripps' sudden death left him stranded in London the Shakespearean volume decided him. He would try the stage.

For anyone without friends, money and influence, that is a hard path even to-day. It was worse then, because the scope was so circumscribed. In 1768 there were, among the proper theatres, only Drury Lane, Covent Garden and the Haymarket open to him, and there was no prospect for an untried amateur in the few outlying unlicensed places.

Henderson applied to Drury Lane. He got a setback at once. He had, by some means, procured a letter of introduction to George Garrick, David's brother, and the letter got him an interview with that gentleman. Greatly condescending to the poor, ill-clad youth, Mr. George gave him an audition, or, in the parlance of those days, watched him go through the scene. Then he gave his opinion. Henderson's voice was too feeble. No audience would hear what he said. He had not the necessary strength. There may have been something in this, for at the time Henderson was fighting against consumptive tendencies in addition to his other troubles.

But Henderson did not despair. He studied and worked hard at odd jobs.

Then he made the acquaintance of a Mr. Beckett, a well-known book-seller. Mr. Beckett's shop was a meeting-place for wits and celebrities, a kind of informal club. Mr. David Garrick was a constant visitor there. It was cheaper than the coffee-houses. Garrick would not be expected to spend money, to stand treat, and this suited his economic mind; also he would not meet many actors—Garrick did not like consorting with his own profession out of business hours. Young John Henderson watched him with awe and reverence and hung upon his every word. Kindly Mr. Beckett introduced him to his hero, and after a while Henderson stammered out his ambition to become an actor and begged Mr. Garrick to hear him. The actor always made excuses and turned him down, even when he waited on him at the theatre. It seemed that Henderson would never get the ear of anyone who could advance his ambition.

But he studied Garrick carefully. His active mind and retentive memory photographed the great actor, recording every movement, every habitual gesture, every tone of voice. For Henderson, like Foote and Garrick himself, was a marvellous mimic.

A Mrs. Phillipine Burton was to have a play of her own done at the Haymarket, presumably by arrangement with Foote. Henderson applied for a part in it. He did not even get an answer. He called constantly at Covent Garden, beseeching George Colman to see and hear him, but he got only refusals.

Then one night a chance came. It was not what he had expected. It was no audition with one of the great ones. It was a performance in a tavern. A very obscure member of the Drury Lane company was being given something of benefit at this Islington inn: he was probably in low water and his friends were "rallying" round.

Henderson heard of it and went along with an offer to perform. His offer was accepted. He recited Garrick's "Ode to the Jubilee," and he did it as Garrick himself used to do. The imitation was perfect. It stunned that audience. A member thereof shouted: "This is either Garrick himself or Antichrist." He was a sensation, and tasted his first public applause, not, as he had hoped, for the performance of a great Shakespearean role, but by an imitation of the leading actor of the day.

Word of this by some means got to Garrick, for the great man now condescended to hear Mr. Henderson "rehearse." He listened with care. His opinion was unfavourable. He told the young aspirant that "he had in his mouth too much wool or worsted, which he must absolutely get rid of before he would be fit for Drury Lane stage." It was probably not his real opinion. Master David was annoyed that Henderson had dared to imitate him. It was a thing he could not endure. He had to put up with it from Samuel Foote, but he was not going to encourage this young fellow. That this was the case is made certain by the fact that he gave Henderson a letter to Palmer, who was running the Bath Theatre, and told him to apply there. It may have been his kindlier nature, but it is more likely that he saw Henderson's talent and thought him better tucked away in the country than hanging about the Lane and giving impersonations of himself.

A letter from Garrick was almost a command. Henderson managed to get to Bath, and delivered the document to Palmer. Thus he got his first job, and his salary was one guinea a week.

For his debut, Henderson chose to appear as Hamlet. There was no mock modesty about actors in those days. They flew at the biggest game right away.

It was in 1772 that Henderson first trod the stage as an actor. He had last-minute qualms. He might fail and he did not want to be damned for ever. Henderson always left a line of retreat open, so that he could try again. He made his first appearance, therefore, not under his own name, but as Mr. Courtney. He need not have troubled. He was an instant success. Nobody had the slightest difficulty in hearing him in Bath. He must have swallowed that wool and worsted which Garrick said was in his mouth, or else he had spat it out—if it was ever there.

He repeated Hamlet by popular desire and at the end he recited Garrick's Jubilee Ode again. Right away, he stepped into fame at Bath. During that first season he played, besides Hamlet, Richard III, Benedict, Macbeth, Bobadil, Bayes, Don Felix, Earl of Essex, Hotspur, Fribble, Lear, Hastings, Alonzo, and Alzuma. He was a resounding success. What a feat of memory his multitude of roles demanded. Such a round of parts, so widely contrasted, would stump most actors to-day. But Henderson took the task in his stride. Those were the days of giants. He also spoke a public address to the city on the night of December 22nd, and he assumed his own name. He was safe now. They called him the Roscius of Bath. Any feebleness or weakness he had once shown was gone now, for he played practically every night of the season—an almost unheard-of thing even then.

During the closed season he came up to Town and stayed with friends. He wanted to conquer London. Still the London managers were obdurate. But one of his friends knew Foote and took Henderson to see that character at his house.

Aristophanes was in one of his bad, impish moods. He kept stalling every attempt Henderson made to show what he could do, by breaking in with a funny story. He appears to have conceived a dislike to him on sight. Maybe he recognised talent and did not want competition. He was star enough for his theatre. He warned the young man against tragedy. Henderson said he could play comedy too. So very grudgingly he listened for a few moments and then shut the actor up with another succession of jokes. When the time came for them to go, Foote took one of the friends aside and in a whisper loud enough for Henderson to hear said that the young man would not do.

Henderson went back to Bath.

There, in the following season, he extended his repertoire and his success. He played all the old roles and he added Pierre (in *Venice Preserv'd*), Don John, Comus, Othello, Archer, Ranger, Sir John Brute, Bellville (in *The School for Wives*), Henry II, Beverley (in *The Man of Business*) and Zanga. His fame spread with his versatility.

He became famous in Bath, too, for something else—his imitation of Garrick. He was always being asked to do it and he never refused. The town buzzed with it and returning visitors chattered about it in the coffee-houses. Of course, the subject of the mimicry got to hear about it, and, like Queen Victoria on another occasion, was not amused. When Henderson applied to Garrick again for a job, he naturally got a firm refusal. The great man, too, was on the eve of retirement.

Old Giffard, who had built the Goodman's Field Theatre and who had given Garrick his first chance, saw Roscius at Bath and told him he was marked for greatness. Henderson was deeply grateful and never forgot.

His luck was now on the turn. A man who had hitherto refused even to see him now had him in mind. That man was George Colman, Manager and owner of the Haymarket Theatre.

He was looking for novelties. What would not have done for the tradition and greatness of Covent Garden would be well enough for the little Haymarket. This new young man might be a sensation. Perhaps he was as good as they said. Anyway, it would attract attention and probably fill the house. Those were the days when the public went to the theatre as much to see the actor as the play. Most of the plays they knew by heart, but they liked to see how various players performed the big roles. A debut, then, by a new actor or actress was an occasion. It filled the house. Colman went to Bath, and arranged with Palmer, who had Henderson under contract, for the young Roscius of Bath to have a trial against sophisticated London audiences.

Thus Henderson was to face that London which had rejected him— for his London, like that of most actors, was composed of the people of the theatre; the public had to be pleased, of course, but he was con- fident about that. Could he make Garrick eat his words? Colman had recanted and engaged him. Well, he would show these London folk what he could do. Doubtless he thought of all the slights he had suffered. Doubtless he remembered another incident during one of his many attempts to get work at Drury Lane. An official there, saying Mr. Garrick was not available, undertook to interview the applicant

himself, quite unasked. He drew out a foot rule and solemnly measured
Henderson from head to foot. "I do not wish to mortify you, sir," was
his verdict, "but you will not do for an actor; no, sir, not by an inch and
a quarter." What if that rule had been applied to Edmund Kean? Or to
Garrick himself? But then we don't know what height would have
satisfied this meticulous guardian of the art of acting.

Perhaps Henderson now called to mind the eulogies of his friends and
admirers, among them Gainsborough, the great artist. Gainsborough
advised him to model himself on Garrick and warned him about his
habit of over-eating. For Henderson had developed a wonderful
appetite—perhaps he was making up for lost time.

Garrick had already seem him—at Bath. He formed a very low
opinion of his capabilities. He made extremely disparaging remarks
about him and his method of delivering speeches. He wrote to a friend:
"I have seen the great Henderson, who has something and is nothing—
he might be made to figure among the puppets of these times. His
Don John is a comic Cato, and his Hamlet a mixture of tragedy,
comedy, pastoral, farce and nonsense." Pretty scathing from such a
critic as Garrick.

It seems that from beginning to end Garrick thoroughly disliked
him, and not only on account of the imitations. There was jealousy in
it, too—the jealousy of the actor on the verge of retirement for the
actor just beginning what is likely to be a great career.

Colman engaged Henderson for an entire season. He must have had
few doubts about it himself.

Henderson was to open in the part of Shylock. He was risking much,
for old Macklin, the greatest portrayer of that role up to that time,
was still about, and his performance was still bright in people's memory.

The night of June 11th, 1777, was blazing hot. There had not been
such weather for years. Yet the Haymarket was crammed and all the
critics had rolled up to see this new actor. Henderson made his entrance
to a house packed with celebrities. His detractor, Garrick, sat in a box.
In the pit was savage old Macklin, with his seamed and corded face,
eager to see what this new upstart might do to his laurels. And all the
notables of the town were there. It was a worse ordeal than the actor had
faced on his debut at Bath, when he had feared to use his own name
and when, on making his entrance, he could scarcely stand upright or
open his mouth for fear. But success had given him confidence. He was
on trial and he knew it. He had gone through much for this night, and
now he was determined to show those who had flouted him that he was
made of the real stuff. He knew the part; he was not afraid of his lines.
His memory was prodigious, as witness that extraordinary first season
at Bath. He could read a column in a newspaper and immediately
repeat it word for word. Once a great philosopher of the time expressed
wonder at this feat. Henderson replied: "If you had been, like me,
obliged to depend, during many years for your daily bread on getting

words by heart, you would not be so much astonished at habit having produced this facililty. . . ." Yet Garrick found fault even with this quality in Henderson; he could see no good in him; he remarked that Henderson "swallowed his part like an eager glutton, and spewed his undigested fragments in the face of the audience."

At last Henderson's cue came, he walked on, and he got his welcoming round of applause. It was observed that he had to make up rather heavily. He had none of the Semitic cast of countenance possessed by Macklin, which was invaluable for this part. Henderson had not wanted to open as Shylock; it was Colman's wish. The actor wanted something more showy and active for a vivid first impression. He had natural obstacles to overcome. He lacked height, he lacked the lung power which the stage in those days demanded—but he had a quality which conquered listeners.

Colman knew what he was about: if Henderson could succeed as Shylock the rest was easy. From the first he arrested the attention of the highly critical audience. They were all measuring him with the Macklin yardstick. Garrick gazed from his box with a quizzical smile to mask his thoughts. But the young actor was conquering. Each familiar scene brought its applause—applause which grew in length and volume as the play proceeded. It was noted that his reading differed from Macklin's in many particulars and even the old-timers had to admit that in certain scenes Henderson had improved upon the older actor. At length it was over and the hot, excited audience rose to its feet to cheer and acclaim. There was a scene such as one seldom sees to-day in a theatre, for in the eighteenth century acting was taken seriously. So excited did one member of the audience become that he climbed into Garrick's box and asked him what he thought of the new Shylock. "Oh, sir," replied Garrick, with a smile, "I am no judge."

Henderson had conquered. This actor, rejected by London's managers, had been elected by London's playgoers as one of the great players. The opening was there, Garrick, Spranger Barry, Macklin and the rest, retired, or ageing, and here was the newcomer to fill the gap. Here too was the star which the Haymarket had brought forth—its first really great actor. John Henderson drank deep of the ovation, and, alight with excitement, pride and gratitude—he never got swollen-headed—went into the green-room.

There was Colman to shake him by the hand and utter his congratulations—no doubt to tell the actor how right his managerial acumen had been in selecting Shylock for the debut. And then Henderson must have felt nervous, for old Macklin came into the room, grim and forbidding as ever. Henderson waited humbly for his verdict, and the fine old actor gave him considerable praise for the performance of the part which he had made so famous, for Macklin had turned the Jew from a figure of fun into the Shylock we know now. Henderson listened with a thrill of joy—this was indeed sweet music to him. "And yet, sir," he

replied humbly, "I never had the honour of seeing you play the part."
"Evidently not," snapped back old Macklin, "or you would have played it
very differently." He was not going to let the youngster get too puffed up.

Then there was a slight commotion at the door and a swirl in the
crowd of visitors (green-rooms in those days were social centres), the
people made room deferentially, for Garrick had entered. Colman bustled
forward and shook his old friend by the hand. Henderson stood by,
anxiously waiting for the great man's verdict. "Well, David," asked
Colman, "what did you think of it all?" Garrick shot a glance at the
young actor who had dared imitate him. "Hey—hey—well—well," said
he, "I thought the actor who played Tubal was very good." It was a
brutal thing to do, and a classic example of professional spite. Garrick,
who could be so generous, who had helped so many, never forgave this
young man. Although he had retired, he could not endure the thought
that here stood the man who was destined to be his successor. . . .
Ungracious, indeed, of Garrick.

Henderson went from success to success. He played Richard III,
Hamlet and Falstaff—and he scored his biggest triumph as Falstaff. It
was a masterpiece of full-blooded comedy. It ranks with the creations
of Quin, of Tree and in modern days, of Ralph Richardson. It was
different from them all, for Henderson had a gift of imparting a touch
of his own. It was a very fine Falstaff indeed.

The whole season was a signal and overwhelming success. The
Haymarket Theatre was completely established now. It was adding its
full quota to theatrical history. But the harmony was marred by one
thing—Henderson's facility for mimicry. It put him in the wrong again.
He had antagonised Garrick that way; now he was to offend Colman,
the man who had given him his great chance. At a dinner which Colman
gave in his own house in Henderson's honour, the actor so far forgot
himself as to imitate his host. It was a good imitation, but in bad taste.
It led to a distinct coolness between the two men.

Colman, as was customary, gave Henderson a benefit. It was not to
be a "clear" benefit—he was not famous enough for that—but one
from which the expenses of the running of the theatre for the night
were to be deducted. The theatre was, as usual, crowded, and in the
green-room later he received congratulations. He was probably working
out in his mind what the financial result might be when Colman came
in, accompanied by the treasurer, who held a piece of paper in his
hand. The two men, it must be remembered, had been estranged.
Colman walked up to Henderson, smiling, and put out his hand.
Henderson took it gratefully. Colman congratulated him and the
treasurer gave him the piece of paper. As soon as he could, Henderson
opened it and took a glance. He knew it was the list of Colman's expenses with which he would be charged. He gave a gasp of astonishment.
It read:

"'House Charges, by Mr. Colman's order. £o os. od.'"

Colman had stood the entire cost and given Henderson a "clear" benefit. It showed his generous nature, for in spite of their estrangement he had let Henderson pick his own night, and then had charged him nothing. That was the real Haymarket spirit. It obtains to-day, carrying on the tradition left by Colman, who brought it such fame and standing.

That season of Henderson's, during the thirty-six performances he gave, brought Colman a revenue of nearly £5,000. It was the biggest money the Haymarket had ever taken. Colman could afford to be generous, but how many people show such generosity under similar circumstances?

Henderson played no more at the Haymarket after that eventful, glorious season. Drury Lane snapped him up, and so did Covent Garden. So he vanishes from the Haymarket story.

But from that beginning he went to the top of his profession. He became the great actor of his day. He met with some adverse criticism at Drury Lane, where they made invidious comparisons between his Hamlet and Garrick's, for he had the temerity to alter Garrick's traditional business. When, in deference to the critics, he put Garrick's business back, they said he was wrong not to stick to his own ideas. But he wore them all down.

His natural modesty never forsook him. He was a good and lovable person, and a man of culture. He had conquered his profession after a desperate struggle—he had even beaten the weather at his debut at the Haymarket, and few actors can do that. One of his claims to fame is that he popularised the famous poem, "John Gilpin," which up to the time he recited it at some public readings which Sheridan had instituted at the Freemasons' Hall had laid unwanted on booksellers' shelves. Henderson's recital of this piece of grand comic verse made it a sensation, and the neglected poem attained a nation-wide popularity.

Henderson could play both tragedy and comedy. In after years, at Covent Garden, King George III brought Queen Charlotte to see Henderson play in *The Mysterious Husband*. Simple old King George was not partial to stage tragedy—he liked to laugh. In the last scene of this play the hero, played by Henderson, dies. The King was so carried away by the performance that he exclaimed, "Charlotte, don't look —it's too much to bear." Seldom has such a tribute been paid to an actor's art. The play—or, rather, Henderson's performance in it—affected the King so much that, at his request, it was never repeated.

Henderson always got into the skin of his parts. It was not Mr. Henderson as Falstaff, Hamlet, Iago or Sir Giles Overreach—the actor was lost in the character he represented. Handicapped by ill-health, a poor figure, a medium voice, he overcame them all. He even conquered his big appetite, and when he found the habit of drinking growing upon him with his increasing success and popularity he conquered that too.

Therein he was greater than many actors. His mind gave him the power to rise above his physical defects. He had a critical, analytical mind, which dissected the characters he studied. When approaching a new part, unlike the celebrated Mrs. Pritchard, he read the whole play through most carefully. Then he learnt his part, a thing he could do with the utmost speed. Then he read the whole play again with the utmost concentration. After that he laid the script aside; he had no further use for it, it was all in his photographic memory.

He is said to have been at his best in Shakespeare and at his very best in the soliloquies. Mrs. Siddons, after she had acted with him, said he was the soul of intelligence. He wrote quite good poetry himself and was a great reader.

He died suddenly—and all too soon—in his thirty-eighth year. His last performance was Horatius in *The Roman Father* at Covent Garden on November 8th, 1785. He was seized by a fever which at first seemed to yield to treatment, but he collapsed suddenly and died in his house in Buckingham Street, Strand, on November 25th, 1785. He had not had time to acquire wealth; his top salary was £20 per week, with benefits.

There was a wild rumour of foul play just after his death and his wife (*née* Jane Figgins), came under suspicion. But it was a cruel canard, and the fact that Mrs. Siddons played at the widow's benefit shows that Mrs. Henderson was held in high esteem.

Henderson's grave was in Westminster Abbey and near the last resting place of his unforgiving enemy, David Garrick. At the funeral high and low crowded into the great church to pay their last respects, and the pall-bearers were Murphy, Malone, Steevens, Whitefoord, Hoole, and the Hon. John Byng.

There we must leave John Henderson, lying in the resting place of the great—as befits a man who was a good fellow, a great actor and throughout his short life a simple, perfect gentleman. He was the first of that great cavalcade of actors who achieved fame at the Haymarket and who contributed to the greatness of that theatre. He should be better remembered than he is by the public and his own profession.

But whilst remembering the great ones of the Haymarket, let us take a further glance at the rank and file who had played there with Foote, Henderson and Colman. Parsons, Palmer, Bannister and Edwin have been chronicled, let the smaller fry take a bow.

Dubellamy has claims to notice. He had been "second singer" at Covent Garden until Colman brought him to the Haymarket. His bad deportment was a handicap. He had a curious habit, when playing or singing, of cocking up his thumbs at the audience, a mannerism he probably acquired in his pre-stage days as a shoemaker. He never forgot his trade. Once he went with some ladies to buy shoes in Cranbourn Alley. The shopkeeper trotted out his wares, and Dubellamy expertly pointed out all the defects. "Come, come, master," protested the shoemaker, "each to his calling. This is telling the secrets of the trade, and that's not fair to one another."

Fearon was a useful minor actor, good in character parts. Mrs. Jewel, probably the treasurer's wife, had been at the Haymarket with Foote. She had played the young ladies in his farces and sung songs. She continued this line of business with success long after her youth had departed. Mrs. Love played comic old women and had a long if undistinguished stage career.

Two others of the old Haymarket company are worthy of remembrance. There is old Ned Shuter, who has figured earlier in the story.

David Garrick said that Shuter was the greatest comic genius he had known. He created Old Hardcastle and Sir Anthony Absolute and Justice Woodcock in *Love in a Village*. He was, as has been stated, a follower of Whitefield, but that did not prevent him from helping Foote to burlesque the great preacher. He got religion after a formula of his own, and spent his time acting, drinking and praying. When drunk he was only restrained with the greatest difficulty from going out into the streets, open spaces or fields—like Wesley—and preaching to the public. Tate Wilkinson records that he spent a Sunday with Shuter, and it was a busy day. At six o'clock in the morning they were at Whitefield's chapel in Tottenham Court Road, at ten at a meeting-house in Long Acre; at eleven they were back at Whitefield's and at three o'clock they went to another chapel, spending the evening at one in Moorfields. Shuter seems to have been athirst for religion too.

He had made his first appearance in 1745 at Covent Garden, billed as "Master Shuter," in *The Schoolboy*, and he was still "Master Shuter" the following year at Drury Lane. He was, for all his odd ways, a remarkably good actor, as Garrick testifies, and he did not praise without cause. He was almost illiterate, it being as much as he could do to read his parts and sign his name. But he was a good companion. He had a fund of stories and was an excellent host. At taverns where he dined he kept the company merry and people would gather round his table in crowds.

Shuter died the year before Colman took over the Haymarket, but he had been a pillar of strength to that theatre under Foote. He made his last appearance on the stage as Falstaff, but between his obsession with religion and his devotion to the bottle his faculties were gone. Wilkinson says that Shuter was more bewildered in his brain by his desire to obtain grace than by his drinking, and he really believed that he had a "call." But Shuter was a great Haymarket character and a very fine actor.

Thomas Weston, his companion under Foote's management, was also a grand performer. His father had been head cook to George II— Betterton's father had also been a royal cook and Baddeley was a pastrycook, although not in the Royal family. Weston, when young, had a job as clerk in the royal kitchen. But he got mixed up with riotous

K

company. He went into the Navy as a midshipman, and on being discharged joined a company of strollers. He had made up his mind, like
so many other comedians, that tragedy was his line. He played Richard
III and if there has been a worse Richard, it is hard to find it. The
following evening they persuaded him to play Scrub in *The Beaux
Stratagem.* He was a real success at once.

He never earned much money and what he did get he spent at once.

He played for Shuter and Yates in their Bartholomew Fair booth,
performing nine times a day for a guinea, and glad to get it.

When Foote engaged him for the Haymarket, he had only inferior
parts, but Aristophanes spotted his talents and wrote Jerry Sneak
especially for him. In 1760 he went to Drury Lane and thereafter he
played at both houses, the Lane in the winter and the Haymarket in the
summer. As comedian he was second to none in his line, save perhaps
Foote, but his success did him little good. He was always overwhelmed
with debt and so hunted and waylaid by bailiffs that he had to climb
over the roofs of adjoining houses to enter the Haymarket. Had he used
the stage door he would have been arrested. Often he was besieged in
the theatre by his creditors.

His Abel Drugger in *The Alchemist* was as good, if not better, than
Garrick's, and so impressed that actor that his managerial gratitude
took the form of a £10 note—a real windfall to Weston. He used a
natural method of acting. He had a very slow smile, which grew by
degrees over his solemn face. He never overplayed and he always kept
right "in the picture." He died in 1776, the same year as his companion,
Shuter. He and Shuter were twin pillars of comedy at the home of
English comedy.

The Haymarket story must say good-bye to Macklin, too. He is
already old, but has years before him. They are to be spent elsewhere,
before he takes his farewell benefit at the age of ninety-seven at Covent
Garden. He was to live on, after his farewell, for another ten years
before finding his last rest in St. Paul's, Covent Garden, the Actors'
Church. A fierce, bad tempered, quarrelsome man who murdered
another actor, Macklin knew not fear and lived his long life to the full.
He had fought for the Haymarket when it was a weak, struggling
theatre and he lived to see it become famous and well-established. That
must have given him joy.

CHAPTER XII

THE HAYMARKET ASCENDS

COLMAN'S preoccupation with the Haymarket did not prevent him from writing the Epilogue to Sheridan's *School for Scandal*, which was produced at Drury Lane in 1777. Garrick had written the prologue. That shows the standing of Colman as a manager and a man of letters.

The Epilogue was spoken by Mrs. Abington in the character of Lady Teazle. It is much longer than Garrick's smart, short prologue. But it is a very good piece of work. It ends with a tag, supposed to be spoken by Sheridan, as author, to Mrs. Abington, who objected to the moral of the play and the awful possibilities of Lady Teazle's country life under the thumb of Sir Peter:

> "*All this I told our Bard; he smil'd and said 'twas clear*
> *I ought to play high Tragedy next year*
> *Meanwhile he drew wise morals from his play*
> *And in these solemn periods stalked away*
> *Blest were the fair, like you, her faults who stopp'd*
> *And clos'd her follies when the curtain dropp'd*
> *No more in vice or error to engage*
> *Or play the fool at large on Life's great Stage.*"

In after years the Haymarket was to have a famous drop curtain, which depicted a scene from *The School for Scandal*. It was quite a work of art, and it was all the more fitting in view of the fact that the Haymarket's Colman had written the epilogue to the great play.

Colman had tried two other players that same season. He gave a chance to Blissett, who, like Henderson, came from Bath, and he employed Mrs. Massey, who is described as a "Squeezy old lady, with features not much more attractive than her figure was majestic, but she evinced sound judgment and a good deal of energy in some grave and tragic characters."

Tragedy, as well as comedy, now walks the Haymarket boards—it is a real theatre offering all the wares in the theatrical larder. And by the end of the season Colman had made a very nice profit.

In the February of the following year (1778) Colman was involved in legal trouble (never very far away from a theatrical manager). He got an injunction in the Court of Chancery to prevent a bookseller from printing and publishing some of Samuel Foote's plays—*The Cozeners, The Maid of Bath, The Devil upon Two Sticks* and others. The enterprising and piratical bookseller had already issued two of them, asking nobody's permission, and was advertising a third. Colman had paid a good sum to Foote for these plays and was much aggrieved. He got the verdict. It was a test case, and the Judge held that Colman had the rights, otherwise there was nothing to stop booksellers printing *The School for Scandal, The Duenna* or any popular play, without paying anything for the privilege.

Colman was putting some of the money he had made back into the Haymarket, wherein he showed his wisdom. Although Foote had made certain alterations, the little theatre was still far from perfect. Indeed, it was hardly fit for the new prosperity and popularity which was coming upon it. So in 1778 Colman had the ceiling heightened and a new roof put on. The slips or awkward side-seats in the gallery were turned into a third tier of front boxes, and for the first time the Haymarket was given a lobby, crush-room or vestibule. It was only a few feet deep and wide, but it served its purpose. Previously the public stepped straight from the street into the auditorium, and the audience were much distracted by the noises from outside, caused by post-horns, street cries and the shouts of newsvendors.

He demolished what his son describes as the ugly facings to the boxes and galleries, and replaced them partly with balustrades and mouldings, gold on a white ground, which made the place much lighter and gayer and did not destroy the feeling of cosy intimacy which meant such a lot to the playhouse. Colman grumbled a good deal at the expense, but he knew it was an investment, and he realised his luck in making so much money at a small theatre with a limited season after his rather disastrous start. For it was still a very small theatre. The corridors leading to the boxes were so narrow that there was always a chance that corpulent gentlemen (and they ran to corpulency in those days) might become jammed whilst trying to pass each other. Young Colman commented that he, when he took over, considered the necessity of providing the side box patrons with a bell which they could ring as they went along, so as to warn people coming the other way and get a clear road. But small or not, the little theatre had charm, and everyone could see and hear, which was not at that time a claim which the two enormous Patent theatres could make with justice.

Colman's second season opened on May 18th, 1778, with a comedy in three acts called *The Female Chevalier*. It had a prologue by Colman —spoken by John Palmer—which made reference to the death of Samuel Foote.

Colman gave them a new play of his own called *The Suicide*, described as a comedy, despite the title, and although Garrick wrote an Epilogue, it failed.

On July 20th of that same year, an episode occurred at the Haymarket which was treated by most people as a joke, but which might have had exceedingly painful, not to say tragic consequences. It was fashionable at that time for ladies with any pretence to smartness to wear extremely

large hats, so large that they were almost out of control. Rowlandson
immortalised them in his drawings and does not appear to have overdone it. The Victorian and Edwardian *matinée* hat must have been a
mere bonnet by comparison.

A lady of importance—her name has not come down to posterity—
wearing one of these creations and sitting in a stage box, turned her
head, causing the brim of her hat to touch the candles and catch fire.
The flames spread to the brim of the equally large hat of the lady
sitting next to her. Both appear to have been blissfully unaware of what
was happening, but the audience, roaring with laughter and instead of
warning the fashionable dames of their danger, watched the progress
of the blaze. The report of this little incident comments: "It is impossible to say where the conflagration might have ended, had not a
gentleman, who seemed to be much interested in the fate of the ladies,
with great dexterity extinguished the flames."

His own play having failed, Colman fell back on *Bonduca*, which he
announced as by Beaumont and Fletcher. There he was wrong; it was
by Fletcher only, and had been first produced in 1613. It had been
brought up to date several times, and once the title had been changed
to the more familiar *Boadicea*. Colman made his own alterations, went
back to the original title, and his friend Garrick wrote a Prologue to it.
The disturbed state of the times gave this patriotic play an appeal, and
Garrick's Prologue did much towards its success. It was one of the last
he was to write, for he died early in the following year. Had Garrick
never done anything else he must have gone down to posterity for his
prologues and his epilogues, for this many-sided genius had a great
flair for them, and his wit and sense of effect never deserted him. His
prologue to *Bonduca* is a trumpet call.

That stirring Prologue to a stirring play had a very great deal to do
with the success of *Bonduca*, which filled the Haymarket for quite a
run. The country was in the midst of the American War, and had
France and Spain against her.

In that year, and during this season, Colman received a play from
one of the leading notables of the day. It was a farce, and the covering
letter betokened a modesty which its author, Horace Walpole, did not
show as a rule. The letter said: "The author of *Nature will Prevail* is
extremely obliged to Mr. Colman for his civility, and sorry he cannot
have the courage to be known for an author. He does not mean to give
Mr. Colman the trouble of correcting his farce, but, as he is very
sensible of the little merit there is in it, Mr. Colman is perfectly at
liberty to make any alteration in it he pleases, as he must be a much
better judge of what is proper for the stage than the writer can be. If
Mr. Colman has anything else he wishes to say, the bearer will attend
him at any time he shall appoint, to receive a note with his commands."

A very sensible letter from a budding dramatist—though one can be
sure that Horace Walpole in his heart considered he knew as much as

Colman. The trifle went on, however, and made very little stir, so Walpole was wise in withholding his name. It was produced, described as a dramatic proverb, on June 10th, 1778. Walpole owned to it later and had it printed in his works.

On August 3rd, Colman gave the Haymarket a comic opera called *The Gipsies*. This was the work of the great Charles Dibdin, with music by Arnold, and was based upon *La Bohmenienne*. The wanderlust of the gipsies, however, was too much for the distinguished author, composer and the Haymarket, for it shortly took itself off. It was not one of the prolific Dibdin's successes. But another comic opera, written by the Rev. Henry Bate—later Sir Henry Bate Dudley—proved much more to the public fancy. This was called *The Flitch of Bacon* (music by William Shield), and was based on the Dunmow Flitch ceremony. It had a good run, and was often repeated.

This Bate was a remarkable man. He was the proprietor of the *Morning Post*, a sporting parson, a duellist, a well-known pugilist, and also a dramatist. He it was that Garrick sent to have a look at "the woman Siddons" when he was pestered to give this unknown strolling player a chance. It will be remembered that Bate put in a good report, with some reservations, after seeing her in the wretched little theatre at Worcester play Rosalind on a tiny stage. He tipped her, however, for "genteel comedy."

Bonduca and *The Flitch of Bacon* made the season another good one for George Colman. He now felt his feet at the Haymarket and considered himself and his theatre well settled in as a regular Town attraction.

But he was getting a little tired of his son, George junior, always hanging about the theatre, and he packed that young man off to Christ Church, Oxford. But young George hankered for the theatre which he was to inherit, and he says that he was delighted when the Long Vacation arrived and he was able once again to come to London. The Haymarket, being a summer theatre, was open just when he wanted it. He is eloquent upon the subject. He says: "While coerced into purer air, I was consoled by thinking I should soon swelter behind my father's scenes, and inhale, through all the coming dog days, the rancid odour of his blazing lamps in the little theatre in the Haymarket. I dreaded him dragging me with him upon his visits to my once favourite Richmond. . . . I detested all his greens but his green-room; all rural scenery which was not painted in distemper, all purling streams but a tin cascade by candle light, and as to refreshing breezes, so playhouse-mad was I in those days that I should have solicited the privilege of entree to the Black Hole in Calcutta, if it had been crammed with comedians." This is spoken like a true son of the theatre. He did not quite live up to his early promise.

But when Master George came to Town he found that a Christian namesake of his was playing havoc with his father's business. For Lord

George Gordon was indulging in his celebrated riots and it was not proving beneficial to the Haymarket Theatre.

Young George no sooner arrived at his father's house in Soho Square than he was all atwitter to get behind the scenes at the Haymarket. He dressed himself—and his hair—with the utmost care and in the height of fashion to impress the players. His father saw it and smiled. Instead of driving his son to the theatre directly after they had dined, he took him for a walk around town, and they saw the camp of the soldiers in St. James's Park. George Colman senior told his son that on the night of June 7th, when the riots were at their height and when London was afire in thirty-six different places, the takings at the Haymarket had been over twenty pounds. This was a very small sum indeed, but it was remarkable under the circumstances. So bad were the riots and such the danger in the streets that most people stayed at home. Yet there were enough determined playgoers to pay twenty pounds at the Haymarket Theatre. It says much for Colman that he kept open. But he did—the show went on, the orchestra played and the actors acted, and the playgoers looked on and applauded, just as they did nearly two centuries afterwards when bombs rained down, flying bombs snarled overhead and rockets exploded nearby. Londoners go to the play despite all perils and dangers. They did so in 1780. They did so in the First and Second World Wars. London always carried on and so does the London theatre.

Henderson came no more to the Haymarket, Parsons had gone elsewhere temporarily, but still there remained Palmer, Edwin and the clever, popular Miss Farren, the Haymarket's first real leading lady. The elder Bannister and Digges were there too and the company was built up with other good actors. The plays that season included a comic opera, *Fire and Water*, by Miles Peter Andrews, who had already scored there in 1779 with another comic opera called *Summer Amusement, or An Adventure at Margate*.

Fire and Water was produced on July 8th, 1780, and was a success. This play took a glimpse into the future, even into the atomic age, for in it was a character called Sulphur, who was supposed to be making an electrical machine to destroy all England.

The Chapter of Accidents was a play by Sophia Lee, originally intended to be a light opera in which the authoress wanted the celebrated Miss Catley to play the lead. There was also *The Genius of Nonsense*, a pantomime written by Colman himself, and also his own curious stage entertainment called *The Manager in Distress*. This was called "an occasional prelude." In this little piece, which was very successful, Colman broke once more the bounds of the proscenium wall, and had his actors in the audience interrupting the show. This is often done to-day in pantomimes, revues and similar entertainments and has also been done in straight plays. It was not a novelty when Colman did it, for it had been used with effect by Beaumont and Fletcher in *The Knight of the Burning Pestle*. Ben Jonson used it too. But Colman revived it.

His *Manager in Distress* portrayed a theatre manager who had been disappointed by some of his company not arriving, they having been kept away by the other two theatres remaining open longer than usual (a sore point always with Colman). The manager appeared on the stage to apologise to his audience. Then the actors, pretending to be members of the audience sitting in front, rose up and suggested forms of entertainment which could be given without the absentee actors. The topics of the day were satirised and there appears to have been lots of fun. Mrs. Webb, one of the leading ladies, spoke up as a lady from "La Belle Assemblée," a pseudo-cultural affair run by the notorious Mrs. Cornelys which did much harm to the theatres. The younger Bannister gave his imitations. It was a free-and-easy, amusing show and quite a success.

Miss Lee's *Chapter of Accidents* was so successful as to become a stock piece. In the original cast were Palmer, Edwin, Aickin, Mrs. Love and Miss Farren. Indeed, Colman had now a first-rate company, for besides those already mentioned there were Bensley, Wilson, Bannister junior, Lamash, Mrs. Cuyler and Mrs. Wilson. Bensley was a tragedian who was always efficient, but who had a stilted walk, a blank stare, and a nasal twang. This hindered him in some parts and helped in others. He was quite a famous Malvolio. Wilson was a comedian with a resemblance in style to old Shuter, but nothing like as good. His wife, however, was an excellent soubrette, pretty, well made and clever. Lamash was the best player of conceited men and also of "gentlemen's gentlemen" of his time.

And other actors came in too. Baddeley, the Drury Lane actor of the famous cake bequest, played at the Haymarket for Colman during the summer, excelling in old men, character and foreign parts, also as Jews (he created Moses in *The School for Scandal*). Wewitzer was there too, the best stage Jew of his time, beating Baddeley in this one particular.

There was Mrs. Cargill, a celebrated beauty, actress and singer, and Miss Harper, who, prior to her marriage to the younger Bannister and retirement, spent most of her career at the Haymarket, making her debut and her farewell there. Mrs. Webb, already mentioned as one of the supposed "interrupters" in *The Manager in Distress*, was a good actress of immense corpulence.

But the rising star was Jack Bannister, son of old Bannister. This brilliant man had made his debut at the Haymarket at his father's benefit in 1778 as Dick in *The Apprentice*. He had not as yet found his true line or shown his full talents. He was now what was called "general utility," but he always gave a good account of himself, even when cast for parts which were right out of his line. Actors then were expected to play anything, and mostly succeeded very well, for type casting was unknown, but Bannister was now pushed about in every play, doing as he was told, playing anything given him to do and gaining tremendously valuable experience. Nor was this all he had to put up with. The wardrobes were not very extensive, and Jack Bannister constantly found himself made to wear a light blue suit, trimmed with silver, with a sword by his side. The audience applauded this familiar suit. No matter what the part or the period, this was what he wore, because it fitted him. And actors since his days have got engagements because the clothes of the management happened to be their size. But he always gave a very good performance, and it was apparent that here was a young man with a future.

Colman's *The Genius of Nonsense* was advertised as an "Original, Whimsical, Operational, Pantomimical, Military, Temporary, Local Extravaganza." Some of the critics referred to it as "The Nonsense of Genius." In this Colman almost returned to the manner of Foote, for he burlesqued many things of the moment, including the celebrated Dr. Graham's "Temple of Health," and the doctor himself had the mortification of being present at the first performance. He had heard of the proposed scene and threatened action. He came to see for himself. During the play they gave away handbills like those he so sedulously circulated, boosting his quack establishment. He kept leaning out of his box, trying to snatch one, but the actors were always too quick for him.

In this production Bannister played Harlequin—a speaking harlequin —and had to transform himself into the character of the quack doctor. Knowing there was going to be trouble, he suggested that he gave a mere impression of the doctor, but Colman senior insisted on a full-length and life-size portrait. So Bannister paid a visit to the Temple of Health to get his details and took Colman junior with him, to that youth's intense delight. The result of that one visit was a perfect representation on the Haymarket stage of the man and his methods, which gave the greatest of delight to the audience and the greatest annoyance to the quack.

Bannister and young Colman were now becoming fast friends and were seeing life together. A good deal was to come of that.

That season of 1780 was also a successful one. The Haymarket was steadily rising in fame.

The next summer Colman presented many plays, but the new ones were *The Dead Alive*, by John O'Keefe, who also provided *The Agreeable Surprise*, *The Baron Kinkvervantkotsdorsprakengatchdern*, a comic opera by Miles Peter Andrews, *The Silver Tankard, or The Point at Portsmouth*, by Lady Craven, and a burlesque ballet, *Medea and Jason*.

The author John O'Keefe was a most prolific writer of all sorts of plays, and Hazlitt went so far as to call him the English Molière. It was, however, Molière and water—lots of water. O'Keefe wrote with a fluency, but with no great wit, although he could contrive situations. He was extremely versatile and no sort of show was beyond him. He supplied farce, drama, light opera, burlesque, pantomime, anything that came along. He wrote his own life and did not forget to blow his own trumpet, either.

The Dead Alive was but a moderate success, but *The Agreeable Surprise* went very well, because Edwin and Mrs. Wells, also Mrs. Webb, were in fine form. *The Silver Tankard, or The Point at Portsmouth* was a failure. Lady Craven, afterwards the Margravine of Anspach, knew little about playwriting and less about Portsmouth Point, where she had obviously never been. After six performances, the play was seen no more. That handy little title to the musical show, *The Baron Kinkvervantkotsdorsprakengatchdern*, met the fate it deserved. How could a play with a name like that succeed? Nobody could pronounce it, even had they wanted to. It ran for three nights, each a stormy, disapproving one. It was an adaptation from a novel by the same authoress as *The Silver Tankard*—Lady Craven—who thus met two complete defeats in a season. She may have been a good Margravine, but she was no good as a dramatist. The audience appears to have thought the play vulgar and suggestive at one and the same time, and would have none of it. Miles Peter Andrews, who was responsible for the stage version, drew a complete blank.

Medea and Jason, the burlesque opera, did better. They were presenting ballet at the Opera House over the way, and Colman's burlesque of it was much to the public taste and crowded the theatre. Delpini, the most popular clown of his day, played in it.

But the great hit of the whole season was that good old safeguard, *The Beggar's Opera*. It was, however, an unusual revival. Colman, working on his policy of giving the public novelties, turned this popular opera upside down. He had all the male parts played by women, and all the female parts by men. The beautiful Mrs. Cargill was the Macheath, the attractive and dainty Mrs. Wilson was Filch; Peachum was played by Mrs. Lefevre; Lockit by Mrs. Webb; old Bannister and Edwin were Polly and Lucy (Edwin, the low comedian, as Lucy must have been unique), Wilson played Mrs. Peachum, and Parsons played Diana Trapes. There was an original Prelude to this topsyturvy version of Gay's work, written by George Keate (so the bills said), which was an amusing but very dirty piece of work.

Young Master Colman, with a foretaste of the prudishness he was to show when later he became Licenser of Plays, disapproved strongly of his father's enterprise in this production. He leaves a very scathing criticism of it. He says:

"The manager's appetite must have been extremely keen when the sacred hunger for gold induced him to bring upon the stage the indecorous catchpenny of the reversed *Beggar's Opera*. It may be doubted, but bold is he who will be responsible for the caprices of any age, past, present or to come, whether the existing state of society would tolerate, throughout the whole play, so complete a perversion of the sexes; or whether theatrical despotism be now so strong as to force a large body of performers into such a simultaneous transforma-

tion, since it is difficult to suppose that they were all volunteers in
this nauseous entertainment. Many of the actresses, for instance,
must have been conscious of their want of symmetry for male attire;
trowsers were not then in fashion; nor were boots furnished for
gentlewomen upon low salaries; those females, therefore, who could
not afford the last articles appeared not only 'en culottes' but in silk
stockings; and certes, among the she-highwaymen belonging to
Macheath's gang, thus accoutred, there were, to quote the song of
Jemmy Jumps in *The Farmer*

> " '*Six feet ladies*
> *Three feet ladies*
> *Small legg'd ladies*
> *Thick legg'd ladies,*'

all with horse pistols in their hands, screaming 'We take the road'—
a feminine phalanx which constituted, as Macheath himself says of
the Judges in the Old Bailey, 'a terrible show.' . . ."

Master Colman, for his pains, was not sent back to Oxford, but up
to King's College in Aberdeen. His father perhaps had had enough of
him at the Haymarket. But whatever the son thought, the public supported the father and this transposed *Beggar's Opera* was a very big
success indeed.

Deprived of the playhouse, the young man took to writing plays, and
sent one to his father, with a view to Haymarket production. He called
it *The Female Dramatist*, and Colman senior was more than doubtful
of it. He gave it a chance at the benefit of the treasurer Jewell in 1782—
not very fair upon a very devoted servant. It was well and truly hissed.
But young Colman was not deterred; he wrote on, and finished another
play called *Two to One*.

Meanwhile the Haymarket proceeded steadily on its upward path.
Colman steered clear of all the rocks and shallows of the theatrical
ocean and held on to a steady course. The Haymarket had progressed
far from the barn of Potter, the battleground of Fielding, and the
rebels' cave of Theophilus Cibber and Macklin. It was a first-class
playhouse, if no longer Theatre Royal. But what was important was the
fact that it now stood on its own feet and had its own policy—and
therefore its own clientele. It provided first-rate entertainment in the
summer, which is the most difficult time of the theatrical year.

There is not much of note about this time save the revival of Lillo's
play, *The Fatal Curiosity*, for which Colman wrote a Prologue and
which Parsons spoke.

But he had again been improving his theatre. Complete redecoration
had made it elegant, gay and well-appointed. It was said that it now
appeared to be "well dressed." It has been so ever since.

The season of 1784, however, opened disastrously. On May 31st,

Mr. Palmer appeared before the curtain and spoke a Prologue to a
play of Colman's. That Prologue gave a short history of the little
playhouse:

> *"Of real novelty, we're told there's none*
> *We know there's nothing new beneath the sun.*
> *Yet still untir'd a phantom we pursue*
> *Still expectation gapes for something new.*
>
> *What though our house be threescore years of age*
> *Let us new vamp the box, new lay the stage*
> *Long paragraphs shall paint with gay parade*
> *The gilded front and airy balustrade.*
>
> *Here late his jest Sir Jeffrey Dunstan broke*
> *Yet here, too, Lillo's muse sublimely spoke*
> *Here Fielding, foremost of the Hum'rous train*
> *In comic mask, indulged his laughing vein*
> *Here frolic Foote, your favour well could beg*
> *Propp'd by his genuine wit and only leg*
> *Their humble follower feels his merit less*
> *Yet feels and proudly boasts as much success*
> *Small though his talents, smaller than his size,*
> *Beneath your smiles his little Lares rise,*
> *And oh, as Jove once grac'd Philemon's thatch,*
> *Oft of our cottage may you lift the latch*
> *Oft may we greet you, full of hope and fear*
> *With hearty welcome tho' but homely cheer*
> *May our old roof its old success maintain*
> *Nor know the novelty of your disdain."*

It knew it almost at once. The play which followed was called *The
Election of Managers*. There had been trouble from the start. The
production followed a real General Election, and at first a licence had
been refused the play because of many topical allusions. But finally it
got by the Censor. Edwin played a character which was very clearly a
man who had figured prominently in the recent election, and he made
up like him too. There were two female characters who had real proto-
types, one being the Duchess of Devonshire, the lady celebrated for
kissing the butchers to get their votes. These parts were played by
Miss Farren and Mrs. Webb. They were also made up like their
originals. The play pleased at first and went quite well, until it met with
unexpected and singular opposition. The word "singular" is used
advisedly, for the whole trouble was caused by one man, who chose to
be a lonely dissentient. He was Bob Monckton, a very fat "buck"—
son of General Monckton, who served with Wolfe at Quebec.

This stout individual sat in a box all by himself, and shouted "Off!

Off!"—the usual terms of disapproval—all through the show. He did it night after night. Why he was not turned out is not on record. Perhaps they thought a disturbance so caused might have led to a riot—a pastime to which playgoers were much addicted and undertook on the slightest provocation. But if so, they were wrong in restraining themselves. For the news, very naturally, of this one-man "bird" got round. Other "bucks" came in to join the fun. The opposition grew until the whole house joined in. Too late now for reprisals. Now any attempt at eviction would indeed have led to general uproar and the smashing of seats, lamps and boxes. There was nothing for it but to take the play off. Colman consequently withdrew it.

It was young Colman's chance. He persuaded his father to stage his new play, *Two to One*—a comedy with songs is how he described it. It saw the light of the Haymarket candles on June 19th, 1784, and had a Prologue written by his father, which Palmer spoke. Now for the first time, father and son appeared as managerial playwrights in the theatre of managerial playwrights.

Young Colman was a very scared young man; he suffered all the terrors common to dramatists whose work is being judged by that hard-headed lot, the general public. He thanked his father for the nice Prologue, he fluttered about a prey to nerves, and he even cried a bit in his overstrung excitement. The curtain went up and the play went on. It was a Saturday. The house was crowded to capacity. And the presentation by Colman *père* of the play by Colman *fils* was a great success.

The father had done the son well. For he had got the great Dr. Arnold to write the music for his son's immature verses. Arnold was Musical Director as well. All the next day, a Sunday, young Colman flaunted through the streets, although it was pouring with rain, hoping to meet acquaintances who had been to the show and would congratulate him. He got only one nibble, and that from a man who knew him by sight, but had never spoken to him before. To young George this was undiluted joy, however.

But he still had the Press to face the next day—and at that time the Press was very plain-spoken. It can be imagined with what trepidation, mixed with bravado, Colman junior sped down from bed to get the papers, with what sinking feeling he opened the first one and then forced himself to take the plunge and read his first "notice." And this was what he read:

"To George Colman, Esq., Junior, on the deserved success of his comedy *Two To One*

"*Another writes because his father writ*
And proves himself a bastard by his wit
So Young declaims—but you, by right divine
Can claim a just, hereditary line;

By learning tutor'd as by fancy nursed
A George the Second sprung from George the First."

He was a success. Here was the man to carry on the Haymarket when the time should come for the father to lay down the reins. Here was the playwright-manager in direct line—Fielding, Cibber, Macklin, Foote, Colman I and Colman II.

CHAPTER XIII

EXIT GEORGE I—ENTER GEORGE II

THE Haymarket plays for the 1784 season were *The Great Mogul Tale, Lord Russel, Hunt the Slipper, The Noble Peasant, The Two Connoisseurs* and *Peeping Tom.*

The Great Mogul Tale is interesting because it was the first play which the celebrated Mrs. Inchbald had produced publicly. Parsons played a cobbler and played it remarkably well. *Hunt the Slipper* was by a clergyman, the Rev. Harry Knapp, but it was not of much note, even as a farce. *The Noble Peasant,* a comic opera, had a bad first night, but survived, and was played often during the season. The libretto was by Holcroft, the music by Shield. Colman wanted Dr. Arnold to do the music, but Holcroft objected, as he was already committed to Shield. The latter wrote a remarkably civil note to Arnold about the matter and all difficulties were smoothed over without offence to any party. Dr. Arnold, an intimate friend of the Colmans, was Director of Music at the Haymarket, having previously held a similar position with Colman senior at Covent Garden. In 1783 he was organist and composer to the King. A very distinguished musician, he died in 1802 and was buried in Westminster Abbey, of which he had been organist since 1793.

Lord Russel, a tragedy by Bayley, was a dull piece of work. *Peeping Tom,* by the ubiquitous O'Keefe, was a big success. Based on the Godiva story, it was in the form of a light opera, and it held the stage for a very long time.

Young Colman went abroad after this season, and on his return discovered that his father was determined to make him a barrister. He found himself accommodated with a set of chambers in King's Bench Walk, up two flights and sparsely furnished, and his name down as a student of Lincoln's Inn. Old Colman was bent on preventing his son and heir following in his footsteps. Young George had become friendly with a Haymarket actress, Miss Catherine Morris, and it was to nip this romance in the bud that Colman senior planned the voyage abroad, to France and Switzerland, and the entry into the legal world. Needless to say, the plans failed. Young George took a trip north to Gretna Green in company with his charmer, and they returned man and wife. They had to live on the small allowance George's father gave them.

George junior at once started writing plays. He began one on the morning of December 20th, 1784, and as he was biting his quill and searching for inspiration, news came that Dr. Johnson's funeral procession was on its way up Fleet Street, *en route* for Westminster Abbey.

He ran out to see the sight, recollecting the grandeur of Garrick's interment, but he was disappointed by the cortège of the great Doctor. The principal mourners were Sir Joshua Reynolds, Edmund Burke, Sir John Hawkins, George Colman senior and the Doctor's faithful black servant, Francis Barber. The young author reflected that after all Johnson was not a man of the theatre. Moreover, Dr. Johnson had never written a successful play. Colman junior had, and, glowing with pride in this distinction, the author went back to his task greatly revived and inspired by the thought. He worked at his play at a great rate, chuckling to himself as he wrote. The last passage through Fleet Street of Dr. Johnson had inspired him to call his piece *Turk and No Turk*.

He persuaded his father to present it at the Haymarket, and he himself says it succeeded better than it deserved. But it ran for only ten nights when it saw the light of the Haymarket lamps the following July. Later, when he took command, he found the old prompt copy, read it—and threw it on the fire.

That season, 1785, which saw young Colman's funeral-inspired opus, saw also the production of *I'll Tell You What*, a comedy by Mrs. Inchbald, which had been pigeon-holed. It was a considerable success and may give hope to struggling playwrights who despair of their dramatic offspring ever seeing the light. Score one success and managers clamour for previously rejected manuscripts!

The Haymarket was flushed with success under the wise guidance of George Colman. Here was a man who knew the ropes, a practical man of the theatre, a dramatist himself and father of a playwright as well. But beyond the sunshine the dark clouds were gathering.

The season ended on September 15th as usual. George Colman, tired by the heavy work of providing London's summer-time entertainment, betook himself to Margate to recuperate. For three weeks he bathed daily in the sea and felt so much benefit that he said he was building up a fine reserve against the coming winter.

Margate then was not the bustling resort it is to-day. It was a quiet little village, with sea bathing as its only attraction, and its link with London was a "hoy," which took its time and which often gave its passengers a rough journey and made them well and truly seasick. If a couple of hundred people visited the place during the year, it considered it had had a busy season.

One day Colman came back from his early morning bathe in fine spirits. As he shaved he commented on his healthy appearance. His friend Dr. Arnold was staying with him, and he was going to take the doctor as far as Canterbury on his return journey in his own carriage. The two ate a very hearty breakfast.

Arnold had already got into the carriage, and Colman, who was following, remembered he had left his keys on his dressing table. Returning to the house, he ran up the stairs towards his bedroom.

Mr. B. Webster as Tartuffe.

John Henderson.

Mr. Suett as Ibrahim.

Mr. Shuter as Lovegold.

Left
Mr. Oxberry as Ma
worm.

Left
Miss De Camp.

Above
Mr. J. M. Barrie (la
Sir James Barrie, O.N

Halfway up he had a paralytic stroke. One side of his body was made powerless. With his good hand, the stricken man held on to the balustrade, but was unable to call for help, for the stroke had rendered him speechless. There his valet found him.

A local doctor was called in, and he promptly put blisters all over the unfortunate Colman. In his more lucid moments he tore the blisters off and threw them about the room, but his power of speech seems to have come back, for he damned the doctor heartily.

The news reached young George in London, and he and Jewell, the Haymarket treasurer, set off to Margate in a postchaise. Colman and Jewell were old fellow travellers, for the steady old treasurer had acted as the youngster's companion when his father had sent him to Scotland a few years previously.

They dashed through the night on what was a long and dangerous journey in those days, hammering on inn doors to awaken the landlord to get fresh horses. They lost about half an hour this way at every stage, and it was eleven o'clock the next morning before they reached Margate, having thus been twelve hours on the road.

Young Colman hurried to his father's bedside, and found him a little better. Immediate danger, it seemed, had vanished. Nevertheless, young Colman dispatched poor Jewell back to Town to find the finest doctor procurable. He was told to get Dr. Warren, the best man of his day and an old friend of the father's. Money was no object.

Dr. Warren could not leave Town, he had so many urgent cases on hand, but he sent a Dr. Harvey, Registrar of the College of Physicians, a medico of the old school. He came at once with Jewell, and they must have presented an extraordinary appearance. The Doctor was attired in a court suit of dark cloth, with a high, stand-up collar, and cut steel buttons all over him, whilst Mr. Jewell was dressed in nankeen and blue silk stockings.

Dr. Harvey's appearance on the scene created a situation. The first doctor took umbrage and matters were not helped by the violent diatribes of the patient about the treatment he had received. Harvey kept his patient at Margate and came down once a week to see him. At the end of a month, the Haymarket manager was taken home.

A curious fact was to come to light later, when young Colman went through his father's papers. In his diary Colman had written this phrase from Virgil, "*Haerat lateri laethalis arundo*," on the space allotted to that date on which he was to be struck down.

This fragment of the description of the stricken deer ranging the forest with a deadly shaft in its side, was almost prophetic. It seems as though honest George Colman must have had a presentiment. Such things are not uncommon in the theatrical profession.

Julian Wylie, the pantomime king, the night before he died, drove home in his car and asked his wife who was the big theatrical producer whose death was announced on all the evening paper contents bills.

L

A search of the papers disclosed no such news. The next day those bills announced Julian Wylie's own death.

It was a very different George Colman that came back to London. What had been a handsome, active man was now a shattered, half-paralysed invalid, whose mind, if not deranged, was certainly un-balanced and subject to bouts of uncontrollable depression and rage.

For the next four years (between 1785 and 1789), George Colman was a prey to delusions and to strange upheavals. He had attacks of epilepsy, too, which they treated by plunging him into slipper-baths filled with nearly boiling water. But he had long lucid periods when his theatre filled his thoughts. He would allow nobody else to direct its policy or select its plays. He was proud of the Haymarket and he clung to it as his hold upon life and upon reason. Young Colman had to exercise considerable tact in seeming always to do his father's bidding. For Colman the younger was getting more and more into control. Old Colman put up a brave fight, if a losing one.

His friends were mindful of him. Horace Walpole, whose play he had presented, sent him a version of *Walpole's Essay on Modern Gardening*, the pages being printed alternatively in French and English. Walpole had his own printing press at Strawberry Hill.

The poet Cowper, an old friend who had drifted away, got into touch with him and asked for his assistance in the issue of a new translation of Homer. It gave old Colman something to think about.

When not occupied with the affairs of the Haymarket, Colman's active mind, in its clear moments, turned to poetry. He published two volumes of miscellanies, he wrote a pamphlet called *Some Particulars of my Life*, and for his theatre he even wrote a musical entertainment *Ut Pictura Poesis, or, The Enraged Musician*.

But he was getting weaker, and young Colman was getting more firmly in the saddle. The latter had staged a play of his own called *The Battle of Hexham*. The father had his doubts about it and asked the son to explain the plot and the treatment. Old Colman shook his head. "George," he said, "I will show you how such a piece ought to be written." And a week later he gave his son a one-act drama on an *Arabian Night's* subject which was a little masterpiece of dramatic construction. It was played at the Haymarket and it succeeded. It was virtually written on Colman's deathbed—he worked for the Haymarket to the last.

In 1787 John Palmer left to open his own ill-fated venture, the Royalty Theatre, in Wellclose Square, Goodman's Fields. This was, of course, an unlicensed theatre and as such could not be tolerated by Drury Lane and Covent Garden—nor by the Haymarket, now an established playhouse and peer of the Great Two! Colman joined with Linley of the Lane (Sheridan's father-in-law) and Harris of Covent Garden in putting up violent opposition. How the times had changed, and how rapidly they had changed! Only a short time before the little

Haymarket itself had been at war on a similar cause with the Lane and the Garden. Now it joined with them in putting down another upstart.

This Royalty venture was an ill-fated one. Palmer made all the mistakes and blunders he possibly could. On the opening night, he addressed the audience and said that when the first stone was laid, no objections were made by the other theatres. In fact, he said, "in the course of last summer when I performed at the Little Theatre in the Haymarket, Mr. Colman wrote a Prologue, which I spoke on my benefit night, and amongst others, were the following lines:

> "*For me, whose utmost aim is your delight*
> *Accept the humble offering of this night*
> *To please, wherever plac'd, be still my care*
> *At Drury, Haymarket or Wellclose Square.*"

This upset Colman, who immediately sent out paragraphs saying he had only written what he did because Palmer assured him he had every necessary authority for his theatre, which he did not intend to open in the summer, and which therefore could not interfere with the Haymarket season. But Mr. Palmer had opened in June!

So the three great managers threatened Palmer that they would lodge information against him "for every appearance he should make in any play, or scene of a play, at any unlicensed theatre, contrary to the statute." Old Colman shows his human weakness in this action. He did not mind, apparently, what Palmer did to the other theatres, but when he opened against the Haymarket he was hot on his trail.

Palmer was scared. He shut the Royalty and reopened on July 3rd, in opposition to the Haymarket only, for the other two were closed. He had old Bannister, who had left the Haymarket, Leoni, the great singer, and young Braham, the pupil of Leoni, Mrs. Gibbs, then only a girl, Mrs. Wells, and Miss Wilkinson (afterwards Mrs. Mountain) in his company.

At the Haymarket on July 7th, 1787, they produced a comedy by Cumberland called *The Country Attorney*. There was trouble with Miss Farren, and a long correspondence went on between the author and old Colman over this. Apparently Colman cast Mrs. Brooks for the part the Farren thought she ought to have.

Colman, on his sick-bed, thought that the author might have a better chance of dealing with Miss Farren's temperament than he. So he asked him to get round her. Cumberland wrote her a very fulsome letter which appears to have done the trick with reservations, for he reports to Colman:

"My DEAR SIR,—I have just received your letter signifying Miss Farren's commands for transposing her introductory scene to the second act; be it so, but I conclude it will be done with the hand of a master, or that you will transpose it yourself, therefore I rest in peace. For heaven's sake, write her an Epilogue. I have plunged from thought to thought in the profound of nonsense, and can fix on nothing; one sense is left me, the sense of your kindness.

"Farewell.

"R. CUMBERLAND."

This is dated from Tunbridge Wells. The way the author hands the baby back to poor sick Colman must be admired.

The Country Attorney was produced and played by Bensley, Aickin, Stephen Kemble, R. Palmer, Miss Farren and Bannister, junior. But it was not a success. And old Colman wrote the Epilogue. It evidently got a bad Press, for Cumberland writes to Colman again with the age-old cry of the author of a failure—a cry, anyway, as old as newspapers. He says:

"I have so long been the public aim of newspaper violence, that they have familiarised a nature originally too sensitive, and cured me of my feelings by the force of corrosives. I read with indignation the pert malevolence of the papers against my friends, but in my own particular, I expect the lash and have learned to bear it. I am glad to see that the Morning Chronicle has spoken so handsomely of the performers, and readily forgive the humiliating account he has published of the author's performance. But of this more than enough.

"Farewell, my dear Sir, and ever believe me
"Your most faithful friend and obliged servant,

"R. CUMBERLAND."

He wrote again, too, full of praise for Colman's kindness.

This Cumberland was a playwright with a heavy hand. He was rather a pompous person. It was he who reproved, publicly, his children for laughing at Sheridan's *School for Scandal*. It was repeated to Sheridan, who said, "I don't know why he should have done that. I laughed heartily all through his last tragedy."

But young Colman, now more and more master of the Haymarket, was busy again as a dramatist. He wrote a play called *Inkle and Yarico*, which was produced during the 1787 season. He had thrown up the law, which he never liked. Nor could his father say much about this, for had he not done the same thing from the same cause?

Having found inspiration in some paragraphs in the *Spectator*, young Colman threw off what he calls his opera, *Inkle and Yarico*.

He had already experienced setbacks. His first play was a success, but *The Battle of Hexham* had not scored, nor had *Turk or No Turk* made much of a stir. His fourth play, *Ways and Means*, had been hissed on its first night at the Haymarket. He had not had the "bird" before and

he did not like it. He had written an Epilogue which had upset the
newspaper critics, for he was very rough on them:

> "*I am a critic, my masters, I sneer, splash and vapour,*
> *Puff parties, damn poets, in short, do a paper.*
> *My name's Johnny Grub—I'm a vendor of scandal*
> *My pen like an auctioneer's hammer I handle*
> *Knocking down reputations by one inch of candle.*
> *I've heard out the play, yet I need not have come*
> *I'll tell you a secret my masters, be mum,*
> *Though ramm'd in amongst you, to praise or to mock it*
> *I brought my critique—cut and dried—in my pocket.*"

That sort of thing did not make him popular with the Press. He felt
very sore on the point, and salt was rubbed in the wound by his friend
Reynolds telling him that a man had met him in Covent Garden and
said, "Your friend Colman has written a shocking bad play. Never saw
it myself, but it's monstrous bad." That sort of thing still goes on.

All this time poor Colman senior had been endeavouring to conduct
the affairs of the Haymarket Theatre from his sick-bed. It was a
curious directorate for a theatre. Then things got worse. The poor man
had to be taken to a place in Paddington, a kind of private asylum, to be
properly cared for.

It says a good deal for young Colman that he stood up to this. His
love for the theatre and his experience of plays and their production
was now of the utmost value to him. The financial position was not
good. George Colman had made money at the Haymarket, but it must
be remembered that the season was a restricted one, the house was
small and profits were not large. And Colman had to live well, to keep up
a good appearance, always one of the curses of the theatrical profession,
in which so much is taken at face value. The long illness made other
inroads upon an uncertain income. Although Colman was never an
extravagant man and did not live above his station, there was little or
no reserve—and what there was went into the theatre.

Old Colman's end was not far off, and he died in 1794. It was a happy
release for him. His passing occasioned grief, for he was a fine, upright,
honest man and greatly respected. Too little is remembered of him
to-day; his plays are largely forgotten, although *The Clandestine
Marriage* is sometimes revived. His record in the theatre is second to
none. He had stabilised and made fashionable and popular the theatre
he loved and served so well, the Haymarket.

The king was dead, and straight into his shoes stepped the heir
apparent, the prince regent of the Haymarket, George Colman, junior.
It had always been his ambition; now it was realised. He was proprietor
and manager of the little theatre, behind the scenes of which he had
peeped so eagerly as a boy. He was now in charge of the house where his

first play had been produced—where, indeed, all of his plays so far had
seen the light. His father had written thirty-five plays in all: he himself
was already responsible for seven. He had a fine heritage, this incoming
or, rather, hame-trained new manager.

He encountered the full blast of managerial difficulties almost at
once. He was inundated with unproduced plays. He says they came
by cartloads. Thus the theatre changes very little. But one play, written
by a sailor, on a nautical subject, appears to have caught his eye.
It was a tragedy in five acts, and during all the principal scenes the hero
remained on the masthead of a ship, spouting his lines and never once
coming down. Colman returned it.

Old Charles Dibdin, that amazing man, had been a Haymarket
playwright. His output was colossal. He wrote over 1,000 songs and
operettas. His songs, such as "Tom Bowling," "The Jolly Young
Waterman," "Fare Thee Well, My Trim-built Wherry," and certain
of the famous sea-songs live to-day. His contributions to the Haymarket
include *The Trip to Portsmouth*, 1773, *The Waterman, or The First of
August*, 1774, *The Metamorphoses*, 1775, *The Gipsies*, 1778, *Reasonable
Animals*, 1780, *None So Blind*, 1782, *Harvest Home*, 1787, and he was
to do one more.

Whilst young Colman was in control (but before his father died) a
disaster had befallen the theatre, for which, however, he was not in
any way responsible.

Theatre Royal, Drury Lane, was rebuilding. Sheridan, Linley and
Ford had arranged with young Colman to use the Haymarket for the
Drury Lane Company until their own home was inhabited again. It was
a windfall for Colman, for it brought him a rental during the closed
winter season.

On February 3rd, 1794, the King commanded a performance at the
Haymarket. A Royal Command in those days, as in these, drew great
crowds. The little theatre was besieged and it was clear that only a
portion of the waiting crowd would ever get in. There was no queueing
then. It was a vast, milling mob round the pit door; the battle (and
the seats) was to the strong. The opening of the pit doors at any
theatre on a big night was always the signal for a free fight, and this
February night in 1794 was to be no exception. But alas! it was not to
be an occasion of cuts, bruises and faintings, it was to be marked by a
real tragedy.

The pit doors opened and at once the mob surged forward. A man
in the front, pressed by the mob behind him, fell down the stairs. Those
following tumbled over him, and in a second or so there was a screaming, struggling heap of humanity being trodden underfoot by the on-
rushing crowd behind. Fifteen people were trampled to death, nineteen
severely injured, and many more slightly hurt.

They did not tell the King and Queen of the disaster, and the show
went on. The news was broken to the Royal visitors after they had

returned to the Palace. There was no further Royal Command after that at the Haymarket until 1803.

The lease of the theatre, having been George Colman senior's for his lifetime, now fell in. George Colman junior purchased it and carried on.

He wrote most of the plays, and his friend Jack Bannister played in them. The two were almost partners. Their friendship had lasted for years when the parting of the ways came in 1796. Bannister had become so popular that provincial tours (in the summer, when the Lane was closed, for he played there in the winter) paid him much better than the small salary Colman could afford at the Haymarket. And Colman also began to write for Covent Garden as well. So the business association died, but not the friendship. Bannister came back to the Haymarket again in 1804.

Tate Wilkinson, that thorn in Foote's side, and now manager at York—Patentee, in fact—coming down from the north to inspect the new Drury Lane Theatre (the one rebuilt during Sheridan's lesseeship and burned down in 1809), took a gloomy view of it. He believed in smaller theatres as being better for the actors. Colman, senior, had taken a similar view. In a Preface to his translation of Terence's comedies, written before he took over the Haymarket, he had said: "By contracting the dimensions of their theatres, although they have a deal abated the magnificence of Spectacle, they have been able to approach much nearer to the truth and simplicity of representation." He was comparing Drury Lane and Covent Garden with the vast open arenas of ancient Greece, but when he got into the Haymarket he knew that intimacy helps plays. But spectacle has always been, and always will be, part of the two Patent theatres' existence, and when young Colman took over the Haymarket Theatre the two great rivals of his were in floodtide of spectacle. He knew his only chance was for his little place to do something which they could not.

And he, the champion of the small house, rammed home his argument in the first play of his new régime, *New Day at the Old Market*. This was an easy-going affair with plenty of songs. He jeered at the vast spaces of the Lane and the Garden by saying:

> "*When people appear*
> *Quite unable to hear*
> *'Tis undoubtedly needless to talk.*"

And continued:

> "*'Twere better they began*
> *On the new invented plan*
> *And with telegraphs transmitted us the plots.*"

For the drama as then presented at the big houses was little more than spectacle and made no intellectual demands on its audience at all.

Animals began to invade the stage, *à la* Astley's, and oxen, both white

and coloured, horses and elephants—both real and "property"—were
included in the spectacles provided.

Colman, sure that he was quite right, rubbed it well in:

> "*But our House here's so small*
> *That we've no need to bawl*
> *And the summer will rapidly pass*
> *So we hope you'll think fit*
> *To hear the actors a bit*
> *Till the Elephants and Bulls come from grass*
> *Then let Shakespeare and Jonson go hang, go hang*
> *Let your Otways and Drydens go drown*
> *Give them but Elephants and White Bulls enough*
> *And they'll take in all the town*
>
> > *Brave Boys.*"

Colman conveniently forgot the many comedies, not least *The School
for Scandal*, which had succeeded at Drury Lane, or *She Stoops to
Conquer* at Covent Garden, whose intimacy had suffered no check, and
whose wit had not been diminished by the huge auditoriums and stages.
Shortly after, Kean and Mrs. Siddons were to have no difficulty in
making Shakespeare "get over" all right. And there is always the case
of Garrick—and the rest.

But then, Colman was boosting his own theatre—the Haymarket—
and that was still, in size, "the Little Theatre in the Hay."

CHAPTER XIV

THE BOY WHO RAN AWAY

ALTHOUGH George Colman jeered at the two big theatres, he was not above writing for them and putting their money into his pocket. In 1796, after his father's death, his resources were low, so he wrote plays for Drury Lane—spectacles at that—*Blue Beard*, a very big success, *Feudal Time*, and *The Forty Thieves*. They were really pantomime dramas on a big scale.

Hitherto he had confined himself to writing for the Haymarket. There was another dramatist there, a regular contributor. This was John O'Keefe, who was the most prolific and most popular writer of funny plays of his time. His output was amazing, for between 1767 and 1798 over sixty entertainments of various kinds from his pen saw the footlights. He has been mentioned before.

Loosely called "the English Molière," the chief laughter-maker of his time, he has passed into oblivion. It was to the elder Colman and the Haymarket that he owed his first chance in London. He had brought his family over from Ireland in 1777, and he sent George Colman a play. He wished to remain anonymous, fearing the humiliation of rejection, so he signed the covering letter "A.B." and asked the manager, in the event of the play not suiting, to leave it at the bar of the Grecian Coffee House, marked "A.B. To be called for." If, however, he did like it, would he leave a note there, similarly addressed, making an appointment?

He spent twenty-four hours of agonised waiting and then called round. Colman appeared to read plays at once, for O'Keefe found a letter saying that the play was approved, would be produced the following summer (it was Christmas-time then) and would the author call on him at Soho Square? O'Keefe was in ecstasies, for a friend who had read the play had opined that it was not worth twopence.

O'Keefe kept that appointment, knocked at the door of the handsome house, and was ushered into the library. There sat Colman, in cap and dressing gown, having his breakfast. He was very kind to O'Keefe, who then disclosed his name and the fact that he was a successful dramatist in Ireland. The play was a farce called *Tony Lumpkin in Town*. It may be that Colman remembered how nearly he had wrecked the original "Tony Lumpkin" play, *She Stoops to Conquer*, and was taking no more chances of that kind.

He was as good as his word, the play was produced in the summer of 1777 and succeeded. O'Keefe thereafter wrote regularly for the little theatre. He had many successes, for he had the knack of fitting

Edwin and Parsons, those two great comedians, with just the right parts and material. His Haymarket plays include *The Son-in-Law* (music by Dr. Arnold), *The Dead Alive*, *The Agreeable Surprise*, *The Young Quaker*, *Peeping Tom* (a great personal success for Edwin), *The Beggar on Horseback*, *The Birthday, or The Prince of Aragon*, *The Prisoner at Large*, *The Basket Maker*, and *The Magic Banner*. Old Colman made a friend of him, and the son followed suit. O'Keefe was very successful at the Haymarket, but not so successful at Drury Lane and Covent Garden. Perhaps the intimacy of the little theatre suited him best.

The year 1796 was an important one for Colman. He wrote a play called *The Iron Chest*, which was produced by John Philip Kemble at Drury Lane Theatre, and Kemble played the lead, Sir Edward Mortimer. The play was a dismal failure at the Lane. Colman, bitter and aggrieved, laid the whole fault at the feet of Kemble, who in turn blamed the play.

Everyone seems to have been to blame to some extent, but perhaps Kemble was the chief culprit. Anyway, there was war to the knife between the leading spirits of the Haymarket and the Lane; the weapons chosen were pens, from whose points torrents of venom flowed.

The Iron Chest received such a bad reception on its first night at Drury Lane that it was nearly condemned to the dustheap. Colman persisted with it. It became a success and was played for years, providing Edmund Kean, at the same theatre, with a very big hit.

Colman had the play published with a most bitter Preface, so insulting to Kemble that it is a wonder that gentleman did not "call him out." Perhaps, however, he had had enough of duelling after his encounter with Aickin—who had played at the Haymarket. Aickin, who stood upon his dignity, took deep umbrage at a remark of Kemble's (who appears to have been drunk at the time) and challenged him. They met in Marylebone Fields, Aickin being seconded by Bannister. Kemble appears to have been passive about it. He allowed the two actors to stand him up, take the necessary number of paces away and then Aickin turned and fired. He missed by miles. Kemble then fired in the air and honour was satisfied. Kemble said afterwards that as soon as he saw Aickin take aim he knew he would be all right.

Be that as it may, he never challenged Colman, although he had good cause to do so. For Colman refers to him in the Prologue as "a scowling sullen black bull, right athwart my road; a master of Bœotian breed, perplexing me in my wanderings through the entangled labyrinth of Drury. He stands sulkily before me, with sides seemingly impenetrable to any lash, and tougher than the dun cow of Warwick; his front outfronting the brazen bull of Perillus! He has bellowed, gentlemen, yes, he hath bellowed a dismal sound, a hollow, unvaried tone, heaving from his very midriff, and striking the listener with torpor. . . ."

A pretty picture of the great John Philip Kemble! Colman goes on to say that the chief proprietor of Drury Lane had agreed to pay him a sum for the play larger than any author had received before. There is no doubt this was Sheridan throwing the money about as usual. And then the Sheridan technique, both of his own writing and management, is followed. As fast as Colman wrote the pages they were taken away to be put into rehearsal—a reflection of the manner in which Sheridan wrote *The School for Scandal*. But there again Colman has complaints, for there never seems to have been a proper rehearsal. He states that not once was the entire company present and that their conduct was more slovenly than that of a barnstorming company. There was no chance of seeing it as a whole, or of doing any "timing" and consequent cutting at all. Colman then went down with a bad chill, for which he blames the newly opened Drury Lane, and he may have been right, for Kemble was stricken down as well, but ordered the rehearsals to go on without him. Nor were the casualties over then, for Storace, who was to do the incidental music—a most important item in drama of those days—now fell sick as well and, indeed, lay on his deathbed. Altogether it seems a most ill-fated affair.

Kemble, as soon as he was better, took a look at the play as it then stood and decided that they would produce on the date announced, now but a couple of days hence. The news was taken to the sick Colman, and scared him. Nor were his fears allayed when he received a note from Kemble telling him to transpose two of the most important scenes in the play—the request being made only three hours before the curtain went up! The reason given was that the machinery required by the master carpenter was not yet ready and that if it could not be altered, there would be a wait of ten minutes between scenes. Colman refused to do it.

Very ill, he got out of bed and went down to the theatre. He went to Kemble's dressing-room and found that actor taking opium pills. Kemble said he was in great pain, but Colman stated that he was in the habit of taking them, and that he had been drinking as well.

The play went pretty well at first, but the audience got restive with Dodd, who had a very long scene to get through—which Colman would have cut had there been a chance. This did not worry the author, because Kemble was to enter almost at once, and he was relying on him. Indeed, the part was written specially for him. The curtain rose on Kemble, and he had dressed the part perfectly—so far as looks and appearance went, nothing was missing.

But for once in his life, Kemble appears to have given a dreadful show. It may have been his illness, it may have been the opium, but it was appalling. Colman entreated him to have an apology made for his indisposition; he did not want the onus to fall on him as author. Kemble refused. There was a row, and finally one of the management went on and made an apology. It did not help much. Kemble got worse and worse as the play proceeded. The audience were more than restive now, the dreaded "bird" was hovering in the air, and then when the already obnoxious Dodd appeared, the "bird" settled and the audience let them have it. Poor Dodd. It was not his fault; he was a good actor. It was bad rehearsal, lack of timing and cutting, and a shockingly bad performance by Kemble.

That worthy now took action. He made a humble apology to the audience and said it was all his fault. The play was announced for a second performance amidst derisive hoots. Colman's blood turned cold. At first he thought Kemble had been generous in taking the blame; then he realised that Kemble had saved his own face and piled the fault on to the author. So he drew up and printed a little bill of what he owed Kemble:

For his illness	Compassion
For his conduct under it	. Censure
For his refusal to make an apology . .	. A smile
For his making an apology	A sneer
For his mismanagement	. A groan
For his acting	. A hiss

That is pretty plain talking. They did not produce again the next night. A week elapsed, so that Kemble could recover and Colman make his cuts. Then it went on again. This time Kemble professed himself quite well. According to Colman, he just walked through the part:

"The devil a trick did Mr. Kemble play but a scurvy one. His emotions and passions were so rare and so feeble, that they seasoned his general insipidity like a single grain of wretched pepper thrown into the largest dish of water gruel ever administered to an invalid. For the most part, he toiled on, line after line, in a dull current of undiversified sound, which stole upon the ear far more drowsily than the distant murmurings of Lethe, with no attempt to break the lulling stream, or check its sleep inviting course. Frogs in a marsh, flies in a bottle, wind in a crevice, a preacher in a field, the drone of bagpipes, all, all yielded to the inimitable and soporific monotony of Mr. Kemble. The most miserable mummer that ever disgraced the walls of a theatre could not have been a stronger drawback than Mr. Kemble."

The whole thing was a failure. Colman and Kemble were to be reconciled in time, but Colman took it very badly. He was determined that his own theatre should see him righted. He meant to make a stir during the forthcoming summer season of 1796. He remembered his father's policy of novelty. He remembered Henderson from Bath. He cast his eye in the same direction and it fell upon a young actor, Robert William Elliston, who was piling up success there. Much was to come of that.

Colman now had many cares and worries, not the least the fact that a coolness seemed to have sprung up between him and that old friend of his family, Dr. Arnold. It was glossed over for the moment.

The Haymarket opened on June 11th, 1796, with *Peeping Tom* (O'Keefe), *The Liar* and a farce called *Banian Day*. Palmer, Fawcett, Charles Kemble, Miss De Camp, Aickin, and Mrs. Gibbs were the principal performers.

Miss De Camp was a lady who always looked very young, much younger than her years. She was practically born in the theatre and was, besides being an excellent dancer and singer, a good actress and a fine mimic. She had a long and successful career. She married Charles Kemble. Aickin was an Irishman and had been a weaver. But he preferred the stage, and it was a wise choice. He started in Ireland and then went to Scotland, where he became a great favourite in Edinburgh. Also in the company was an actor called Stayley, who had a puffed-up idea of himself and gave himself airs and temperaments. So much trouble did he cause that he got the sack. But he had become very friendly with many of the students in the town, and to them he appealed for help, toadying to them and representing himself as very hardly done by. Very little encouragement was needed then to start a riot and wreck a theatre. The management got to hear what was brewing and advertised the true facts. It made no difference; the students attended in force, to make their demands at the sword's point if need be, and compel the management to re-engage their unworthy favourite.

The curtain went up, and at once yells of "Why is Mr. Stayley not engaged?" came from the malcontents of the pit. The management lay low, so the determined students yelled for Aickin, who was "top of the bill." Aickin came on the stage, dressed as Romeo, which part he was playing that evening. He tried to explain matters as tactfully as possible, but the enraged Scots audience would have none of it—or him. There was a cry of "Damn your soul, down on your marrowbones and ask pardon of a British audience." That was too much for Aickin, who was also being a target for fruit, cabbages and less pleasant missiles. He came forward and said his piece, with a good deal of force. "Gentlemen," he shouted, "I know of no offence either my fellow performers or I have been guilty of, which, if you would but listen to me, I should soon be able to explain to you. As to going on my knees, it is what I never will do but to God and my King. If any gentleman insists on it, he must rip from me this heart which inspirits this declaration."

They took him at his word, they swarmed on the stage with drawn swords. But Aickin had seen them coming. One or two he would have faced, but the whole pit was far too many. He prudently beat a retreat and escaped by a window. But they wrecked the theatre thoroughly and everyone was out of work. A similar episode occurred under Garrick at Drury Lane.

Aickin managed to reach London. He got a job at Drury Lane, but was only given indifferent and very poor parts. It was when Foote first engaged him for the Haymarket that his great talents became observed, and from that time he never looked back. He was excellent in both comedy and tragedy, and although never quite in the very front rank, was a leading man of standing and repute, with an ease of manner and a gift for natural acting which took him to heights at the Haymarket, Covent Garden and Drury Lane.

On June 21st Colman presented O'Keefe's *The Magic Banner*, but for once the writer of comedy did not quite hit the mark. The stage was, however, set for his novelty—the presentation to London of the new actor, Robert William Elliston. A new star, designed for the highest possible altitude, burst upon the town by way of the Little Theatre in the Hay. The night was June 25th, 1796.

Robert William Elliston was born in Orange Street, Bloomsbury, on April 7th, 1774, so that he was only twenty-two years of age when he became a star actor. Aries was his birth star, and if there is anything in that curious astrological belief, Elliston goes far to sustain it. Arians are said to be impulsive, brilliant, somewhat erratic at times, but born leaders and people who get their own way. Robert William Elliston was all of that.

His father was a watchmaker, and the younger son of a Suffolk farmer. The eldest son, young Robert's uncle, was the big noise of the family. He was a member of St. John's College, Cambridge, and a master at Sidney Sussex. Another uncle was in the Royal Navy and became a commander. Young Robert's father was the only one to lack distinction. It missed him, but settled on his son. For he was to become more famous than even a great-uncle, who was notable for having lived in the same house he was born in for eighty-six years.

Robert's father was an indolent fellow given to low pursuits and the neglect of his watchmaking, which required more concentration than he was disposed to give it. But the uncle at Cambridge befriended the boy, who saw very little of his worthless father. He was sent to St. Paul's School and the Church was to be his future. The kind uncle encouraged the lad to learn long pieces for declamation—with a view to the pulpit. But it did not work out that way.

Young Elliston declaimed in public at school on Speech Days and got to love an audience. The first seeds of the stage were shooting up. He was sent to learn French from a Mme. Cotterille, and there he met young Charles Mathews. This Mme. Cotterille had lodgings over a pastrycook's shop, and there she gave her French lessons. Her methods seem a little difficult to understand, because twice a year she coached her students in an English play—in their native tongue—and had it performed to the parents and others who were interested. This was a delight to the boys Mathews and Elliston. They shone very brightly. They were always the success of the night, highly praised by the no doubt indulgent audiences. Then they appeared together in *The Orphan*,

Elliston playing Chaumont and Mathews The Chaplain. Elliston made a tremendous hit, eclipsing all he had ever done before. He was intoxicated by it, and now his mind was made up—an actor's life for him.

He sneaked off to the theatre whenever he could, to watch, to study, to see how the players got their effects, how it was all done. His preoccupation was noticed by his schoolmaster. Questions were asked. But Elliston had taken his decision. He would run away and go on the stage. One thing only deterred him, the thought of the uncle who had been so kind to him. But he considered that when he had become famous the uncle would relent, and as he meant to become famous, that was that.

One morning very early he slipped out of his father's house, and ran away—not to sea, as so many boys then did, but to the equally troubled and perilous waters of the theatrical profession. Bath was his objective; that was the place for a promising lad to start—Nance Oldfield, Henderson, so many had come from there or won their first fame there. He knew all about the theatre. He sped to the coach office. To his horror and dismay, the Bath coach was full up. He feared pursuit, and had to work quickly. To get clear of London was the main thing. So he managed to get a place in the other Bath coach—"The Invalid Coach," whose passengers were visiting that lovely city, not in search of Thespian fame, but of health. This coach was certainly a slow one; it took two days over the journey, because the people who travelled by it must not be jolted over the stones at speed, and had need of rest and recuperation—to say nothing of refreshment—at every stage.

Tucked away amongst groaning, complaining, short-tempered, suffering travellers, the young hopeful started on the long road which was to bring him, he believed, fame and fortune. It was not an auspicious or spectacular start, but at any rate his boats were burned and he was off.

That night he got on excellent terms with the landlord and landlady of the inn where the coach stopped. His bright, entertaining conversation, his delightful manner and his reciting charmed the host and hostess. Then and there, they had an impromptu concert. Elliston had got an audience, and that always, all his life, acted as a tonic. He pleased so much that he ate and slept free of charge. So confident had he now become that he let the slow invalid coach go on without him, and caught the day coach when it arrived. He wanted to get to Bath in good style. He knew the value of an "entrance." Even if nobody in the whole city was aware of him, there was his own self-respect.

Arrived in Bath, he sought out a friend with whom he had been in correspondence and who had promised him an introduction to Dimond, who had succeeded Palmer at the Bath Theatre Royal. He got the letter, he saw Dimond, but nothing came of it. Elliston did not despair; he knew he would win. His charm of manner got him a job in a lottery ticket office and he laid persistent siege to manager Dimond. That man surrendered at length and on April 21st, 1792, Robert William Elliston walked the stage, a full professional for the first time, as Tressell in *Richard III*. And he made quite a success.

But the Bath season was nearly over and Elliston looked like being out of work. An actor in the company named Wallis (father of a Miss Wallis, who was then the reigning toast of Bath) took a fancy to him. He gave him a letter of introduction to that same Tate Wilkinson who had been with Foote at the Haymarket. Tate Wilkinson, now Patentee of the Theatre Royal, York, and controller of the whole circuit of Northern England, had a keen eye for talent.

He gave young Elliston a job right away and the young man toured the North. Now he felt established, so he wrote to his uncle, confessing what he had done and stressing that he was a success. The uncle, an understanding man, not only forgave him, but sent him a letter of recommendation to the great John Philip Kemble of Drury Lane. Elliston got into touch.

Kemble was very polite, but nothing ensued. Little did either of them dream that one day—and that day not so far distant—the young applicant would control Theatre Royal, Drury Lane, and be known as the Great Lessee.

Elliston finished his tour and went back to Bath. Dimond re-engaged him. He was a success as Romeo, he was a success in all that he played. His lucky star, that forceful ram, looked after him. A house caught fire. In it was an old, bedridden man, at the mercy of the flames. Young Elliston rushed in, burst through the flames, and carried the helpless old creature out in his arms. Sensation upon sensation, and very good for him materially and from the point of view of publicity.

Naturally, too, he fell in love and had quite a little romance. He was saving money too, a habit he soon abandoned, and had both his eyes on London. London, in the person of George Colman, of the Haymarket Theatre, had its eye on him. Colman wrote to the young actor and offered him a London debut at the Haymarket. Elliston, his heart bounding within him, showed a sound business sense. He did not appear to leap at the offer. He made terms; he could come if he could play the parts of his choice—Octavian, Sheva, and Hamlet. Colman agreed readily to the first two, but demurred at Hamlet, and Colman won. Indeed he shook Elliston's confidence in his ability to play it. With his certainty of Bath success whenever he wanted it, his London engagement in his pocket, and, in his optimistic, dashing mind, a sure triumph, Elliston got married. He kept business in that romance too. It was to be a partnership in more ways than one. He was to act and she was to run a school. Elliston always had his eye on the main chance.

On June 25th, 1796, Elliston appeared at the Haymarket Theatre, the first real novelty in the way of actors that George Colman the Second had presented. He played Octavian in *The Mountaineers* by Colman himself. It may have been tact which suggested Elliston's choice of this

Miss Kelly as Lady Savage.
From an engraving dedicated to the Duke of Devonshire.

Mr. Phelps and Miss Glyn
in Act III, Scene 4, of
Hamlet.

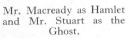

Mr. Macready as Hamlet
and Mr. Stuart as the
Ghost.

part and play, but it was an established success and had been produced at the Haymarket in 1793. He also played Vapour in the farce, *The Grandmother*, by Prince Hoare, another tried and popular Haymarket stock piece. So he gave two examples of his art—for *The Mountaineers* is a melodrama in blank verse and Octavian is a hermit. He was a success.

The Press spoke well of him:

"This young performer has claims that fully entitle him to the favourable reception he has met with from a London audience. He appears to possess that first requisite to an actor—good conception of his character. Many passages in his performance of Octavian were marked by energy and feeling. His pathos made a successful appeal to the audience, and discovered effects beyond common artifice. His delivery in general was good, except that, when he was desirous of being impressive he was occasionally too rapid. In Vapour he disclosed some power of whim and humour."

Elliston played Octavian again on June 28th, with even greater applause than at his debut. The first-night nerves, that had occasioned that too rapid utterance, had worn off. On June 30th, he played Sheva, and this established him firmly in favour. He was now one of the élite. He read with pride: "no performer of better promise has presented himself in London for many years." He played on for several nights and completed his engagement, which had only been for a limited number of performances. He had to return to Bath to complete his season there and on July 15th he had a letter from Colman:

"MY DEAR SIR,—I shall be very happy to see you again, the moment your affairs will permit you to return. I will either defer settling terms till we meet or fix them with you by letter. If you prefer the latter, pray propose, and nothing that I am able to effect shall be left undone to meet your wishes.

" 'Octavian' and 'Sheva,' you might, I am confident, repeat with increase of reputation to yourself and advantage to the theatre. Hamlet too (of whom you seem a little afraid) has nothing in the character which is not within your scope. If you fancy my hints can be of service to you in any part, I think they may be so in this, for I have been reading *Hamlet* with no small attention, on your account, since your departure.

"I am, my dear sir, sincerely yours,
"G. COLMAN."

That was a real Haymarket letter. Elliston was at the cross roads. Here in Bath and neighbouring towns he was certain of continued success and employment. He had just cleared over £100 by his benefit at Bristol, a hitherto unprecedented sum for that town. There was his

M

wife and her school, there was the ease of achievement at Bath—there was the lure of London, the joy of triumph in the capital, the heights to be reached. . . . London won. Elliston went to Colman and the Haymarket.

Now perhaps Colman was not altogether altruistic concerning Elliston. His old failure of *The Iron Chest* at Drury Lane still rankled bitterly and deeply. He longed to be revenged on Kemble, to show the world that it was the actor and not his play which had failed. In Elliston he saw just the right man for the part. He saw his way to victory.

Meanwhile, after Elliston's departure, the Haymarket went along quietly. Colman re-staged his old entertainment, *New Hay from the Old Market* under the title of *Sylvester Daggerwood*, with the added attraction of Caulfield, the mimic. It had done very well. Cumberland supplied a play called *Don Pedro*, but that had failed. Colman's careful reading of *Hamlet* had another result too. For he persuaded his friend Jack Bannister, the magnificent light comedian of his day, into playing the part at the Haymarket. The bills announced that he played for that night only. A critic observed: "So much the better." The same applied to the mercurial Jack's other Shakespearean attempt on the Prince of Wales in *Henry IV*, although it was considerably better than his Hamlet.

Whilst Elliston was weighing his chances in Bath, he received a letter from a great friend, a Mr. Gore, a man of wealth and position, who was in London.

"Why have you not replied to Colman's letter? [asked Gore]. Sense of security is mortals' frailty; and a man who has behaved so kindly to you as Colman has a claim on your best attention. I see no reason why you should stand in awe of Hamlet; you have every qualification for it, except perhaps features, and art may do much for you, even in this. . . . Cumberland and myself have met—we chatted together last Friday behind the scenes very freely, upwards of an hour. He talked much about you; and do not blush that I praised you highly as a good son. Last night, I was behind the scenes, at Colman's. Jack Bannister bow'd again, *en passant*, more coolly than he was wont to do. Perhaps he has heard of my attendance on you; and rooks will smell gunpowder. Charles Kemble asked very kindly after you; he seemed pleased to hear of your probable return this season. Waldron, the renowned 'Sir Walter Raleigh,' rapped out some dozen oaths—swore 'by Gad' he could never have thought there was so much stuff in you—that 'by Gad' you had taken them all in; and that you were an astonishing young man. He talked of Garrick, of whom, to his teeth, he knows no more than I of Sanconiatho. He said, too, he had heard you were engaged at Covent Garden, at £20 a week. . . ."

That is a nice little picture of life at the Haymarket and the contrasted

types of people there. Waldron was the Prompter and Sub-Manager.
He had his benefit on the closing night of that season. Gossip went on
then as now, everyone was full of news, or making it up to start something. It is the same to-day. There is little doubt that this letter from
Mr. Gore, a man who loved the theatre and the society of actors, had
much to do with Elliston's decision. The position at the Haymarket is
clear. Colman wants him. Kemble is friendly and Jack Bannister
jealous. Waldron the Prompter, who could make things very unpleasant
(for Prompter then was the stage director of to-day), was on his side.
He came to London to finish the season.

George Colman put the idea of *The Iron Chest* before him, but let
him play himself in first with his old successes, so as to give him
confidence. It paid them both very well. What Elliston thought about
this resurrection of a play which had been "damned at the Lane," had
caused so much trouble and was now to be tried again, cannot be put
better than by using his own words. He wrote to his Uncle:

> "Here I am once more in the metropolis, and have again paid my
> respects to a London audience by whom I have been received with
> renewed—with increased demonstrations of welcome. Colman's *Iron
> Chest* which has made some noise in the dramatic world, is published
> and with it a 'preface'—or a Prescription which the author no doubt
> intended for Kemble's malady. *The Iron Chest* is now to be performed
> at the Haymarket and I am fixed on to take the character of 'Sir Edward
> Mortimer.' It is thought by many a bold attempt and by none more
> so than myself. Young Bannister, eaten up with spleen, has positively
> refused my repeating Sheva, which he claims his unalienably own;
> and as I do not think it prudent to perform Hamlet, or indeed any-
> thing I could not confidently offer to the public, I am at a stand. *The
> Iron Chest* engages all my attention. I am already in the stirrup for
> my purpose—wish me, dear Sir, success."

Colman was terribly anxious about it all; the whole town was talking.
It was looked upon as an affair of the greatest interest and importance
in the theatre. It was the great morsel of gossip and discussion everywhere. Here was a young man, young in years and experience, who was
to try conclusions with John Philip Kemble, the admitted leading actor
of the day. He was to try to succeed where Kemble had failed; in other
words, he was to teach the great tragedian his business. Quite certainly,
Jack Bannister was assiduous in spreading talk to upset Elliston. He
was obviously jealous, as Mr. Gore had hinted, otherwise he would not
have stopped Elliston playing Sheva so effectively. These were the days
when certain parts belonged to certain actors in each theatre by right
of seniority as well as by merit. Bannister had staked his claim, Elliston
must perforce stand down. But, by all means let him rush headlong to
his doom in *The Iron Chest*.

For nobody except Colman believed in the play. It had been seen;

even allowing for Kemble's indisposition at the opening performance, it had been no better on succeeding nights. It could not be, people argued, the actor's failure, as Colman said in his Preface. For the *Mirror*, the great theatrical oracle of the day, had condemned it as a play, had said it was beyond all hope, a most defective piece of work, which nothing, under any circumstances, could ever make a success.

George Colman was blamed for his rude Preface; he evidently could not take his punishment. They were sorry about this, of course, but—well, everyone has to have failures, and *The Iron Chest* was one of Colman's.

But that astute man of the theatre and experienced playwright thought differently. He knew what was in his play, he knew what could be done with it, he knew how ill-rehearsed it had been, how poorly cast, how very badly played by Kemble. He knew that the real play and the real part had never yet been seen. He considered too that it would make a better appeal at his smaller theatre. And he hoped and prayed that his judgment was right and that in this new Haymarket discovery, Robert William Elliston, he had the very man to play Sir Edward, to revenge him upon Kemble, to shame the overproud and confident star and to give him—and the Haymarket—full satisfaction for the disgrace put upon them. For a reverse for Colman was a reverse for the theatre he managed and loved.

This time he cut his play; he rehearsed it himself with every care and in every detail. He explained to Elliston the finer points of the character and the way he wanted them brought out. He never showed a moment's lack of confidence, either in the play or in Elliston's ability. He went straight ahead, with his mind made up. He would win through.

This confidence did not impart itself to Elliston. He had heard all sides, he knew all there was to know about it; his fellow actors saw to that. He had only felt as despondent once before in his career, when, in his very early days, he believed himself, for the moment, a failure and that his uncle had cast him off. He remembered some words of Colman's own: "A new play redoubles the hazard to a new actor." Did Colman mean to sacrifice him and his future on the altar of his own pride, in an attempt to be revenged on Kemble? Was that it? He knew what he himself was facing—a play which had been condemned at Drury Lane and was now offered to a Haymarket audience, which would contain many people whom he had pleased in a few familiar parts, now standing on trial for his very theatrical life, in a part which had humbled the greatest player of the day. He grew to dread the time when the attempt must be made.

And that day, July 29th, came all too soon for him.

CHAPTER XV

A NOTABLE VICTORY

THERE was no drawing back for Elliston now. The house was full, and seething with excitement. Colman himself was on tenterhooks. His status as a manager, his judgment as well, his fame as a playwright and the prestige of the Haymarket were all at stake. He had flung down the gauntlet to Drury Lane the Great, he had challenged the greatest actor of the day, and his champion was a new and only partially tried actor from Bath. It was a tremendous gamble. But he had faith.

The play began, the chatter stilled, the house was tense. The story in its opening stages was followed with interest. But all were waiting for the entrance of the young man, who, on Colman's behalf, would challenge the great John Philip Kemble and try to succeed in a part where the mighty one had failed—and failed miserably. The cue came, all eyes were on the wings—and Elliston entered as Sir Edward Mortimer.

There was no trace in his face or his demeanour of what he was feeling. He took the stage nobly and with assurance—and a most encouraging round of applause greeted him. It acted like a tonic; it steadied Elliston's nerves. He began to play this important part and to play as he had never done before. In each act he transcended that which had gone before, the applause grew, the play gripped and held and Elliston went on to triumph. At the end all was glory. Colman had succeeded, the despised play had succeeded, the Haymarket had succeeded where Drury Lane had failed, and young Robert William Elliston stood assured of fame—for he also had succeeded where John Philip Kemble had failed. The house rang with cheers. It was a great Haymarket victory—and it was to take Elliston far.

From that night onwards *The Iron Chest* became a stock piece in every theatre (including Drury Lane) and was played for many years. Irving played it at the Lyceum. It was so successful at the Haymarket that no more plays were wanted that season. Elliston promptly received offers from Sheridan to go to Drury Lane, and from Harris to go to Covent Garden, when his Haymarket engagement should be over. He made an appointment with Sheridan which that worthy kept—but seven hours late. Harris—and Covent Garden—got him.

There was still a carping spirit shown in certain quarters after the vindication of *The Iron Chest*. The *Mirror* had a curious paragraph:

"Had Mr. Kemble played Mortimer infinitely better than he did, *The Iron Chest* would, nevertheless, have been condemned at Drury

Lane. Had Mr. Elliston not played half so well as he did *The Iron Chest* would have been successful at Mr. Colman's *'own theatre.'* "

The suggestion is, of course, that Colman had "packed" the house and possibly engaged a claque. The answer is that after its rebirth at the Haymarket *The Iron Chest* was performed hundreds of times at Drury Lane, with great success. There was no retort to that.

Early in 1797, Colman wrote an entertainment which he proposed to play at the Haymarket in Lent, but the Lord Chamberlain would have none of it. This Lenten closing was always a sore point with the theatre managers of those times. Over a century before there had been an uproar because Charles II had permitted a French company to play at the Cockpit during Lent, whilst his own company—His Majesty's Servants—at Drury Lane were not allowed to open.

Colman published the entertainment in book form as *My Night Gown and Slippers; or Tales in Verse, written in an elbow chair by George Colman the Younger*. There were three tales, and it sold very well.

Colman had a special reason for wanting to play during Lent. He was very short of money. Successful though the little theatre had become, Colman was a bad business-man and spent as he received.

Finding himself prevented from earning money in Lent, he tried to become a borrower. He applied to Dr. Arnold for a loan. The letter is typical:

"Sunday Night, Piccadilly.

"MY DEAR ARNOLD,—I feel more unpleasantly than I can tell you (so I leave you to conceive it) in writing to you on money subjects. Take therefore a plain tale; though tales, now-a-days, according to Lord Bishops and Lord Chamberlains, are of ill-omen. I am so thrown back in consequence of the failure of our Lenten entertainment (which I reckoned on as a certainty) that I am obliged to apply to those who are more blessed with affluence than I am. Can you, my dear Arnold, lend me two hundred pounds? for the repayment of which, in the summer (or before) I give you the word of an old friend and any other security in my power. I am in need of this occasional supply to take up a bill, which is soon becoming due; and I have everything but an absolute promise of a renewal of accommodation after I have honoured my acceptance, so that you see I am not hasty in saying that I might probably reimburse you before our Haymarket season commences.

"They who ought to hunt for me upon these emergencies are bad dogs at best, or I should not apply to you. I am going on Thursday to Mountains. Please send me a line in the course of to-morrow.

"Truly yours,

"G. COLMAN."

Colman wrote again to Arnold on the Tuesday asking him to use any influence he had to get theatres open in Lent and asking him to call, but apparently the doctor did not call and did not let Colman have the £200. For Colman's next letter is in regretful tones. It is dated from Piccadilly on March 7th, 1797, and it says:

"I cannot leave town, and I am just going, without sending you a line to thank you, my dear Arnold, for your letter. Alas! we are two unlucky dogs! Could you have assisted me now, it would have rejoiced me; and I am sure you would if you could. I feel your explanations and intentions to be most kind and friendly.

"Ever truly yours,
"G. COLMAN."

Colman was getting into deep water. His season was so short and even if he did well—and he mostly did very well—it left little margin. He was careless in money matters; he always said money meant nothing to him and that he hated it, but he managed to get hold of it all the same. But in the end, his instability in money matters was to bring him down. There is a good example of how he "raised the wind" in another letter to the friendly and perhaps somewhat long-suffering Arnold. Evidently his first rebuff by Arnold had not put him off and he had propounded another scheme, for he writes on May 18th, 1797, as follows:

"MY DEAR ARNOLD,—I appointed to meet your friend Savignac on Thursday next, that we might go to Blackfriars that day at eleven, but we neither named the precise time nor place of our meeting. Will you be so good as to fix this matter with him and send me a line? He mentioned to me that you had drawn out stock which would make our matter up, about eleven hundred pounds instead of the thousand, and you said I might have it if I had occasion for it. On deliberation, and on looking over my arrangements, I will, if you hold in the same mind, accept the offer, and make the annuity accordingly; and now, my dear Arnold, let me thank you (although I am awkward at thanks and say much less than I feel) for your goodness and real friendship on this occasion. I hate all money transactions in general; they are damned, nauseous, nasty, sour things that go against my stomach; but you have contrived to throw into your draughts such a mixture of warmth and kindness, that I shall never think of it without pleasure. I return to town on Wednesday and am working tightly for the summer. I was in some hope that Robin might have dropped in on me. Remember me to him, and all yours.

"I am, my dear Arnold,
"Yours truly and affectionately,
"G. COLMAN."

The Robin referred to was Dr. Arnold's son, christened Robin because of the first successful afterpiece, *Auld Robin Gray*, which was produced at the Haymarket.

When the theatre re-opened in 1797, Colman engaged Munden, the great comedian. Bannister had gone, but Munden did not replace him, rather he filled the gap left by Parsons. Readers of Lamb know all about Munden, whom the gentle Elia adored. He cannot say enough wonderful things about him. And truly Joseph Munden was not only a fine comedian, but a fine actor. He came to the Haymarket fresh from his great London successes at Covent Garden. He was high in public regard when Colman engaged him. He had succeeded to the mantle of Edwin, and so it was fitting that he should play at the little theatre where Edwin had won such fame. He was no newcomer, in a sense, to the Haymarket; he had played there before when unknown and unobserved—or almost unobserved. But a short sketch of his amazing career to the date when he makes his first real entrance at the Haymarket belongs to that theatre's story. For he is a great name.

Joseph Munden was born in 1758, the son of a respectable poulterer in Brooke's Market, Leather Lane, Holborn. His father died in the lad's infancy. A loving mother brought him up, and at the age of twelve years old put him to work for an apothecary, where he only stayed a month. He did not like medicine, either to take or to sell. This time there was some show of consulting his wishes and because he was a very good penman he was put into an attorney's office in New Inn. He left there for a law stationer's in Chancery Lane. Here he got his articles and was apprenticed for five years. The stationer died at the end of the first two years and young Munden was taken over by his successor, whom he did not like at all. In fact, he hated him like the medicine from which he had flown. There was continual battle between them, and young Joseph sought relaxation at the play. What he saw in the theatre fired his imagination. He hung about on the off chance of getting to know the actors and met other stage-struck youths like himself. He developed a gift for mimicry. One of these would-be Thespians actually got an engagement, in Liverpool. He persuaded young Munden to try his luck and come with him. Munden agreed and went off to Liverpool, deserting his articles, the obnoxious stationer and Chancery Lane. But Liverpool did not receive him gladly. He could get no work at first in the theatre, but finally his penmanship won him what his talent could not—a job writing out the actors' parts in each play, for which he received eighteenpence a night. He stuck to it, longing for a chance of getting on the boards instead of simply writing out parts for the luckier ones—and at length the luck came his way. He "went on"—that is all that can be said of his first public appearance, for it was as a "super" without a line to say. But it filled him with joy, for there he was actually on the stage, before a real audience who had paid for their seats (some of them) and who might possibly be looking at him. But when the season closed and the company went to London, Munden could not go with them. He had not got the fare.

He fell back again on his writing, he got a job in the Town Hall, where he made himself useful to the Town Clerk. But could one who had seen the glory of the footlights—however dim—and felt the thrill of facing an audience be content in such humdrum surroundings? Not Joseph Munden.

A play was got up for a tradesman in difficulties by a number of youths as stage-struck as Joseph, but amateurs, not semi-professional like him. They selected *Henry IV* to show off their talents and Munden joined them. Thus he spoke his first lines on the stage. He doubled the parts of one of the Carriers and Bardolph—and he was a success. The Town Hall was now unendurable. He heard of a company at Rochdale which wanted recruits—to Rochdale he went, got the job and did very well indeed. But the engagement did not last very long—the salary was negligible; it was not a very good company and was largely composed of local amateurs with stage ambitions. So back he went to Liverpool. They took him on again at the Town Hall—his writing was so good— and there he stopped for two years.

But it was irksome to Joseph Munden. His brief encounters with the "profession" had settled his fate. For him it was the stage—or nothing. It was very nearly nothing. He had saved a guinea. With it he went to Chester, hoping for a job in the theatre. The guinea went, shilling by shilling, and finally the time came—not very tardily either—when young Master Joseph found that his 21s. had dwindled to the last odd "bob"! But so great was the call of the playhouse that he spent his last coin on a ticket for the Chester Theatre. Little did it know or he think then that one day he would manage that same theatre.

His shilling spent, his play seen, he found himself outside, with no prospect of supper, bed or breakfast. He stood in the street, his head still full of the play he had seen, but his heart beginning to fail him, when a man stopped and spoke to him. It was a butcher with whom he had formed a slight acquaintance. The kindly man, on hearing his plight, put him up for the night.

Next day he tried the theatre again for a job, but there was nothing for him. He went to a stationer's and offered himself as a clerk. There were no vacancies. He wandered about the streets, getting hungry and desperate. He was quite penniless and, except for the butcher, absolutely friendless in the town.

Then Fate took a hand. He met a man he knew—a man from London —who helped him. Munden determined to go back to Town. His friend decided to do likewise. That friend was a real one. He was short of money too, but he had a ring, and he pawned it. Even so, it was not enough for both their fares to Town. But it would and did buy a donkey, and, mounted together on the poor beast, they set out for Town. Chester had brought neither luck. Eventually they reached

Birmingham, and there Munden and his companion parted. For Birmingham is near Stratford-on-Avon and Joseph could not resist the temptation of going to see Shakespeare's birthplace. Funds, of course, were not available. But ingenuity found a way. Munden joined a group of militia-men bound for Stratford. He got his board and lodging, and entertained his fellows with excerpts from plays. In the morning, when they reached Stratford, the bugles blew for assembly, but Munden did not answer the call. He had served his military career.

The wanderer got to London at last and went straight to his mother, who received him as all mothers do all prodigals. To please her, he went again into the employ of a law stationer for some months. But the stage forever beckoned to him. He met a man who was running a company at Leatherhead—of all places—and left Town again with thirteen pence in his pocket. He was told he would participate in the night's takings. The barn which was the theatre was not ready; there were no seats. Thirteenpence was soon spent. The next night the barn was all ready and waiting, but no audience turned up. The company appealed to the manager for funds, only to learn he was as penniless as they were. On the third night, which was a Saturday, a local gentleman bespoke a play. The profits gave each performer the sum of 6s. and a couple of tallow candle ends each. Yet to Munden it was glorious. It was his first real salary. The manager decided to carry on and as Munden had distinguished himself, he and another actor were given a benefit. They were robbed of their anticipated reward because the barn was burned down. The manager then got up a petition to the people of the neighbourhood, asking for help. This was Munden's idea. Quite a sum was collected, the company got 5s. each and the manager went to London to buy costumes and properties. He never came back.

Munden walked to London and went to the Black Lion in Russell Street, Drury Lane, where the lower ranks of unemployed actors congregated. He got a job with some strollers, who went around the Berkshire villages and then reached Windsor, where they were quite successful. This time, Munden had a new experience. He "got his Notice" as actors say—in other words, he was discharged for refusing to play a very important part at far too little notice. He said he would only give the best and this would not be possible. So once again he walked back to London and his mother.

Later he went to the Haymarket, where some private plays were being performed, and then a man called Hurst, Manager of the Canterbury Theatre, engaged him for the season. It was the turning point in his career. He was to have played "second" tragic parts, but a comedian falling out, he got the job and was a big success. From Canterbury he went to Brighton, where he scored a further success.

Then he was engaged as principal comedian at Chester Theatre, the house where once he had spent his last shilling. He made a big hit there and later toured the whole of the North of England becoming a great favourite.

He was of a careful turn of mind and saved money rapidly. With a Mr. Whitelock he purchased the controlling interests in the theatres at Newcastle, Lancaster, Chester, Preston, Warrington and Sheffield.

But Munden did not like management. He wanted to act. In the winter of 1790 he was engaged at Covent Garden. His success was immediate. He remained a star up to the day of his death, and inspired Elia to write an epic as to his acting. Munden is an immortal of the theatre and it was at the Haymarket that he got his first real piece of luck.

In 1797 he was playing all the leads at the Haymarket—where once he had made small appearances in tiny parts. The biggest hit that season and one of the biggest the Haymarket ever had, was Colman's play, *The Heir-at-Law*, which contained the character of Dr. Pangloss. There is little doubt that Colman based this play on an older one which he had read, and the part of Dr. Pangloss too. But that was the custom then. Mrs. Inchbald, a somewhat captious critic, said the play contained everything a play should have—except taste. But it was very much to the taste of the audiences and it lasted for years. Another play that season which succeeded was *The Italian Monk*, in which John Palmer, Charles Kemble and Miss De Camp were on top of their form.

And Colman wrote a clever prologue which was spoken at Covent Garden where the management had lured the famous Mrs. Abington back to the stage. It was fitting he should do so, for she herself had made her first stage appearance at the Haymarket with Theophilus Cibber in 1758, but under the name of Burton. She was not seventeen at the time, but the little theatre was her stepping-stone to Bath and then to Old Drury itself.

The Haymarket and the Colmans did not show up too well when O'Keefe wished to publish a complete set of his works, under a subscription list headed by the Prince of Wales. Poor O'Keefe had gone blind. Harris of Covent Garden gave permission for all the plays which had been performed there. But Colman refused to allow *Dead Alive*, *Son-in-Law*, *Agreeable Surprise*, *Peeping Tom* and the *Young Quaker* to be so printed. Colman the Elder had bought them cheaply, in the first instance, to prevent them being played elsewhere, and had tied up the agreement so tightly—he had legal knowledge, it will be recalled—that O'Keefe found the copyright was not vested in him, as it would have been had they been published; copyright in those days only lasted with publishers for fifteen years.

Colman the Younger was now writing for Drury Lane and Covent Garden as well as for his own theatre. One of his pieces, *Blue Devils*, failed at the Garden, but succeeded later at the Haymarket.

The season of 1798 opened on June 12th with *The Deaf Lover*, *The Battle of Hexham* and *Blue Devils*. These were followed by a drama called *The Inquisitor*, which was said to be by Holcroft, but after its reception nobody would own it.

The Haymarket had another success in a drama called *The Cambro-Britons*, in which an all-star cast embracing Munden, Suett, J. Johnstone, Charles Kemble, Henry Johnson, Robert Palmer, Miss De Camp, Mrs. Gibbs and Mrs. Bland made a big impression.

On August 11th came still another success, *False and True, or The Irishman in Italy*. In this John Johnstone, the Irish comedian, drew all London with a song which Colman wrote for him.

The stage suffered a loss in this year when John Palmer, a great Haymarket actor, fell dead while performing in Liverpool. There was a benefit for him at Covent Garden (for he played there as well as at the Haymarket and Drury Lane), and 700 guineas were raised for Palmer's orphan daughters.

Charles Kemble appeared as Shylock at the Haymarket on August 18th, 1798, and Mrs. Henry Johnston, wife of the Scottish Roscius, played with success there as Ophelia and Roxalana. It was a most successful season.

Colman published another edition, the third, of the celebrated play, *The Iron Chest*. Having proved his play a success, he omitted the attack on John Philip Kemble. That chapter was closed.

At the beginning of the Haymarket season of 1799, Colman, whose play, *Feudal Times*, had failed at Drury Lane during the winter, tried a translation of a drama by Kotzebue called *Family Distress*. He was inspired to do this by Drury Lane's terrific success with *Pizarro*, but his venture did not hit the mark.

For the summer the Haymarket fell back on its staple, comedy. A farce called *Fortune's Frolic*, by Till Allingham, succeeded largely because Fawcett the actor played the lead. John Fawcett was the son of an actor who had shone in Garrick's days. He was apprenticed in the City, but the stage blood came out and he ran away from his master, joined some strollers and appeared with them under the name of Foote. At Tonbridge he attracted the attention of Cumberland, the dramatist, who helped him.

He rose steadily and was engaged at Covent Garden, where he did good work. When Bannister left the Haymarket in 1795, Fawcett went there and showed himself to be so reliable that Colman made him Stage Manager. He married Mrs. Mills, the widow of another celebrated actor. Each season, if not each month, he got better and better and developed into a really first-rate comedian.

On July 30th, Colman presented a comedy called *Sighs, or The Daughter*. This pleased very well, and a song, "'Twas in the Solemn Midnight Hour," sung by Mrs. Bland, became the hit of the Town. The words were by Cumberland. Mrs. Bland was the daughter of an Italian Jewess named Romanzini, a very popular artist and singer. Bland, whom she married, was brother to Mrs. Jordan.

Whilst the Haymarket was closed Colman was busy. He supplied Covent Garden with a play called *The Poor Gentleman*, which was a tremendous success and set the whole town laughing. Munden, Fawcett, Lewis and Mrs. Mattocks appeared in it. But despite this and the continued success of the Haymarket, Colman was getting out of his depths in money matters. In February, 1800, there was further recourse to Arnold; we find him insuring his life as security for an advance from that gentleman, and blaming the success of *Pizarro* as the reason for his need. Fawcett concocted a pantomimical drama called *Obi, or Three Fingered Jack*, and it proved something of a novelty. Charles Kemble played Three Fingered Jack, and pretty Miss De Camp (afterwards Mrs. Charles Kemble) showed her talent—and her delightful figure— in boy's clothes. The music was by Dr. Arnold and the scenery by Whitmore. It was an out-and-out success and the credit was Fawcett's.

Holman's comic opera *What a Blunder* was produced—a brisk, bustling affair which kept the audience in happy mood. Johnstone had a fine Irish part and played it as only he could. Mrs. Mountain had a striking success in this light opera. Her simple manner, her good looks and her sweet voice made instant appeal.

The Haymarket was getting all the stars. And it had yet another success up its sleeve. This was a play from Colman's own pen called *Review: or The Wags of Windsor* and produced on August 31st. It was one of those strange freaks of the theatre which are hastily thrown together, probably as stop-gaps, and which turn out to be much greater successes than productions on which much care and expense have been lavished.

Colman wrote it at a sitting at Dr. Arnold's house in Duke Street. Dr. Arnold supplied the music from some scores he had by him, and characters were written in to sing them. Samuel James Arnold, the son, supplied two songs, one sung by Mrs. Bland and the other by Miss Decamp. It had no plot, no story; it was just a show, light, airy and amusing—the sort of thing called "intimate revue" to-day.

On July 24th, 1801, the theatre opened with a musical entertainment, *The Gipsy Prince*, with Kelly, who composed the music, as the hero— a forerunner evidently of Ivor Novello.

The nineteenth century, however, was not dawning too well for the Haymarket. The season of 1802 was not so successful as some which had gone before. A comedy called *Beggar My Neighbour* did its best to beggar Colman and was hooted from the stage. Fawcett made a big success as a musically mad footman in a farce called *The Sixty Third Letter*; there was an adaptation from the French called *The Voice of Nature* and a little burletta, *Fairy Revels*, played principally by children. But things were not good at all.

Colman looked around him and deplored the change in manners and customs. He could not decide if they had improved or deteriorated— nobody in his position ever could—but in his heart he thought they had taken a turn for the worse. Ladies' hoops had vanished from fashion—he thought this no improvement—and pigtails for men were a thing of the past. He took a gloomy view of this too. It was the old story of the changing times and the dislike for new ways by a conservative man and manager.

There was a very material grievance, too. The changing fashions meant alteration and replenishment of the wardrobe—and consequent expense.

Those majestic playhouses, the Patent Theatres, were again giving trouble. Instead of keeping regular hours or regular seasons, they now carried on until well into summertime, which was the harvest period for the Haymarket. It was very hard upon Colman. He was accustomed to engage the actors from the two Patent Theatres for his summer season. Now they never knew when they would be free, and consequently he could not be sure what sort of a company he could get. The situation was summed up by Fawcett in the Farewell Address at the end of the 1802 season:

"When a Royal Patent was about to be granted to the late Mr. Foote, it was enquired, with that justice which characterises the English Throne, what annual extent of term might be allowed him, without injury to the theatrical patents then existing in the metropolis. The proprietors of the Winter Theatres were interrogated on this point and in consequence of their documents, a patent was granted to Foote for his life to open a theatre annually from May 15th to September 15th inclusive. The Winter Theatres never closed precisely on the commencement of his term, but Foote was unique, and depended chiefly on his own writing and his own acting. A licence was given to the older Colman, on Foote's death, for the same annual term; but being aware that he could not, like his singularly gifted predecessor, depend on his own individual powers, he engaged a regular company of comedians, chiefly selected from the Winter Theatres, for whose assistance he was obliged to wait till those theatres closed. He ventured in every shape very deeply on a limited privilege, which this mode of speculation rendered still more limited. The younger Colman, our present proprietor, succeeded his father in the licence, but bought the property at the expense of several thousand pounds; and thus came into a theatre where the custom of depending on the movements of the Winter Theatres has now curtailed his short season of nearly one-third. The object at length in view is, to remedy the evil, without invidious and vain attempts to attack much more powerful theatres, who have an undoubted privilege of acting plays all the year round. The proprietor has no intention of tiring the public ear by a querulous appeal; he admits that others have the fullest right to make their property as productive as possible; he wishes merely to follow their example, and solicits your support in his efforts for establishing a company of actors totally independent of them. There are but three houses permitted to give you regular batches of plays in London; and this house (by far the most humble) sees no reason, when they will all be making their bread, on May 15th, why even three of a trade should not perfectly agree. Should his arrangements succeed, which are, even at this early period, actively forming, you will, on the re-opening of this theatre, greet the return to London of some favourites, who it is trusted will find no diminution of your protection. You will witness new and rising merit, which it is your marked practice to foster. There is no theatrical town in the United Kingdom which will not be resorted to, in the hope of procuring you the choicest produce; and in addition to other authors, you will be entreated, early in the season, to show your indulgence to the proprietors further attempts at dramatic composition; whose pen, he humbly hopes, not withstanding the long duration of your encouragement, is not yet quite worn out in your service."

This statement, it is chronicled, "was received throughout with frequent marks of approbation and concluded amidst loud and long-continued applause."

It has a familiar ring to-day, this manifesto of Colman's, but it was the somewhat novel means then whereby he hoped to cope with the inroads of the Lane and the Garden, and keep the Haymarket flag flying.

CHAPTER XVI

THE TAILORS' RIOT

A BRIEF mention has been made of Dicky Suett, a member of the Haymarket company. This actor is worthy of more than a passing reference. Born in Chelsea in 1755, he was a choirboy at Westminster Abbey at the age of ten, and at fourteen he was performing at Ranelagh. Soon afterwards he was a member of Foote's company at the Haymarket, and was also working at Marylebone Gardens and Finch's Grotto Gardens. Then he joined Tate Wilkinson, Foote's old friend or antagonist, now the patentee of the York Theatre, a great power in the North and about the best trainer of players the country ever had. Wilkinson saw his talent and brought him along well.

In 1780 Suett signed for a further two years with Wilkinson and almost immediately afterwards got an offer from Drury Lane. The generous Wilkinson, who remembered his own early struggles, put his own contract with Suett in the fire, and sent him to Town. Suett was an immediate success. He often deputised for Parsons when that fine actor was laid low with asthma. George III admired him very much— as a comedian. He played many of Parson's parts very well indeed, but he was best when he had a character to create. He was a real "low" comedian, popular with his fellow players, but his tragedy was drink. He seldom went home sober, and there was always a bottle on his breakfast table. He was tall, thin and ungainly, given to gagging and pulling funny faces. He was a good musician and wrote much music. A great popular favourite, he was a star at the Lane, the Garden and the Haymarket. He was followed at the latter theatre by a man whose talent was to outshine his own—Charles Mathews. Dicky Suett's father was a butcher with a most suitable name who had another job utterly dissimilar—that of guide in St. Paul's Cathedral. As a comedian, Suett was next to Parsons. He had a most notable collection of wigs of which he was very proud. A good singer, a good comedian, a good musician and a good joker—he punned even on his deathbed—he was buried in St. Paul's Churchyard.

Colman's company at the Haymarket was indeed a starry one, but he could not be sure of keeping them together, nor indeed of having them with him when he opened each season. Hence his decision to form his own exclusive Haymarket company of players. It was a fine idea, and the Haymarket was worthy of such a company. But it needed capital if it was to come to fruition, and Colman was short of money. He looked round for support.

He had been in touch with Tom Dibdin, the son of Charles Dibdin.

Once before Dibdin, who wrote plays at express speed and songs on the spur of the moment, had sent the Haymarket a play which had been refused.

Dibdin had lately written a five-act comedy which Harris, of Covent Garden, had rejected. Colman accepted it. He also gave Dibdin's sister-in-law an engagement at the Haymarket at £4 a week.

Colman then approached Dibdin with the offer of a quarter share in the Haymarket for £4,000. Dibdin was tempted, but he had just incurred much expense over Sadler's Wells Theatre, where he and his brother had bought a quarter share for £1,400, so he had not the ready money available. He borrowed £2,000 towards it and then heard the property might go into Chancery. Various delays took place, and ultimately Dibdin cried the bargain off. He always regretted it.

Colman still had to find his Haymarket company, and he decided once again on provincial novelty. Henderson, Elliston, Johnston and others had won London honours at the little theatre, and filled his coffers, so why not the provinces again? He fixed on an actor named Charles Mathews, then playing at York. Colman wrote him:

> "THEATRE ROYAL, HAYMARKET.
>
> "*14 Sept. 1802.*
>
> "SIR,—Your merits as an actor having been mentioned to me, give me leave to propose an engagement to you for next year at my theatre. It is my intention to commence the season positively on 15th of next May and to continue it to the 15th of the following September. Should you think it eligible to embrace the opportunity which I now offer you, of performing for four months before a London audience, I beg you will be kind enough to inform me on what terms you will give me your assistance. At all events, I shall thank you for a speedy answer, directed to me at Mr. Jewell's, 26 Suffolk Street, Charing Cross.
>
> "I am, Sir, your obedient servant,
>
> "G. COLMAN."

A very courteous letter indeed, but Mathews did not jump at the bait. To Colman's surprise, there was quite a correspondence before he could get Mathews to state his terms, and when he got them they took his breath away. Mathews wanted £10 a week and a benefit. Colman perceived that the times were changing with a vengeance. Here was a provincial actor with no London name at all demanding a star salary and a clear benefit.

Colman capitulated, with one condition. He gave Mathews an ordinary benefit.

> "SIR," he wrote on October 8th, 1802, "the terms which you have proposed are certainly high, and perhaps unprecedented, for a performer who has not yet felt the pulse of a London audience, but the

N

reasons stated for thus fixing your ultimatum appear to be founded on justice, to put vanity out of the question. I waive therefore all mention of any risk incurred on my part in my new speculation and embrace your offer. But to prevent all mistakes, permit me to state precisely what I conceive to be the engagement. Ten Pounds a week and a benfit, of which benefit you pay the usual charges. You will perform from the 15th May to the 15th September inclusive. If you engage in London after your appearance with me, you give me the preference on a re-engagement. If you think any short legal memorandum requisite between us, I am willing to enter into it. If you conceive the letters that pass between us as sufficient, I am quite content that it should remain an agreement upon honour. Pray send me two lines speedily, which will be conclusive. I will, when we meet in the summer, do everything in my power to contribute to your reputation with the public and your comfort in my theatre.

"I am, Sir, your obedient servant,

"G. COLMAN.

"PS.—Of course your attendance will be expected in town a week or ten days previously to opening the theatre, as I begin with novelties."

Mathews accepted, but was concerned with the part he should play for his debut. He asked if Colman was quite determined to open with new plays? Colman wrote him a long and characteristic letter. He sent to Mathews, in confidence, an outline of his plans, his ideas for new plays and ballets, and a lot of good advice as to how a player new to London should make his choice for a debut. He said that Mathews called himself a low comedian. He wanted to know what sort of low comedian he considered himself, in which particular line he shone. And his mind evidently ran on what are now called "stunts" with which to establish his new star. For he says:

"First impressions often make or mar. I remember, soon after Munden's first appearance in London, he ate, with uncommon success, a hundred pounds weight of plum puddings in *Two Strings to Your Bow*. This feat was new to a London audience. He had a good character in it, in which nobody had been seen before. Do you recollect anything in which you might make your appearance, under the same favourable circumstances?"

Mathews had no recollection of such a thing himself and probably no desire to rival Munden in his pudding-consuming feats. But to show that there is little new in the theatre, a century and a quarter afterwards London playgoers were to read of the number of sausages consumed on the stage at the Haymarket Theatre during the run of a play called *The Phantom Light* by that magnificent comedian, Gordon Harker.

In the March of 1803, Colman and his son (a captain in the Army) went up to York to see for himself what manner of actor he had engaged in Mr. Mathews. A friendship began between the two men which lasted a lifetime. They liked each other and Colman was vastly impressed by Mathews both on and off the stage. So much so that Mathews' request for his wife to be engaged at the Haymarket as well as himself was instantly granted. Tate Wilkinson, who had recommended Mathews, had made no mistake. Colman read the whole company his new play, *John Bull, or An Englishman's Fireside*—and let them play it too. Afterwards it scored a tremendous success at Covent Garden. Mathews delighted Colman with his imitation of Suett. They were the best of friends.

On May 10th, Mathews arrived, and found that Colman had also secured Elliston to return to the theatre of his former triumphs. He was not putting all his eggs into the Mathews' basket. Elliston was leading man and also Stage Manager.

The new and exclusive Haymarket company opened on May 16th, 1803. They performed a prelude called *No Prelude, The Jew*, with Elliston as Sheva, and O'Keefe's *The Agreeable Surprise*.

Charles Mathews played Jabel in *The Jew* and Lingo in *The Agreeable Surprise*. His success was immediate and tremendous. Press and public acclaimed him. Colman and the Haymarket had done it again. The New Company was an established success right away, for a very signal honour was paid to the theatre, the manager and the actors. The very second night was "By Royal Command," a hitherto unprecedented thing. The new comedian drew Royalty at once, and Royalty had not been near the Haymarket for nine years. And what is more, His Majesty —and Her Majesty—came thrice in the first fortnight. It was indeed, Theatre Royal, Haymarket.

Mathews made a huge hit in a farce called *Mrs. Wiggins*. It had a very stormy reception when first introduced, but was persisted with and finally grew into a big success. This was due to the way in which Mathews built it up. Colman wrote a farce under the *nom-de-plume* Arthur Griffinhoofe called *Love Laughs at Locksmiths*. Again Mathews and Elliston scored heavily. There was also a drama called *The Maid of Bristol*.

But despite Royal visits and Elliston's and Mathews' immense success, the company was disbanded when the season closed and Colman went back to his plan of picking from the two big theatres.

Mathews went on tour and eventually to Drury Lane. This did not affect his friendship with Colman nor his frequent performances at the Haymarket summer seasons. He was a star, thanks to that theatre, and he remained one.

Charles Mathews (now known as "The Elder" because of his brilliant son Charles) was born at No. 18, Strand, London, for so long the Street of Actors, in 1776. The site of his birthplace is now covered by Charing

Cross Station. His father was a bookseller who specialised in religious books and also preached sermons. He and his wife, although good people, were surrounded by a host of fanatical followers. Young Charles's first bit of histrionics was imitating some of these characters, which did him little good at home, and his subsequent imitation of a man selling eels in the street got him such a sound thrashing at the age of ten that he remained tender for weeks. He went to St. Martin's School and afterwards to Merchant Taylors. He imitated the masters. He received French lessons from the Mme. Cotterille mentioned previously and there he met Elliston and performed plays with him. Strange that the two should be together when Mathews came to make his London debut and strange that both should win fame at the Haymarket. Mathews was now bursting to go on the stage. He played in private theatricals in a loft in Short's Gardens, off Drury Lane, and here he met Charles Young, who will shortly enter the Haymarket story. Three great Haymarket stars had their youth intertwined.

Young Mathews and a youth named Litchfield paid £15 15s. to be allowed to play *Richard III* at the Richmond Theatre. They fought such a tremendous combat, both being proud of their swordsmanship and both refusing to be killed, that the audience revolted. Mathews finally got a job in Dublin with a defaulting manager.

It was in Swansea that he met the girl who was to be his wife. She was in distress. He was earning 12s. a week, but so much did her story move him, so much did her charm and beauty enthral him, that he proposed and was accepted. They married. She tried to augment their small income by writing novels, by which she earned a tiny sum, but she contracted consumption. On her deathbed she asked her husband to marry her friend, a girl in the same company, for whose kindness she had much to be thankful and for whom she had a deep affection. In due course, that girl became the second Mrs. Mathews.

From Swansea Mathews joined Tate Wilkinson, and his salary there was £1 per week. Nor was Wilkinson's reception of him very encouraging. Mathews got an appointment and said he was a low comedian. He was very tall and very, very thin. "Ugh, what a maypole!" exclaimed Wilkinson. "Sir, you are too tall for low comedy. I never saw anything so thin to be alive. Why, sir, one hiss would blow you off the stage." The old manager advised him to go back to his father and earn his living at an honest trade. It took much persuasion before he would give him a job. But Mathews got his chance and took it. Wilkinson admitted his mistake handsomely. He praised him and encouraged him. He gave him opportunities. So well did Mathews please the York audience that his benefit reached £96 15s., a second-best record. And from his engagement with Wilkinson he went to the Haymarket.

During the winter, when he was playing in Liverpool, he entreated Colman to give an opportunity to a friend of his, Mr. Young—Charles Mayne Young. This was the lad with whom he had acted as amateur in the loft in Drury Lane. Colman played with the idea, thought it over, and wrote that he could not do it. The expense was too great. He had Elliston for at least two seasons, and things were pretty close as regards profit. Although he did not tell Mathews, he was in low water.

The season of 1804 was without incident of importance. Mathews was back and was consolidating his success. Elliston was getting famous and as Stage Manager was already beginning those speeches before the curtain, those appeals to the audience, for every conceivable reason and often for no reason at all. They were his hall-mark throughout his whole career. Elliston was a born showman.

Colman now made his financial decision. He had been treating with Tom Dibdin to bring in capital and be a partner. Well for him, and for Dibdin, if this had happened. But it did not. So Colman took in his brother-in-law Morris, a man called Winston and an attorney named Tabourdine. This was the beginning of the end of Colman.

For some reason the Haymarket had always responded to personal management. This is true of so many theatres. One manager, or perhaps a joint captaincy, can succeed. But in the multiplicity of counsels there is theatrical disaster. Theatrical history emphasises it over and over again. The Committee at Drury Lane brought that theatre as low as it had ever been. Despite the success—the overwhelming success—of Edmund Kean, they got into financial difficulties. It is true that the Triumvirate at the same theatre consisted of three people, but they were actor-managers and practical folk, who knew their business at first hand and worked in their own playhouse.

The Haymarket had been an individual house and its steady success was due entirely to this. It had been a house where the control was either in an actor-manager or in a manager-dramatist. Fielding, Theophilus Cibber, Samuel Foote, George Colman Senior and George Colman Junior were all practical men of the theatre, all of them dramatists and some of them actors too. The Haymarket, a theatre with a personality, responded to personal care. It had no time for amateurs. Now it was saddled with three, who could outvote and control the one man of the theatre amongst them. And the 1805 season, under the new régime, started with storms and was stormy throughout.

Colman had engaged Dowton to strengthen his company. This fine actor was the son of an innkeeper in Exeter and had been well educated. He was apprenticed to an architect, but devoted more time to perform-ances at a so-called private "theatre" run by some of the stage-struck youths of Exeter. In a performance there of *The Revenge* he made a terrific success as Carlos. The plaudits decided him. He would be an actor. He skipped his articles and joined up with some strollers at Ashburton, a place of no theatrical importance then or now, and there he made his debut in the part mentioned above. So eager was he to act that he gave a new coat off his back to another actor to get that player to stand down in his favour. The troupe had a bad time, even for strollers, and Dowton, nearly starved, had to give it up and go home. Here he was welcomed, but, with good food and comfort, the urge revived, and he was off again, this time to Weymouth. He did well, and he came back to his own city to play Romeo, Macbeth and all the leads in Shakespearean tragedy. And Exeter applauded its Thespian son. He went to Kent, joining a company run by a Mrs. Baker, who controlled that area. He married her daughter. He was now settled in life.

Cumberland, the dramatist, whose gift as talent-picker was better than his talent for plays, recommended him to Drury Lane and he was engaged there. He had heard that Elliston had made a great success as Sheva in *The Jew*, and he chose the same part for his debut. He made a wise choice and a big success. His portrayal of the old Jew, never burlesqued, never overplayed, never out of the character, was a thing of beauty. He was not a one-character man by any means, for he stood supreme amongst his contemporaries for his playing of Sir Hugh Evans in *The Merry Wives*, Old Hardcastle in *She Stoops to Conquer*, Clod in *The Young Quaker*, Sir Anthony Absolute and many more. He was a truly great Malvolio and Falstaff. There appears to have been great charm and richness in his acting, and a gift of real characterisation at a period when there was tendency to buffoonery. He had a peculiar characteristic, very unusual amongst star actors—he would never allow his name to appear on the bills larger than those of all the rest. He detested star billing as a means of publicity. Of course, it may have been that his objection was in itself good publicity.

With such a trio as Dowton, Mathews and Elliston, things should have been fine at the Haymarket. But, probably because there were too many masters and considerable interference, there was constant trouble back stage.

Despite their long friendship, Mathews and Elliston had a first-class row. Elliston was never averse to a fight, and he was also a man of dictatorial methods and ideas. He was Stage Manager, a position equal to general manager of to-day. He chose to call Mathews to order. He did it in a public and peremptory manner. He told Mathews that he was not doing his best in the part he played in *The Village, or the World's Epitome*, a new comedy by Cherry. Mathews resented this, and replied that all concerned in the play had done their work as well as Elliston had done his—and some of them better. Elliston's answer was a very rude word, sometimes described as a form of military adieu, and he got a good sound, well-aimed punch on the head from Mathews. There was, of course, a tremendous scene and gigantic trouble, for a back-stage fight has enormous repercussions. The two men were estranged and the discipline back stage suffered. However, after a while, a reconciliation was brought about, not by Colman or his partners in management, who appear to have been supine in the matter—or perhaps afraid—but by two mutual friends of the combatants, Warner Phipps and Sir John Carr.

Things had hardly settled down from this trouble than a fight of a

far larger and more general kind ensued. There was another good
old-fashioned genuine Haymarket riot.

Dowton was to have a benefit. He chose, as his vehicle for the
occasion, that old play which Foote had presented (and of which he may
have been author, although he denied it) *The Tailors, or a Tragedy for
Warm Weather*. The moment the announcement was made the trouble
started. The tailors of London considered this play a scandalous slight
upon them and their necessary, if undistinguished, profession.

Letters poured in upon Dowton and Colman, demanding the
cancellation of the performance, the substitution of another play, the
shelving for ever of *The Tailors*—or forcible steps would be taken to
stop it.

Sturdy old Devonshire Dowton scoffed at the idea. A pack of tailors
to interfere with him? Perish the thought! What Colman had to say is
not on record, but Dowton was very decided—he would play *The
Tailors* and be damned to them for a pack of snips.

The London tailors held indignation meetings. Feeling ran to fever
heat. Dowton got a letter which informed him that 17,000 tailors would
be in the theatre to hiss the show. How 17,000 tailors were to be found
in London at that time, and how they would all have got into the little
Haymarket Theatre needs some explaining. Dowton treated the threat
with contempt. So another letter came for Dowton, bearing the menacing signature of "Death," informing the actor that if he did not think
the wrath of 17,000 tailors in the theatre would be enough, there would
be another 10,000 tailors outside the theatre, all intent on destruction.
Their indignation seems to have made the arithmetic of the tailors very
faulty, unless the tailoring business at that time was considerably
overcrowded.

Neither the management nor Dowton was at all perturbed. The evening came, and it was apparent at once that if there were actors pretending to be tailors on the stage, there were tailors who were not pretending
to be angry in the audience. The theatre was full of them, even if they
did not reach the astronomical number threatened, and they made
enough noise as if they had been up to the full-estimated strength. And
outside, too, if there were not the reported 10,000, there was a sizeable
angry milling mob of gentlemen of the needle and shears, all anxious
to make a proper misfit of the theatre, the play—and Dowton.

Inside there was pandemonium. Actors of those days were used to
this and the play went on. Dowton entered as Francisco. The din
reached a crescendo, and a pair of shears, hurtling through the air,
stuck in the stage perilously near to Dowton. This was past a joke.
Downton immediately came down to the front and offered a reward of
£20 for the apprehension of the scoundrel who had thrown the shears.
The tailors ignored him and the row went on. The crowd outside, too,
got very ugly. Not a word could be heard inside, and outside there was
talk of firing the theatre.

Mr. Aaron Graham, the principal magistrate at Bow Street, was sent for. He came post-haste, bringing his constables with him. But he could not make himself heard nor were his men a sufficient force to cope with the rioters. Reinforcements were sent for, but they too were powerless against the now infuriated and dangerous mob. Mr. Graham called out the military and along came the Dragoons. They charged the mob in the street whilst others dismounted and entered the theatre. The redcoats did what the constables could not. The tailors were no match for the soldiers. They broke and ran, but not quickly enough for some of them. Sixteen scared and sorry tailors appeared before Mr. Graham the following morning after a night in the cells, to which they had been taken none too gently. They were held to bail in £50 each and had to find two sureties in £40 each. They paid large fines. The Tailors' Riot was over.

But there was a brighter spot at the Haymarket towards the very end of the season. Another new star was found and made his debut—a man destined to go right to the top of the tree. For Liston made his London debut there on September 15th, 1805, just before the season closed. He played Sheepface in *The Village Constable*, and he leapt into fame. He became a great figure of the stage of his day, and he raised the status of comedians as a whole. Up to the time of Liston, the tragedians got the big money and the comedians were less well paid. Liston was the first comedian to draw a salary greater than any tragedian—other than an actor-manager. And he began at the home of comedy, the Haymarket Theatre.

John Liston was born in 1777. He was well educated and he came of a respectable family. He began his career as an usher at St. Martin's School, Castle Street, Leicester Square. He did not remain there long, and even while schoolmastering, he was in the habit of providing an extra turn for players taking benefits at the Haymarket. Naturally, the excitement and applause of the theatre outweighed the attractions of trying to teach unruly boys, and he left his scholars to become a strolling player. He played heroes in tragedy, for which he was totally unfitted in appearance, but he persisted. No comedian ever thinks he is properly cast. They all want to play tragedy or heroics. Finally, he got an engagement with Stephen Kemble, the fat brother of Mrs. Siddons, who was running theatres in Edinburgh, Newcastle and the North. Kemble saw the possibilities of Liston and persuaded him, with some difficulty, to play old men, comic rustics and the like. Liston did not like it, but the public did, and when he found his fame increasing—and his salary—he shed his heroic ideas and worked with a will. But from time to time, in his career, he would play tragic or heroic parts, just to show them he could.

Colman, always on the look-out, heard about him, probably remembered him from his obscure benefit days and gave him his chance. No better part than Sheepface could have been his for his debut! It described him.

Liston was a great, a very great comedian, and his face was no small part of his fortune.

Lamb said: "There is one face of Farley, one face of Knight, one (but what a one it is) of Liston. . . ." It was long, it was vacant, it was laughter-provoking, and it was very grave. For Liston was a very grave comedian. He was of grave demeanour on and off the stage. What he said was of less value than the way he said it. He was a quiet comedian, and when a quiet comedian is good he is the best. Liston could take what liberties he liked with his audiences; he had them in the hollow of his hand. His appearance was always greeted with yells of laughter long before he spoke. His manner was deliberate and he never gave the slightest suggestion that he was playing for or getting laughs. He got them with unconcerned ease and he never descended to buffoonery. He was said to suffer from a nervous complaint, which made it necessary for him, very often, to drink a whole bottle of brandy during the course of the evening's performance. But it made no difference to his acting—he was most reliable.

He was a great practical joker, he had a quick wit and he was a punster too. But it was hard to get the better of him in repartee, despite his looks and his slow manner. His idea of fun was sometimes embarrassing to the recipient. One day he was walking across Leicester Square with a friend, Miller, the bookseller, and was talking with relish of the tripe he was to have for supper. "It's beastly stuff," said Miller. Liston stopped and stared. "You don't like tripe?" he queried in a very loud and astonished voice. "No," was the reply. "You don't like tripe?" bellowed Liston at the top of his lungs. People began to stare, and stop to listen. "Ssh! For goodness' sake," said the now embarrassed bookseller. "Don't speak so loud." But Liston took no heed. He turned to the passers-by and, pointing at Miller, he shouted: "There's a man who doesn't like tripe." It takes a very short time for a crowd to collect in London and this yell of Liston's brought people flocking. Miller, unable to bear the indignity, made a bolt for it. "There goes the man who doesn't like tripe," shouted Liston, whilst the interested onlookers took up the cry and heartily booed the unfortunate victim of the actor's trick. Then Liston departed on his way to eat his stewed tripe, quite happy in what he had done.

In his time, there was an old gentleman who regularly attended the annual dinners of the Royal General Theatrical Fund who always insisted on telling the same long, pointless and interminable story. As is their wont, the actors guyed him. It was left to Liston to bring things to a head. The annual banquet came, and the old man rambled along with his story. Liston slipped out of the room. As the saga ended its seemingly nonstop course, a messenger entered the room and announced that His Excellency the Persian Ambassador was without and begged admittance. He had heard that a gentleman at this banquet had a most wonderful story, the fame of which had penetrated to his own land.

Could permission be given for him, the Ambassador, to be allowed to come in and hear this story at first hand from its reciter? Permission was accorded, and the Persian Ambassador, in full Eastern finery and blazing with diamonds, made a stately and impressive entrance. The old bore, very proud, a little nervous, but highly elated, told his story all over again, to the almost painfully suppressed amusement of the rest of the company. But the Ambassador listened in dignified silence, not a flicker of an eyelid, not a muscle moving in that impassive face. At last it was over and the Ambassador, through his interpreter (also in Eastern costume), expressed his gratification and his thanks. He made a slow and dignified exit. The banquet bore was overwhelmed with congratulations. Then Liston returned to the room, having got rid of his costume and make-up. He approached the story-teller. He said how sorry he was to have been called away when such a marvellous thing was happening and added gravely: "I am delighted, sir, that you rendered the story so effective to a person so particularly ignorant of the language." "Oh, yes," said the victim of the joke, "and so particularly ugly, Mr. Liston."

He went from the Haymarket to Covent Garden and then to Drury Lane, under Elliston, where he had £40 a week. When Mme. Vestris opened the Olympic, she engaged him and paid him £100 a week. Talfourd said that when he played Launcelot Gobbo, and Kean played Shylock, it was one of the richest combinations of talent ever seen.

He left the stage in 1837. He spent the last years of his life standing at the window of his house, which faced Hyde Park Corner, with his watch in his hand, timing the omnibuses. If one of them was late he was most annoyed. He died a rich man.

Boaden gives perhaps the best description of him:

"He must be seen to be comprehended. Other actors labour to be comic; I see nothing like labour or system in Liston. In person, he is stately and even grave in expression . . . he does not concur in general effect—he is alone, as well with others on the scene as when he enters to soliloquise, or rather enjoy himself with the audience. . . ."

Liston once asked Mathews to play at his benefit. Mathews had another engagement and excused himself by saying, "I would if I could, but I can't split myself in halves." "I don't know that," retorted Liston. "I have often seen you play in two pieces." With all his peculiarities he was highly respectable and—brandy apart—led a very good life. He was happily married to Miss Tyrer, of Covent Garden Theatre.

John Liston takes his place in the portrait gallery of great Haymarket actors, not by any means the least of them.

Liston was there the next season, too, in 1806. Elliston and Mathews were with him—it was a galaxy of stars. The summer seasons of the

little theatre were now an eagerly looked-forward-to event, not at all
surprising with three such artists to entertain, with excellent support
as well.

At his benefit that season Mathews gave, for the first time, a ven-
riloquial entertainment. It was such a success that Colman asked him
to repeat it every now and again, because he was short of plays and
novelties. Mathews did so with pleasure and it remained a popular
Haymarket item.

The only new play of note was *We Fly by Night*, by Colman himself.
The Haymarket was succeeding, but Colman was being swamped. His
partners were interfering more and more, and his financial position was
getting steadily worse and worse. Ruin was facing him—and he hoped
that it might not engulf his beloved theatre as well.

CHAPTER XVII

THE AMAZING "ROMEO" COATES

WHEN 1807 arrived, Colman was getting tired. He promised himself a complete week off, during which he would do no work. He was just starting his idle holiday when his old friend Jack Bannister turned up, an immense manuscript under his arm. It was the script of a show which he had written and which he called "Bannister's Budget." He wanted Colman to knock it into shape and he wanted it done at once. Colman could not refuse his Jack. He did the work and Bannister went off rejoicing.

Some months afterwards Bannister returned to Town. Colman asked him how the "Budget" had succeeded. Bannister said it was likely to last him all his life as a vehicle, and in virtue of what Colman had done towards it, he cancelled a bond which Colman had given him for money lent.

Colman was amazed; he had not looked for any payment. But Bannister was in earnest. To make sure, he wrote to Colman:

"For fear of accidents, I think it necessary to inform you that Fladgate, your attorney, is in possession of your bond to me for £700. As I consider it is fully discharged, it is proper you should have this acknowledgment under my hand. J.B."

What a friend—and what a relief to Colman! For he had a lot of debts now and he was in real trouble. He had been assailed in *The Dramatic Mirror*, which had said that his admission of partners "enabled the proprietors to completely liquidate all the demands which had for some time past involved the house in temporary embarrassment." Colman was most annoyed about this. He maintained that the theatre was never embarrassed, but that on the contrary it was a most profitable speculation. It was a different matter when it came to his own affairs. As the Haymarket was, until he took partners, his own property, it seems a little difficult to separate the two things. True, the Haymarket could and did pay its way, but its limited season could never keep pace with Colman's needs. It was Sheridan and Drury Lane all over again on a smaller scale.

He did not start the season in 1807 until June 15th. He had had the theatre newly decorated and the pit enlarged by doing away with some waste space in front of the proscenium. This had been made possible by the new capital.

He wanted a new star, however, and at last he yielded to Mathews'

-equest and engaged Charles Mayne Young. The company also included Mathews, Fawcett, Liston, De Camp, Chapman, Taylor, Mrs. Grove, Noble, Palmer Junr., Waddy, Bennet (a singer from Bath), Mrs. Gibbs, Mrs. Taylor, Mrs. Mathews, Mrs. Liston, Mrs. Powell, and Mrs. Litchfield. This latter lady was a tower of strength. She was the only daughter of a clergyman, John Sylvester Hay, who held the living of Maldon in Essex. He appears to have been a doctor as well, for he had been ship's surgeon on a famous East Indiaman and for a time Head Surgeon of the Royal Hospital in Calcutta. In her extreme youth she had seen the Siddons' play *Isabella*, and from that moment, despite all family opposition, she determined on the stage as a career. She started at the Richmond Theatre as Julia in *The Surrender of Calais*. The audience included no less a person than Mrs. Jordan, who was delighted with the young debutante. She played more parts there and then went to Scotland, where her success was considerable. Dumfries adored her and when she left she had a letter from Robert Burns, asking her to pay a return visit. Aicken engaged her for Liverpool, but she quarrelled with him and came to London. She then married a Mr. Litchfield, a light of the literary world, and left the stage. But she came back to play at Mrs. Davenport's benefit. Here Harris of Covent Garden saw her and engaged her for that house, where she made a big success as Lady Macbeth amd afterwards scored very heavily in a very difficult part, Ottila in the tragedy of *Alfonso*. Upon the playing of her part the whole success of the play depended. She scored a triumph. She was leading lady to Master Betty, the infant Roscius. She had been at the Haymarket before, and now returned to play opposite Young.

For it was the debut of this actor which was the chief event at the Haymarket that season. And once again new actor and old theatre scored a joint triumph. Young joined the ranks of the great ones who had graduated at the Little Theatre in the Hay.

This fine actor is little remembered to-day, and that is a pity. He was an actor of the Kemble school—with the grand manner. He was born in Fenchurch Street in 1777, a year which seems to have brought forth fine actors and fine plays—for it is the year of *The School for Scandal* and many fine players. His father was a surgeon. As a child he was taken to Copenhagen to visit his uncle, who was Court Physician there. The King, Queen and Queen Dowager were so taken with the child that they wanted to keep him always with them. When he left they gave him a purse, which the Queen had made, filled with gold, a watch and his portrait, of which a replica stood upon the King's own table.

He went to Eton, but financial trouble at home cut short his education there and he was sent to Merchant Taylors. His father had taken to bad ways, and so desperate did the position become that young Charles and his brothers took their mother away and Charles charged

himself with her support. He got a job as a clerk. But he evidently
fancied himself as an actor, for he met and performed with Mathews
at the loft theatre in Short's Gardens. He got tired of the monotony
of commercial life and took the plunge. In 1798 he made his pro
fessional debut at Liverpool, under the name of Green, as Young
Norval. He must have been pretty good, for he was engaged for "leading
business" at Manchester directly afterwards. From thence he went to
Edinburgh, where he took the town by storm and became a social lion
as well. In 1802 he was a guest of Sir Walter Scott, and their friendship
thus begun, was lifelong. In 1804 he married Julia Grimani, a beautiful
woman who had played Juliet at the Haymarket in that year. She had
gone to the provinces after that and found herself in the same company
as Young—back again at Liverpool. They played opposite each other.
Their stage love became a real thing and they married. They were
deeply and passionately devoted to each other, but fifteen months later
she died, giving birth to a son, afterwards the Rev. Julian Young.
Charles Mayne Young never married again. He survived her for fifty
years, but he kept her memory always in his heart. As he grew older his
love for his dead wife grew even more intense. He would take out her
miniature and gaze at it with tears running down his cheeks. And he
would handle tenderly a lock of her chestnut hair, which was always
with him. When he died in his turn, his last words were: "Thank God,
I shall soon see my Julia."

This was the man whom Mathews had recommended and with whom
Colman at last got into touch. Again the manager's breath was taken
away. He had been shocked when Mathews had demanded £10 per
week. Young wanted £20, and a benefit. This was almost too much for
Colman. He wrote Young one of his letters. He said the terms asked
"much exceeded any bargain formed within my memory between a
manager of the Haymarket Theatre and a performer coming to try
his fortunes upon the London stage." But he did not want to lose
Young, and made a counter-offer, which is probably what Young
expected. Said Colman: "We propose, then, £14 a week and a benefit,
you to take all the profits of that benefit, however great, after paying the
established charges. Should there be a deficiency, we ensure that you
shall clear £100 by it. This, upon mature deliberation, is all we think
prudence enables us to offer." Young accepted.

He played at the Haymarket for the first time on June 22nd, 1807.
He played Hamlet. He was young, handsome, graceful and dignified.
He had a fine voice and a grand manner, and consequently was a very
great success.

Amidst the applause which greeted him at the close there came one
clear, distinct, decided, venomous hiss. Young gazed at the part of the
house from which came this solitary sound of dissent. It was as he had
thought. The man who was hissing him, who was doing his best to mar
his success, was his own father. That man had never forgiven his

children for siding with their mother against him and for rescuing her
from his disgraceful treatment. He pursued Charles and tried to harm
him, to disgrace him wherever he could. He did the same to his other
sons. One of them he assaulted before a coachload of onlookers. The
young man stopped the coach and told the passengers it was his father
who had struck him.

But that hiss in the Haymarket Theatre was drowned in the great
applause and the father got no revenge that, or any other night. Young
was a Haymarket star. He played Hamlet, Don Felix, Osmond, Sir
Edward Mortimer, Rolla, Hotspur, Petruchio, Gondibert, the Stranger
and Harry Dornton that season, besides several other original roles in
new and now-forgotten plays. What actor to-day could stand up to it?

He had critics, as had all new actors of quality. *The Dramatic Mirror*,
Colman's enemy, carped a bit about him, pointed out some defects,
but had to admit they were the defects of youth, and it was expected
he would conquer them. He did. He had a slight tendency to lisp, but
there was great and untiring energy, animation and ardour—and a lot
of sound common sense.

Young had a great career. He was engaged by John Philip Kemble for
the Garden, and even with Kemble and Cooke in the same company
Young held his own. He played Cassius to Kemble's Brutus and many
people preferred him of the two. The last time they ever played together
was in this play. Kemble came to Young's dressing-room after the performance and gave the young actor several of his "props" that he had
used in favourite characters. He begged him to keep them as memen-
toes of their many battles on the stage. "We have often had high words
on the stage, Young, but never off," he said. Young was immensely
touched and stammered his thanks. Kemble wrung him by the hand and
hurried from the room. Young stayed at Covent Garden until 1822.
Then a dispute as to salary, brought about by the emptying of Covent
Garden through the success of Kean at Drury Lane, caused him to
leave there. Drury Lane engaged him at £50 a night and he played with
Kean in *Othello* and other plays. Covent Garden had to pay him the
same salary to get him back. He would have accepted £25 previously,
but they cut him down to £20. Now they had to pay his terms.

He refused a lucrative tour in America because he wanted to retire.
He made his farewell as Hamlet at Covent Garden in 1832—the part he
had played at his Haymarket debut. Mathews appeared as Polonius,
Macready as the Ghost. So great was the demand for seats that the
orchestra was used for the public and the receipts were £643. The sum
of £81 was returned to those who could not even find standing room.

Young died in 1856 at the age of seventy-nine. His private life was
beyond reproach, his generosity something to wonder at. Even when he
lay sick with his final illness, beside his bed stood a mahogany table with
an ever-open drawer. He could not be better pleased than when someone asked for help for a good object. His hand would go into the

drawer. "What will you have?" he would say, and gold and silver would be showered out. His parting injunction was always: "Mind you let me know when you want more for the poor creature." He lay there in a richly brocaded dressing-gown, a black velvet cap, with dark eyes gleaming from under strong, bushy eyebrows. His mouth was always firmly closed, except when some joke or antic of his adored grandchildren made him laugh, or he thought of a funny story, of which he had a great fund. One who knew him aptly wrote: "He wore the grand old name of gentleman unsullied to the end, and died in the fullness of his years beloved, honoured and lamented."

Such was the Haymarket actor who had been hissed by his own father at the testing point of his career.

During the same season there were two musical pieces by Theodore Hook, *The Fortress* and *Music Mad*. And there was a very successful revival of *The Critic* with Fawcett as Puff, Mathews as Sir Fretful Plagiary, and Mrs. Liston as Tilburina. Liston played Don Ferolo, Mathews made a great success as Sir Fretful. Leigh Hunt wrote a wonderful pæan of praise about it.

The year 1808 saw a long-drawn-out battle by correspondence between Mrs. Inchbald, the dramatist, and Colman, the manager-dramatist.

It was to be a disastrous year for Colman, in almost every sense. He was now feeling the adverse effects of his partnership and things are to happen which would affect him and also his theatre.

There were changes in the company when the season opened on June 15th. Those changes were not altogether for the better. But Young was there as leading tragedian, whilst Fawcett, Mathews and Liston remained the trio of comedians unequalled in Town.

The first new play was a farce, adapted from the French by Charles Kemble and called *Plot and Counter Plot*. It did pretty well. But a revival of Lillo's *Fatal Curiosity* staged for the purpose of letting Young play old Wilmot was killed by a spell of very hot weather.

Much faith was placed in a play by Colman called *Africans, or War, Love and Duty*. It was far from being Colman's best play. It was an unbalanced affair, with highfalutin dialogue where simplicity would have been best. Colman had tried to graft his poetic gift on to a thing which required speed and action, and the two things, as usual, tripped each other up. Young, Farley and Fawcett played three brothers and Fawcett did the best—he almost saved the show. Liston was dragged into the story to play a character called Henry Augustus Mug—a careless bit of interpolation. But Liston was himself, and that was all that mattered. He supplied the humour and he sang a song which always got a treble encore.

But the Haymarket was now in a most curious situation. Colman, its guiding genius and its moving spirit, its manager and its dramatist, was endeavouring to steer its course from a debtor's prison. His embarrassment had closed upon him. He was in the King's Bench Prison. He had

been put there because of a debt which his father had contracted to the
father of the man who had him locked up. That was the main cause, but
there were contributory causes as well. Colman's finances were in a
shocking state. So here was one of the three great theatres of London
being directed from inside prison walls. This might have well deterred
an ordinary man, but the hopeful, mercurial disposition of Colman
rose above it. A letter from him to Charles Mathews speaks volumes.
Mathews had asked him to dine—and Colman had promised. Then he
remembered that he was not a free man and the following letter arrived
for Mathews:

"November 11th, 1808.

"DEAR MATHEWS,—'I 'gin to pull in resolution.'

"When I talked of holiday Sundays, I felt bolder than, upon
reflection, I ought to do, with a due respect to the regulations of our
college, into which I have more particularly enquired since we met.
So another day, in the course of the month, I will, if you please,
attend you, and be kind enough to look out a moon for me, for I
incline to the party of the Lunatics, and am no follower of the Prince
of Darkness, on the King's Highway. So, Sheridan and Hood for
ever! No Paull! God Save the King! Bless the crier! Huzza! Huzza!

"G. COLMAN."

Not a very depressed letter from a man in a debtor's jail. The invitation was to a cottage which Mathews had taken out at Colney Hatch—
then in the heart of the country. Hence Colman's desire for a light
night. The "college" was, of course, the King's Bench, and the reference
to Sunday holiday was because on that day debtors were immune from
arrest.

Colman treated his residence within the "Rules" as a great joke. It
is likely that he could have raised the money to get out, but it is also
more than likely that his affairs were so involved that he was much
safer inside. He was, as it happens, only just inside, for he lived in the
last house of the "Rules" on the Westminster side—and he said he
would stop there to prove he could keep within the "Rules," no matter
what people thought. But all of a sudden he left that house and moved
further in. One of the windows looked on to the free world outside and
Colman said that he might, one night, fall out of it, on his way to bed,
and so "fix his bail."

But whilst the activities of Colman were thus circumscribed, his
partners were actively working against him and endeavouring to get
the Haymarket entirely into their own hands. As is so often the case,
they could not agree amongst themselves. Colman's real antagonist was
David Morris, his brother-in-law. Morris was jealous of him every
way, and a more undesirable partner could not well have been found
At one time Colman got very dandified in his dress and assumed
extremes of fashion. Morris would at once go to his tailors and have a

O

suit made exactly like Colman's. He was a dashing young man of no particular ability—except that he aped Colman. He even had his hair dressed in the same way. Colman knew all about this, and would ring the changes as often as he could, for the joy of seeing Morris try to keep up with him. Once, on his way to the theatre, Colman got badly splashed with mud. He arrived at the theatre with the mud still on him, waiting for it to dry before he brushed it off. Morris saw it, went outside and promptly splashed mud over himself so as to match up with Colman.

The plot to unseat Colman was a considerable time in the hatching, but his enforced absence in the King's Bench gave the conspirators every chance. David Morris saw in himself the proper man to control the little theatre and was determined to do so.

Prison or no, the Haymarket went on. In 1809 Liston, for his benefit, determined to play Octavian in *The Mountaineers*. It will be remembered that he had started off by playing heroic parts before he became a comedian, and the old urge still persisted. So he played this hero! What is more, he played it well. But the public would not believe it. They roared with laughter all the time and their amusement affected the rest of the company. Mrs. Johnson, who was playing opposite him, had the hardest job in the world to keep a straight face and must have suffered considerably. After *The Mountaineers*, they played *Dr. Last's Examination*, *Blue Devils* and that old Haymarket success of Fielding's, *Tom Thumb*. In all these Liston scored as a comedian and also spoke an address written by Colman.

Here a word is due to Mrs. George Colman. He had married into the Haymarket Theatre company, as previously stated, and his father had not increased his allowance. But his wife was a good woman and went on with her acting. She was a godchild of John Palmer's and had made her debut when very young at the Haymarket as Sally in Colman Senior's farce, *Man and Wife*. The title was prophetic. She and the dramatist's son did become man and wife. Her name was Logan, but when George Colman Junior married her she was already a widow, Mrs. Gibbs.

She went with Palmer to the ill-fated Royalty and supported him there as she did when that theatre was suppressed and he had to play where he could. She was a loyal soul. Later, she played at Drury Lane and Covent Garden. But, when her husband succeeded to the Haymarket, she went back there. He wrote special parts for her in his plays and she played and sung them very well indeed. She could depict the artless, languishing maid of the period or the bustling tomboy equally well. In later life, she played broad comedy parts excellently. Colman was lucky to have such an actress in his theatre, for there is no sign that she ever interfered or presumed on being the manager's wife, and she was an excellent wife at home, an honest, affectionate and big-hearted woman, with a pretty face and beautiful eyes. A contemporary

says of her: "Mrs. Gibbs was ever cheerful: and in any kind or charit-
able actions in the theatre, or elsewhere, she was always liberal and
unostentatious."

In 1809, the company at the Haymarket included Young, Mathews,
Liston and Jones, a fine team. A play by Theodore Hook, called *Killing
No Murder*, was banned by the Censor, but on alteration it was produced and ran for thirty-five nights—a long run then. *The Foundling of
the Forest*, by Dimond, ran for twenty-five nights, so the season was
prosperous. But the rift within the lute had widened and now gaped
open. There was internecine war. Morris declared against Colman, but
Winston sided with him.

The first sign the public had of the battle of the Haymarket was an
advertisement in the newspapers of the day, dated January 29th, 1810.
In this Morris flung down the gauntlet with a vengeance:

"THEATRE ROYAL, HAYMARKET.
"As joint Proprietor and Treasurer, Mr. Morris thinks it right to
apprise all Persons engaged at this theatre for the year 1809 (except
Mr. and Mrs. Liston) that such engagement terminated on the
15th September last."

This was a nice state of things for the Haymarket. It may seem
strange that the announcement should be retroactive. The reason was
that Morris was trying to snatch power and was acquainting everyone
that unless they had a contract to which he was also a signatory they
were not properly engaged. Colman did not worry about contracts—
his letter to Mathews shows that. He had no contracts with anyone.
The actors took his word, and he kept it. By his gage of battle, Morris
intended to stop all that and show that Colman was not sole arbiter of
fate at the Haymarket.

But manifesto or no manifesto, Colman for the time being pursued
his way. In the disputed 1810 season he got his old friend Jack Bannister
back again to the Haymarket. He played his old parts with great
success. This might have upset Mathews, but Colman's tact and careful
judgment prevented any collision. Liston remained on; he had not
been in dispute, anyway; not even Morris would want to dispose of that
tower of strength. Jones, a useful actor, but indistinct and restless, was
engaged and Charles Kemble returned after an absence of eight years,
to play Don Felix in *The Wonder*—the last part in which Garrick ever
appeared.

The Doubtful Son, or Secrets of a Palace, a serious drama which
introduced Sowerby, from Bath, to the Haymarket, proved a success.
It ran nineteen nights. Sowerby was a bit of an eccentric and had a very
unfortunate habit of unconsciously misplacing his words. For instance,
when playing in *The Iron Chest* as Mortimer, he had to say to Wilford,
"You may have noticed in my library a chest." At which Wilford starts
and Mortimer continues: "You see, he changes at the word." Sowerby,

when playing the part, had his mind on other things and said, "You may have noticed on my chest a library."

The actor playing Wilford burst out laughing, but Sowerby, quite unconscious of anything wrong, continued with a correct line: "You see, he changes at the word." Wilford capped this with the next line (correctly as it happened) by saying, "And well I may"—and that was too much for the audience, who roared with delight and gave a cheer. It was only then that Sowerby woke up to the fact that something was wrong.

Bombastes, by Rhodes, also succeeded—and Liston, Mathews and Taylor in this provided a feast of fun. Taylor was a native of Bath and of that famous 1777 vintage. He was an excellent singer and a good actor into the bargain. He got his Haymarket engagement through Elliston's recommendation. Despite Morris's challenge, the season was a success.

The internal dissension notwithstanding, there was a bright interlude at the Haymarket during the 1810 season. It may not have done the theatre much good, but nevertheless it gave the whole of London a gigantic laugh, the memories of which still echo. Perhaps it was right that the home of comedy should supply this hilarity, although not in the regular course of its business, but as an "added attraction," which no doubt brought a bit of rent to the coffers.

For one of the most extraordinary actors—if he can be so called—that ever trod the boards of the English stage, chose the Haymarket to give London a glimpse of what he believed was his transcendant talent. He was not a professional, but an amateur, and the talent was apparent only to himself. But as a laughter-maker, in spite of himself, he has had no equal. In that respect the name of "Romeo" Coates is immortal.

This strange man, Robert Coates, was the son of a sugar-planter in Antigua. The father having died, the son returned to this country and determined to cut a dash. It was an age of eccentrics, but he was one of the oddist of them all. He frequented all the fashionable places. He was already thirty-six years old when he burst upon the town—old enough to know better. He looked older, for he was sallow and wrinkled, possibly as a result of the West Indian sun and also possibly because of the life he led. He was not ill-looking, but had a crafty expression. He had quite a good figure, and a contemporary of his, who was by way of being a friend, says that he had received a good education and was quite an agreeable man, although very conceited and very egotistical. As a man, when people got used to his eccentricities, they liked him. The trouble with him was that he persisted in acting, and like so many persistent players, he could not act at all.

He made sensation enough, without his acting, by his amazing dress, appearance and general behaviour. He wanted to cut a dash—and he succeeded. But he never succeeded in his acting.

His clothes were outrageous even amongst the Regency bucks. Summer or winter, he covered himself with furs, and diamonds gleamed from his costume wherever room could be found for them. His buttons were diamonds, as were the buckles of his knee breeches. He had lots of clothes and every suit was a remarkable creation.

He drove about in an amazing vehicle, which was made like a triumphal car, but which some say was also shaped like a tea kettle. He called it a curricle, but it was like nothing else on the road. Its general idea was that of a scallop shell. It was painted a rich lake colour and it bore his coat-of-arms, a crowing cock. Two fine white horses pulled the carriage, which looked as though it had come out of a circus or a pantomime. On their necks the steeds bore a life-sized silver crowing cock, with wings outstretched. There was another silver rooster on the splinter-bar between the horses and emblazoned on the coach was his motto: "Whilst I Live, I'll Crow." The interior of the turn-out was richly upholstered and very highly sprung on two very large wheels. Wherever he drove he was accompanied by a retinue of dirty little street-boys yelling "Cock-a-doodle-do" at the top of their voices. And he liked it.

There is a general belief that it is vanity which makes people go on the stage. There is a grain of truth in this as a rule, and a little vanity is no bad thing in an actor either, but it was vanity pure and simple which made Robert Coates consider himself the equal or superior of David Garrick and all the others.

He *would* be an actor—nothing should stop him. The vanity was there, the urge was there, but the talent was not. But he always thought it was and was delighted by his own performances, so nobody was the worse off.

He had been sent to England as a boy to be educated, and had gone back to Antigua in the year of Trafalgar. Then his father died. Coates, considering himself a rich man, could not wait to come back to London. Antigua meant nothing to him. All the time he was there he was thinking of the glories of Town, of the delights of the fashionable world and the celebrity attendant upon a man who was a part of it, but more still of the glamour and the fascination of the stage and the effulgence surrounding a great and popular actor. He got back to this country as fast as he could, and burst upon an astonished world at Bath. There was a great deal of natural curiosity about him. He appeared to be fabulously wealthy, but to have no friends—quite enough to set tongues wagging in the Pump Room.

Then Bath got a surprise. It was announced that for the evening of February 9th, 1810, the Theatre Royal, Bath, had been taken "By a gentleman of Fashion who will make his first appearance in England." He was to play Romeo. This was a sensation for Bath, and the theatre was packed. It was discovered that "the gentleman of fashion" was this strange creature who was already the talk of the town. Bath went to the play expecting a thrill—and got it. They never stopped laughing from curtain rise to curtain fall.

The next day his name was on everyone's lips and he was christened "Romeo" Coates. He liked it. He fluttered about, basking in what he thought was glory. Let them think what they liked about his acting (he had his own views on that); he was being talked about, stared at, spoken to, and that was what he wanted. The fashionables, on coming back to Town, spread his fame far and wide. They laughed as they told the tale; they laughed as they recounted that at the end of the show he had come forward and said, "Haven't I done well?" and also that he had informed the amazed and laughter-weary audience that his reading of the character improved on the original.

He performed at Brighton as well, and at Richmond, always with the same results. His notoriety grew. His great ambition, next to being recognised as the leading actor of his day, was to meet the Prince, the First Gentleman in Europe, "Prinny, the Prince Regent."

Meanwhile, he drove around in his amazing curricle, his diamonds flashing, the sunlight glittering on his rings, his buckles, his buttons, brooches and sword hilt, and always with the attendant mob of cheering, dirty, crowing little boys. Workmen raised a derisive cheer, and joined in the cock-crows. He acknowledged the attentions with pride and felt that this was Life.

But he soon adjudged it time to let London see his histrionic talent. So he took the Haymarket Theatre, and there he staged *Romeo and Juliet*.

A company was engaged to support him, the event was advertised, and the crowd turned up, all anxious to see the fun. "Romeo" was delighted.

That audience got it money's worth. It saw what was probably the most extraordinary performance of Shakespeare's tragedy ever beheld in any theatre. Truly, the tragedy compelled tears—but tears of laughter. For the audience split their sides. His appearance alone was a riot. He dressed the part in a sky blue spangled cloak, red and very tight pantaloons, muslin vest, a full-bottomed wig and—an opera hat.

It was a surprising make-up, herald of surprises to come. The Haymarket audience soon discovered that Coates could not act at all. He was wooden to a degree, yet he could not keep still for one moment —the hall-mark of the amateur! Interest and laughter grew as his reading and business developed. They laughed continuously and uproariously. Then came the cry of "Cock-a-doodle-do." Coates interrupted his speech and crowed back at them in delight.

"Ah, you like my acting, do you?" he asked. "I'm a good actor."

"Never seen anything like it," came the delighted response, and Coates went on from absurdity to absurdity. Nobody could hear a word, so great was the laughter, and the other actors and actresses felt their position acutely. Coates interrupted his labours to take a pinch of snuff. More, he passed the box to the people in the stage box, asking them to honour him by taking a pinch and to pass the box round.

Farce reached its height in the tomb scene. He dragged the unfortunate lady playing Juliet round the stage like a sack by the hair of her head. A climax came when he split his red pantaloons with a resounding noise. But the real high spot was his own death scene. He was determined to do this well. But first he spread an enormous silk handkerchief on the stage, on which to expire. This brought roars of delight. Coates stopped, came down to the front and addressed the audience. "Ah, my friends," said he, "you may laugh if you like. But I'm the sensible one. Do you think I'm going to spoil my nice new clothes on these dirty boards? Not I." And he went on with his preparations, to applause and shouts of "Cock-a-doodle-do."

He took the poison, and he acted like mad, giving an entirely new reading by pretending to be sick! Then he lay down carefully, very carefully, on the handkerchief, and expired. Not finding it at all comfortable, he raised his head and put his opera hat under it for a pillow. Then, with tremendous writhings and contortions, he re-died a most painful stage death.

The audience were in uproar. They yelled, they cheered, they crowed, they applauded. Then somebody cried, "Encore!" which was taken up by the rest of the house. Coates was in triumph. He scrambled up and was just starting to die all over again, when the poor girl who was playing Juliet, and who had had more than enough of it, put a stopper on the whole thing. She was quick-witted in her agony. Stepping down to the front she said: "Ladies and gentlemen, please don't encourage him, I beg of you.

> "Dying is such sweet sorrow
> That he will die again, until to-morrow."

This witty paraphrase brought down the curtain to the only genuine applause of the show.

But Coates had tasted blood. He considered it an enormous success. He took the Haymarket again. He staged that fine old crusted play, *The Fair Penitent*, by Nicholas Rowe. He himself sustained the role of Lothario, in which Garrick had defeated Quin in their battle for supremacy. What cared "Romeo" Coates? He was greater than Garrick, but he had a job to get anyone to act with him, and could only get together a scratch company. A tall, skinny boy with a whine and a bad cold played Altamont, a man with a voice like the bark of a dog played Sciotto. But what of the Lothario, that "dear, perfidious one"? Well, there he was—"Romeo" Coates, dressed all in white satin—a male Tilburina, and as mad as she. He cut an extraordinary figure as he ambled about the stage. Then came the leading lady, the Callista, and she proved a fitting partner to the "haughty, gallant, gay Lothario," for she was a painfully thin person with a thinner voice who ran about the stage like a frightened hen. A wag suggested she was Mrs. Coates, and this was received with cheers. The play went on, full of the most curious happenings, whilst the audience in turn wondered, laughed and hooted with joy. At long last came Lothario's death scene. It was in such moments that Romeo Coates fancied himself and really let himself go. He spread no handkerchief this time, he used no opera hat as a pillow. But, like Charles II, he was an unconscionable time about dying. He writhed in mortal agony and the audience cheered. He writhed the more, he staggered, he gasped, and more and more heartening cheers and hearty laughter rewarded him. The worse he got the more they applauded. He dropped on one knee and scuttered about, making the most extraordinary noises. And finally, when he could think of nothing more to do, he fell flat on his back with a resounding whack which shook the house. The finale of the play did not matter. But he had not finished. He rushed off, changed his clothes, reappeared dressed as a soldier. He recited a poem, which he announced as "Hobbies." What little of it—it was mercifully short—could be heard seemed to be a statement that his own hobby was doing good to others. If laughter was the food of goodness, as Shakespeare said it was of love, he succeeded in his hobby.

He continued for a while his endeavours to prove himself an actor. Nobody would pay and the house was "given away." Coates said he gave the proceeds to charity, but what small takings there were he pocketed as a tribute to his art. But he became in great request at benefit performances. There his recitation of "Bucks, have at ye all" was the laugh hit of the evening and was a sure draw.

The time came when he thought he had achieved his ambition. He received an invitation to a party at Carlton House. At last he was to meet the Prince! Guineas flowed like water to provide a costume such as nobody had ever beheld before. He got as far as the door. The invitation was a forged one. But for that one occasion the Prince Regent appears to have lived up to his name as "The First Gentleman in Europe." He heard the noise, asked the reason and on being told, had Coates admitted and treated him civilly.

Coates, however, found that what are riches in Antigua may not be riches in London. He became hard-up. He moved to shabby lodgings in Craven Street and went to cheap eating-houses. Trouble in the West Indies further reduced his income. He went to Boulogne. There he met a woman whom he induced to marry him. Eventually he returned to London and died, as the result of an accident, at the age of seventy-seven.

He is perhaps the most comic character that the home of English comedy—the Haymarket—has to show.

CHAPTER XVIII

A HOUSE DIVIDED

IN 1811 Colman tried again to form an independent company. This may have been a challenge to Morris in his turn, or it may have been Morris who insisted on it. Elliston was engaged again—he had refused to go to the Lyceum with the Drury Lane Company, who took refuge there after the Lane had been burned down.

The company included John Cooper, a good all-round actor, another Jones who came to the Haymarket from Edinburgh, Barnes, who came from York, a first-class performer who never got a real chance at the Haymarket, and Miss Bellchambers, making her debut and looking handsome. Later, when the "winter theatres" closed down, Liston, Munden and Jones rejoined.

There was a farce called *Trial by Jury*, a fair success. In June, Colman presented Dimond's play, *The Royal Oak*—founded on the adventures of Charles II. And then came a sad affair. Old Charles Dibdin, the victim of Fate, the man who wrote so many masterpieces of song, who earned such fame but little money, tried his luck again. He was desperate, he was penniless, he was ageing. He brought Colman a musical piece called *The Round Robin*. It was his last hope, his last throw against Fortune. He who had written "Tom Bowling," "The Jolly Young Waterman," and hundreds of other songs which had swept the country, whose operas had been the rage, whose sea songs had kept up the morale of the nation during the French wars was almost starving. He had been actor, manager, musical director, opera singer, song-writer, composer, music publisher, novelist all in turn. He had built his own theatre—the Sans Souci—wherein he had given a one-man show, written, composed, sung and played by himself. His songs were sung by the whole nation. Yet luck was always against him; he never had a break. He had quarrelled with his family over his love affairs. He had been given a pension by one Government, only to have it revoked by the next. His works had filled the pockets of many, but never his own. Now he brought along his last effort to the Haymarket, where he had succeeded before. Alas! it failed and failed miserably. Brave, stubborn, indefatigable Dibdin was on the spot the very next morning with new songs and new lyrics for it—but all to no purpose. *The Round Robin*, of which he had hoped so much, failed completely. Dibdin was down at last and only a public subscription saved him from a pauper's death.

A farce called *The Outside Passenger* was not much better in result. Then came drama in realistic form. An extravaganza was announced, called *The Quadrupeds of Quedlinburgh, or the Rovers of Weimar*. The bills announced that it had been long in preparation and that every effort had been strained to SURPASS NATURE.

Be that as it may, ill nature took a hand. War flared up again amongst the proprietors of the Haymarket. It was to have been produced on July 22nd, 1811. But it did not appear. Instead there was issued a bill of a most curious nature. This time it originated from Colman and Winston, allied against Morris. It read as follows:

"THEATRE ROYAL, HAYMARKET

"Messrs. Colman and Winston, from a sense of respect and duty to the public, and in justification of themselves, are under the necessity of giving a short detail of circumstances which have occasioned the new piece (intended for reproduction this evening) to be withdrawn and three of the most principal performers to withhold the further assistance of their talents from the Theatre.

"On a motion brought forward in the High Court of Chancery, on Saturday last, it was deemed proper by the Lord Chancellor to order that Mr. Morris (the Treasurer), who is one of the Proprietors, should be obliged by his partners to pay the salaries of certain performers with whom Messrs. Colman and Winston had entered into engagements. This matter will undergo much future question in a Court of equity; but in the present stage of business, Mr. Morris refuses to pay Messrs. Elliston, Jones and Munden the emoluments for which they have agreed to perfom, and they have consequently retired from exertion without profit, giving the manager all the timely notice in their power of their intentions, that their conduct may not be misconstrued into any disrespect to the town. Messrs. Colman and Winston have only to lament that they are (for a time at least) thus restrained from procuring these novelties, and that number of prominent performers which may merit the patronage of an English metropolis."

This was a bit startling. It would seem that Morris had resented the engagement of these three stars, two of whom had come from the other theatres. Elliston had been engaged for the whole season beforehand. But he was probably anti-Morris—and pro-Colman.

The battle raged between the rival managers for some days, and then came a further bill on July 25th.

"RETURN OF MESSRS. ELLISTON, JONES AND MUNDEN

"Messrs. Colman and Winston most grateful for past patronage and solicitous to deserve its continuance by every effect in their power, are happy in announcing to the public that they have surmounted the great difficulties opposed to them by their partner, and effected the return of the above gentlemen."

The Battle of the Bills was over—and victory rested with the allies—for the moment.

The next night the strangely-named entertainment about which all the fuss had arisen was presented to the public. It was by Colman, and was a satire on the management of Covent Garden for introducing animals on the stage of that great theatre and making it into a kind of Astley's Amphitheatre with horses and elephants. Colman drew up a comic playbill which had such an effect on the public that it led them to expect far too much—a piece of over-publicity for a show which is a lesson many theatre folk have still to learn. Consequently, the extravaganza fell a bit flat. But they perisisted with it and kept it going for thirty-six nights.

Colman, battling with the continued encroachment upon his summer playing time by Drury Lane and Covent Garden, petitioned the Crown through the Lord Chamberlain, and got an extra month tacked on to his licence. For the first time he introduced the half-price-at-half-time system at the Haymarket. But he put the original prices up a 1s. to make it pay him better.

Theodore Hook supplied a successful farce called *Darkness Visible*. Mrs. Gibbs (Mrs. Colman) scored in a piece called *Travellers Benighted, or the Forest of Rosenwald*.

Mathews, it will be observed, was an absentee from the Haymarket this season. Colman, who looked upon him as his trump card, had tried to secure him, but failed. Mathews was now such a success elsewhere and had so many engagements that he could not fit it in. But Colman made overtures for succeeding seasons.

All this time, whilst all this was going on, the writing of plays, the production of them and the battle with the inimical Morris, Colman was still in the King's Bench. No less a person than His Royal Highness the Duke of York took compassion on him, asked him to dinner at Carlton House and got permission for him to go. He even did Colman the honour of calling for him personally at the "Rules" and driving him to dine. As they walked through the Royal apartments, Colman remarked to his host: "What excellent lodgings. I have nothing like them in the King's Bench."

Colman behaved like a boy out of school. After dinner, he exclaimed in a very loud voice: "Eh, why, this *is* wine. Pray, do tell me, who is that fine-looking fellow at the head of the table?" Full well he knew it was the Prince Regent. The good-natured Duke, who sat next to him, nudged him and said: "Hush, George, you'll get into a scrape." "No, no," said Colman in an even louder voice. "I am come out to enjoy myself; *I* want to know who that fine, square-shouldered magnificent-looking agreeable fellow is, at the head of the table." The Duke was a bit alarmed. "Be quiet, George," he urged. "You know it is the Prince." "Why, then?" said Colman in a voice which he knew the Prince would hear. "He is your elder brother. I declare he don't look half your age. Well, I remember the time when he sung a good song, and as I am come out for a lark, for only one day, if he is the same good fellow that he used to be, he would not refuse an old playfellow."

The prince heard him, and laughed. The flattery, though gross, pleased him. And perhaps he had a fellow feeling for a debtor, being always up to his eyes himself, though never in danger of King's Bench. He obliged with a song. "What a magnificent voice," exclaimed Colman. "I have heard nothing to be compared to it for years. Such expression, too! I'll be damned if I don't engage him for my theatre." None of which gave any offence to "Prinny," who, indeed, treated Colman afterwards with great kindness.

In 1812 Colman was much alarmed by a report that Mathews had engaged himself at Covent Garden. He wrote him a long letter, appealing to their past and present friendship and saying that he was banking on having him at the Haymarket. The letter showed only too plainly, also, what was going on at that theatre. Colman says: "You cannot have forgotten that at our last parting I told you that I considered our engagement as concluded, and that although I must, *pro forma*, put the proposition to Mr. Morris, yet I and Mr. Winston had maturely deliberated upon your terms and had made up our minds upon the expediency of acceding to them, for the good of the theatre, we should, as the majority of the firm, ratify them should Mr. Morris's answer turn out contrary to our expectations upon the point . . .!" and much more to the same effect. It is plain what was going on. Morris was opposing them at every turn.

Meanwhile, the suit in Chancery dragged its weary length along the months, and caused general unrest and disruption. Colman wrote again to Mathews, hoping to secure him. He has another hit at Morris in the second letter.

"Morris is like Scrub," he writes, "and will say nothing 'pro or con' till there is a peace. In other words, he will neither be an 'ass' nor 'dissenter' to any engagement till the point of management is settled, so, as I am advised by my counsel, 'learned in the laws of the land,' I go on without him; and you are engaged by me and Winston, in behalf of the theatre; by me as the Director and by both of us as the majority of partners.

"The Master's report as to my capability of managing under my present situation is most particularly strong against Morris. This is the last of his two grand points and he is licked upon both."

But the difficulties were very real. Morris was putting up a fight and putting everyone in difficulties. He was sending out proclamations and notices of his own to all and sundry, and nobody knew how they stood. Mathews had one and wrote to Colman about it. The latter replied urgently. Things were getting serious.

"I have unavoidably lost a day before I could answer it, by waiting for my solicitor's opinion, who advises that you should not answer

Morris's notice. And had Morris's notice the effect (which they have not had in any one instance) of inducing performers to throw up their engagements, Mr. Grove, to whom he does not object, would distance longo intervallo, as a favourite with the town, all the remaining actors and actresses of the grand Haymarket company. He endeavours to mislead you in respect of Munden, to whose terms he also objected; and he only gives them to you as he [Morris] is willing to have them, and so, probably, he may misrepresent your terms to others. As to what steps you are to take, he *might* pay you the salary as it has been agreed upon by the majority of his partners. He attempted to play the same silly game last year and was foiled. He objected to pay Elliston, but was obliged to pay him every shilling."

It was quite clear what was going on. Colman and Winston were making engagements and agreeing terms, Morris was writing to the players and telling them this was all wrong and illegal under the circumstances of the current lawsuit and making his own proposals to them as being the proper ones. He was disclosing terms of one actor to another and trying to beat both down by so doing. That was Colman's interpretation.

When trouble arose, as a non-agreeing partner, but as Treasurer, he would not pay. It does not seem a very sensible course of procedure, but then Morris was not a man of the theatre, but only out for commercial ends. Such things have happened since. The theatre is not a business, and cannot be run on hard and fast commercial lines. It is a gamble and there must be give and take and latitude. Personalities must be studied. Morris apparently did not know this.

But Morris was depending for his victory upon the law and the terms of his partnership agreement. This was another matter. It might bring him on top, but at a ruinous cost to the whole goodwill of the theatre. Anyway, he was going to risk it and put it to the touch. And he went into open battle again on May 5th, with a public announcement, stating his case for all to see and read.

The people of London read in the public prints on the morning of May 6th, 1812, the following manifesto, in which the dispute raging behind the doors of the popular and well-loved little theatre in the Hay were made general knowledge:

"LITTLE THEATRE IN THE HAYMARKET

"Whereas by the Agreement, dated 4th day of June, 1805, entered into by the proprietors of the above theatre, it was agreed that no author, performer, or other persons should be employed, retained or discharged, in, for, or from the said concern, without the assent of the proprietors and that no repairs of alterations should be made, nor orders to tradesmen given without the assent of the proprietors.

"Now I, the undersigned David Edward Morris, one of the proprietors of the said Theatre, do hereby give notice to all persons
whom it may concern, that I am not answerable nor will be responsible for any engagement whatever, already entered into by my
co-proprietors, George Colman and James Winston, or either of them,
or which they, or either of them may enter into, with any author,
performer or other person, touching the said concern, unless such
engagement be in writing, and signed by me; and I am not and will
not be responsible for any repairs or alterations in or to the said
theatre, nor for any orders given to tradesmen unless such repairs or
alterations, and orders to tradesmen respectively, be made or given
by directions in writing, signed by them and me.
Dated the 5th day of May, 1812,
"D. E. MORRIS,
"26 Suffolk Street, Charing Cross."

This caused talk and concern. It was washing dirty linen in public.
It was damaging to the theatre, to its popularity, to the prestige of its
management and especially to Colman, cooped in his debtor's prison.

But the credit of the Little Theatre in the Hay stood high. Its record
was magnificent. It had been the jumping-off place of stars—it had
given the stage of England so much. It had been run by distinguished
people, it was an institution of London. During the ninety-two years of
its existence it had climbed steadily from an unlicensed little barn of a
place into a theatre which had gained a Royal title and now stood
shoulder to shoulder with the two great ones. It had marked itself as
the fostering-place of opportunity and the home of comedy. It had
shown Henderson, Elliston, Mathews, Liston, Charles Mayne Young,
Johnston and many more to the public for the first time. In Samuel
Foote and Charles Mathews it had produced the two greatest solo
performers—men who ran their own show by themselves—that the
stage had ever seen. It had, whilst encouraging young talent, also
fostered music and dancing. It had survived oppression, bad times and
riots. It had been the cause of a special Act of Parliament—the Licensing
Law, but it had fought for freedom in the theatre.

Now it was menaced by internal dissension. It had reached its
height because up to now it had been run by practical men who knew
their job and were of the theatre. Now the outside hand was creeping
in. Now the house was divided against itself. Could it survive that?

George Colman and James Winston went steadily on their way.
Despite the attack by Morris, they opened the theatre as usual for the
season, and they brought another new star for London's consideration,
and once again the judgment and foresight of Colman as regards
theatrical matters was fully justified.

This was Daniel Terry, born in 1789, and the son of parents who
intended him to be an architect. They placed him under Wyatt, with

whom he studied for five years. But he determined to be architect of his own fortunes and went on the stage. He did not succeed very well and went back to architectural work. Still, however, the stage called and he joined a company managed by Stephen Kemble in the North of England. He worked hard, he tried hard, he made slow progress. But it was good enough to get him a job in Liverpool, where by sheer hard work and good reliable performances he grew in favour. He knew his job now; he was sure of himself. No lightning success had come to him, what he had won he had fought for. He went to Edinburgh. The critical audiences there liked him. He met Sir Walter Scott, who was ever afterwards a very good friend to him, and proved it by deeds as well as words.

It was whilst playing at Edinburgh that he got the offer of the job at the Haymarket. Naturally, he jumped at it.

Being primarily a character actor, he elected to appear as Lord Ogleby in *The Clandestine Marriage*, written by the elder Colman and David Garrick. He opened at the Haymarket on May 20th and he was approved by the Haymarket audiences. It was not the startling success of Henderson, Mathews, Young or Liston. But it was hearty appreciation of a sound and excellent actor. And as the season went on he got more and more popular. He played Shylock, Job Thornberry, Sir Edward Mortimer, all the round of the routine leading parts. And the Haymarket liked him and came to see him.

Afterwards, he went into management, acquiring the Adelphi Theatre with Yates, and it was Sir Walter Scott who guaranteed him good for the purchase money of his share. He had small but expressive features and, perhaps out of affection for Scott, he acquired a Scottish accent, though born in Bath.

A farce called *The Sleep Walker*, written by Oulton, was produced on June 15th, and in this Mathews, who was back again at the Haymarket this season to support Colman, made a most tremendous hit, so great that the show was repeated for the unprecedented run of fifty-three nights during the short season. There were two failures, a drama called *The Child of Chance* and a comedy called *The Fortune Hunters*. Towards the end of the season, a comedy called *Look at Home* was a very big success. Again the Haymarket permitted half-price during the last month of its playing time.

But things were getting worse between the partners. All through the preceding season, nothing had been staged without a struggle, no action had been without dispute, there was chaos where there had been order and success. Worse was to come.

For the case between Morris, Colman and Winston had now got really before Chancery, than which nothing could be slower. Day followed day, argument followed argument, adjournment followed adjournment, and the worst thing that could happen to any playhouse happened to the Haymarket in the 1813 season. Although bills had announced the opening and that Mrs. Jordan herself had been engaged, the Haymarket remained closed all the year whilst its management performed unwillingly in the Courts of Chancery.

Nor did it reopen in 1814 until July 18th, having lost much valuable time. Then a farce by Baron Langsdorff was staged called *Come and See*, which ran for thirteen nights. But Mathews, to show his versatility, played Falstaff with much success. Bad luck dogged the little theatre, for the season was further marred by a bad accident to Mathews and Terry, who were thrown out of a gig. Terry broke two ribs. Mathews had his hip joint dislocated, which left him lame and suffering for the rest of his life.

Colman was truly distressed. He was very fond of Mathews and he had the further anxiety that a harlequinade upon which they set much store would now be in jeopardy. Mathews wrote and told him that he would, if necessary, play on crutches. It was already August and the big theatres would open in September. It was a pretty state of things. Colman was being driven by Morris and predicted disaster if that man got his way. He had looked to this pantomime to put him right and here was Fate intervening with an accident to Mathews, its prop, stay and hope.

Mathews, good friend and good trouper, said he would play, come what may. He knew that if the thing were delayed, the shows at Drury Lane and Covent Garden would swamp them. For harlequinades were in the air and Covent Garden was to stage one. So it was arranged that, although Mathews was suffering all the time, they would open, and chance it.

They got it open on August 12th and it was called *Hocus Pocus, or Harlequin Washed White*. Mathews played a speaking Harlequin, but an apology was spoken by Terry:

"Ladies and gentlemen, before the curtain rises I am requested to say a few words to you on behalf of an invalid. Mr. Mathews still continues to suffer much, very much, from his late severe accident; but he trusts that his anxiety in coming forward thus early to perform his duty to you and to fulfil his engagement here will atone for his deficiencies in bodily activity, requisite to the character he is about to sustain. A former very celebrated proprietor of this theatre once enjoyed the fullest favour as 'a devil upon two sticks,' and it is hoped, nay, it cannot be doubted, that you will now extend your utmost indulgence to a harlequin upon one."

Much had been hoped of the show, much trouble had been taken. Here is a notice of it:

"It is a species of performance that defies criticism, partaking at once of farce, comedy, tragedy, and pantomime and possessing the novelty of three harlequins, and apparently designed for the purpose

A Stalwart of the Haymarket: John Baldwin Buckstone.

E. A. Sothern in his favourite role of Lord Dundreary.

of introducing Mr. Mathews to the public again, after his recovery
from his late severe accident. It is needless to add that Mr. Mathews
on his appearance was greeted with the loudest applause. He is still
extremely lame, and requires a crutch stick for his support. His right
side seems to have particularly suffered, and it was difficult to separate
the idea of pain from even his happiest efforts.''

And another paper, like Silas Wegg, dropped into poetry:

> *"It seems, if obliged on his crutches to play,*
> *At Harlequin Mathews will aim,*
> *If so, very fairly the public may say*
> *'Tis the first time his efforts were lame."*

It was a success for Mathews, especially when he gave an imitation
of a child of six, but it is doubtful if it added much to the exchequer.
It showed one thing, however, that a great performer was willing to
make a great sacrifice for a manager he liked and esteemed when that
man was in dire need. And the effort of performing in this piece, to
help Colman, his friend who had given him his first London chance, and
to help the Haymarket, where that chance had taken place, left Mathews
lame for life. How many actors would have made the effort?

Mathews played again that season. Colman staged a play called *Love
and Gout*. It was written by Jamieson. It may have been that the
original play was altered to give Mathews the chance of playing a
gouty man so that his supporting stick should seem a natural necessity.
He played the part whilst suffering considerably. It was not a good
play, but the brave comedian got magnificent Press notices for his
performance—and deserved them.

Colman became very anxious to keep Mathews at the Haymarket
when the other theatres closed for the summer. But his hands were
much more tied, for whilst that unselfish actor suffered actual pain for
sake of the theatre and his old friend and manager, Morris was still at
war with those whose real objects were the same as his own. Colman
wanted Mathews in 1815 to join the Haymarket before Covent Garden,
to which he was contracted, actually closed. He had a little scheme and
Mathews' presence, through his engagement by Colman, seemed
imperative.

Mathews played for him that season, but little of note happened.

Probably what Colman wanted was to show that, without him,
Mathews would not be there. The chief event of the season was,
indeed, Mathews' benefit, when he confounded certain critics who
would persist in regarding him chiefly as a mimic and only secondly as
an actor, by playing Sir Archy Mac Sarcasm, Macklin's old part in his
own play, and playing it magnificently.

Still the fight between the partners went on, still money flowed into
the pockets of the lawyers, but the theatre opened in 1816 on July 1st—

P

the disputes made the short season get shorter and shorter. They had a good company, too, which included Fawcett, Jones, Terry, Tokely, Russell, Duruset, Mrs. Glover, Mrs. Davenport, Mrs. Gibbs and Miss Carew. A debut was made by Miss Copeland—and very successfully. She became known as Mrs. Fitzwilliam.

Tokeley was a good comedian who made a success that season in a comedy by Jamieson called *Exit by Mistake*. Mrs. Glover was to become a very famous actress indeed. She became the rage of Bath when only sixteen, in 1796. She appeared the next season at Covent Garden. She was a better player in comedy than in tragedy, but in light plays and parts she was the nearest thing to Mrs. Abington. After Jane Pope, she was the best player, in her later years, of such characters as Mrs. Candour and what were technically called "old women." She had some of that quality which had shone so brightly in Garrick's days. Yet she made experiments. She played Hamlet at the Lyceum, and earned Kean's praise. She essayed Falstaff too, but that was a mistake. Her life was not altogether a happy one. She had a father who took all her earnings and kept her on short commons. That father, too, married her off to a man she did not like and who was supposed to be wealthy. He not only lived on her salary too, but kept another family on it as well. She got a separation from him, but he persecuted her for years. She herself led a most upright life. She had been an unselfish and perhaps too dutiful daughter, she was a badly treated wife, an admirable mother to her children (whom her scoundrel of a husband tried to take from her), but no breath of scandal ever touched her. Her last benefit (at Drury Lane) was under the immediate patronage of Queen Victoria, a most unusual honour. She died in 1850, almost on the stage, working to the last.

Mrs. Davenport was another good actress, in the same line of business as Mrs. Glover.

The company was strong, the summer very wet, so the Haymarket had a good season, short as it was. The season closed with *A Chip of the Old Block*, *Exit by Mistake*, and *The Dead Alive*, Russell taking a benefit. Mathews appeared at this performance—his first and only that season—as Chip and Motley.

Colman wrote a closing address, which Terry spoke:

"Ladies and gentlemen, I am deputed by the proprietors of this theatre to offer you their most cordial thanks for the patronage with which you have honoured them during their very short season. They lament that the increased speculations of the higher theatrical powers, whose influence at present must regulate their motions, so very much curtail the period of exertion on this spot, to merit your favour. But one material ingredient in theatres should be wit, and brevity, we are told, is the soul of it; if so, the proprietors here should feel particularly obliged to their neighbours for rendering their seat of dramatic exhibition wittier and wittier."

There was a good deal of sting in this. Colman was still holding on and still wanting Mathews to sign on—or promise on, for he needed no contract, for the entire season. And he got him. More than that, Colman wrote him a show called *The Actor of All Work*, in which Mathews made a most astounding success. It gave him an opportunity of showing his tremendous versatility.

The season opened on July 7th. Mathews, back again after two years as a regular member of the company (he had played only on odd occasions during the last two years), played Scout in *The Village Lawyer* and was acclaimed. On 15th of that month, he was announced to appear as Rover in *Wild Oats* and to give also his celebrated imitations. He fell ill at the last moment. The hastily posted announcement was not seen by the majority who crowded into the house, and when another actor appeared as Rover there was a first-class row and yells for an apology. It was some time before quiet was restored. In spite of all this, Mathews, in picking up his newspaper the next morning, read a detailed account therein of his performance (which he had never given) and a summing up that it was most inefficient and a deserved failure. A nice example of dramatic criticism of that period, but not without parallel in modern times. A certain very well-known critic, not many years ago, who wrote for a Sunday paper, begged to be allowed to witness the dress rehearsal of a revue. He was let in and saw it all through. Playgoers reading his notice on the Sunday were amazed to find a slashing attack upon a certain scene which they, who had been present at the first night, had never seen, because between the dress rehearsal and the first night it had been entirely cut out. He had not taken the trouble to find out.

When, a few nights afterwards, Mathews did at last play Rover, he was a great success.

But the triumph of the season was *Actor of All Work*. This was a vehicle for Mathews' imitations and impressions. He played seven widely different parts, including a remarkable imitation of Talma, and was a sensation. Amongst his gifts, Mathews had the power of completely altering his face and features without the aid of make up. This *Actor of All Work* was a great piece both artistically and physically, for the changes of costumes were effected at lightning speed. At times, Mathews would alter his voice so that three people seemed to be carrying on a conversation. The receipts beat all records.

A little "press" impromptu of this performance of his is worthy of note:

> *"If, by acting one part so much honour be gained*
> *Pray tell, if it be in your power*
> *What honour, what meed, shall by him be obtained*
> *Who acts seven parts in the hour."*

Another honour was also in store for him, and let the letter speak for itself:

"21 UPPER BAKER STREET.
"*August 26th.*

"DEAR SIR,—I have heard so much of the *Actor of All Work* and have so great an admiration of your talents, that I cannot resist troubling you with a request that I am sure your good nature will pardon; it is that you will have the goodness to procure a private box to give me that pleasure. Allow me, sir, to assure you, that if your compliance is likely to be attended with the least inconvenience, I shall attribute your refusal to those motives of propriety that are indispensable, and not to any disinclination to gratify.

"Your sincere admirer
"and obliged humble servant,
"S. SIDDONS.

"PS.—Mr. Colman has always been so kind as to admit me to the theatre and I flatter myself he would not be adverse to favouring me with a box any day this week, except Friday."

The writer, of course, was Mrs. Siddons. That is how one star wrote to another star in the early nineteenth century. So great was Mathews' success in this Haymarket piece that he took it to France and succeeded there. Indeed, he entertained the British troops with it, a forerunner of the E.N.S.A. of the Second World War.

The company was, that season, practically the same as the preceding one. Tokely made another success in a comedy called *Teasing made Easy.* Nor did it change much in 1818. The only important event was the production of *Nine Points of the Law*, not a big success, and *The Green Man*, a considerable one.

The reign of Colman at the Haymarket was growing very short now.

CHAPTER XIX

THE OLD ORDER CHANGES

THE change came in the year 1817. Colman could no longer resist; Morris was too strong and too clever for him. George Colman Junior surrendered control of the Haymarket to D. E. Morris. Another king now held sway, but for the moment Colman remained on as Manager, clipped of his power, but there in name. And that name had raised the Haymarket very far. From 1777 to 1819, for forty-one years, a Colman had been in command, son had followed father. Both had written plays performed in the theatre they controlled, both had found new stars, both had added to its fame, its success and its quality. In the last Colman season very little happened. There was trouble at Drury Lane, where the amateur committee had got into a mess, and the Drury Lane Company played at the Haymarket. Its own season did not start until July 20th, but the company was up to the usual Haymarket standard, and included Jones, Liston, Terry, Mrs. Edwin, Mrs. Gibbs and Mrs. Davenport. A new play by Theodore Hook called *Pigeons and Crows* was a big success. Then Colman relinquished power to Morris. He was out of the King's Bench now, and a free man. He had lost the commanding position of chief of the Haymarket, but he had powerful friends. In the succeeding year, 1820, he was made Lieutenant of His Majesty's Guard of Yeomen of the Guard. This was one of those little Court sinecures which were usually bought for a nice price, but George IV made a present of it to George Colman.

On the King's Birthday next succeeding his appointment, Colman attended Court in full uniform. The King seemed pleased to see him and said: "Your uniform, George, is so well made that I don't see the hooks and eyes." Colman at once unhooked his coat. "Here are my eyes. Where are yours?" he demanded. He held his Lieutenancy until 1831, when he received special permission from the King to sell it. So he did very nicely out of it. At the Coronation of George IV a rumour went round that Colman was to be knighted, but it never happened. Colman was made Examiner of Plays in 1824. He got two guineas for every play so examined. It was a splendid source of income. The fee, by the way, is still the same.

He took his office very seriously. He succeeded a man called Larpent, who was of a religious turn of mind and had been held a difficult nut to crack. He had mainly concerned himself with political allusions, as to which he was very stern. Actually, the drama of the day, such as it was, had shed much of the dirt of the previous century and was, if somewhat artless, at least fairly clean. Colman's appointment was hailed as that of the right man in the right place. Here was at last a practical man of the theatre who would know what was what. His exact title was "Examiner of All Plays, Tragedies, Comedies, Opera, Farces, Interludes, or any other entertainment of the stage, of what denomination soever." It was a pretty lucrative job, and he saw to it that everything spoken or sung on the stage went through his hands. He had a bit of a difficulty at first. The minor theatres were now beginning to fight that battle with the Patent Theatres which ended in their favour and the removal of the Patent's monopoly. What Colman had to decide was: "What was a burletta?" Burlettas were allowed at the minor theatres as not being legitimate stage-plays or operas and therefore not infringing the Patent rights. But the minor theatres had a lot of tricks: they played regular plays in such a way that by the interpolation of songs here and there they could claim them as burlettas. But what *was* a burletta in the legal sense? Nobody knew. There was no dictionary definition. Colman gave a long and involved judgment and burlettas went on. He said that they had been allowed so long, there seemed no real reason to stop them. Colman did not want them stopped. They meant a lot of guineas to him. His view was that a burletta was "a drama in rhyme, which is entirely musical; a short comic piece, consisting of recitative and singing, wholly accompanied, more or less, by the orchestra." That "more or less" made everything perfectly clear, of course. But those who had hailed the appointment of Colman as Examiner of Plays soon regretted it. He became a real tyrant. He was a man who had to be in the limelight, he loved publicity, he loved to be a public figure. As proprietor of the Haymarket, he had been always in the news. As Examiner of Plays he saw to it that he was still in the news. He was a most captious censor. He had put plenty of spice into his own plays; he would have none in other people's. He was ultra-censorious about anything touching the Deity. Be it direct or indirect, out it had to come. He refused to allow the heroine of a play to be alluded to as an angel—an angel, he held, was a character in Scripture, so had no place in a profane play.

If an author allowed a character to appeal to Providence, Colman cut that out. He said that it was the Providence of God which was meant and that this was irreligious. The words "Heaven" and "Hell," however used, were at once blue-pencilled. The word "damn," of course, was taboo. He would not even allow "Oh, Lord" or even "Oh, Lud." The expedient of "Demme" never got by him. Once a play came before him in which there was a scene where monks and nuns chanted in a cathedral. He cut it out at once. He was asked to explain the position as regards the National Anthem. He ruled this was an anthem, and sanctified by custom, but not to be used as a precedent. As censor he was a very tough nut indeed. As a manager he had been approachable, human, understanding, honest and generous. He put on no "side," he was on friendly terms with his entire company from lead to small-part player. But he held the public in proper respect and was always in fact and deed their obedient humble servant. An author himself, he never obstructed other authors by giving preference to his own work. He encouraged his company to be on good terms with each other.

He founded and ran a little club back stage at the Haymarket called the Property Club. Here the players could get refreshment at the right price with sociability thrown in. Here the social precedence of the green-room did not function; it was free to all. It opened directly the first act was over; it remained open until the curtain fell. The chair was taken in succession. People outside the theatre belonged to it, writers, drama-tists, literary men. And the ladies of the company were also allowed the privilege of membership. One of them used it to make a little pin-money, by giving the Press reports of what went on. She was expelled. That was the only occasion on which the harmony of the Property Club was marred.

In private life Colman was a most sociable man, good-tempered, very intelligent and a master of repartee. Though he suffered ups and downs of fortune and even imprisonment for debt, he was never in want of money. His trouble was extravagance to keep up with associates whose means were far greater than his own. His loss of the Haymarket was the price he paid for this. He was not a good business-man, but he knew how to get the best results out of a theatre.

He suffered much from gout towards the end of his life. This attacked him violently in 1830 and brought on complications. He had to give up prolonged physical exercise and all social activity. He went to live at Greenford. But increasing illness and the necessity to be near his doctor brought him back to Town, to Brompton, where he died on October 17th, 1836. He was in great pain, but perfectly conscious and perfectly resigned. His wife was constantly with him. He could not bear her to be out of his sight. He was calm, clear and brave up to one hour of his death, when intense agony made him lose consciousness and thus his passing was easy. He was buried in the vaults under Kensington Church, beside his father. So two pillars of the Haymarket, two men who had done so much for it, were together at the end.

The passing of the name of Colman, curiously enough, was contem-porary with the passing of the old Hay Market, as it had stood for so many years. John Nash was improving London, and the old places were coming down. All the houses from the theatre southwards were to be rebuilt. Morris was to rebuild his theatre in accordance with the new plan for the street. Nash persuaded him to shift a little from the old site, to just a shade more southward. It only meant going next door. For Nash had an idea and wanted to carry it out properly. He wanted the portico of the theatre visible from St. James's Square, along the whole length of Charles Street (now Charles II Street), so as to make a dignified vista of approach. Morris agreed; he could probably do little else. He got a lease from the Crown on June 20th, 1821, of "a plot of ground on the east side of the Haymarket and West Side of Great Suffolk Street, with a Theatre and a Messuage thereon." It was granted for ninety-nine years and the rent was £356 9s. 6d. It seems incredible to-day.

The rebuilding started in 1820. The new theatre, grand and noble, arose beside the now forlorn Little Theatre in the Hay. For a time they stood side by side. It was a fitting picture of the advance of the years. There was the little playhouse, whose spirit had grown until it had been forced to expand its body. There was the humble, plain little building, where Fielding, Theophilus Cibber, Macklin, Samuel Foote and the Colmans had successively added to its fame and prestige, now handing over to the handsome, imposing playhouse which we can see to-day. It passed on its atmosphere too, its charm, friendliness and its curious intimacy, together with its own life. Its soul passed into the new theatre, which took on the patina of the years, as if there had been no break. The Haymarket Theatre was still the Haymarket Theatre, although it had gone into brand new premises. Even the invisible ghosts of the old ones moved next door, for there was no change in its feeling, it still had that queer tranquillity, that mellowness which dimmed down the freshness of the building and the paint. It might be new, brand new, but it took on the glamour of the years and the sense of continuity. It was still the Haymarket Theatre—though no longer the Little Theatre in the Hay. But then that word "little" had only applied to its size for many a year.

It was ready for opening on July 4th, 1821. The outside looked as it does to-day, over a century and a quarter later. The six Corinthian pillars were there, with their portico carried over the pavement, covering practically the whole front. It was just as it is to-day, with the exception of that small circular window in the tympanum of the pediment. That is modern. The columns, it is believed, are of brick covered with a patent mastic. Nash liked cast-iron, but it may be that there was difficulty in making the pillars in one piece of that material.

The three middle doors under the portico led to the boxes, the door on the right to the box office, and the door on the left to the pit. There were four large gas lamps in the spaces between the doors. The gallery entrances were on each side, outside the portico. The "gods" were not given any shelter in case of rain. All the interior is, of course, quite different to-day. But reference to those gas lamps shows how conservative and loth to change the Haymarket was, and how it clung to tradition (a thing it does still, for which all may be thankful). Gas was not used in the auditorium until 1850. It was the last theatre to surrender. Up to then it used oil lamps and spermaceti candles, in beautiful cut-glass chandeliers. It was slow in taking to electric light, too. But candles, gas or electric lights, the old world charm has never faded.

The interior, when it reopened, was very handsome. The ground floor was, naturally, all pit, from orchestra to back wall. There were three tiers of boxes along the side walls; there was at the back a 2s. and a 1s. gallery. The Haymarket had an apron stage, with two proscenium doors, above which were two tiers of stage boxes, two on each tier. The proscenium was supported by pillars shaped like palm trees. A very handsome house indeed. The ceiling bore painted symbolic figures and there were ornate panels.

It took four months to build—that also seems incredible to-day— and the cost is said to have been £18,000.

But the old theatre did not vanish; it only changed its calling. It had once been a tavern, it now became a restaurant, later on still the Pall Mall Restaurant, with a little bar which was almost a public green-room, where famous actors—those appearing at the Haymarket predomina- ting, but many others as well—used it as an unofficial club. It was a small but cosy and joyous place, where strangers were not much wanted and where everyone knew everybody else. It was presided over by a lady who knew and understood her clientele. She was tact personified; in her business she was an expert. The place had the real Haymarket atmosphere and she was part of it. Her name was Macdonald, but every- one called her "Mac." The Pall Mall was a real "West End" bar and she was real "West End" herself. The great charm of the place was that you were actually in the walls of the Little Theatre in the Hay, where so much that was theatrical had happened. The shop next door, Messrs. Farrow and Jackson, was part of the old theatre, too, as was the smart well-run Pall Mall Restaurant, a meeting-place for the best of Bohemia, literature, art and theatre—all in the atmosphere of the famous old playhouse, as it was actually within its walls. It has all gone now, but Haymarket Theatre No. 2 stands, and retains all that made great Haymarket No. 1. The soul of the theatre is untouched.

The new Theatre Royal, Haymarket, as they called it grandly, held upwards of £300 in money. Its prices were: boxes, 5s.; pit, 3s.; gallery, 2s.; upper gallery, 1s. In addition to the points already mentioned, it had straight side walls, so that the boxes ran straight along the tiers, but the end of the auditorium farthest from the stage was curved, though not very much. The scheme of decoration was gold, pink and crimson. It still had a very small vestibule, and it still has a small one even to-day.

The half-price introduced during certain seasons by Colman was abandoned. The play began at seven o'clock, although the doors opened at six.

Morris had a more resplendent and larger theatre than his pre- decessors. He started off well, with a revival of *The Rivals* played by a fine cast. Terry, Oxberry, Jones and Miss De Camp were in the com- pany. Oxberry was for long a Drury Lane stalwart who excelled as comic countrymen.

Before the reign of Morris starts, a backward glance should be taken, and a few things worthy of note put on record, before the Little Theatre in the Hay vanishes for ever. Some of the old bills have nice little stories to whisper. There is one dated July 7th, 1778, when, just over a year after its original production, they staged *She Stoops to Conquer*. There was in the cast Mr. Palmer, Mr. Griffin (from Theatre Royal, Bath, that royal nursery of players), Mr. Gardner, Mr. Jackson, Mr. Massey, Mr. Painter, Mr. and Mrs. Webb (from the Theatre Royal, Edinburgh), Miss Farren, Mrs. Poussin, and "A Young Gentlewoman" (being her second appearance on any stage). She was Miss Powell. They followed this with a burletta in one act (for the fourth time) called *Buxom Joan*. It was played by Bannister, Brett, Massey, Mrs. Edwin, Mrs. Brett and Miss Twist. The bill adds:

"Books of the Burletta to be had at the Theatre. The doors to be opened at Six O'clock, and the performance begin precisely at Seven. Servants to keep places are to be at the door in Suffolk Street by Five O'clock."

In the year in which these words are written (1947) quite a sensation was made by a performance given in Whitechapel of *The Merchant of Venice* played in Yiddish. There is very little new under the sun, or in the theatre. A Haymarket bill dated March 10th, 1806, proclaims:

"By Permission of the Lord Chamberlain, Theatre Royal, Haymarket, For the Benefit of Mrs. Barre (from the Theatre-Royal, Cheltenham). Will be performed the Play of *The Merchant of Venice*; Shylock . . . Mr. Sherinbeck (who will for the second time, attempt that character in the JEWISH DIALECT)."

One presumes it was Yiddish; the ancient Hebrew language is scarcely a dialect. History is silent on the fame of Mr. Sherinbeck. What the playgoers made of it all one does not know. Anyway, they had plenty else for their money. At the end of the fourth act of the play, just to liven things up a bit, there was "A Fancy Hornpipe by a Young Lady (her First Appearance)." Her name has not survived, but the bill goes on: "End of the Play, 'Bucks, have at ye All,' " by Mr. Dalton (which was a famous piece of the time, much in request and often recited by "Romeo" Coates). But that was not all, for "In the Course of the Evening Mr. Grossete will sing a Comic Song, after which a Pantomime in One Act (by Mr. Delpini) called *The Life and Death of Pantaloon*. Harlequin, Mr. Auld, Pantaloon, Mr. Grossete (from the Theatre Royal, Richmond) and Columbine, Miss Bryson." The Clown did not get a look in. It was not over even then, for the bill states: "To which will be added (compressed in One Act) the favourite Farce of *Lovers' Quarrels*," with Wouldsley, Auld, Mr. Barre, Dalton, Miss Burton, and Mrs. Barre, the beneficiary who had also played Portia to the Yiddish Shylock, duly appeared. She sold the tickets, it states, from 5 Stafford Street, Bond Street, or you could get them from Mr. Rice, at the Theatre. There was no increase in prices (5s. to 1s.), but the doors opened at 5.30 and it commenced at 6.30.

The Haymarket, like all theatres then, gave value for money.

Cyril Maude, in his delightful book, *The Haymarket Theatre*, gives some good instances of the discipline—or lack of it—obtaining in Colman's days: "Mr. Ledger came too late for his scene in *Inkle and Yarico*, in consequence of his mistaking the order in which the pieces for the evening were acted." Even that has its counterpart to-day. At one West End theatre, not so long ago, where the management, or part of it, were of a very sporting turn, there was never a matinee on the Wednesday on which the Derby was run. A Thursday matinee was substituted. One of the company never turned up at all. He had forgotten all about it. And, not so long ago either, one of our beautiful and most talented leading ladies of the musical comedy stage suddenly discovered that she was still at lunch in the Savoy Grill when she should have been on the stage performing. The audience at the Winter Garden Theatre were amazed, and gratified, to see an understudy sing the first verse of an early song, and a breathless leading lady arrive to sing the second.

Another strange Haymarket happening Mr. Maude quotes is the following: "N.B.—It being so late this evening before the farce could be begun, the first scene was omitted." There seems to have been no demonstration from the audience—at least, none is on record. Perhaps they did not mind. It is possible to see plays to-day where it would be much better if a few of the acts were omitted. The players were temperamental too, and would refuse to play, and things were held up until someone could be borrowed to perform in their place. And unpunctuality seems quite a common occurrence, not only by the players, but by members of the orchestra too.

There are one or two of the old players of that time, some of whom lasted into the new régime, who claim their share of notice. There was Wewitzer, for example. He was a Londoner brought up and trained as a jeweller. But the sparkle of the player's life had a greater appeal. He, too, strolled the country and got to Covent Garden to play Ralph in *The Maid of the Mill* for his sister's benefit. He was at Dublin, and tried afterwards to run the ill-fated Royalty Theatre. Of course, he failed, and so he joined the Drury Lane Company, playing often at the Haymarket in the summer months. He wrote or invented pantomimes with some success. He specialised in French and Jewish parts (he was probably a Jew). His line was dry humour. He had not much sentiment, so failed as Sheva, but succeeded very well as Moses in *The School for Scandal*. He was a specialist in his own line and presented delightful little cameos, but was not an actor of big dimension. In private life he was a good companion, an inveterate punster (puns were esteemed then) and could keep the table in a roar.

William Oxberry, to whom a brief reference has been made, was born in 1784 in Moorfields, exactly opposite Bedlam, as he was proud of claiming. His father was an auctioneer, and intended his son to be

an artist. His son preferred painting his own face to those of other
people. But his father disapproved of this, and tried to nip his son's
histrionic leanings in the bud. He bound him 'prentice to a printer. The
boy turned the printer's establishment into a theatre, for it so happened
that his employer was as stage-struck as himself. Young Oxberry was
ambitious. Before he was even a professional actor he became an actor-
manager. He performed in a stable in Queen Anne Street, and he took
an outhouse at Edgware, made some attempt at fitting it up as a theatre,
and began operations. He published no prices: the admission money
was exactly what the customer wanted to spend; no money was turned
away. He had some lads with him, as keen and as inexperienced as
himself. Oxberry took all the leads and all the money; or at least he
took it at the doors as it came in, for he doubled leading business and
money-taker—probably a wise precaution. One evening there must
have been quite an audience because he was still taking cash at the
doors when his cue came. He dashed behind the scenes and made his
entrance—he was already dressed in his costume covered by a cloak,
which he shed as he stepped on the boards. A puzzled audience watched
him play Othello with a perfectly white face. He had no time to make
up. Everything went well until he came to the line, "Haply for I am
black," when universal indignation stopped the performance. The
venture closed down very shortly after.

He went through the usual routine; he played in small towns and
villages with small companies and smaller audiences, and with him
were many players destined to make their names. One was Edmund
Kean. Eventually he got to Worthing, and there Mr. Siddons—
husband of the immortal Sarah—saw him. His good offices got Oxberry
a chance at Covent Garden. He made a success, but his chief job was as
understudy to Emery (who comes into the Haymarket story as well)
and Munden. He then played all round Scotland with Mrs. Glover and
Johnston. Returning to Town, he was at the Lyceum and then went to
Drury Lane. He played summer seasons at the Haymarket.

A good comedian, he also fancied himself a tragedian. He was over
average in height, very dark and had a pair of small but very expressive
blue eyes. Towards the end of his life he got very fat, largely because
of his love of good living. He was also fond of the bottle, was often
drunk on the stage, and frequently in trouble thereby. He was good
company and much in request. Often he stayed too long at table and
was late for his entrance. That meant more trouble, for audiences in
those days were outspoken, and if an actor was drunk, they told him so.
On one occasion, Oxberry, dining with friends, was very late indeed.
He missed his part in a play called *The Suicide*. But he played in the
final farce, and when he came on there was a stormy reception for him.
But Oxberry addressed the house:

"Ladies and gentlemen, it may appear that I have been guilty of a neglect towards my patrons, the public, but if you, ladies and gentlemen, will grant me a moment's indulgence, I can, I trust, clear myself from such an imputation. I came early to the theatre and was sedulously employed in studying a new character. I was not wanted until the last act. This is, I believe, the only acting comedy that is in four acts—that, and not my negligence, misled me. As my moments were employed in studying for your amusement, may I trust you will forgive my inadvertency?"

He spoofed them completely, and they cheered him. Turning to Johnston, he said with a wink, "Damn it, Sam, go on. I thought I'd settle 'em."

On another occasion when he was almost due to go on, he was nowhere to be found. Terry had to ask the audience's indulgence for another actor to read the part. This man, Ebsworth, dressed for it quickly, and then had to undress again as Oxberry dashed in. He jumped into the clothes and went on the stage to face a highly incensed audience, furious at the delay. There were yells of "Apology, apology." Oxberry took off his hat—he was never at a loss. "Ladies and gentlemen," he said, "deeply do I feel your disapprobation, but I am sure the cause of my absence will be, with you, a sufficient excuse. Ladies and gentlemen, I have but within a few minutes received information, that my only—my darling son, has met a severe accident; riding a spirited horse, he was thrown, and at the moment I now address you, I know not whether he is alive or dead." The shouts of disapproval now turned to cries of sympathy and forgiveness. So convincing had artful Oxberry been in his speech that his own daughter, who was in the audience, despite the knowledge she had of her father, was completely deceived and rushed home in distress of mind. For days kind inquiries from the public rolled in, which Oxberry answered in the gravest possible manner. Had his memory been as good as his inventive power, he would have been a great actor. As it was, he was a good comedian, who always believed he was a fine tragedian. He frequently "dried up," even in parts he had played hundreds of times. He had a gift for writing and journalism, and founded and ran The Dramatic Mirror, which was often a thorn in the side of Colman and his brother managers. He had a hasty temper and made enemies, but when he had money he was generous to a degree. His breakfast was a bottle of soda water, followed an hour afterwards by a pint of milk. He dined on a chop and spent the rest of the day sustained by ale and brandy and water. He only drank tea when in the theatre, when he imbibed it by the pint. He died, not surprisingly, of apoplexy on June 9th, 1824. He is buried in St. Clement's Danes, Strand.

Charles Kemble, whose name figures so often in Haymarket annals as actor and playwright, was a younger brother of Sarah Siddons. As with his elder brother, his father tried to keep him away from the stage. He went to Douai, as John Philip Kemble had done, for his education. A position was then found for him in the Post Office. But it was no good. You could not keep a Kemble off the stage.

He played with some small companies and then appeared, either in 1792 or 1793, at Sheffield in *As You Like It*, playing Orlando. After a round of parts there, he went to Newcastle, and thence to other provincial cities. His brother John then brought him to Drury Lane, where on April 21st, 1794, he appeared as Malcolm in *Macbeth*. The Press comment was: "As Malcolm appeared a tall, awkward youth, with what is termed a hatchet face, a figure badly proportioned and evidently weak in his limbs. His acting was even worse than his appearance." The Kembles were never well received when they started. That year he was probably the worst actor at Drury Lane, or elsewhere. When ten years had passed, he was one of the best anywhere. It was at the Haymarket that he began to improve and develop into his real prime.

At the Haymarket his Wilford in *The Iron Chest* and his enormous success in *Three Fingered Jack* placed him in the front rank there; he also began to have his plays produced. He played a lot at the Little Theatre, and later became one of the great figures of the English theatre. The Haymarket was truly his nursery, as it had been of so many great players. That hatchet face and ungainly figure became handsome and noble. His wife, Miss De Camp, was also of the Haymarket Company.

And as a tail-piece to these men of the Haymarket, of whom only a few can be picked, there is the great figure of John Emery, one of the best actors who ever walked the British boards. He came of acting stock. His father, Mackle Emery, was an actor, his mother was an actress, of the Haymarket and Covent Garden, but not in the first rank.

Emery was born at Sunderland on December 22nd, 1777—that vintage year in stage annals. He received his education in Ecclesfield, a small Yorkshire town, where he also acquired a North Country accent, so useful in later life. His parents wanted him to be a musician, but he decided that what was good enough for his parents was good enough for him, and that he would be an actor.

He made his debut at Brighton, and then he went to York, under that maker of stars, Tate Wilkinson, who saw and recognised this talent and prophesied greatness for him. Wilkinson made few mistakes.

Covent Garden got to hear of him and offered him an engagement. Wilkinson let him go, but put on record in his Memoirs, *The Wandering Patentee*, his dislike of the system which caused the Patent Theatres to rob him of his best people with such astounding regularity.

He appeared at Covent Garden on September 21st, 1798, as Frank Oatlands in *A Cure for the Heart Ache*, and Lovegold in *The Miser*—two widely contrasted characters. It needed pluck to make a debut such as this, but he was backed, of course, by the confidence of youth. He was a big success. Knight, who had just left the theatre, was a favourite Frank and Parsons and Quick were celebrated Lovegolds. Emery stood up to big guns like this.

In his early days he was overshone by Munden and Fawcett, both of whom excelled in the comic rustic parts which were Emery's *forte*.

But in 1799, Munden and Bannister left the Haymarket and Emery and Fawcett replaced them. It was at the Haymarket that Emery really came into his own.

There at the summer theatre, he got the parts he wanted and he played them to the delight of the public. He was a West End star when he was twenty-one, made so by his own talent. He married Anne Thompson, who was not of "the profession."

Emery's great talent, his sterling worth, his hard work, made him a great and general favourite. He owed much to a play by Morton, which gave him a part in which he found full scope. He was immensely popular on and off the stage. He played with ease and naturalness when much around him was stilted and artificial. He was reliable in all that he did. Not for him the shifts, absences and excuses of men like Oxberry, and all too many more. But on one occasion even he was not there when he should have been. The story is Cyril Maude's (whose wife, that beautiful woman and actress, Winifred Emery, was a granddaughter of this fine actor). Emery was at Drury Lane and was playing The Sentinel in *Pizarro*. The curtain did not rise and the audience manifested their displeasure in the usual way. The manager went before the curtain and apologised. The delay, said he, was occasioned by the non-arrival of a principal actor. He asked for a few minutes' indulgence. He had hardly got off the stage when John Philip Kemble himself came forward. It was evident that he had come because of annoyance by the rest of the company, who were present and who feared unjust reprisals if the name of the delinquent were not made public. So Kemble informed the audience that, at the request of the principal members of the company, he had to inform them that the absentee, whose lateness had caused the trouble, was John Emery. He bowed and retired. And he was almost immediately followed by John Emery himself, in a dishevelled state, hot, muddy and with perspiration streaming down his face. He was so much out of breath that he could hardly speak. But at last he managed to gasp out his own announcement. "Ladies and gentlemen," he puffed, "this is the first time I have ever had to appear before you as an apologist. But, ladies, for you I must particularly address, my wife was but an hour since brought to bed, and I ran for the doctor."

The sympathetic audience responded at once to this simple, homely statement. It was just what they liked, and he hurried off to shouts of "Bravo!" and roars of applause.

The play proceeded, but Emery had not quite done with the incident yet. Being "named" by Kemble evidently rankled a little. His chance for a "come-back" arose in a scene with Kemble himself. That stately actor, as Rolla, inquires of the Sentinel: "Have you a wife?" "I have," replied Emery.

"Children?" came the query. It was Emery's chance and he took it. "I had two this morning—I have three now," he replied. And the delighted audience cheered to the echo, whilst Kemble retired in confusion.

Emery never gave trouble. There are few stories about him because his life was as orderly as it was exemplary. He did his job, he gave perfect performances and he was universally esteemed. Tyke in *School for Reform* was perhaps his most famous part—but he never gave a poor performance in his life. He died all too soon, on July 25th, 1823. Inflammation of the lungs caused the rupture of a blood vessel. He was buried in St. Andrew's, Holborn. He left a wife and seven children, and he had not had time to make provision for them. There was a benefit on their behalf. Despite torrential rain, the house was packed as soon as the doors opened. People who could not get into the auditorium were content to pay to stand in the lobbies, so that they could show their material respect to the dead man and aid his family. There was a performance of *The Rivals* with Munden, Young, Kemble (C.), Liston and Jones in the lead. Others were Egerton, Mrs. Davenport, and Mrs. Edwin. Bartley spoke an ode written by George Colman, and there was a concert provided by the artists appearing at the English Opera House (the Lyceum). Such was the tribute paid by public and players to John Emery.

So the Little Theatre in the Hay makes its bow and departs, handing on its greatness to the newer and younger edition of itself, standing almost on the same ground, much finer, much bigger, much more elaborate, but starting with the advantage of the prestige which the little old theatre had won. But it was still only a summer theatre.

Methods did not change much at first. When the lovely new theatre opened, its customs would have seemed strange to a Haymarket play-goer of to-day. There was not that tranquillity which is now such a feature of the present playhouse. The times and the manners were more robust.

On that night of July 4th, 1821, the lighting was still by candles and oil lamps, and women sold the book of the play, the music, if any, also fruit to be consumed or thrown at the actors. And the gallery still demanded, and got, liquid refreshment served to them in their seats.

Morris was in charge; Colman had gone at last. Of the other two partners, Winston clung to his shares, but had no power or say in actual management. Tabourdine had only been a nominee of Morris, who was now the absolute cock of the Haymarket walk.

He had his own methods of management and he appears to have been a bit of a despot. He was evidently doing some thinking about the way to run the theatre and the best sort of attractions to find. He got into touch with Tom Dibdin, who had been offered a share in the Haymarket

Mr. S. B. Bancroft (later
Sir Squire Bancroft).

Miss Marie Tempest.

Below
Mrs. Lily Langtry.

Two Studies of Beerbohm
Tree in the role of
Svengali.

Miss Dorothea Baird
Trilby.

Mr. H. V. Esmond as
Little Billie.

long before, and who never ceased regretting that he had let the opportunity go by. Morris bought a play from Dibdin, and it was produced at the Haymarket in 1821. It was a success, because Dibdin was a good writer and a real man of the theatre. Its title was *Rise and Fall*, and Jones and Terry made successes in it. Dibdin was paid £100 for it by Morris.

Morris kept Dibdin in his mind, but that mind was not working on very original lines—or perhaps it was. He was thinking of staging a play in which animals had a part. There had been a craze for this at Drury Lane and Covent Garden—even John Philip Kemble and Mrs. Siddons had gone with the tide. It will be remembered that Colman had written a burlesque on the subject and had overdone it. Now Morris thought that the time had arrived when the Haymarket might make some money out of this Astley-ish idea. So he went to Dibdin about it.

But Morris was not thinking of elephants, horses and camels, such as the other theatres used. He had a much better stunt—he was going to have a play featuring reindeer—that at least was novel. Reindeer were scarce; few people had ever seen them. He had managed to get hold of some from a Mr. Bullock, of the Piccadilly Museum, and he wanted Dibdin to write him a play in which they could be introduced. He had got all the scenery painted, with some rocks for them to leap about on (if that is one of their habits) and some painted mountains for their grazing grounds. This was a bit of a staggerer to Dibdin, more especially when Morris presented to him a man, his wife and son, little podgy people, like barrels on pegs, whom Morris claimed were either Laps or Esquimaux (much the same to him). Dibdin asked what on earth they could do on the stage? They promptly danced, sang and played the violin. Morris thought it was all right, though Dibdin had his doubts. However, he was not the man to turn work away, although he was running the Surrey Theatre at the time.

They went ahead. Dibdin wrote the play, Erskine, his Surrey musical director, composed the music, the dresses were made in the Surrey wardrobe from designs lent by the accommodating Mr. Bullock, and when everything was ready, Morris, the reputed Laps and all the Haymarket company were invited to the Dibdin office at the Surrey to hear the play read. He had called it *Lapland*. He waited for over an hour. Nobody arrived. Then appeared Terry of the Haymarket with a little note and a long face. The reindeer had all died— possibly they had gone to work for Father Christmas. According to Morris, the whole thing was off. Dibdin told him that the writing, the composing and the making of the dresses was a contract job definitely commissioned by Morris. Morris pooh-poohed all that. It was just a risk authors, composers and the like had to take. He could not pay anyone anything.

That was how Mr. Morris did business—not in the approved Haymarket way. Dibdin, having stated his claim, bided his time.

Q

CHAPTER XX

THE NEW RULE AT THE HAYMARKET

MORRIS apparently bore Dibdin no ill will for demanding payment for work done, probably because he had no intention of paying. Very shortly afterwards he approached Dibdin to come to that theatre in the position of Stage Manager—now General Manager. The terms he offered did not attract Dibdin, for not only was that clever man expected to run the theatre, but also to write a one-act farce for the opening, and a two-act farce and three-act drama to be performed during the season, for the total sum of £200. Dibdin turned it down. He promptly got a letter from Morris offering a "clear benefit" as well, and an engagement for Mrs. Dibdin to run the wardrobe, though at a small salary. Morris was not generous as to terms.

Now, Dibdin, through no fault of his own and largely through unfair competition at the Coburg (now Old Vic) Theatre, had had very bad luck at the Surrey and in an Irish venture. So he closed with the new offer, and signed for three seasons. Morris told him repeatedly that his partner, Winston, strongly objected to both terms and engagement. They evidently ran a Spenlow and Jorkins act, for Winston had no power at all and Morris used him as a bogy.

Dibdin set to work on his Haymarket plays. He completed the one-act farce, which he called *The Bill of Fare or Inquire Within*, and the two-act farce, entitled *Love Letters*.

He took his seat in Morris's office as Manager for the first time on Saturday, June 8th, 1822, and he read the one-act farce to the company. Before he was allowed to read them the two-act play, *Love Letters*, he had to read it in private to Morris and Madame Vestris. He found that petticoat government reigned at the Haymarket. If Madame Vestris did not like him, or his play, it was all over.

Dibdin had been his own master for seven years, and this sort of thing did not appeal to him at all. When he had worked for Colman, nothing of the kind happened. What he wrote was good enough for presentation at once. Dibdin soon found that the New Haymarket was not the Old Haymarket by any manner of means. He found, too, that he was not to be allowed to use his own judgment or discretion, but that Madame Vestris was "the boss." Well, she was accustomed to wearing the trousers. However, on this occasion she liked the play and said so.

Morris sat through the reading of the farce with a perfectly solemn face: no smile hovered, no muscle twitched—a nice ordeal for any author.

The Haymarket opened on June 15th, 1822, with *The School for*

Scandal and Dibdin's *The Bill of Fare*, for which Parry composed the music. Charles Kemble was to have played Charles Surface, but his brother Stephen (the fat man) died, and he could not appear. Dibdin put in Russell, who did very well. His own little farce was a success.

On June 24th his longer farce, *Love Letters*, was produced and Madame Vestris's judgment was justified. If Morris had not laughed, the public did so heartily.

Dibdin now set to work on his three-act play, running the theatre all the while, conducting rehearsals, stage-managing, and doing all the hundred and one things a general manager has to do. He got an idea from a book of travels and he wrote an opera called *Abyssinia*.

On the day he finished it, he was asked to dine with Morris, *tête-à-tête*, in his office. By way of dessert, he was to read his play. Morris was not giving him any time off. They had a good dinner and some good wine. Dibdin read his opera and said he thanked Morris for the dinner, of which he highly approved. Morris replied gravely that he could not say the same of the opera—he entirely disapproved of it. Dibdin swallowed hard and replied, "Very well, sir. Then I'll try another." He set to work the very next day writing a fresh one, called *Morning, Noon and Night*.

Whilst working on it, he heard from Elliston, now at Drury Lane, who wanted him there as Stage Manager. And he heard also from his old musical director, Erskine, desiring to know when he was to be paid for the music he had written for the ill-fated *Lapland*. Dibdin laid this before Morris, who disposed of it in a way all of his own. "As the piece was never played," he declared, "I say once again that no money is due." Once again Dibdin pointed out that this was a direct commission, not something written on speculation and that both he and Erskine had a just claim. Morris, in his pompous way, begged to dissent from Mr. Dibdin's opinion. So that worthy held his horses and advised Erskine to do the same, although Erskine could at that time have been paid off for a small sum.

In September, 1822, Dibdin's *Morning, Noon and Night* was produced. It had undergone the ordeal of Morris's judgment—although Dibdin did not dine this time—and also Liston's. It was a very big success, and, although late in the season, ran for eleven nights.

That season had been a busy one for Dibdin. He had, besides writing three plays and producing them, staged five other major productions and all the usual stock pieces. And he had trained Miss Paton, who made a successful debut in her opening play.

The Haymarket closed on October 15th, and Dibdin spoke the address. In this, whilst thanking the public on behalf of the proprietors, he also thanked the performers on behalf of the proprietors. That brought the wrath of Morris upon him. He was informed it was a most unusual thing to do and, indeed, that he ought not to have done it at all. All through the season, Morris had not approved of anything Dibdin had done. All sorts of petty little things were used as pinpricks. He had, as did all stage managers in those days, a private box at his disposal. But nobody but himself was allowed to go into it. His wife could, but she was always too busy. His two sons were refused admission and the box-keeper even withstood Dibdin's remonstrance. Dibdin took his boys home and wrote to Morris that if such things went on he should leave the theatre. After an angry scene, he got a half-satisfactory answer by letter. And he was heavily reproved for having stuck some lists by means of wafers on the grey whitewashed walls of his office—which measured nine feet square. He was glad when the season ended, and he went back to Drury Lane.

Dibdin was back at the Haymarket for the season of 1823 in no very happy frame of mind. He opened with a trifle of his own called *The Will for the Deed*. A two-act piece was wanted next. Dibdin put up six or seven, all of which Morris turned down. One of them, called *King Charles the Second's Merry Days*, pleased Madame Vestris, and she said she would like to play in it—but Morris would not have it. It went to Covent Garden, where it was a big success. The meretricious Morris also would have nothing to do with an adaptation from the French called *Sayings and Doings*. Yet later he accepted another version—and a much inferior one—done by his own secretary, a mere literal translation. All the others that he had banned succeeded elsewhere.

Dibdin protested violently against the rejection of his pieces. Morris took refuge behind his company; he said the players did not like them. It was no good appealing to them; they were frightened of the tyrannical manager. Dibdin suggested Colman as arbitrator. That displeased Morris more than ever.

Morris liked cracking the whip, he liked showing these clever professional people that he was master. So he selected the play himself. This was *The Vicar of Wakefield*, which Dibdin had already produced at the Surrey. Liston played in it. It had been given for over fifty performances at the Surrey, so did not have a long run at the Haymarket.

Mrs. Smith, an adaptation from the French, followed, and then *The Heir-at-Law*, by Colman, in which Mrs. Jones made her debut. She showed great promise as an actress, but died young. *Sweethearts and Wives*, adapted from the French by Kenny, was a big success, however.

Dibdin was having plenty of trouble. His old friend Erskine was again pressing for the *Lapland* money and again was advised to wait.

A farce called *Spanish Bonds, or Wars in Wedlock* failed miserably. Dibdin condemned it before production, but Morris overruled him and told him he was obstructive. Another farce, *The Great Unknown*, to which he also objected, was approved by Morris, out of his great experience. It ran one night only. The chief scene was a snowstorm and the whole thing was a frost.

Ebsworth's melodrama *Rosalie* saved the season. At the end Dibdin spoke the usual address. He was not allowed to write it, however, but it

was given him by Morris, who had probably written it himself. It was
a dull, pompous affair, but Morris praised Dibdin's speaking of it in the
green-room afterwards, the first bit of praise Dibdin had received since
coming to the Haymarket.

Yet there had been an occasion when he had deserved many thanks
and got censure instead. It is a nice little bit of back-stage Haymarket
history.

Morris sent for Dibdin one afternoon, and told him to be dressed and
at the theatre early to receive and light to the Royal Box Her Royal
Highness the Duchess of Kent. Dibdin was delighted. He knew the
Duchess very well; she had often visited the Surrey Theatre. Morris
told him he must light her forth again at the end of the show.

This business of "lighting" meant that the responsible manager of
the theatre received the Royal visitors with two candles—a very necessary thing on account of dark passages and stairways—and walked
backwards before them into the Royal Box, doing the same thing, in
reverse, when they left. Dibdin duly received the Duchess of Kent,
who was glad to see him. When the time came to send her away in her
carriage, it was discovered, to Dibdin's dismay, that another coach,
belonging to a lady member of the company, was standing just opposite
the door from which the Duchess was to emerge. Dibdin told the driver
to pull up a bit. The driver, who was drunk, refused to do any such
thing, although told whose carriage he was obstructing. Dibdin sent for
an officer of the law to make the ultra-democratic coachman move, and
whilst awaiting the removal, tendered his apologies to the Royal
Duchess, who was charming about it all and treated it as a joke. Had
she not known Dibdin, it might have been serious, and if the Court
frowned on a theatre in those days, it was almost extinction for that
playhouse. But Dibdin's tact smoothed it all over.

Now it is almost certain that the obnoxious carriage was that of
Madame Vestris, that remarkable woman who had, at the time, a considerable hold upon Morris. She exerted her sway over so many.

So much is known about her, so much has been written about her that
there is no need of a detailed account of this fascinating woman here.
Singer and actress, and the possessor of the loveliest legs in London,
Lucia Elizabetta Vestris was the granddaughter of the great Bartolozzi.
Born in 1797, she was a most precocious child and had her first "pro-
tector" at the age of fifteen. She was much married, and much loved.
She had made her debut at the King's Theatre, Haymarket, the Opera
House of Vanbrugh, and before she came to the Haymarket Theatre
she was a great star. Her Giovanni in London at Drury Lane was a
furore, so was her Macheath in *The Beggar's Opera*. Her beauty, her
voice and her legs made an irresistible appeal. The more she showed
her legs the more the Town loved her. Covent Garden, Drury Lane,
the King's Theatre, all added to her fame, and she to theirs, and then in
Morris's time she came to the Haymarket for summer seasons. Here she

played Shakespeare. In 1825 at the Haymarket she was seen in *The Beggar's Opera*. It was one of her great successes. She was criticised by the purists for wearing the male costume of the time instead of the period of the play. What did she, or her audience, care about that?

At the Haymarket she played another "breeches part." The opera was *Alcaid*, a story of Spain, and she played Don Felix. The *London Magazine* reported:

"Madame Vestris enacted Don Felix in a good loose dashing rake-helly fashion. She is the best bad young man about town, and can stamp a smart leg in white tights with the air of a fellow who has an easy heart and a good tailor. We remember once seeing Madame Vestris in female attire, and thought her a very interesting young person in that solitary instance, but we presume that she herself inclines to pantaloons and prefers to contemplate the daring knee and boot, to the neat and modest foot veiled below the ankle. The music was composed by Isaac Nathan. It was pretty but Mr. Nathan is one of those composers who require poetry to inspire them."

Other plays Vestris did that season at the Haymarket were *Intrigue* and *Sweethearts and Wives*. She also sang in *The Marriage of Figaro*, in which Susanna suited her perfectly.

Ebers, who ran the King's Theatre, had trouble with the structure of that place and, pending repairs, went over to the Haymarket. But that house did not suit his super-aristocratic clientele. The boxes were not entirely separated from each other and he put it on record that—

"persons of fashion suffer the pain of being seen by the next door neighbours as plainly as if they were exposing themselves in the public boxes of vulgar theatres,"

as if that was not the main idea of sitting in a box! But in Ebers' opinion, the Haymarket was vulgar.

Another mistake was the announcement that the balcony "had been fitted up in a commodious manner to communicate with the boxes and the pit." It turned out to be just the old 2s. gallery, for which he was charging 10s. a seat. This brought a mass of complaints, one of them being that an attendant of the house stopped everyone wishing to pass from the so-called balcony to the pit. If they said they came from the gallery, out they went. It caused a lot of trouble. Ebers went back to the fashionable rarefied atmosphere of his Opera House as soon as he could and left the vulgar Haymarket.

Vestris's career at the Haymarket was notable for her incursion into the legitimate drama, too. She played Letitia in *The Belle's Stratagem*, and she was not very good. She played Mistress Ford in *The Merry Wives of Windsor* and she played Rosalind in *As You Like It*. Said a learned critic: "Madame Vestris cannot play Shakespeare because she evidently cannot comprehend Shakespeare—and those who saw her

Rosamond must confess this." A critic, who calls Rosalind, "Rosamond," does not comprehend much more about Shakespeare than did Vestris. She probably wanted to play Rosalind because she could show off her legs.

She did better in *The Lord of the Manor*. She had a chance to use her voice—and she sang Bishop's "Dashing White Sergeant" with terrific effect. She wore women's clothes too. Press comment is that she appeared in—

> "her natural and becoming habiliments. To the shame of the age we protest that we never saw this lady perform but once in female attire; we therefore had more than ordinary pleasure in witnessing her performance of Anette in *The Lord of the Manor*, though we thought the stamping sort of saucebox air with which she marched away to the tune of 'The Dashing White Sergeant' was too much in keeping with her notorious male attire exhibitions."

The paper, which was called *The Sovereign*, got quite cross about it: "This theatrical system of putting the female sex in breeches is barbarous and abominable." What that critic would have thought if he could come back to-day and walk along any street is intriguing.

Neither Madame Vestris nor the management took the slightest notice of the critic's censure, for later in the season she appeared in a play called *The Epaulette*, in which not only she, but seven other women, wore the breeches. She was in male attire and on familiar ground with *The Beggar's Opera*, and she showed her delightful figure to the greatest possible advantage when playing Apollo in *Midas*. This drew some unfavourable comments, in an indirect manner, for, commenting on Maria Foote as Ariel in *The Tempest*, *The Dramatic Mirror* said: "Always excepting Madame Vestris's Apollo, we know no dress so indelicate as that chosen by our heroine." But it did not upset everyone—certainly not the public—for the *London Magazine* said: "She is a very tight little person in her dress and indeed looks a mighty dapper Daphne-hunter."

So much for Vestris at the Haymarket in 1825. But something big was to come and she was to participate in it.

This event was the production of the famous *Paul Pry*. This play by J. Poole, produced at the Haymarket on September 13th, 1825, was a terrific success. Liston scored the greatest of his many triumphs in it; indeed, he made the play. His odd figure, his odd dress, with its baggy breeches, Hessian boots, black gloves, ungainly umbrella, tickled the house. His catchwords, "I hope I don't intrude" and "I just popped in," not only swept the town, but became part of the language. And what a company performed the play: Mrs. Waylett, Mrs. Glover, William Farren (who had joined the Haymarket the year before), Madame Vestris and Liston. Liston's performance of the intrusive, interfering, inquisitive busybody achieved one of the great creations of the English stage. It ran for 114 performances to packed houses. Never had there been such a success at the Haymarket—and seldom elsewhere.

But what makes it the more memorable is something which Madame Vestris did in the play. She had to have a song, of course. She could not decide what to sing from a mountain of ballads which lay before her. She was trying them over with George Perry, a well-known musician of the day. There seemed little to please her. Song after song they tried, and then when Perry had played one through and she had just hummed it, he said, "Really, madame, that's a very pretty song." She tried it again; this time she sang it. "I think so too," she said. "I shall sing it to-night." She did, and it rivalled the success of the play. It was "Cherry Ripe"—always associated with Vestris, and still sung to-day. It still recalls the charm of its singer in its own grace. *Paul Pry* and "Cherry Ripe" were a famous Haymarket "double." It was the work of C. E. Horn, a delightful song-writer, also remembered by "I Know a Bank" and "I've Been Roaming."

The Haymarket wanted no more plays that year. In 1826 Vestris had gone to Covent Garden, but *Paul Pry* remained as popular as ever. Mrs. Humby played Phœbe, the part Vestris had created. But Vestris returned to the Haymarket for the last performance of the 1826 season, and as soon as she stepped on the stage, the orchestra struck up "Cherry Ripe." She ran down to the footlights, bathed the audience in one of her ravishing smiles, and spoke the epilogue which always ended the season. In this she poked fun at Farren, who was to have done it. She said:

"Pray don't be alarmed, but sit quietly there
I'm not going to sing 'Cherry Ripe,' I declare.
But those fiddles, though quietly placed on their shelves
Would from habit squeak out 'Cherry Ripe' by themselves.
No. My visit just now is in kindness and pity,
To save you from almost so hackneyed a ditty.
The tribute of thanks in the self-same dull strain
You've endured, patient victors, again and again.
I saw it impending—this ominous hat—
A true type of the usual address—dull and flat.
Farren dressed all in black, with a grave solemn face
And these four cruel pages of trite commonplace. (*Holds up a paper.*)
Hang such dull undertakers—like work. Whence the reason?
We're not going to bury the Haymarket season.
Can't we part as we met? In good humour? If he be
Black on this night—then my name isn't Phœbe. . . .

And there we must leave her. Morris paid her thirty guineas a week, a huge sum for the Haymarket, but she earned every penny.

She flashes across the Haymarket sky like a comet. She does not stay long, but she makes the impact of a meteor. She was beloved and she was much loving. Although she affected male attire so much, she was herself all woman. Though she graces the Haymarket story for so short a time, that theatre was inextricably bound up with her life. There she sang the song by which she is always remembered, and later, when she found her true level and revolutionised stage *décor* at the Olympic, Covent Garden and elsewhere, and gave burlesque to an eager public, laying the foundation stone of the musical comedies and plays to come, she married a man whose father had made his name at the Little Theatre in the Hay. For Charles J. Mathews, whose life she linked to her own at last, was the son of the Charles Mathews who looms so largely in the Haymarket story. Alas! that the end of the lovely Vestris, whose voice, eyes, limbs and talent fascinated London and enslaved so many hearts, should have been so tragic. Perhaps the best epitome of her career was spoken by three other actresses in a green-room gossip. They were Mrs. Humby, Mrs. Orger and Mrs. Glover. They were chewing over the Vestris-Mathews marriage. "They say," said pretty little Humby with much simplicity, "that before accepting him, Vestris made a full confession to him of all her lovers. What touching confidence." "What needless trouble," commented Mrs. Orger. But Mrs. Glover capped it. "What a wonderful memory!" quoth she.

But Vestris herself is a wonderful memory, sharing romantic eminence with Nell Gwynne herself.

Paul Pry, "Cherry Ripe," Liston, Vestris, Farren—that was the successful, happy side of the Haymarket which the public knew. Behind the scenes it was not so pleasant.

The long and increasingly bitter feud between Morris and Dibdin came to a head. Thomas Dibdin, blunt, straightforward and belligerent, true son of the father he had cast off, was not to be bullied and badgered and cheated by such a pompous, petty tyrant as David Morris.

At the close of the 1823 season he had wanted a full settlement of his salary. There was a bit of demur about this. It was pointed out that of the plays he had contracted to do, only *Summer Flies* and *The Vicar of Wakefield*—not a new or a cash-productive one—had been accepted. Dibdin replied that it was not his fault. Morris suggested arbitration. Dibdin named a Mr. Williams as his champion. This man was a solicitor, a friend of Morris's, and knew all that went on in the theatre. The facts were laid before him. Dibdin's claim was for his full salary, the full night's takings of his benefit and £100 for plays, as stipulated in his contract. After weeks of discussion, all he could get was £50. He took this and he signed a receipt, the full implication of which he did not understand. It was a trick, for it tried to make out that, by accepting this meagre sum, he did so in full settlement of all matters between them. That was to be fought out later.

Bad luck was pursuing Dibdin. Besides being ill-treated by Morris, Elliston at Drury Lane, where he worked in the winter, turned against him too.

Before the Haymarket opened again, Morris wanted his help. He had got involved in a lawsuit with a Mr. Paton over the engagement of that gentleman's daughter at the Haymarket. Morris actually called upon Dibdin and wanted him as a witness. He was subpœnaed by Morris with the 1s. payment. He was subpœnaed the same day by the other side with a guinea as payment. Morris lost his case. It did not decrease the tension between them.

In preparation for the Haymarket season, Dibdin wrote a play in three acts based on *St. Ronan's Well*. Morris refused it. Dibdin wrote a comedy called *India Pickle*. Morris refused that too. Morris then gave him some volumes of an old French novel and told him to make a play out of them for Liston. In three weeks, the play was read to Morris. That magnificent judge approved the first act, suggested alterations in the second and finally said if Liston would play the part, it could be produced. Liston said he would do so. Morris, however, finally refused the play. So the pinpricks of Dibdin went on. Play after play, suggestion after suggestion were turned down. When they did get open, it was with a sketch as to which Dibdin had warned Morris, without any of the stars and only Wilkinson in a part unsuitable to him. Naturally it failed.

At the end of the first week of the season Dibdin sent to the Treasury for his salary and was refused, because of the failures and also because it was stated that he was not entitled to any payment as author, and, anyway, his engagement was a weekly one. His agreement stipulated that the season's salary should be paid in weekly instalments. Dibdin was in a hole. He had a lawsuit with Drury Lane over Elliston's battle with him, he had earned no money all the winter and he had his family to keep. He put his pride in his pocket, went to Morris, laid his situation before him and asked him to pay him what was due, including the old disputed sum over *Lapland*. All he got was a note referring him to Morris's solicitors. Try as he would, he got that answer every time. Overworked and worried, he fell sick. But ill as he was, he still went down to the theatre to do his duty. He had to ask indulgence over the non-appearance of an actress. He begged the audience's permission to substitute another opera for *The Beggar's Opera*, which could not be put on because of the the non-appearance of Miss Paton. The audience would have nothing but the opera which made Gay rich and Rich gay. Dibdin got through somehow.

He got not a word of encouragement or thanks. The next day, on his way home for dinner, he felt a hand on his shoulder. He was arrested for debt incurred in legal action. There was no bail in these matters; it was payment or imprisonment. He had money owing to him—quite a lot—at two places, the Haymarket and Drury Lane. He applied to both in vain. He was kept at Carey Street, and taken to the King's Bench, where he borrowed money at 40 per cent. on the security of his library.

Mrs. Dibdin rushed to Morris to ask for her husband's salary. She was referred to the solicitors. Mrs. Dibdin had to continue her day and night work in the wardrobe—though her family were ill—for £2 a week and submit to petty tyranny from Morris all the while. Dibdin wrote demanding the money due to him, and expressed himself very forcibly. Morris replied taking umbrage at the tone of the letter and refusing to do anything. Much correspondence passed, belligerent on the part of Dibdin, artful on the part of Morris. At last Dibdin had to take legal action.

He managed to get out of prison. He left the Haymarket, he left Drury Lane, but Covent Garden was glad to get him. Then he and Erskine joined hands over the unpaid account for *Lapland*. They took Mr. Morris into Court. Twelve good men and true on a British jury awarded Erskine and Dibdin their money, and Morris had heavy costs to pay. It was not a creditable affair for any manager of the Haymarket.

Morris was not destined to control the Haymarket for much longer. He gave up the search for novelties and fell back upon stock plays. He had Madame Vestris, as we have seen, he had Liston, to whom he paid £60 and £70 a night, and he had William Farren.

William Farren was a fine actor of quality who excelled in old men parts. His Sir Peter Teazle was unsurpassed. He had an air, he had distinction, he had dramatic power and he had comedy. He was supreme, too, as old Lord Ogleby in *The Clandestine Marriage*. He raised the wages of actors. He knew his value and insisted on getting it. Alfred Bunn, who had the utmost aversion to paying anyone, was very bitter about Farren. "Is Mr. Farren a better actor than Mr. Munden was, and is he, *per se*, more attractive?" he demanded. "Decidedly neither. Upon what principle, then, is Farren to receive £40 per week when Munden only received £14? Suppose some blockheads are to be found who maintain that Farren is the better actor—at all events he can't be £26 a week better. The joke, originating in Farren himself, of his being the 'only salmon in the market,' and consequently worth so much more per pound, cannot be borne out. For people would soon get sick of salmon, as Farren knows they have been, when it has been stuffed down their throats day after day."

That was Bunn of Drury Lane's moan, but the Haymarket public did not get sick of salmon *à la* Farren—who called himself the "cock salmon." He demanded his price, and got it. But there were, indeed, differences of opinion about him. He delighted in playing Shylock, but it was not one of his best parts. He was on the lean side, and at one of his benefits, when he nearly always elected to play the Jew that Shakespeare drew, he got a rude interruption. He came to the line:

> "*The pound of flesh that I demand is mine*
> '*Tis dearly bought and I will have it,*"

and a gentleman in the gallery called out: "Let old Skinny have the pound of flesh. You can see he wants it bad enough." He was criticised as an actor without range. He sought to disprove this by playing comedy parts in which Dowton and Terry had shone. Too intelligent and observant to give a bad performance, he never really succeeded in that line. But he had great ingenuity and skill and understood his art. It was when he came to the characters of old men that he excelled—and one critic said that whenever he played something unsuitable, he was forgiven because his Lord Ogleby atoned for all. By the time he got to the Haymarket he had made a large round of parts his own and the public asked nothing better. He was indeed the "cock salmon" of the market. Morris relied on him a great deal, and not in vain. But novelty went by the board. The old stock pieces were played, with perfect casts, led by Farren. One innovation, however, was embarked upon in 1833, when Mrs. Glover attempted the part of Falstaff in *The Merry Wives*. She had been a good Hamlet, as women Hamlets go, but she was not a good Falstaff—fat, artful and robust old Sir John was beyond her—the part is so essentially masculine. One critic was unkind enough to say that she needed no make-up, as regards padding. She was indeed portly, but hardly Falstaffian.

But novelties or no novelties, they had a fine company. Farren, Mrs. Glover, both the Vinings, Mrs. Waylett, Mrs. Honey—good people all—Liston and John Reeve, a couple of unexcelled comedians: it was rich fare. Charles Kemble was there in 1835, playing a wonderful round of parts, and in 1836 Morris did something worth while by presenting Sergeant Talfourd's *Ion*, with Ellen Tree in the title role and Vandenhoff as Adastrus.

Ellen Tree, who became Mrs. Charles Kean, was a better comedienne than tragedienne, but naturally preferred tragedy. Her great days were to come. Vandenhoff was a terrific actor.

But there was someone else—someone of glory and greatness, thought by many the greatest of all—who came again to the Haymarket at this time. That flaming torch of the drama, that brilliant meteor, that thing of fire and flame which lit the theatre for all too short a time—Edmund Kean—came to the little theatre in 1830. The glory was dimmed, the flame was flickering, the white heat of genius was dulled, but, despite loose living, drunkenness and debauchery, that name still drew. The public had seen its idol rooted upon the stage, his memory gone; it had seen him fail so miserably as Henry V at Drury Lane as to make it incredible that he could ever act again. Yet he was at the Haymarket, and the house was packed. One never knew. That living spark might rekindle, that great volcano of power might erupt, for he was a genius and unpredictable—and, at any rate, he was Edmund Kean. So when Kean took the stage, London went to see—to hope and to wonder.

He had been at the Haymarket before, but few of them knew it. In 1806, by the influence of Miss Tidswell, he had played there, a strange little man playing tiny parts. It irked him, he hated it for he knew his power. But at the Haymarket in 1806 he counted for nothing; he was just one of the crowd, with a few lines to say. And when he said them at rehearsals and tried to make them worth while, it was resented by the players of major parts, who looked upon the small part people as so much rubbish, existing merely to make continuity for the entrance of the stars. It was at the Haymarket that Rae was to belittle young Kean. Rae, not a great actor by any means, made things very unpleasant for this dwarfish, large-headed, black-eyed minor player—and that big head never forgot. Those eyes flashed fire and that memory recorded. The time was to come when insults at the Haymarket were to be repaid at Drury Lane. . . . Rae and Kean had known each other as children. Rae held him in contempt. He was to learn. . . .

But those days were gone. Edmund Kean had risen like a glittering sun. Now that sun was setting, was very near the horizon again, the light had gone, night was soon to fall. And those who saw him at the Haymarket in 1830 might well have murmured as an echo to one of his greatest achievements, "Othello's occupation's gone."

He had spent his great gifts with prodigality—nothing remained save a memory, and a hope. And still that hope gave him life. Still people came. Poor in pocket, broken in reputation, he trod the Haymarket boards. He played Richard III, Shylock, Sir Giles Overreach and King Lear.

He was making a struggle, he was still Edmund Kean, there still stretched a few years of fight and grimness before him. And he packed that little summer theatre with people who had seen Kean in his heyday and by people who had never seen him before and who wished to say in after years: "Yes, I saw the great Edmund Kean at the Haymarket." For the moment, it was enough for him. He had to be content with little now—he had squandered his chances. But once again he played his great parts, and remembered how he had been a minor player in the other little theatre which bore the same name, and now was, thank God, a star in the new one—yes, still a star.

He came again in 1832—very near the end. His very face had changed, he was bloated and heavy, his flashing eye was sunken and misted, his voice and his power alike were almost gone. Yet, at times, when the great scenes came, the actor triumphed over the man and the old Kean would show through the wreck of the present Kean—and the applause would come roaring over the footlights. But such moments were few— he struggled rather than moved upon the stage. That sword which once he flourished so nobly and so well had now become his staff; he used it as a stick to help him move about. It was pitiably sad, this decline of genius, this self-destroyed man, who still fought a hopeless battle and yet would suddenly compel a catch in the throat and eager applause. But it was almost the end, very near the final curtain of his life—and he played no more at the Haymarket.

Still he belongs to its story, still his spirit is entitled to a place with

Haymarket ghosts, and his mighty name is on its pages, near his beginning and near his end, the wonderful journey of which the glory began at Drury Lane and the curtain fell at Covent Garden. But to those who love the Haymarket it is comforting to think that Edmund Kean played there—and belongs in part to them.

But happier names appear after that sad exit—names destined to rise to heights and to shine, to write pages for the Haymarket which no shame dimmed and no dishonour smirched. Not so grand, not so epoch-making, but perhaps more in the tradition of the Haymarket, that more peaceful and serene story which, full of humanity as it is, has not the storm and stress of the two great Patent theatres, with their Bettertons, Macklins, Garricks, Siddons, Kembles and Keans.

Two men joined that company of Morris's, both about the same time, and both were fated to raise its prestige to greater heights. Their names were Benjamin Webster and John Baldwin Buckstone. They are of the true Haymarket tradition and two of its most glorious sons. Webster went on to the Adelphi, to make history there, but Buckstone— Buckstone never left the Haymarket. He is there yet—although he has left all managerial and worldly cares behind. Yet his spirit lingers at the theatre he loved—and his gentle kindly ghost hovers in the room he inhabited in earthly form, unable and unwilling to break the ties which always bind it thereto.

Benjamin Webster and John Baldwin Buckstone are names written in letters of gold in the story of the Haymarket Theatre.

CHAPTER XXI

A GOLDEN AGE DAWNS

THE Georgian age was dying—dying in the person of old King William IV—the Sailor King who had had an actress for a lover—when in 1837 a new man took over the destinies of the Haymarket Theatre. The new times were coming to the country and to the little theatre. A young Princess—Victoria—was soon to ascend the throne and to start an epoch which was to become great and glorious. And in the Haymarket Theatre there was a man, a young man as managers go, who was to raise the fortunes of that playhouse to the height at which it stands to-day. He was to make it something it had never been before. He was to place it on a par with the two Patent theatres—shortly to be shorn of their tyrannic power—in every sense of the word. He was to make it, during his management, the theatre of quality it still remains. During his time it was consistently the only theatre in London where quality was always to be found. For the Garden and the Lane were in a period of twilight—flashes came from them, but there were bad patches too. But at the Haymarket the sun shone always whilst Benjamin Nottingham Webster was in charge. Indeed, his rule of the Haymarket might be likened to the glories of the Triumvirate and of David Garrick at Drury Lane.

In 1837, this practical man of the theatre took over the reins from the ineffectual and inexperienced hands of David Edward Morris and the Haymarket blossomed at once. Benjamin Webster stands high in Haymarket annals. Indeed, he stands high in the history of the British theatre—and descendants of his still play to-day.

Once again the Haymarket had an actor-manager-dramatist in charge, for if Webster was not much of a hand at new plays, he knew all about adaptations and play-doctoring and with a few deft touches could make all the difference between a bad and a workmanlike script. He knew his theatre job backwards and, a man of quality himself, he stood for quality all the time. He gave quality to his patrons at the Haymarket, and they immediately responded, as audiences always do to the right stuff.

Benjamin Nottingham Webster was born at Bath in 1798, so he was only thirty-nine when he took command at the Haymarket. He had no "backers"; he stood alone to risk money which he had earned himself at the job of acting. But he had no fears, for he knew exactly what to do.

He had made an inauspicious start in life—for at the age of nineteen, when just entering his profession, he had married a widow who already had a family. That needed pluck, but he shouldered the responsibility. He was fighting for a bare livelihood, tramping after jobs and seldom getting one. He heard that Beverley, an honest manager, was doing a season at Croydon. He hurried there, on foot, of course, to ask for work. But Beverley had all the actors he wanted. Things were desperate with Webster. He inquired if there were any vacancies in the orchestra and was asked what he could play. He reeled off a list of instruments and was told to show what he could do on the violin. What he could do, got him a job at one guinea week. It was wealth to Webster. He was living in Shoreditch. He walked from there to Croydon and back again every day—a matter of twenty odd miles— and he lived on 2d. daily, one pennyworth of milk and one pennyworth of oatmeal. On Sundays he and the family had a little shin of beef for a treat.

Nor was his job all honey. The "gods" of the Croydon Theatre had a playful way of pelting the orchestra. Sometimes, however, the missiles took the form of meat pies—and then Webster had no complaints. He ate them and regarded them as manna from Heaven.

He pleased Beverley, and in response to his repeated requests was allowed to leave the orchestra pit and show what he could do on the stage as a dancer. He tried a hornpipe, but the combination of anxiety, nerves, fatigue and weakness from hunger was too much for him. But he had done well enough for Beverley to see his talent, and Beverley understood about hardships himself. He made Webster an actor and appointed him what was then called "walking gentlman"—a most suitable post for one who tramped his twenty miles a day on 2d.

But Beverley got him a job in London, at the old Coburg Theatre— now the Old Vic. There, coming events cast their shadows before. He made his first appearance in Town in a Haymarket play—Colman's *Heir-in-Law*, although, for the purpose of evading royalties, the title was altered to *The Lord's Warming Pan*.

Webster got on. From the Coburg in 1818 he went to the Regency (now the Scala). Then he managed to get into the Drury Lane company and he made a success. He took over the part of Pompey in *Measure for Measure* at very short notice (because Harley was ill) and scored a hit.

He became a leading actor at the Olympic when Madame Vestris queened it there so magnificently. There he starred with Liston and Mrs. Orger. He was also at the West London Theatre. In 1833 he came to the Haymarket, although he may have played there occasionally before in minor parts as early as 1829.

But on July 17th, 1833, he made a very big success there in Douglas Jerrold's *The Housekeeper, or The White Rose*, and followed it up by appearing with Farren and Mrs. Glover in a farce called *Uncle John*.

This was by John Baldwin Buckstone—and thus two men, both destined to be famous at the Haymarket, came together. In December, 1833, he was back again at Drury Lane, playing in another Douglas Jerrold play, *The Wedding Gown*. He was there also in 1834, in *Henry*

IV, Part 2, and in distinguished company—for Macready played in it and so did Farren. Webster's part was Bardolph. He was with Charles Kemble at the Haymarket that year too, supporting that fine actor in his round of great Shakespearean parts. Once again, in *Much Ado about Nothing*, did Webster and Buckstone come together—Webster as Dogberry and Buckstone as Verges.

Perhaps during their "waits" these two men discussed future plans and ambitions, and formed ideas which later brought fame to the Haymarket. And yet another coming event cast its shadow.

In October, 1834, Webster went to the Adelphi. And in a play called *The Yellow Kids* he stepped into the front rank of actors. The *Athenæum* said of him:

> "He displayed so much original humour as to clearly entitle him to be taken by the Press out of the class of 'useful actors' and to be placed amongst 'the attractives.' "

Later, Webster was to rule the Adelphi and start a new tradition there.

Then Webster was at Covent Garden with Macready, in Lytton's drama, *The Duchess de la Valliere*, the cast also including Vandenhoff and Helen Faucit.

By this time Webster had made up his mind to go into management and to take the Haymarket. He had settled his policy. He was going to do things well. He was going to give the best in every way. Macready was at the height of his fame. Webster decided that Macready should be his star at the Haymarket. He could not fly higher. This again showed courage. For not only was Macready a very expensive actor but also a very difficult man to handle.

William Charles Macready was a great actor who never wanted to be one, but, having become one, decided that there must be no others. He did not like being an actor—he did not like actors at all—he referred to them, including himself, as "a vile set." He had no love in his heart for his calling, and the happiest day he spent in a theatre was the day of his retirement. Yet such was the character of the man that he set a higher standard of attainment than anyone else had approached and was self-analytical of his own performances to a degree which amounted to dissection. He scarcely ever pleased himself with what he had done, as his most revealing "diaries" show. Although one of our greatest actors, he was never really of the theatre at all. When in management, his productions reached an altitude of artistry which nobody else had attained, yet he still disliked his calling and considered it beneath him. He was a snob. He loved the society of the great—but then he had claims to greatness himself. He never mixed with his own profession and it almost broke his heart when the Athenæum Club at first blackballed him. There were far too many actors at the Garrick Club for him to be comfortable there. Yet his whole background was theatrical.

In justice to him it must be borne in mind that he became an actor

R

against his will. His father had been an actor and manager. There was good Dublin blood in him. His mother was a granddaughter of a Governor of Montserrat and came of a family which had ruined itself for the King in the Civil War. Young Macready was born in 1793 in Mary Street, now vanished into Stanhope Street, off the Euston Road, London.

There was no idea of making the boy an actor. When he was old enough, he was sent to Rugby to be educated. His father was then Manager of the Birmingham, Leicester and Stafford Theatres and doing well. The lad showed ability in school entertainments, but had no desire for the stage. He was destined for the Bar. But bad times came upon Macready Senior and the boy had to come home. Then he showed his mettle, that stern sense of duty which was his all through life. He renounced all hopes of the Bar, and went to do all he could for his struggling father. He succeeded beyond all expectation, and when he comes into the Haymarket story he stands at the pinnacle of his profession, a place which he had attained, not with ease, but by hard, grim fight.

Once he was upon the theatrical path, he followed it unswervingly, for he was a man of great strength of purpose and of high character. He was a good husband and a good father. He was extremely pious and much given to asking God's blessing and guidance upon every undertaking. Once, when struggling with a heavy cold, he dressed quickly and hurried downstairs, to be stricken with horror and remorse when he remembered that he had omitted to say his prayers—a thing he rectified at once. It took him a long time to overcome the feeling of shame engendered by his knockabout fight—if fight it could be called— with the egregious Mr. Bunn of Drury Lane. He felt himself besmirched. He was terribly respectable, very moral and extremely badtempered. His conscience never let him alone. He went out of his way to appease and tranquillise it when once he spent an evening in the room of Miss Huddart, a very handsome actress. It was all perfectly harmless, platonic and respectable, but he was worried over the proprieties. Miss Huddart always flattered him—she had an eye on jobs, and who shall blame her—and retailed to him all the latest theatrical gossip.

This he pretended to dislike, but he drank it all in. For he was, without realising it, a true actor at heart. He had his vanity—and no actor is much good without it—he had a very sensitive spot for criticism, and he both disliked and feared the Press—when it trounced him. He had a poor opinion of his fellow professionals and put down what he thought of them in his diary. He considered Farren ignorant and was delighted when someone told him that Vandenhoff's Hamlet was coarse, ill-bred and vehement. His opinion of Charles Kemble was of the very lowest, and was not helped by the fact that Kemble, at Covent Garden, took a special "call" which Macready was sure was meant for him. He wrote down Kemble as "sordidly base."

He loathed Edmund Kean. In their duel for supremacy at Drury Lane, that fierce little genius had outmanœuvred him and defeated him. Kean, indeed, treated him like dirt. Yet Macready was a pall-bearer at his funeral—it was the correct thing to do. He records that he was forced to give two guineas to a testimonial to Charles Kemble and that he never grudged money more. He disliked Charles Kean, for he was a rising star. Macready was scared stiff of him and never lost an opportunity of decrying him. Charles Mathews he never forgave when that grand comedian failed to attend a dinner given in Macready's honour. He spoke and wrote slightingly of him ever afterwards. He was perpetually at war with every company with whom he appeared. He always imagined they were trying to kill his lines and business in order to score themselves. He was probably right in so thinking, and his diary reeks with complaints of this kind.

When in management he was a martinet, and at rehearsals a holy terror. He was checked once, for over-insistence on his way of doing everything. An actress driven to revolt cried, "God help us. If this goes on we shall all be Macreadies." That gave him pause.

He liked to be referred to as "the Eminent Tragedian."

Yet such was his sterling worth, both as actor and as man, his uprightness of character, his courage, his determination to give the best and the best only, and such was his work in raising the whole level of the theatre of his time that one must—and one does—hold him in the highest respect. There is nothing whatever against him, save only the professional faults of the actor.

This was the man upon whom Webster had his hopeful eye. He did not know what Macready thought of him, that it was recorded in the eminent one's diary that "Webster was as coarse and unreal as a clown of an amphitheatre, a most unartistic performance," and that his opinion of Webster in the very play they were in at that moment was "very unmeaning and inefficient." Macready had been told by a Mr. Pritchard that Webster had tried to assault him—which Macready did not believe. The tragedian was apparently sickened by the actors of his day, which shows itself in an entry: "Dined at that vulgar place, the Garrick Club, where the principal conversation is eating, drinking and the American presidency. It is really a disgusting place." His heart was in the Athenæum, which had scorned him, but did eventually admit him. It was Webster, quite unwittingly, who caused Macready to shake the dust of the Garrick off his feet. When he found that the actor-manager had been made a member he was disgusted. "This puts the seal upon the door," he said. "I will have no more to do with it." Yet there was no reason on earth why Webster should not have been so honoured and every reason why he should.

Yet despite all he said, wrote and thought of Webster, that clever man knew exactly how to handle him and to use him, and Macready played much at the Haymarket. For one thing, Webster paid well, and

Macready always had an eye to business. There grew quite a mutual respect between them at last.

The terms and conditions under which Webster took over the Hay market from Morris are not known. But he was making his plans and had made up his mind when he was appearing with Macready at Covent Garden in 1837. Indeed, he asked to see Macready and told him of his intention. And then he shook the eminent one by proposing that Macready should enlist under his banner for the summer season. Macready wanted no other Richmonds in the field, but he never refused work. He had his family and position to provide for.

The next day Webster called at Macready's house to talk business. Macready poured cold water on the whole scheme. In his heart he did not want Webster to succeed and he did not want to play for him, but he never liked to turn business away. So he asked very high terms indeed. Webster tried to beat him down, but Macready was adamant. Webster went away to think it over. He was not long about it, for the next night he went to Macready's dressing-room and renewed the attack. He wanted Macready, because Macready was the best. But the price was high. They argued a long time. Macready got his terms—but Webster got Macready.

He was a manager who was prepared to pay for what he wanted, be the price steep as a hillside, rather than get an inferior article at a cheaper price. He got Macready for the Haymarket for two months, at £20 per night, to play three nights a week for the first fortnight.

Now, Macready had a pet play, *The Bridal*, which he wanted to do in London, and he saw a chance here. If Webster would produce it in the first three weeks of Macready's engagement he offered to forgo £10 but stipulated that he was to have an additional £12 a night for appearing in it if it succeeded. If, however, it failed, he would play a fourth night every week for £10. This is what he meant by forgoing £10. Webster closed with the bargain and went off full of joy and hope. He had a breeze with Macready the very next night, however, over "call" at Covent Garden, but no trouble came of it.

Macready wanted a big say in the supporting company at the Hay market, and Webster did not demur at this. Macready probably told him he could get them on better terms. He went to Miss Huddart to persuade her to join the company. But the lady proved more difficult than he thought. However, he got her to agree to £9 a week—that was more than she got at Covent Garden, if Webster would agree. Webster agreed.

There was another young lady at Covent Garden whose name Macready never mentioned, but who appears to have spent her time endeavouring to vamp the eminent tragedian. He could not understand her advances at first, but eventually it became clear to him. He wrote "Miss ——, in her nightly flirtation, told me that she thought of going to the Haymarket, and chiefly because I was to be there. *Nous verrons*.

That young lady did get there all the same, but her vamping came to nothing—she was up against an unvampable man.

Macready spoke to Webster about engaging Helen Faucit as leading lady. Webster at once agreed. One of his reasons for getting Macready was that the great actor would attract other great ones round him, which would redound to the credit of the Haymarket.

For he meant to do things at the little theatre as they had never been done before. He decided to open with Macready as Hamlet and to put *The Bridal* in the bill as soon as possible. He made all his arrangements with the greatest care. *The Bridal* was a version of Beaumont and Fletcher's *The Maid's Tragedy* and had been handed to Macready with a parcel of plays when he was at the Lane by Bunn. Macready had picked out *The Bridal*, but Bunn would not hear of it. Macready had put others to work on the version and had got Sheridan Knowles to touch it up. That dramatist had worked on it, but had not been able to spoil the genius of Beaumont and Fletcher. Macready had tried it on tour with indifferent companies and still believed in it as a potential success. It had always been a bone of contention between Bunn and himself. But now, at the Haymarket, he saw the chance of putting his judgment to the test at Webster's expense.

Webster went ahead fast. There was much excitement around Town about the new management. Webster had become popular as an actor and as a man. He was evidently going to do things well, said the theatre-minded public. You could not have better than Macready, and here was the great Drury Lane and Covent Garden actor now opening at the Haymarket. Webster put his fame and fortune to the touch on the night of June 12th, 1837. He staged *Hamlet*, with Macready in the title role, Miss Huddart as the Queen, and Elton as the Ghost. The actor-manager contented himself with the part of The Gravedigger. The whole thing was acclaimed. It was a brilliant and auspicious opening. Elton was a fine actor. Parenthetically, he was drowned at sea, a fate he shared with Theophilus Cibber, Gustavus Brooke, Tyrone Power, and, in more modern times, Laurence Irving. And by a strange coincidence, all those men, except Brooke, were Haymarket actors.

How proud of himself Webster must have been at the Haymarket. It was a long stride in a short time, from guinea-a-week stroller to actor-manager, with the greatest tragedian of his time under contract to him. And he was to be a success all the time and to bring much fame and fortune to the Haymarket—which prospered as theatres always do when guided by a practical man.

Preparations for *The Bridal* were pushed on. Macready read it to the Haymarket company and they were very interested.

But Webster had a worry. It seemed likely that William IV was about to die. A royal demise in those days was a very serious thing for the theatres, and to have this happen just as he had opened was a frightening prospect. Whilst he worried, Macready was unperturbed. He had a poor opinion of monarchs in general and of this one in particular. He gave his mind to Othello, his next Haymarket part, which he played there on June 16th—and considered that he played it pretty well too. He got a "call" and took it, but he thought Elton a very bad Iago.

After that performance something of note happened in his dressing-room. His friend Forster called round to congratulate him and brought a young gentleman with him whom he desired to present to Macready. The young man was introduced by the name of Dickens, Mr. Charles Dickens—*alias* "Boz." That Haymarket dressing-room meeting started a friendship between actor and novelist which lasted a lifetime.

On June 18th Macready entered the Haymarket stage door wondering if they would play or not. The King was dying; it was a question as to whether the play would go on before the King went off. When he was half-dressed somebody exclaimed, "The King is off!" It was not official, so they put the play on. It upset them all, and the uncertainty had its effect on Macready (who cared not two hoots about the King). He chronicles that he was very bad as Richard III. The next day, however, the news of the royal demise was given to the world. The theatre closed. But they rehearsed *The Bridal.*

On June 26th, 1837, Macready appeared in his favourite play, *The Bridal.* He played Melantius, but was not pleased with himself. He considered that he gave a crude, unfinished performance. He was always his own sternest critic. If a newspaper had dared to say of him what he said of himself the heavens would have fallen. Whatever he may have felt, the audience liked him, and the play. He was given a "call" and he led on Miss Huddart. Browning, Forster and Dickens came round to congratulate him. All the best people were going to the Haymarket now.

The Times, usually an anti-Macready paper, gave him a fine notice for Melantius—"his rough frankness was touching—his anger terrific."

Miss Huddart, as Evadne, made the success of her life. Elton was magnificent as Amintor, and Miss Taylor as Aspatia. And the cast included such people as Buckstone, Farren, Mrs. Nisbett and Mrs. Glover. That is how Webster did things.

The next play was *The Provok'd Husband*, with Macready and the company at full strength.

Miss Huddart was an excellent actress who would have been more famous had she not lived at a time of so many other great actresses. A very handsome and good woman, she married a man called Warner, who was of no account at all. He treated her badly and was always in debt. Later she fell a prey to cancer and, although always in great pain, she worked and struggled on, paying the debts her husband kept contracting, which threatened her and her children, suffering always, but breathing no word, even to her intimate friends, of either domestic troubles or desperate illness. At length her husband's excesses landed her in the Bankruptcy Courts. Then her true state was revealed. At

once her profession rallied round her and saw her through. Even Queen
Victoria took a hand, although she was not very interested in the stage
or stage folk. But she was told the circumstances and she admired the
courage and fortitude of the woman who had borne so much. Not as
Queen to subject, but as one woman to another, Victoria sent, not only
a handsome donation, but placed a carriage at the actress's disposal for
her to use each day, so that she could have the carriage-exercise pre-
scribed by the doctors, but which she could not afford. It was the act
of one great and gracious lady to another.

Macready's mind was now on things other than the Haymarket. He
was thinking of his forthcoming managerial season at the great Covent
Garden Theatre. He was getting his cast together. When next he played
Melantius at the Haymarket, he admitted doing so badly because his
mind was busy elsewhere. He made a mental note to guard against this
tendency. He was merciless in his own self-analysis.

If the eminent tragedian was thinking of the future, so was Webster.
So far he had got what he wanted. He had opened the Haymarket with
Macready, and it had taken the trick. He had played the ace, now he
must play the king—but who was that to be? He remembered the
Haymarket's reputation as a place where unknown actors made their
names and made money for the managements who gave them the
chance. He recalled Henderson, Elliston and others. He would do this
again. And he turned his mind to a provincial actor—a tragedian—
called Samuel Phelps, with whom he had already been in touch.

Macready soon heard all about this. You cannot keep a secret in the
theatre for more than twenty-four hours. He asked Webster if the
rumour were true, and Webster confirmed it. Macready began to
wonder. He, too, had heard stories about Phelps. This new man might
be a rival, and he wanted no rivals now. He had fought so many, and
new ones must be kept away.

Phelps was making a great name for himself up and down the
country. Webster and Macready were not the only two men thinking
about him. Bunn of Drury Lane was doing the same.

Shortly before this, Phelps himself had come to Town. His idea was
to see Mr. Bunn and, failing him, to see Webster. Phelps thought it a
little early to aspire to Drury Lane, but Webster would want someone
to succeed Macready. He made an attempt to see Bunn, but was unlucky. He did not worry very much. He had heard Bunn's reputation.
He got a letter of introduction to Webster from a mutual friend.

Armed with this letter, Phelps and his nephew, who had come to
Town with him took a walk around London, saw the sights and gazed
at the outside of the theatres. Phelps was to know the inside of them
before long.

This was actually before Webster had opened the Haymarket, and
whilst he was still at Covent Garden. His engagement of Macready,
however, had been announced.

To Covent Garden they went and Webster saw them at once. He had heard a lot about Phelps and actually knew some of his relations in Bath. The two men got on famously together. Webster had also seen a notice of Phelps's performance of Richard III at Plymouth, which said he was better than Edmund Kean. That is as may be, but an agreement was soon made whereby Webster agreed that Phelps should follow Macready at the Haymarket.

Filled with delight, Phelps went back to the road again. Almost immediately he heard from Bunn. In theatre business, it is always either a feast or famine. Phelps told Bunn he considered himself under contract to Webster. Bunn was very annoyed.

Macready had not yet seen Phelps, but Phelps had seen him, for after their interview Webster had given him and his nephew seats for the show and for the first—and last—time, Phelps saw Macready from the front. He was to see him on the stage as a fellow actor hundreds of times, but he never saw him from the front again.

Whilst he was still on tour and playing at Southampton in *The Iron Chest* he got a surprise. A note was brought round. Mr. Macready himself had come down to see him act. He received the great actor with some confusion and much respect. Macready proposed that Phelps should join him at Covent Garden. Phelps replied that he was contracted to Webster. Macready said he knew all about that, but the Haymarket was only a summer theatre and that he could do more for him. He said also that Webster knew all about his approach to the provincial actor (which was untrue). He agreed that Phelps must play for Webster first, but suggested that he should not bind himself for any length of time, so that he could come to Covent Garden. Now, Webster had not stipulated any definite length of engagement to Phelps. It was to be determined by success or failure. But then Webster expected, and very rightly, that as he was giving Phelps his first chance, he should and would have first call on his services. Phelps, overcome with excitement and ambition at the prospect held out to him by the great Macready, let his eagerness run away with his sense of loyalty. He agreed to come to Macready as soon as he had played for Webster. He would not fix a salary, that must be dependent on his London success.

This was Phelps's first big mistake, from which he was to suffer for years. He should have stuck to Webster. That man was not troubling about rivals, but only determined to get the best for his theatre. Macready, on the other hand, was determined to keep all other claimants to fame well clear of his own road.

Webster soon sent for Phelps. On the night of August 28th, 1837, that actor made his London debut on the stage of the Haymarket, billed as follows: "Mr. Phelps (of Provincial Celebrity) will make his first appearance at this Theatre in the character of Shylock this evening."

There was a fine cast and supporting bill. Webster gave him every chance. Vining was Gratiano; Haines was Antonio; Miss R. Phillips was Nerissa; J. Faucit Saville was Bassanio; Mr. Collins was Lorenzo; Miss E. Taylor played Jessica and the Portia was Miss Huddart. Webster played Launcelot.

Shakespeare was further supported by a musical burletta called *West Country Wooing*, starring the celebrated Mrs. Waylett, and a farce, *Make Your Wills*, with Farren as Uncle Foozle. It was a marvellous evening's entertainment, but the main interest was in the new actor. Would he add another successful debut to this home of successful debuts? He was playing Shylock, as Henderson had done at the Haymarket before him—and as Kean had done at Drury Lane. What would he make of it? He had an ordeal to face and he knew it. The house was packed with all the celebrities and critics of the day. Phelps had come to Town armed with letters to the London critics from their provincial colleagues, speaking on his behalf. He had delivered none of them. Nor had he one single friend in front. He wanted to be judged on his merits.

He got the usual round of applause on his first entrance: it was the kindly custom of those days so to greet newcomers. He started well. Soon the applause was spontaneous, and for him. It grew until, after his exit in the fourth act, he was called before the curtain and cheered to the echo. It was a night of triumph for him.

But what would the Press say? Eagerly he looked the next morning. He opened *The Times*: "The moment he entered upon the scene you could discern the practised actor ripe for judgment, and he might have been certain of a favourable reward even from a Daniel. In his costume on this occasion he wore a strange straw hat." The hat was a mistake, although quite correct. The *Morning Chronicle* said: "His representation of the character was correct and judicious, but not remarkable or striking. . . . He performed the Trial Scene very ably and gave great effect to several passages. . . . Upon the whole Mr. Phelps' performance of this part is entitled to considerable praise and shows him to be a valuable acquisition to the London stage. . . . He was extremely well received." No doubt the notices were read eagerly by Macready, who may have felt slightly reassured. Phelps was not another Kean. But they pleased Webster. They would fill the Haymarket.

The critics had made no allowance for first night and debut nerves. Phelps had suffered terribly in this respect, and the actors knew it.

When he was rehearsing as Sir Edward Mortimer in *The Iron Chest* (his next part), old Farren said to him, "Keep up your pluck, my boy, and you'll be all right. Those who were acting with you in *The Merchant of Venice* told me you were so dreadfully nervous the first night you could not do yourself justice. I wish I'd been near you; I was in front, however, and did what I could for you there." A very kindly speech from an actor of eminence to a beginner in London. Farren was with him in *The Iron Chest*, and Phelps did very well indeed. He got a good Press, and it must be remembered that he was playing parts in which they had seen Edmund Kean. Farren foretold that he would be the leading tragedian of the day. Phelps now played Hamlet, Othello and Richard III. His Press and his performances got better and better. Webster was asked how Phelps was getting on.

"He is filling my treasury," he said, "and I don't think a better proof could be given of his success. I am only sorry that I did not positively secure his services for as long a period as I could avail myself of them, instead of allowing another manager to profit by his abilities."

That other manager was Macready, and he was not desirous of profiting thereby. He wanted to suppress Phelps, and when that actor joined him at Covent Garden, he proceeded to do so. So bad was his treatment that Phelps asked to be released from his engagement. Macready would only agree if Phelps would undertake not to play in London. This Phelps could not do, so he dragged away his time in bad parts at Covent Garden. Macready was frank with him. "Your time *must* come," he told him, "but I am not going to try and hasten it. I was kept back by Young and Kean and you will have to wait for me." Certainly Phelps knew where he stood and was not too comfortable. He knew that Webster was offended because he had joined Macready and he knew Macready's point of view as well. If only he had stuck to the Haymarket!

Meanwhile, Webster was keeping the Haymarket busy and full. He produced, in October, 1837, Sheridan Knowles's *The Love Chase*. Mrs. Nesbitt starred and Webster gave himself a leading role too—that of Wildrake.

He got into trouble with the critics over this. Said the *Athenæum*: "May we enquire of Mr. Webster what on earth could have induced him to cast himself into Mr. Wildrake? It is as great a piece of insanity as if he had cast himself into the Thames. We should have soon as thought of his playing Lady Macbeth." Well, he was not the first nor the last actor-manager to cast himself badly. But whatever the critics said, the play was a success and was a standby of Webster's for years.

In 1838 he did another play by the same author, *The Maid of Mariendorpt*. Webster was establishing the Haymarket as the peer of the two Patent theatres, and except when Macready was in actual management, doing better work than either.

In 1838 Macready was back again for the summer. He played there for five weeks, commencing on July 23rd with *Every Man in His Humour*, in which he played Kitely. On August 4th Webster produced Talfourd's *Athenian Captive* with immense success—Macready playing Thoas and Mrs. Warner (Miss Huddart) as Ismene.

The Haymarket season of 1839 was to be important. It brought Macready again, it brought Phelps, and it brought to the Haymarket another great name—Helen Faucit. Phelps had to play second fiddle to Macready both as regards parts and as regards billing. This was only fair. But if Phelps had stayed at the Haymarket, he would have been on his own as lead and on his own in the billing. There was no love lost between Macready and Phelps, and not much between Macready and Webster. Phelps felt awkward about Webster, because he knew he had treated him unfairly. Webster had the whip hand, so long as he kept the peace. It was a nice three-handed bit of theatre intrigue.

He took special pride in his announcement of Helen Faucit as a Haymarket leading lady, for she was already one of the very great ones of her day. She was Macready's leading lady at the Garden. She had been there before he took over the management of the theatre and he found he had to take her—and her contract—over with it. Her salary was £30 per week. Macready was thunderstruck! But Osbaldiston, the retiring Manager, said it was that or nothing. Macready was in panic. Such a position and such a salary would give her too much power. Besides, he could not afford it. He approached her about it and he found her charming and gracious. She loved the theatre and she did not want to embarrass him in his endeavours, so she agreed to take £15 per week. She was still under twenty-one, she had plenty of time, and she did not want to make things too hard for the new Manager. To his credit, it must be said that at the end of the season, although he had lost money, he paid her full salary. When she agreed to go to the Haymarket, he told Webster he must pay it too. Webster made no demur.

Helen Faucit, who thus becomes one of the shining Haymarket names, was born in London in 1819. She was the daughter of an actress, Mrs. Faucit, and a younger sister of another, Mrs. Bland. Both were well-known. She got a chance through hearing her sister rehearse and reading the opposite lines to her during an engagement at the Richmond (Surrey) Theatre. So well did she do this that the Manager, overhearing her, decided she must be given an opportunity—as an amateur. So she played there Juliet, as Mariana in *The Wife*, and Mrs. Waller in *The Stranger*, parts which one would have imagined far beyond her. Her success was such that she determined to become a real actress. She made her debut at Covent Garden as Juliet in *The Hunchback*. It was sheer triumph and she immediately received a contract for three years (the one Macready had to take over). She became his leading lady and was universally successful, a special triumph being in *The Lady of Lyons* as Pauline.

She became one of our greatest actresses and retired after a most distinguished career. She often gave dramatic readings and was a friend of Queen Victoria's. She married Sir Theodore Martin, K.C.B., K.C.V.O. Her last performance was at a benefit. Although really ill, she responded to the cause of charity. She died on October 31st, 1898. and Queen Victoria sent a wreath with an inscription in her own hand. Seldom has an actress been so beautiful, so gracious, so talented, so respected and so well loved.

All that, however, was far away in 1839, when she, Macready and Phelps filled the bill at Webster's Haymarket Theatre, and when he opened the season with Macready, Phelps and Helen Faucit in *Othello*. The eminent tragedian played Othello, the rising tragedian played Iago and Helen Faucit was a lovely Desdemona. A few nights after, as was the custom, the two men exchanged parts. This time Phelps, as Othello, put Macready entirely in the shade. The Press said that Phelps as Othello was as much better than Macready as that gentleman was better than Cooper as Iago. A nasty pill for Macready to swallow. And he could not get it down. He demanded that Webster should at once withdraw *Othello* from the bills. Webster did not want to upset Macready and perhaps he wanted to rub a little salt into Phelps's wounds. He agreed. Phelps played Othello no more that season and, indeed, very little else of importance. He was indeed paying for his earlier mistake.

CHAPTER XXII

AUTHOR, MANAGER, AND ACTOR TOO

M ACREADY had approached the whole season in a very bad frame of mind. He had lost a lot of money at Covent Garden, and that did not improve his temper, which was never of the best. But he had been his own manager and that made him contemptuous of other playhouses not so spectacular as Covent Garden. When he went to the Haymarket to rehearse he commented: "I sensibly feel the descent from Covent Garden into this dog-hole of a theatre—dirt, slovenliness and puffery make up the sum of its character."

That was utterly untrue. Webster ran his theatre beautifully and it was a lovely house. It was also making money for him, which the lordly Covent Garden was not doing for Macready, or anyone else.

Dog-hole or not, Macready was drawing £100 a week from it. And he was glad of the money, a vast sum then.

Webster had, too, gained a signal victory. He had raised the prestige of his theatre so high that he had been able to get the Lord Chamberlain to agree to an extension of his season, right beyond the summer months. The Haymarket was no longer just a summer theatre, and it had Webster to thank for that.

There was the scrap about *Othello* and Phelps dropped into the background, playing leads with Ellen Tree on non-Macready nights. On those, however, Helen Faucit played. She appeared as Mrs. Haller, Mrs. Oakley, and Pauline (in *The Lady of Lyons*), sometimes—indeed often—appearing on five nights a week. She played Portia to Macready's Shylock, and he said he was an utter failure in the part. Be that as it may, it was repeated eight times. Perhaps they wanted to see Faucit as Portia.

She broke down in health, however, through a play of Lytton's, *The Sea Captain*, which was not a big success, despite fine performances on her part and Macready's. That tragedian played Shylock again, and Phelps, who had been so successful in the role, was relegated to Antonio. Buckstone was Launcelot.

The Haymarket was not all Phelps, Macready and Faucit, however. It was making other stars and giving other performers a chance.

In 1838-9, it gave London that extraordinary actress, Madame Celeste. She was born in Paris in 1814. She started her career as a girl in the United States and there she married a Mr. Elliott. She came to the English stage in 1830, when she appeared at Liverpool, and then at Drury Lane in a ballet called *La Bayadére*. She was at Drury Lane again in 1837, when she appeared as the dumb boy Maurice in *Child of the Wreck.* She carried the whole production on her shoulders and scored a resounding success. She specialised in mimed parts, speaking no words, but her gestures and expressions were remarkable. She did this also at the Haymarket. In 1838-9 she appeared there in a melodrama called *Marie Ducange*, which had been written especially for her, and in *The Quadroon Slave*. In 1842 she appeared there in *The Bastille*, a one-act play, and she co-starred with Webster in 1843 in *Louison*. This began a partnership between them which culminated in after years when Webster founded the melodrama tradition at the Adelphi, where Celeste's greatest fame lies. But she has her place at the Haymarket too.

Another Haymarket star was Tyrone Power, one of the best exponents of Irish parts the stage has ever seen. Despite his Irish name and his wonderful brogue, he was a son of Wales, hailing from Glamorganshire, and owning to the name of David Powell.

His first attempt was at tragedy. His strong Welsh accent did not help him at all. An old Irish actor in the same company proposed to teach him elocution for a small fee—and his drinks. The drinks were a much heavier item than his fee. Powell, however, worked hard with this man and took careful note of everything he said. The result was that his Welsh accent entirely disappeared, as his tutor had promised, but it was replaced by a brogue richer and juicier than that of the Irishman who taught him.

He could not detect it himself and imagined that he was now fully cured of the offending accent. He essayed Romeo and emptied the house. He was at his wit's end when he was advised to take an Irish name and specialise in Irish parts. He became Tyrone Power and was just what the public had wanted. There had been no first-class "stage Irishman" since the days of Johnstone. So popular did he become that Webster paid him £150 a week at the Haymarket, more than he paid Macready. Alas! the career was short, if brilliant. He made his last appearance at the Haymarket on August 1st, 1840, when he took his benefit and departed for an American tour. He planned to return to the Haymarket, but it never saw him again. His American tour finished, he was to have come back at once, but his one great failing delayed him. He was a snob; he loved a lord. A peer of the realm was to cross the Atlantic on the boat after the one Power had booked on. He waited for that boat, the *President*. He would at least be in company with a lord, and it was almost certain that he would scrape acquaintance with him. But his snobbishness cost him his life. The *President* foundered with all hands. Nobody was saved. That was the end of Tyrone Power, whose London success, said Webster, was the most instantaneous he had ever known.

Other things happened during that 1839-40 season, too. There was the production of *The Tragedy of Glencoe or The Fate of the Macdonalds*, by Talfourd. Miss Faucit was back for this—on May 23rd, 1840. She played the heroine, Helen Campbell. There was a good deal of trouble about this play all through its rehearsals. Macready drove the company and was in a bad mood. Miss P. Horton (afterwards Mrs. German Reed) told him that he was the subject of general abuse in the green-room. Macready was not surprised. "I have had enough experience of players to know that their ignorance and their vanity combine to make them a most ungrateful set of persons." What they had to be grateful to Macready for does not appear. He was justly annoyed, however, when some of them, including Phelps, missed rehearsals. There was confusion all through the early stages, it would seem, and, according to the eminent tragedian, it was rushed on without due care. Macready played Halbert Macdonald. At one rehearsal his friend Forster prompted him, and that annoyed him very much, for he was probably indulging in one of his celebrated pauses. They tried to keep secret the fact that Talfourd had written this play, but at the same rehearsal that Macready got the unwanted "prompt" he was also told by Webster that Sheridan Knowles had been to the box office, saying he must have seats to see his friend Talfourd's play. This added to the general annoyance.

The first night came and for a couple of acts the show held them. But it was a long-drawn-out, pompous, wordy affair of prolix speeches, and Macready says "the persons in the front were disposed to be ill-natured." However, there was a sufficiently good reception for him to get a call and he made a speech concerning the authorship of the play and disclosed the secret, which got applause. This pleased Talfourd, who took Macready to supper. The tragedian said it was a heavy one—it must have matched the play.

Much more history at the Haymarket must be disregarded to make way for a really important event, the production of Bulwer Lytton's *Money*. This play holds the stage to-day, when a big command performance or similar occasion is toward, because it gives a chance, in the "Club" scene, for the introduction as "guests" of all the celebrities who have not got speaking parts and cannot give time to rehearsals. This lucky chance has conferred some degree of immortality on a play which, after much trouble, disaster and strife, first saw the footlights at the Haymarket Theatre on December 8th, 1840.

Benjamin Webster, good manager, had spared no pains or expense to make this an outstanding show. He got together a magnificent cast and he had a special production built and painted, a most unusual thing then, when players and audience were accustomed to stock scenery.

But *Money* was not destined to be coined the easy way. There was trouble and disaster at every stage of the proceedings. There was trouble over the casting. Webster, Lytton and Macready all wanted Wallack, the celebrated actor who was at the Haymarket at that time, to play Captain Dudley Smooth. He read the play and refused. Macready then read it to him as *he* saw it. Wallack still refused. However, he suggested Wrench, a good actor who was also of the company,

for the part. Wrench got it and played it very well. Wallack did not
believe in the play. It was too long, he said, and if played as written,
it would take three weeks to get through. Incidentally, the part offered
him was about eight lines long.

Money came into the hands of Webster and from his into those of
Macready in the September of 1840. Macready started to read the play
on his way home from the theatre and was deeply interested. But things
were not too pleasant between him and Webster at the moment.
Macready's suspicious mind unjustifiably laid things at Webster's door.
Webster countered by accusing him of trying to sell *Money* to Covent
Garden. There was a good deal of bickering, but Macready went on
preparing an acting version. There were disagreements over the casting.
Macready was displeased that the author wanted Webster himself to
play Graves. Things were smoothed over, and Macready, a stickler
for accuracy, learned to play picquet because he had to do so in the
play.

As preparations proceeded, Macready got more and more difficult.
He would have nothing to do with the choosing of the furniture or
costumes; he would not look at the scenery. He complained when
Webster was away from rehearsals. Then he began to have doubts
about his own part—Alfred Evelyn. He decided that Strickland and
Webster had much more to do and much better scenes than he had
himself. He was further upset because he had to play Werner with
Wallack and Phelps. He said of them: "Both think themselves great
actors and imagine one great evidence of their talent is to frustrate or
weaken the effect of their superiors." He found fault with everything
Webster did. They never seemed to get a move on. Macready altered,
Bulwer Lytton (or as Macready called him, Lytton Bulwer) made suggestions and re-wrote, Forster gave advice, the cast bickered and
Macready fought with everyone. Webster got on with things as best he
could.

The famous Count D'Orsay was called in to give advice. He even
designed a waistcoat for Macready—which greatly impressed Charles
Dickens, who loved flamboyant things. Five years afterwards he wrote
to Macready about it:

"You once—only once—gave the world assurance of a waistcoat.
You wore it, sir, I think, in *Money*. It was a remarkable and precious
waistcoat, wherein certain broad stripes of purple disported themselves, as by a combination of extraordinary circumstances too happy
to occur again, I have seen it on your manly chest in private life. I
saw it, sir, I think, the other day in the cold light of morning, with
feelings easier to be imagined than described. Mr. Macready, sir,
are you a father? If so, lend me that waistcoat for five minutes. . . .
I will send a trusty messenger at half-past nine precisely in the
morning. He is sworn to secrecy. He durst not, for his life, betray

me, or swells in ambuscade would have the waistcoat at the cost of his heart's blood.

"Thine,

"The Unwaistcoated One."

Troubles went on. Macready had his own private setbacks too. His darling son Henry was taken ill. This drove the actor nearly to distraction. He besieged the Almighty with prayers, he called in doctors, his mind revolted against the rehearsals of *Money*. He also, with his usual foresight, settled new terms with Webster. Then he had another row with him. Poor Webster answered back, forgetting his usual forbearance and tact for once, and Macready said he would throw up the whole thing and withdraw. But better counsels again prevailed. So the rehearsals went on.

The play was tentatively announced for November 5th. The bills read:

"A New and Original Comedy by Sir Edward Lytton Bulwer had been accepted and would be produced as early as the scenic arrangements, etc., would permit."

On November 12th they announced the title, *Money*. Expectation was running high.

But still *Money* could not take shape. Little Henry was ill again—much worse, in fact—and Macready was beside himself. *Money* was announced and re-announced, but they never got it on. Something always cropped up. It was finally announced for November 28th. On the 22nd they all worked hard. Macready by now was thoroughly out of feeling with his part, Alfred Evelyn. He said it was "a damned walking gentleman." On 23rd there was talk of giving up altogether. Only Webster's persistence and tact saved the day. These were anxious times for him—he had much at stake. On November 24th, little Henry was a bit better. Macready, always on the look-out for someone to admonish, spoke to Lytton about the way that author had spoken to Miss Faucit. Lytton apologised. Macready got a hat from Ashmead's and found that D'Orsay had ordered it for him, which pleased him, but not much progress was made. The date of production grew ominously nearer.

Then, on November 25th, a terrible blow fell. Little Henry was better, but Macready's daughter Joan, who had been unwell, now became seriously ill. Both his children at death's door was too much for any man, let alone Macready. Worse was to come. Little Joan died.

Macready nearly went mad. Of course, *Money* was postponed once more. Webster was sympathetic, but in despair. Wallack and Phelps stepped into the breach. They played a round of parts to fill the gap. Everyone did what they could and for the time being left the bereaved father, who still expected Henry to die too, alone in his grief. Webster kept all theatre troubles away from Macready, but he himself was very

s

worried. The whole season's plans were upset. He had banked on
Money and had nothing to follow. At last he went to see Macready and
got him to agree, now that little Joan was buried, that unless something
fatal happened to Henry, he would appear in *Money* on December 8th.
Macready said it must depend on Henry's condition.

Henry took a turn for the better. On December 2nd Macready was
able to rehearse again, but still it depended on Henry's health if *Money*
would be produced. December 5th saw a relapse—Henry had the
thrush. Macready regarded him as gone already. But on December 6th
the little sufferer was a bit better. Macready sent for Webster. He said
that unless Henry got worse again he would be ready for the 8th, and
this was the first bright spot in Webster's life for weeks. On the next
day there was a great improvement. Macready attended the theatre and
played Werner that evening.

December 8th dawned. Henry was no better, but no worse. The
plunge must be taken. And, feeling anything but ready to face a new
play and a new part, Macready went down to the Haymarket to play
in *Money*. The company could hardly believe that the curtain was to go
up at last. Webster, with the double care of a part in the play and as
manager of the theatre, still feared there might be some last-minute
calamity. He had never had such a time before in his well-run playhouse. But this time there was no turning back, no last second's postponement. The company were there, the overture was played, the house
was packed with an audience keyed to a high pitch of excitement. They
had been waiting for this play, and had followed its ill luck with
interest. Would it turn out well? Would it be worth the waiting—or
would it be a failure?

It was a fine and distinguished company that played that night.
Macready was Evelyn, Strickland played Sir John Vesey, Walter Lacy
was Sir Frederick Blount, B. French sustained the part of Smooth,
which Wallack had justly scorned. David Rees was Stout and F. Vining
the Lord Glossmore. Benjamin Webster played Graves, Miss P. Horton
was Georgian Vesey, Mrs. Glover was Lady Franklin and Helen Faucit
played Clara Douglas.

Macready himself said he played Evelyn badly. He felt he wanted
lightness, self-possession and in the serious scenes, truth. He knew that
Helen Faucit stole the play entirely in the last scene. She had not a
good part, she had little or no chance until the last scene, and then she
took it with both hands and brought down the house.

The final curtain fell and the Haymarket rang with enthusiasm.
Whether Macready was good or bad, the public liked *Money*. Perhaps
the long-delayed production had whetted appetites, although as a
general rule a postponement is bad for a play. This one had been
postponed over and over again, but rode to triumph. Webster's
heart was as full as his house—and the Haymarket had the greatest
success of its career so far. It was triumph all along the line. Even

little Henry got better. *Money* lived up to its title for the Haymarket.

It ran for eighty consecutive nights—a marvellous thing then—and the Lord Chamberlain extended the season right up to March 13th, an extra couple of months.

It was revived again when Macready returned on May 3rd, 1841, and it ran for another twenty-nine performances. But this time it had another Clara Douglas, no less a person than the great Mrs. Stirling.

Mrs. Stirling's name is famous in the annals of the British theatre. There are plenty of people alive who saw her act; there are still more who remember her passing, for Lady Gregory, as she became, lived to be eighty-two. She was born, Mary Anne, in 1813 in Queen Street, Mayfair, London, the daughter of Captain Hehl, Third Captain of the Regiment of Foot Guards and Assistant Quartermaster-General, Horse Guards, London.

The post of Quartermaster-General did not do much for the pocket of the gallant Captain Hehl, for he ruined himself, and poverty stared the family in the face. They had to go to work. Mary Anne was well educated and pretty. She started to learn the business of acting and singing. Authorities differ as to the actual beginning. There are rumours of the ballet at the Surrey Theatre, of the old Coburg Theatre, and even of the so-called Grub Street Theatre, *alias* the City Theatre, *alias* the City Pantheon, which was a disused chapel in Fore Street, Cripplegate, London, where dramatic instruction was given and where the pupils appeared before such patrons as they might attract to see the show.

She called herself Fanny Clifton at that time, and probably her first professional stage appearance was made at the East London Theatre in Whitechapel in 1829. This theatre is better known as the Pavilion. She got some Press notices there. One scribe commented:

"Mdlle. Aubry (in *The Man in the Iron Mask*) was given to Miss Fanny Clifton, a pretty piece of uninteresting matter with just enough ability to speak her lines and no more."

But she had already found favour in other eyes, those of a young actor in the same company, Edward Stirling. They were married whilst working together at that old East End Theatre, and then they left it to go on tour. At Manchester and at Liverpool (under Davidge) they made successes, and Stirling showed signs of that versatility which was later to make him manager and playwright as well. Mary Anne made a success in Birmingham, and Bond, Manager of the Adelphi in the Strand, made her a London offer. There she played in *A Dream at Sea*, following the distinguished Mrs. Nisbett in that famous melodrama which was written by another who brought glory to the Haymarket— J. B. Buckstone. In 1836 she appeared in *Rienzi*, Bulwer's novel dramatised by Buckstone. Mrs. Stirling had not much of a part in this, but Press reports speak of Mrs. Honey as—

"appearing as a page in a very superb tunic of blue velvet and gold,
with yellow silk stockings and her countenance is most appropriately
beautified by a pair of mustachios, a species of ornament not used by
the other Romans. In regard to the costumes generally, we imagine
that, if one of the gentlemen of Rome were to arise from the dead, he
would be exceedingly puzzled to recognise his own countrymen'
(*Sunday Times*).

That gives a nice little picture of theatrical production in those days
and shows the value of the work done by Macready and Webster
towards a better stage. The care taken over the production of *Money*
has been shown.

Mrs. Stirling went on tour again after the Adelphi season was over,
but returned there with a better company, which included C. Pope,
Mrs. Yates, John Reeve, Buckstone and Hemming. She appeared in,
amongst other plays, that curious *A Flight to America* in which the
celebrated Jump Jim Crow took the town by storm. Mrs. Stirling
blacked her pretty little face for this show. Indeed, that part of Sally
Snow was an early success of hers.

She then went to the New Strand, as it was called. Here she began
to show her real versatility, and her husband wrote her a play called
Batchelor's Buttons, in which she appeared as a tomboy schoolgirl, a
jockey, a sportsman and garrulous maid of all work. She got wonderful
notices.

She was now but twenty-four and hard work caused a breakdown.
Later in the year she was engaged by Braham for his own theatre—the
St. James's. She showed a turn for sentiment and drama, and the mis-
guided Manager cast her for a tough Italian brigand.

Things were, on the whole, pretty poor theatrically about this time.
So bad were they, indeed, that Mrs. Stirling retired. But she came back
in 1839 to the Lyceum (then called the English Opera House). She
went from there to Drury Lane, under the banner of the ill-starred and
short-reigning W. J. Hammond. She made her debut there as Beatrice
in *Much Ado about Nothing*. She had a bad Benedict in Marston. She
got plenty of applause, but the critics disapproved—they nearly always
disapprove of a Beatrice who is not Ellen Terry or Winifred Emery.
Her next play there, *Women's Trials*, missed fire, as did the pistol
which the heroine—our Mrs. Stirling—had to fire at the villain. The
whole thing "got the bird." Drury Lane was in one of its bad patches
and she went to the Olympic, round the corner. There she became a
great favourite. Her next step was to the Haymarket. She joined
Webster's company and came under the eye and the direction of
Macready. She made steady progress and an especial hit in *The
Road to Ruin*. Although her part of Sophia was not a very good
one, this clever and very pretty young artist made it something
worth seeing.

So, when *Money* was revived and Miss Faucit was not there to play Clara, the mantle fell on Mrs. Stirling.

Macready commented: "Was much pleased with Mrs. Stirling in Clara. She speaks with a freshness and truth of tone that no other actress on the stage can now do." Perhaps she did not steal quite as much of his limelight—being less well-known—as had Helen Faucit.

She stayed on at the Haymarket, where she was a popular favourite, and she was still there when, in 1842, Webster had the theatre redecorated and made it what it is to-day—the prettiest, smartest and most elegant house in London. Her later career is theatre history; not least among her many triumphs was her Nurse (in her old age) to Ellen Terry's Juliet at the Lyceum under Irving. She has to her credit, another Haymarket triumph, which will be referred to shortly, and she was well known at Drury Lane, the Strand, the Lyceum and the Olympic.

By the beginning of 1842 the work of Benjamin Webster was bearing fruit. The theatre was acknowledged the social equal of Covent Garden and Drury Lane, and well ahead of all the others. Indeed, it was rightly said to be the only place in London where the banners of the national drama still waved. Webster played comedies, poetic drama and Shakespeare. He gave the stage the variety it needed and he gave it, above all, quality. In June, 1842, he produced Sheridan Knowles's *The Rose of Aragon*, and no lesser persons than Mr. and Mrs. Charles Kean played the leads. It failed, but was a brave attempt to give the best. He also had with him for a long time that fine actor, Creswick, together with Farren, Charles Mathews, Strickland, Buckstone, Tyrone Power, Mrs. Glover, Madame Vestris, Mrs. Nisbett, Madame Celeste—and, of course, Phelps, Macready, Helen Faucit, Wallack, and Mrs. Stirling. He had taken Charles Mathews and Madame Vestris into his theatre when they had ruined themselves with their beautiful, ambitious and ill-managed productions at Covent Garden. He put on such plays as Jerrold's *Time Works Wonders*, Westland Marston's *Heart of the World*, *Strathmore* and Sheridan Knowles's *Love Chase*. He encouraged new talent and was always improving, not only the appearance, but also the standard of his theatre, until he had brought it right to the top. In addition, he gave excellent performances himself.

In 1843 he offered a prize of £500 for the best comedy of British life and manners. He did this to encourage the drama and young dramatists. It was widely advertised—Webster understood publicity—and a most important and representative committee of judges was formed. It included Charles Young and Charles Kemble (now veterans), G. P. R. James, P. R. Moran, H. Ottley, J. Clarke Searle and the Rev. Alexander Dyce.

These gentlemen pondered and deliberated on no fewer than ninety-eight comedies which were submitted—to-day the number would have run into thousands—and then were unanimous in their decision. They chose *Quid Pro Quo, or The Day of Dupes*, by a Mrs. Gore. It was given a fine cast and produced on June 18th, 1844. The audience were no less unanimous in their verdict. It was laughed off the stage with groans, hoots, hisses and ribald merriment. In his end-of-the-season speech, Webster said:

"For three years no comedy was to be got for love or money and Mrs. Gore's was the best of those submitted. None of the judges ever supposed it could have been so egregious a failure."

Naturally not. It goes to show how nobody has ever been able to predict the taste of the public. One would like to know what the rejected plays were like, and can imagine the gloating of the disappointed authors—all of whom were quite sure it would have been different had his or her play been selected.

The public did not blame Webster. He had done his best. His company showed what they thought of him by presenting him with a very costly epergne "as a mark of esteem for his private and professional worth."

Webster was no longer content merely with the Haymarket, which he had raised to such heights, and he now took on the Adelphi as well. J. B. Buckstone, who had been there for some time, became his right-hand man. This fine and upright, honest performer has made occasional entrances in the story. He was in the cast of the lamentable *Quid Pro Quo*. But he was scoring as dramatist as well as actor. He was writing nearly all the farces produced at the Adelphi, and they were uniformly successful. He was constantly being called before the curtain to receive the plaudits of a delighted audience.

He and Webster were colleagues and fast friends. They played together at the Haymarket, successful actors both. There, and later at the Adelphi, Webster the Manager produced the farces and plays of Buckstone the dramatist. It was an ideal combination of two men who liked and understood each other just as well as they understood their business—the theatre.

On October 30th, 1849, Webster presented a play called *The Serious Family* (adapted from the French), playing the lead of Mr. Charles Torrens himself. This was a huge success, which held the stage for years. He played Coolcard in Douglas Jerrold's comedy, *The Catspaw*, and many other parts as well.

Macready returned to what he had called "The dog-hole of a theatre" in 1849, to make his last appearance there. He played Macbeth, Hamlet, Lear and Othello. Webster gave him as supporting company James Wallack, Howe, Rogers, Keeley, Mrs. Warner, Miss Reynolds and Miss Priscilla Horton (an old friend). Macready was now getting £40 per night, three nights a week, £30 for every extra night, a benefit and the authority to write an "order" for two at every performance. His retirement was near, and this was a preliminary farewell. He opened with Macbeth on October 8th. He says that Webster staggered him by saying that the house was not full, but he himself could see no room anywhere. There was great cheering on his entrance, but Macready, always on the look out for faults, did not think it so good—not that wild abandonment to a delighted feeling that he had known elsewhere. "It may be, I think it is, the difference of a Haymarket audience—the stock part is false in its habits, I never noted better." He told Mrs. Warner so. She said that the audience were uneducated, which he took to mean that they were not used to anything so good. He was, he admits, greatly cheered at the end. He played Hamlet next and again the house was good, but not great. He put it down to the bad example of Charles Kean at the Princess's. He could never stomach Charles Kean. He was, as usual, full of complaints. At a rehearsal of Lear several actors were missing and some of the parts not cast. He also was bitter about "these stage managers" who "frittered away their lives in self-important displays of vacuity of mind." When he played Macbeth again, he said he was indifferent in the first two acts, but, on hearing that Peel was in the house, played the last three acts in his best style. He admits to having played Lear fairly well. He had a row with Wallack over a repeat of Macbeth with which he finished the season.

His retirement was now upon him and his spirits were rising in consequence. He bade farewell to the Haymarket during the season 1850–1. The house was again not full for the first of the series of performances. This time he played Hamlet, Othello, Shylock, Richelieu, Werner, Virginius, Brutus, Cassius (with Howe, who made a big success of Mark Antony), Wolsey, King John, the Stranger, Benedict, Henry IV., Mr. Oakly and (for the first time in London) Richard II. This caused little interest. E. L. Davenport, the American actor, appeared in it. Macready's last appearance was as Lear. There was a great scene at the end and he spoke to the people:

"Ladies and gentlemen, the period of my theatrical engagement is reached this evening, but as my advertisements have signified, there is yet one occasion more on which I have to appear before you, and to that, the last performance in which I shall ever hope to strive for your approbation, I reserve the expression of the few words of acknowledgment and regret that I may desire and endeavour to offer you, my true, patient and long approved friends."

He bowed himself off amidst immense applause. His final farewell was at Drury Lane. But, except for that one night, his last actual engagement was at the Haymarket Theatre—there his career really ended.

There was a very important Haymarket engagement in 1852 when Barry Sullivan made his first appearance in London. This actor, born in Birmingham, had won fame in Ireland and then in the provinces. He played Hamlet at the Haymarket on February 7th, 1852, and also appeared there as Angiolo in *Woman's Heart* and as Alfred Evelyn in

Money. He was back there again in 1853, and later his Hamlet was acclaimed but his greatest triumphs lay elsewhere.

Before Webster left the Haymarket, he produced one of his greatest successes, a play which still lives to-day. On Saturday November 20th, 1852, Webster put on *Masks and Faces*, by two dramatists, Tom Taylor and Charles Reade, now famous names. It was a story of Peg Woffington, the great actress, who was played by Mrs. Stirling, since when nearly every famous actress has played the character at some time in her career, until the present generation, whom it may perhaps again tempt some day. In this very delightful play, Webster reached his zenith as an actor. He played Triplet—a starving poet, living in a garret with his ailing wife and equally starving children. He gave a really great performance, showing every phase of sentiment and emotion, and scored a great success.

Masks and Faces was the joint effort of two young authors who had only recently met and become friends. Reade went to stay with Taylor at Chiswick, and would write the play by day, whilst Taylor, who knew more stagecraft than Reade, cut it about mercilessly at night. This led to friction. Mrs. Sirling adjudicated between them and took it to Webster, who accepted it at once. Both these experts sided with Taylor in arguments about the play which sent Reade away from Town in a huff. He came back to find the play on the eve of production. And what a success it was, hailed by Press and public, with two beautiful, sparkling performances—Webster's and Mrs. Sirling's—not to mention Mrs. Leigh Murray as the wife. Webster was a little uncertain of his words on the first night—quite usual for him—and every now and again his Somerset accent would assert itself, as it did in moments of excitement. But he and Mrs. Stirling swept the audience off their feet.

Nobody was more delighted than Charles Reade. All the fights and the rows and the hurt feelings were forgotten in the moment of triumph. He rushed back stage and embraced Mrs. Stirling, Taylor and Webster before all the company. Then he heard the audience demanding him and his co-author by name. It was his first experience of a "call." Taylor dragged him in front of the curtain and the two men received an ovation. Charles Reade said he cried for joy.

Webster's reign at the Haymarket, splendid throughout, was ending in a blaze of glory. On February 12th, 1853, he produced Lytton's *Not So Bad as We Seem* (originally written for the Guild of Literature), and he played Sir Geoffrey Thornside. Again play and actor triumphed. His performance raised what might have been a poor part into a real, live one. The production was very beautiful—he had made Haymarket productions a standard of excellence, and the company was, as usual, first rate.

He brought his tenancy to a close with a triple bill on March 14th, 1853, with *The Roused Lion*, *A Novel Experience* and *The Pretty Girls of Stilberg*. For sixteen years he had controlled that theatre—sixteen years of continued progress and success, during which the Haymarket had ceased to be simply a summer theatre and had become, owing to the prestige he had given it and the respect in which he was held, a full-time theatre in every sense of the word. He had got the summer seasons disregarded and extended to cover the whole year. Now the recent Act repealing the Patent rights of Drury Lane and Covent Garden had brought freedom for all, largely owing to the ceaseless battle of the Haymarket Theatre, and particularly of Webster, to get the old shackles broken and justice proclaimed for the drama.

He stood on the stage of the Haymarket as actor-manager there for the last time, listening to the roars of applause which greeted him, and sensing the wave of good feeling which rolled towards him over the footlights. Let him sum up his progress and career at the Haymarket for himself:

"To authors I find I have paid nearly £30,000, if not more. 'Tis said, 'Uneasy lies the head that wears a crown,' but far more un-easiness was the head begirt with the tinsel crown of theatrical sovereignty, where every popular favourite is a viceroy over him, and where the ways and means are not compulsory, but solely dependent upon the will and pleasure of our sovereign the public. However, if my labour in the case of the drama, which has been a labour of love, has met with the approval of you, my tried and valued friends, it will not have been love's labour lost. Those who remember this theatre when I first took it, sixteen years ago—of course, I exclude the ladies from so long a remembrance—must perceive the extensive alterations, and I think I may say improvements, that I have accomplished during my tenancy. Abrupt angles have given way to curves, and my circles, especially from their present occupancy, appear graceful in the extreme. I have backed the pit and could in another sense—for respectability—against any pit in London. I have stalled off what was originally the orchestra, sometimes discoursing sweet sounds, though sweeter music in my ear has supplied its place in the audible approbation of my exertions as, to quote the words of Triplet, 'author, manager and actor, too.' The proscenium I have widened eleven feet and entirely remodelled it, and introduced gas for the fee of £500 a year and the presentation of the centre chandelier to the proprietors; and behind the curtain money has not been spared to render the stage as perfect for dramatic representation as its limited means will furnish; in fact, I have expended, with no ultimate advantage to myself, on this property over £12,000, besides paying more than £60,000 in rent."

It was an honest speech of an honest man, and he got his meed of praise and his place in history. He was popular with everyone; even the grudging, grumbling Macready always went back to him. No wonder they called him "The Guv'nor"—a name later bestowed on George Edwardes.

Webster had presented always the best; he had made the Haymarket a star house. Macready, Phelps, Charles Mathews, Helen Faucit, Mrs. Stirling, Madame Vestris, Charles Kean, Ellen Tree, Mrs. Warner, Mrs. Nisbett, Mr. and Mrs. Keeley and Charlotte Cushman (who will be referred to shortly) were a few of the names amongst so many glittering plays and players. He had treated authors well; he numbered amongst them Lord Lytton, Talfourd, Sheridan Knowles, Buckstone, Marston, Boucicault, Charles Reade, Tom Taylor and many others.

Above all, Benjamin Webster had been his own backer. He had put his savings into the Haymarket, he had worked with his own money and he had prospered well. He passed on to the Adelphi, where he did more magnificent work. But his name is in gold on the Haymarket story.

CHAPTER XXIII

A GALAXY OF STARS

BEFORE the new man of the Haymarket takes the centre of the stage, there are some others who must receive a "call" and take a bow. There was James Anderson, the Scots actor, born at Glasgow on May 8th, 1811. He had been a stroller and became a manager, during which time he met Macready, who offered him an engagement. This gave him his London debut at Covent Garden as Florizel in *A Winter's Tale*, in which he was very successful. He played a lot there and remained on under Vestris and Mathews when they took over. He was a good Romeo, the original Fernando in Sheridan Knowles's *John of Procida* and the original Charles Courtly in *London Assurance*. In the latter role he got a bad Press.

Anderson was with Macready at Drury Lane. He made a huge success as Titus Quintus Fulvius in *Gisippus* and also played Othello. He was one of Macready's most successful actors. He went to the Haymarket in 1845–6 to play opposite Helen Faucit. He also appeared in *Romeo and Juliet*, *Much Ado about Nothing*, *Lady of Lyons* and *The Hunchback*.

Webster's letter to him about this engagement shows back-stage Haymarket politics:

> "T. R. HAYMARKET.
> "23 *Sept.*, 1845.

"MY DEAR ANDERSON,—I have heard from Miss Faucit, Maddox told her that 'Mac' (Macready) positively commences on the 13th October and she wishes to begin as soon after as possible. Can you play on or before 20th October? Make an effort, as I want to take the wind out of Mac's sails! The plays she names at present are *Lady of Lyons*, *Romeo and Juliet*, *The Hunchback*, *As You Like It* and, if I like, *The Patrician's Daughter*, but I don't know the play. She is also ready in *Macbeth* if required. There is my budget and now for the reward of merit. It is understood between us that you are to have One hundred Pounds for twelve nights, to be played off at three nights a week, and a clear third of a benefit. Wishing you well through it, and expecting an answer by return, I remain,

> "Yours truly,
> "B. WEBSTER."

He got his answer very promptly as follows:

"16 High Street, Camden Town.
"*Sept. 24, 1845.*

"My dear Webster,—I will write to Manager Simpson to let me off my Liverpool engagement, which I have no doubt he will for a consideration; then I am yours. Mind, everything must be on a fair 'give and take' principle. If it is left to be supposed that I am engaged merely to support Miss Faucit, I must decline the engagement altogether. I am thus explicit to prevent any further misunderstanding. No one can have more respect for Helen Faucit, or a greater admiration of her talent, than myself, yet I must have assurance that there will be no partiality shown, no difference in the announcement of either in playbills and advertisements, or in any other way. Your reply in the affirmative will finish the business, the remuneration part of the affair being perfectly understood.

"Yours faithfully,
"J. R. Anderson."

Back came Webster's reply next day:

"You shall have a clear stage and no favour, so set your heart at rest. Miss F. merely mentioned what she would wish to be done. In the announcings and all you shall have fair play."

And he got it. They played to fine business for twenty-four nights.

Anderson, who did much good work both here and in the States, became Manager of Drury Lane and produced Shakespeare and big spectacular plays. He had varying success, but he scored a bull's-eye with *Azael, the Prodigal.* But Drury Lane broke him in the end to the tune of nearly £10,000. He starred at the old Britannia Theatre, starting there at £25 a night and finally receiving £100 a week. He played all over America, he ran the Surrey Theatre here, he was back again at the Lane—indeed he played all over the world, perhaps the first star actor to visit such places as Ceylon, Aden and Malta. His round-the-world trip earned him £3,000. And he wrote plays too. They were actors of parts in Anderson's day.

Of Charles Kean little mention need be made here; his fame is so widely known. The son of Edmund Kean, going on the stage against his father's wish, he made slow but determined progress, but eventually, as actor-manager, he did more to bring stage setting and spectacle to a fine art than anyone before him, even Macready. A good but not great actor, he ran the Princess's superbly and trained his people so well in their business that he made it a nest of stars. Ellen Terry started with him as a child. He laid the path which Irving was to tread.

Mr. and Mrs. Keeley, two more of Webster's stars, had a long, happy and prosperous stage career together. They both excelled in comedy. She had made many hits in parts which also called for sentiment and drama, being a very famous Smike in a version of *Nicholas Nickleby.* At the Adelphi she made a vast success as Jack Sheppard, a part she repeated at the Haymarket. In *The Roused Lion* she and Webster caused a sensation. She appeared with Mr. and Mrs. Charles Kean at the Haymarket too.

Mr. (Bob) Keeley had an expressionless face, which gave contrast and point to his great comic gifts. He spoke with queer jerks and was greatly imitated. He saw an imitation of himself once, and watched it through with his poker face betraying no expression. When it was over, Keeley remarked, "Well, if I'm like that, dem'd if I like it."

He was born in Carey Street, London, but that was his only appearance there! He ran away to go on the stage. His first big success was under Elliston at the Olympic, after which he never looked back. He was tried out to play Shylock, and took it very seriously, but the audience did not. Dickens was a great admirer of his comedy work, and if he could not play Shylock he was a magnificent Dogberry. As Jacob Earwig in *Boots at the Swan* he had no equal, and was a magnificent Sarah Gamp in *Martin Chuzzlewit*. He played *Box and Cox* at the Haymarket.

William Creswick, born in 1813, had made his London debut at the old Queen's Theatre (now the Scala) in 1835. Soon after he and Marston took an extraordinary little theatre in Oxford (in Magdalen Street). It was more barn than theatre, and to get to the boxes the audience had to enter through the fruiterers' shop next door. Here he played Macbeth, Banquo, etc. His London triumph, which made him, was his Hotspur at Sadler's Wells, under Phelps, in 1846. At the Haymarket he did very well indeed, especially in Westland Marston's *Heart of the World*, in which he played lead opposite to Helen Faucit. Another success was in *The Patrician's Daughter* (Webster had apparently heard of it by that time), again with Helen Faucit. He went into management at the Surrey Theatre and had a long and distinguished career.

J. L. Toole, at the very beginning of his career, played Simmons in *The Spitalfields Weaver* at the Haymarket. This was in 1852, and it was Toole's first London appearance as a full-fledged professional actor.

Charlotte Cushman was, in her time, the most celebrated actress America had produced. She went on the stage for much the same reason as Mrs. Stirling—the bankruptcy of her father. She had a fine contralto voice and decided to take up the musical side of the "profession." And she did quite well in opera, until her singing voice suddenly failed her. Stranded at New Orleans, miles from friends or help, she was advised to try her luck as a dramatic actress. She applied to the manager of the theatre, who realised that she had qualities, but could never draw them out. But one day he got her into a rage and she blazed out in fury. It woke her up—she had let herself go, and the acting followed. She played her first part—Lady Macbeth—at this manager's (Mr. Barton's) benefit. She was so poor that she had not the means of

buying a proper dress. At the last moment, she had to sink her pride
and borrow one which did not fit her.

Misfortune followed her to New York, where she got an engagement
at the Bowery Theatre and at once fell ill. As soon as she recovered
sufficiently to play, the theatre was burned down. All the theatrical
wardrobe which she had managed to get together was destroyed.

Apart from these disasters, her path was hard enough. She had no
beauty. Her face was plain, she had a protruding chin and a beaky
nose, and a big, rawboned figure like a man. Her speaking voice was
inclined to be deep, if not gruff. But she made an immense hit as
Nancy in *Oliver Twist*. And by hard work and sheer talent she got to
the very top, and starred with Macready in America. His acting
influenced her greatly.

In 1844 she determined to conquer London as she had conquered
New York. She arrived here quite unknown, took lodgings in a by-
street near Covent Garden, made a couple of mutton-chops last her for
three days, and called on the London managers. None would look at
her. She tried Maddox at the Princess's as a last resort, and he too
turned her down. She was nearly at the end of her tether. She went to
Paris, failed to get an engagement, and came back to London. It was
now a matter of life and death; she must get work. Rebuffed again by
Maddox, she turned on him. So forceful was she that the manager
woke up to the fact that he was in the presence of something unusual.
So he let her play as a trial and then engaged her. She carried all before
her and completely put her compatriot Forrest in the shade. The
greatest of all her successes was as Meg Merrilees.

When she appeared at the Haymarket, late in 1845, she made a
sensation. After her outstanding success, she had sent for her sister
Susan, who played Juliet to Charlotte's Romeo. This was amazing.
Mrs. Glover had played Falstaff there, but failed. Miss Cushman as
Romeo was terrific. She looked the gallant youth, her figure suited the
part, and what her face lacked in looks it made up for in fervour and
expression. She drew all the town. Her playing of the difficult balcony
scene is said to have been unsurpassed. This woman's strange career
reads like a thriller, and is worthy of a book in itself. It is surprising
that it has escaped the eyes of the film magnates, but maybe they do
not read our history, except where it concerns royalty or courtesans.

Before passing on to the days of Buckstone, a glimpse of the state of
the theatre in general at this time is worth while.

It was a strange, patchy period. Macready had gone, almost the last
of the great classic actors. But Charles Kean was now filling the gap.
Drury Lane was in the hands of mediocrity. Anderson had fallen
bravely. Gye was attempting to make it the Grand National Theatre
and coming a cropper. Three speculative managers lasted less than a
week each. And E. T. Smith, that odd figure, was doing all sorts of
productions and presenting Gustavus Brooke, the tragedian. Under

him the great playhouse was practically a booth. Phelps was making
history at Sadler's Wells. There, at this outlying theatre, he played
Shakespeare and the drama in a manner which won him enduring
fame. It became the Mecca of all who loved quality and acting. If he
did not make much money, his artistic achievement was peerless and
his example and courage a shining light. Charles Kean, at the Princess's,
contributed a page of theatre history as glowing in colour and richness
as an illuminated missal. But by and large there was not much else in
the London theatre—save at the Haymarket.

Covent Garden had lost money for so many, and had ruined Vestris
and Mathews. It was ceasing to be a theatre and in process of becoming
what it is to-day, an Opera House. Delafield and Gye were tenants in
turn, and in 1856 it was burned down. Farren, Wigan and Robson were
names at the Olympic, never a lucky theatre; the Adelphi was a drama
house; Mathews and Vestris were playing their last (with Mathews constantly being arrested for debt) at the Lyceum. It was a miserable state
of things nearly everywhere. The drama was at a low ebb. The plays
were stilted, artificial, or bombastic and pompous. Little of any value
was to be seen. But the Haymarket had kept up the standard when the
two great Patent theatres had let it down badly.

The truth was that the theatre was nearing the end of an epoch,
for theatrical affairs run in cycles. An age was petering out, waiting
for a new force. That force was to come before long; new life was
to breathe in playhouses, but for the moment it was sawdust and
fustian.

The newly obtained freedom of the theatres meant that Shakespeare
and the legitimate drama could be played openly everywhere, and this
did much to kill the attraction of the works of the playwright who was
not for an age but for all time. When his plays could be seen in their
true form at only one or two playhouses he drew the crowds. But when
everyone could play them and everyone could see them, satiety was
reached and a revulsion set in. It was still, however, an age when actors
counted for far more than they do now. Crowds would flock to see an
actor in a new part—they went to see the man, not so much the play in
which he appeared. The old plays were done over and over again; it was
the new people in the leading roles that brought the audiences. A bad
play would run provided it had a fine actor or actress. Nowadays a great
actor in a poor play soon "puts up the notice." But at this time long
runs were unknown—*Money* was remarkable for its eighty performances—and bills were changed almost nightly. The actors really
worked and the public eagerly responded.

The best people shook their heads over the theatre at this time. It
was dead, they declared. But it did not die. It never does; its life is
preserved through these recurring bad periods by a few main arteries,
and then suddenly comes the great transfusion and power flows back.
The theatre of our country is like our country itself. It droops, it loses

lustre and energy, and then—the man for whom it is waiting arrives and it goes forward to new greatness.

One of the conduits which at this period carried the life blood of the theatre was, without question, the Haymarket Theatre.

A new man now stood there. He was not new to the theatre; he was known there as actor and playwright. Once again the actor-manager-playwright was in command of what had been the Little Theatre in the Hay. It was John Baldwin Buckstone, who took over the sceptre from his old friend and colleague, Benjamin Webster, and was now in command of the Theatre Royal, Haymarket.

Buckstone was a Londoner, born in Hoxton in 1802. He went on the stage as a stroller in 1821, opening at Wokingham as Gabriel in *The Children in the Wood*. From there he joined the Faversham, Folkestone and Hastings Circuit for three years. He had other jobs too and many vicissitudes, of which he was proud. In 1855, when he had controlled he Haymarket for two years, he told some stories when making a speech at a banquet of the Royal General Theatrical Fund—that oldest and best of theatrical provident institutions. His remarks throw a nice light on what touring actors went through then, and also of how they learnt their business. Young people in "the profession" may contrast them with their own experience to-day.

"I was a country actor," he said, "and amongst other vicissitudes, once walked from Northampton to London—seventy-two miles— on 4½d. As it may interest you, gentlemen, I will describe my costume on that occasion, and how we got to London. My costume consisted of a threadbare whitey-blue coat, with tarnished metal buttons, secured to the throat, because I wore underneath it what we term a flowered waistcoat, made of glazed chintz, and of a very showy pattern, generally adopted when playing country boys and singing comic songs, which at that time was my vocation. I will not attempt to describe my hat; while my trousers must only be delicately alluded to, as they were made of what was originally white duck, but as they had been worn about six weeks, and having myself been much in the fields, there was a refreshing tint of green and clay colour about them which imparted to that portion of my attire quite an agricultural appearance. I carried a small bundle. I will not describe its entire contents, except that it held a red wig and a pair of russet boots. Under my arm was a portfolio, containing sketches from Nature and some attempts at love poetry; while on my feet, to perform this distance of seventy-two miles, I wore a pair of dancing pumps, tied up at the heels with pack thread. Thus equipped, I started with my companion from Northampton and before breakfast we accomplished fifteen miles, when we sat down to rest under a hedge at the roadside, We felt very much disposed to partake of the meal I have alluded to, but were rather puzzled how to provide it. Presently a

Mr. Beerbohm Tree (later Sir Herbert Tree) as Sir John Falstaff.

Miss Julia Neilson as Drusilla Ives in *The Dancing Girl*.

Cyril Maude as the Rev. Gavin Dishart in *The Little Minister*.

cow-boy appeared, driving some lazy, zigzagging cows, and carrying two large tins containing skimmed milk. We purchased the contents of one of the cans for ½d. A cottage was close at hand, where we applied for bread, and procured a very nice, though rather stale, half-quartern home baked loaf for 1d. The cow-boy sat by us on that roadside to wait for his can. The cows seemed to regard us with a sleepy look of mingled pity and indifference, while with the bottom of the crust of that loaf and three pints of skimmed milk, I assure you, I enjoyed the roadside breakfast of that summer morning more than I have enjoyed the sumptuous banquet of this evening. On the first day we walked forty miles, in which my pumps and what they covered, as the Yankees say, 'suffered some.' Our bed for that night was in one of those wayside hostelries called 'a common lodging house for travellers,' for which accommodation we disbursed 2d. Late in the evening of the next day we completed the remaining thirty-two miles, and found ourselves at the 'Mother Red Cap' at Camden Town, with enough in our pockets to procure half a pint of porter. Thus, you see, gentlemen, I have experienced some of the vicissitudes of a country actor."

That journey to London was to end with the command of the Haymarket Theatre—and a brilliant, good, honest period of command it was to be.

Whilst a struggling stroller, Buckstone had met Edmund Kean, who gave him praise and encouragement. His first appearance on the London stage was at the Surrey Theatre, in 1824, as Peter Smirke in a play called *The Armistice*. He proved a very excellent low comedian and he received many offers. He played at the Peckham Theatre and the Union in Catherine Street. He was at the Adelphi in 1828, when Yates and John Reeve ran it, and during that time blossomed out as a dramatist, performing in his own plays. He now devoted much time to writing plays and adapting them, both for the Adelphi and the Haymarket. His two big successes at the Adelphi were *The Green Bushes* in 1845 and *The Flowers of the Forest* in 1847. There were many farces and adaptations which enjoyed popularity in their day. *Forgery* or *The Reading of the Will*, gave him dual success as dramatist and as actor, for he scored in the comedy part. In the same year his *Ellen Wareham*, with Mrs. Yates in the lead, was played at the Haymarket. In 1833 he played at the Haymarket in Douglas Jerrold's *The Housekeeper, or The White Rose*, a Jacobite play, in which he appeared with Vining, Miss Taylor and Benjamin Webster. He was there too with Charles Mathews, the younger. In 1834, besides plays at the Adelphi, he had *Rural Felicity* and *Married Life* at the Haymarket, with Mrs. Faucit, Mrs. Glover, Mrs. Humby, Vining, Farren and himself in the casts.

He went on writing for both the Adelphi and the Haymarket, and in the same year or very shortly after he became a permanent member of

T

the Haymarket company. Then he wrote all the farces performed there, or practically all of them, and an outstanding success was *The Irish Lion*. In 1840 he went to America and returned two years later after a moderate success. Of his return, the *Athenæum* said:

"Buckstone showed his comic phiz again on Wednesday, after his long absence in America, and literally 'tipped the wink' to the audience, who responded with a roar of laughter. After playing Dove in his own grotesque piece, *Married Life*, he was called forward, and expressed in a becoming and feeling manner his acknowledgments of the welcome."

He played at the Haymarket with Madame Celeste; he was in the ill-fated *Quid Pro Quo* and he created Bob in Boucicault's play, *Old Heads and Young Hearts*. He was Tilly Slowboy in Webster's adaptation of *The Cricket on the Hearth*, and he was with Charlotte Cushman and her sister when they did *Twelfth Night* in 1846, playing Sir Andrew Aguecheek. His own farces were universally successful. He took a farewell benefit, playing Scrub in *The Beaux Stratagem* before leaving for the Lyceum. This was one of his famous parts.

In 1847 he was one of the representative actors chosen for the special performances to raise money for the purchase of Shakespeare's house at Stratford-on-Avon. He returned to the Haymarket in 1848-9, playing in Shakespeare with Charles Kean and his wife. But his performance as one of the Weird Sisters in *Macbeth* caused much amusement, to the horror of the company, but to the delight of the audience. He could not resist being funny. In January, 1850, he wrote a very successful play for the Haymarket called *Leap Year*, in which he appeared with the Keans. He added success to success and was one of the pillars of the house under Webster.

So it was not surprising that, when Webster went to the Adelphi, Buckstone should succeed him at the Haymarket.

He had a clear-cut policy of his own. He did not care about tragedy or heavy fare, although he was a very expert writer of melodrama. He was a comedian himself and he decided that comedy was to be the staple at the Haymarket. Under his control it became the leading comedy theatre of London, a position it still holds firmly and unassailed.

He began his managerial career on Easter Monday, 1853, and he had collected a magnificent company. They included Barry Sullivan, Henry Compton, Chippendale, Corri, Howe, William Farren Junior, Tilbury, Rogers and Arthur Payne, Miss Reynolds, Miss Louisa Howard, Mrs. Buckingham, Mrs. Poynter, Mrs. Stanley, Miss A. Vernon, Miss E. Romer, Miss A. Vining, Mrs. Caulfield, Miss E. Bromley, Miss Grace Leslie and Miss Laidler.

The comedy theatre opened with *The Rivals* and a burlesque by Planché called *Buckstone's Ascent of Mount Parnassus*.

He was true to his idea of the Haymarket as a purely comedy house for a long time. In fact, he only departed from this policy on particular occasions and for particular reasons. A great comedian himself, he knew the value of laughter. Webster had introduced many improvements into the building (it is interesting to note that the Haymarket had been the last theatre to be lighted with candles when all the others had installed gas), and Buckstone kept up the standard with his company and plays. And he was not a jealous limelight-grabbing actor-manager (contrary to modern opinion, very few of them were). He collected other comedians round him. He kept up comedy and he kept up pantomime—the Haymarket pantomimes were institutions, although they did not attain the spectacular magnificence of Drury Lane.

An early production of Buckstone's in 1854 was *The Knights of the Round Table*, by J. R. Planché, the master of that sort of extravaganza. G. Vandenhoff and Buckstone himself scored well in the piece. This Vandenhoff was the son of the elder actor whom Macready despised. He was not destined for the stage; his father did all he could to prevent him following that career, but he threw up a very nice sinecure—Solicitor to the Trustees of the Liverpool Docks—to take to the boards, and he succeeded. He got right to the top and then, having had enough of it, went back to the law and became a barrister. George Vandenhoff was a man of mettle.

At this time, however, he had just returned from a most successful American tour and Buckstone offered him an engagement. George Vandenhoff agreed and said he would open as Hamlet. Buckstone immediately demurred. He did not want Hamlet or any other Shakespearean character at the Haymarket, "for," he declared, "it doesn't matter if you play it as well as John Kemble, a Shakespearean play keeps money out of the house." This was a bit of a staggerer to Vandenhoff, a great Shakespearean. To him such a view seemed sacrilegious. One of the three best theatres in London refusing to stage Shakespeare! It was eleven years since he had played in London and things appeared to have altered, especially at the Haymarket. He stuck to his guns, and, much against his will, Buckstone gave in. It was a special occasion.

There was another Hamlet in London at this time, at the St. James's, where the German actor, Emile Devrient, was playing it in his native tongue. Vandenhoff and his father, Shakespearean actors and Hamlets both, went along to see it. It was a strange affair to them, but the climax was reached when Hamlet said to the Ghost (in German, of course): "Go on, I'll follow thee," and started to do so. There was a little applause and the German actor promptly stopped when nearly "off," came down to the footlights, and bowed three times. It was his habit to acknowledge applause whenever he got it, despite the play's situation. Vandenhoff believed he was the better Hamlet of the two.

He played it at the Haymarket, to the grave doubts of Buckstone, on

October 25th, 1853. Buckstone had opened his house the previous evening with *A Cure for Love* and *The Beggar's Opera*. The part of Macheath was played by Miss Featherstone (afterwards Mrs. Howard Paul). She had been drawing the town to the Strand and now did so at the Haymarket. A lovely creature, with a magnificent figure and all dash and fire, she had also a fine voice in addition to being a first-rate actress. As Macheath she rivalled Vestris—indeed, artistically she probably beat her. It was said that she sang the part better than Sims Reeves—of whom she could give a perfect imitation. She was a tremendously popular Macheath for years and equally acclaimed as Apollo in *Midas*. But it was not only in singing and light shows that this lady shone. She went to Drury Lane and amazed the theatre world by playing in *Macbeth*—and more, she doubled Hecate with Lady Macbeth and was magnificent in both parts.

On the evening of Vandenhoff's Hamlet that actor realised that the strong point of the company was not tragedy. Why should it be? Buckstone's policy was comedy. Vandenhoff puts on record that he never saw so weak a cast—that the Queen was played by a young lady of fine figure, considerable personal attractions, whose appropriate line of business was genteel comedy, gay widows and sprightly *intrigantes*. Horatio was weak, and played by an actor who admitted he had never played in *Hamlet* and had never even seen it. The Ghost was all right; so was Howe (possibly the only Quaker to become an actor). Chippendale (also Stage Manager) was a good Polonius, Louisa Howard was a competent Ophelia and Compton a grand Gravedigger. Despite all this, Vandenhoff was so good that he received an ovation. Buckstone complimented him and rushed out an announcement:

> "Mr. George Vandenhoff having on his first appearance created a sensation equal to that made by any tragedian of the day, will repeat the character of Hamlet on Thursday and Monday next."

He got a fine Press as well. Although it was a tragedy, and consequently against Buckstone's ideals, it was a good enough theatre sensation to play again and get the money whilst it was going.

Vandenhoff was lucky in having Compton as the Gravedigger. Henry Compton was a magnificent actor and probably the finest exponent of Shakespeare's clowns the stage has ever seen. He was a great character actor and created many parts. His real name was Charles Mackenzie. He was born in 1805, his father being a well-educated man, a great book-lover, a fine public speaker and a remarkable debater. His mother was a Symonds of Worcester and a connection of Rowland Hill, of postage-stamp fame.

Compton was born in Huntingdon and was, after a good education, put into the cloth trade, under his maternal uncle. But he never took kindly to business and eventually became an actor. He got a job at Leicester and, having to walk there, he arrived too late for rehearsal and was told to walk home again. But he got a free pass for the theatre and became one of the audience instead of one of the actors. In the theatre he met a man who knew his family at Huntingdon and who prevailed on the manager to give him another chance. He got it. He went through all the vicissitudes of the touring actor of his day. Eventually he got on to the York Circuit and made himself very popular there, so much so that seventy-eight Leeds playgoers presented him with a snuff-box. He got to London at last, after eleven years' hard provincial work, and he achieved success. He reached Drury Lane in 1837. There he made hits as Master Slender (with Dowton as Falstaff), as Tony Lumpkin, as Gnatbrain in *Black Eye'd Susan* and as William in *As You Like It*, the Touchstone being Dowton. It was as Touchstone that Compton was afterwards to become so famous—and a better there has never been. He played many parts at the Lane, including the First Gravedigger, which he later played with Vandenhoff at the Haymarket and later still with Irving at the Lyceum. It was at Drury Lane that Compton and Buckstone met. Compton had a row with Macready, and got the better of it. When, later, he was at Drury Lane with Macready, they had several passages of words. Macready would instruct everyone. He instructed Compton, who was playing a sailor. Said the eminent tragedian: "Mr. Compton, I do not speak without due consideration and thought on the subject, and you will therefore excuse my saying that you have never been still for more than a minute at a time the whole of this scene."

The answer from the experienced character actor came pat: "Mr. Macready, I do not speak without due consideration and thought on the subject, and you will therefore excuse my saying, 'Did you ever know a British sailor just come on shore after a long voyage who *could* keep still for more than a minute at a time?' "

Collapse of Macready.

That was the sort of man Henry Compton was. His descendants grace the stage and literature to-day. Fay Compton, his granddaughter, is one of the best actresses of the contemporary stage. He went to the Haymarket with Buckstone in 1853 and he remained there for nearly eighteen years, doing magnificent work. He performed at Farren's last appearance and benefit there in 1855, when that fine old actor said farewell to the stage. The performance was under the immediate patronage of Queen Victoria. The "cock salmon" had a grand farewell, his profession rallying round him. Compton played in *Where There's a Will There's a Way*; with him were Mrs. Stirling and Leigh Murray, and the bill included *King Rene's Daughter*, with Helen Faucit, Barry Sullivan, Howe, W. Farren Junior, Villiers; *A Moving Tale*, with Mr. and Mrs. Keeley and Miss Keeley; the first act of *Flying Colours*, with Benjamin Webster and Madame Celeste; the second act of *The Clandestine Marriage*, with Farren himself, Alfred Wigan, Chippendale, Hare, etc.; *Box and Cox*, with Buckstone, Harley and Mrs. Griffiths. As makeweight, there were Perea Nena and Marcos Diaz, the Spanish dancers, with their "twelve unequalled coryphées," a selection by Albert Smith from *The Ascent of Mont Blanc* and "The Bay of Biscay" sung by Sims Reeves. And all for the usual prices!

Señora Perea Nena and her partner, Señor Marcos Diaz, were a couple of Spanish dancers who did much to revolutionise stage dancing and ballet. There are very few records of them nowadays, although they figure largely on the Haymarket bills and made a great and far-reaching impact in their day. Ballet was sinking in interest and losing its hold. Splendour and show palled; something new was wanted to reawaken it. Ballet lost its attraction through its unchanging insistence on the classic correctness of Taglioni, Grisi, Cerito, and the others.

Into this static atmosphere burst the Spanish woman. She was speed, she was vivacity, and the rapidity and variety of her steps, together with her method of working up to a frenzied climax, made the sylphlike gliding of the *figurantes* seem anæmic. She had grace and voluptuousness at the same time. Her swirling skirts, her ever-moving, eager toes captivated everyone and breathed a new ardour and vitality into the ballet as a whole.

Vandenhoff gives a description of Perea Nena himself, which is possibly a little tinged with the jealousy of a tragedian who found that a dancer was a greater attraction—and also discloses a little bit of Buckstone's managerial methods:

"The Spanish Dancers, headed by the agile little Andalusian Perea Nena, were the next novelty at the Haymarket Theatre and such was their—or rather her—attraction, for her *corps de ballet* were shocking contrasts to her rapid, flashing, coquettish movements, now like the curvettings of an Arab barb, fretting on the bit, anon like the bound of an antelope, and now and again like the whirl and whiz of a steam engine—such was her attraction, that actors and acting became of quite secondary importance. Mr. Buckstone took advantage of the opportunity to rid himself of all salaries that it was inconvenient to pay, and with all services he could now dispense with, by the expedient of a notice in the green-room, closing the season on a Saturday night, and re-opening it on the Monday following, as a summer season! Ingenious and ingenuous!"

But to return to Vandenhoff. After his experience of the Haymarket comedy company playing tragedy, he decided that his successful Hamlet was enough, for the moment, to show London what sort of a tragedian he was, and he gave in to the wishes of Buckstone. He had been most thrilled by his own father's criticism, that famous actor-father who had not wanted him to be an actor at all. The veteran had seen his son's performance and had watched it with keen eyes. He told his wife, who told her son, how delighted he was.

Vandenhoff next played Alfred Evelyn in *Money*—following in

Macready's footsteps. This was roses all the way, for the Haymarket company were just right for this Haymarket play. Vandenhoff again awaited his father's comment, and again his father confided to the mother, who passed it on to the son: "It was as good as the Hamlet, and more I cannot say." He next played Claude Melnotte in *The Lady of Lyons* and disapproved his leading lady. But the show was a success. Then he insisted on Shakespeare again, and played Benedick in *Much Ado*. Charlotte Cushman came again to the Haymarket and he appeared with her. She played Bianca, but he would not play Fazio; he appeared with her in *The Stranger*, and as Wolsey in *Henry VIII*.

Cushman got Buckstone to produce a play called *The Duchess Elanour* by Chorley, the music critic of the *Athenæum*, but it was hissed off the stage on the second night, to Charlotte Cushman's great mortification. It dragged its way through four acts, but the audience would not stand the fifth.

Town and Country, and *London Assurance* followed for Vandenhoff and then Planché's *Knights of the Round Table*. It was an elaborate production, one scene being a view of London from Hampstead Heath. It ran for fifty-four consecutive nights. Compton's scene, in which he outwits and cheats a landlord, was the talk of the town.

During this season a tower of strength was lost to Buckstone when Mrs. Fitzwilliam died of cholera. She was his friend and business partner.

Buckstone was a bad business man and was to pay for it in the end. He gave too much value and did not watch expenses—two things which, although they helped the theatre from the public point of view, were to bring him to financial disaster in the end.

But that was not near yet. A short description of a Haymarket pantomime is of interest, and Henry Morley has left us one:

> " 'Little Bo-Peep, who lost her sheep' is the heroine of the Haymarket pantomime, and the introductory burlesque is a neat little story very elegantly put on the stage with Arcadian shepherd scenery and bursts of fairy splendour. The succeeding pantomime is not too lively, but it is carefully and handsomely got up, is well worked, and without omitting all allusions to the war [the Crimean War] contains less reference to it than occurs in many other houses. . . . Señora Perea Nena, the popular Spanish dancer, who shakes her petticoats and observes curiously the twinkling of her swift, impatient toes, has left us, and the manager of the Haymarket has brought back the young lady who so delightfully imitated her at the St. James's Theatre, Miss Lydia Thompson, the little Silver-hair of last year's Haymarket pantomime. A better representative of Little Bo-Peep could scarcely have been found. The best performer in the Harlequinade was the Pantaloon, Mr. Barnes, a name honoured in pantomime. The scenery throughout was excellent, and one particular

transformation, of a party in a ballroom, with couches and chairs, into the same party accommodated with a coach and horses, was the cleverest thing of its kind done at our theatres in Christmas, 1854."

It seems that the Haymarket did good pantomimes.

There was a little scene at the Haymarket which, although it did not happen in pantomime, was worthy of it. They were playing the musical farce, *No Song, No Supper*. The business of the play demanded a boiled leg of mutton every night, and this, according to theatre tradition, became the perquisite of the property man after its use on the stage, where, of course, practically none was eaten. Some of the "flymen" coveted this joint and thought how nice it would be to have it for their families. So a plot was hatched. One evening, when Farren, who loved a joke, had carved the joint, as the "business" demanded, he fell in with a suggestion made by the flymen. They asked him to attach a hook, which they would lower, to the joint, and leave the rest to them. He did it with glee. Just before the scene "closed in," as the parlance then was, and the property-man was waiting to dash forward and get his leg of mutton, the piece of meat slowly ascended in the air, without any visible means of support, to the great joy of the audience and the ill-suppressed mirth of everyone on and off stage, save the thwarted property-man. But the hook, which Farren had only fastened in the fat, came out, down fell the mutton into the dish, spraying everyone with gravy. Amidst rounds of applause, the triumphant property-man dashed forward and secured his joint after all. Never again did the flymen try to pirate his "perks."

Buckstone's first season, despite the trick mentioned by Vandenhoff, extended for five years.

CHAPTER XXIV

THE ERA OF BUCKSTONE

To attempt anything like a complete record of all that Buckstone did—and left undone—at the Haymarket would fill volumes. Only outstanding events can be chronicled here. He made Tom Taylor a regular Haymarket dramatist, he did plays by Stirling Coyne, such as *Everybody's Friend* (in which Buckstone was the original Major Wellington de Boots, and which afterwards gained fame for J. S. Clarke, who was to succeed him at the theatre) and *Black Sheep* (in which he played Mr. Bunny), *The Family Secret*, by Edmund Falconer (in which he played Bubbles); *The Wife's Portrait*, by Westland Marston; *Silken Fetters*, by Leicester Buckingham; *A Hero of Romance*, again by Westland Marston (in which he played Dr. Lafitte) and many others. But two outstanding Haymarket dramatists were Tom Taylor and W. S. Gilbert. Taylor should be taken first because of some very remarkable happenings.

Of Taylor's plays, Buckstone produced many, and played in many too. There was *The Contested Election*, in which he was Mr. Peckover, *The Overland Route* (with Buckstone as Lovibond), *The Babes in the Wood* (with Buckstone as Beetle); *New Men and Old Acres* (with Buckstone as the original Bunter), but most important of all was *Our American Cousin*. The production and history of this play is a story in itself. Before it is told, the position should again be looked over, for this attraction did not see the stage until 1861.

Buckstone believed in value for money. His shows began early and lasted until one o'clock in the morning. It was a period of late hours. It was strenuous work, but as several plays were presented during the course of the evening, it did not fall too heavily upon anyone in particular, and gave much employment. If such a system were revived to-day it would go far to solving many theatrical difficulties. But London no longer keeps such late hours. There was half-price at nine o'clock, even after which time it was possible to see more than one can get to-day for double the money. Audiences leaving a full evening of opera at the Haymarket's neighbour (but never rival) would drop into the theatre to see the closing farce, which rarely began before midnight. There was always a good comedian in it. One of them, Wright, got £50 a week for playing in these closing farces, and the receipts after midnight always averaged over £100 a week.

It was a happy, leisurely London in those days. Playgoers went to the theatre mainly because there was hardly any other form of entertainment to attract them. Music-halls were just beginning their great popularity, but respectable husbands did not take their wives there. If they were people of moderate means, they went half-price to the play, had a little supper afterwards and then strolled home. Mostly they lived nearby, and not in distant suburban dormitories. And nobody minded walking then; their legs were good and had not been rendered weak and wilting by the use of buses or cars. Buckstone took full advantage of the times. He would give four plays an evening.

Another important Haymarket event about this time was the success of Amy Sedgwick in Tom Taylor's *Unequal Match*. In 1861 Buckstone presented Booth, the famous American actor. Here again he let Shakespeare tread the Haymarket stage, but it was not a great success. Booth played Shylock, but did not set the Thames on fire, nor did he succeed any better as Sir Giles Overreach in Massinger's *A New Way to Pay Old Debts* or in *Richelieu*. Money was lost, yet Gustavus Brooke was pulling them in with Shakespeare at Drury Lane. It seemed that good luck was deserting the Haymarket and its cheery manager-dramatist-actor. Things had been going against him. Perhaps he missed Mrs. Fitzwilliam, his good adviser; perhaps he found that the demands of his backer were too great. Buckstone had not run the Haymarket with his own money, as had Webster. His friend Geness had put up the funds. Buckstone had made an excellent start, for he persuaded the owner of the theatre, the widow of D. E. Morris, to let him have it for £500 a year cheaper than she had charged Webster. It is probable, however, that his own business methods were to blame. He gave too much for the money; he did not cut down salaries; he wanted everyone to be happy—he was a good natured, happy-go-lucky man himself. Perhaps, too, he was failing to observe that sound Haymarket tradition of star names—equally there were not many to be had at this time—and was playing too much himself, not giving enough variety for box-office pull. At any rate, he was in pretty low water when, in 1861, he produced the play called *Our American Cousin* referred to earlier in this chapter. It was one of those dramas within dramas which happen in the history of the theatre. It was by Tom Taylor, the chief Haymarket dramatist, but it had already been produced in America. Although Tom Taylor wrote it, the chief factor in its astounding success was not the plot or dialogue, but the performance by and the gags of an English actor called E. A. Sothern. This remarkable performer, who made fortunes and put a new type and a new name into the English language, started a fashion, and left a memory which endures to-day. It was Sothern's creation of the character of Lord Dundreary which saved the play, saved the Haymarket and created a legend which so many people believe really existed.

Edward Askew Sothern was born in Liverpool on April 1st, 1830, a fitting birthday for a man who was to create the character of an immortal fool. He first appeared at Jersey. In 1851 he went to America and was successful. In 1852 he was in New York at Laura Keene's

Theatre. Here they had a play by an Englishman called *Our American Cousin*. In it was the character of an old man, Lord Dundreary. It was a small part that consisted of only forty-seven lines, and Sothern was asked to play it. He refused. The management pressed, and he agreed on condition that he was allowed to alter the part, write it and play it on his own lines. To this the management consented. Sothern began by putting into that part everything he had ever seen which had struck him as being funny or absurd.

He declared that not one thing in it but had been observed by himself in real life. The play opened and was not a success. But the management persevered. The public could not understand that Sothern, whom they had always seen in serious, dramatic, and even pathetic parts, was to be taken seriously in his attempt at humour. But they found themselves laughing in spite of themselves; evidently Sothern meant to be funny, and it was all right to laugh, and they laughed immoderately at what they now came to regard as a typical English character. Sothern built it up steadily. Everything which had got a laugh anywhere went into the part. One day, during the rehearsals, in order to keep warm, he was hopping about at the back of the stage. Laura Keene, who by no means approved of what was going on, asked him if he meant to put his antics into the part of Dundreary? Sothern looked at her and replied gravely: "Yes, Miss Keene. That is my view of the character." Having said this, he felt bound to do so. He now made his creation walk with a curious kind of hop, and found that not only the company but also the stage hands roared with laughter. So did the audience. Because of Lord Dundreary the play caught on. It ran for months, it ran for years, it swept right across America. And its fame swept across the Atlantic to London, where Buckstone became very anxious to make His Lordship's acquaintance. In due course it was announced that *Our American Cousin* with E. A. Sothern in the part of Lord Dundreary, "as acted by him with enormous success over eight hundred times in America," would appear on the Haymarket stage on November 11th, 1861.

Buckstone was doing what so many managers do when they find themselves "up against it." He was taking a chance. He was by no means certain about it. Nor, to tell the truth, was Sothern himself. He had his doubts as to whether the English would like Lord Dundreary. For, in Sothern's hands, that gentleman, with his wig, his whiskers (which started the male fashion of "Dundreary whiskers"), his eyeglass, his faultless yet eccentric clothes (the long frock coat he borrowed from Boucicault), the lisp and stutter, the queer little hop or impediment in the gait, the mixed metaphors and proverbs *à la* Malaprop (never mispronounced, only mixed up), that gentleman was like nothing on earth, although he was eventually hailed, both in America and in this country, as the true type of inane "swell" or "man about Town" which it was fondly believed could be met with in quantities in the West End clubs and fashionable resorts.

Actually, Lord Dundreary was unlike anything. The "typical man" of any nationality never is.

Before he left America, Sothern wrote to a friend in England:

"I have received a point-blank offer from the Theatre Royal, Haymarket, London, and conditionally have accepted, to open in October next. I commence as Lord Dundreary. Everyone foretells a hit, but I am doubtful. The whole past seems like a dream to me. Who (when I first played Beverley as an amateur) ever imagined I should take to the stage as a profession—come over to America, remain nine years and return to star in London."

But over he came and found the whole company at the Haymarket quite convinced that the play would be a failure. They included Buckstone, who cast himself, most unsuitably, for Asa Trenchard, Chippendale, Rogers, Clark, Baird, Mrs. Charles Young, Miss M. Oliver, Miss H. Lindley and Miss Henrade. Sothern commenced the rehearsals and the gloom grew. He was rehearsing a scene in which he read one of the letters from his mythical brother Sam—a character never seen, but almost as famous as Dundreary himself. The leading lady, after waiting impatiently, walked on the stage. Sothern turned to her, saying, "My dear madam, don't come on here until you get your cue. In fact, on the night of the performance, you will have twenty minutes to wait during this scene." The lady was satirical. "Why?" she sneered. "Do you expect so much applause?" "Yes," said Sothern. "I know how long this scene plays." "Ah," said the actress sharply, "but suppose the audience should not take your view of the matter?" "In that case," returned Sothern, quietly, "you won't have to bother yourself, for I and the piece will have been condemned a good hour before your services are required." But it shook him, all the same.

The first night came and with it came first-night nerves *in extremis*. No company is ever happy when it expects to appear in a pronounced failure. Buckstone was worried, and Sothern was scared stiff as to how he and his travesty would be received. It was one thing to make America laugh over a caricature of an Englishman, another thing to present an audience of his own countrymen, who knew nothing of him as an actor, with something they might well regard as an insult. But the curtain went up and the play started.

There was no demonstration. Sothern played for all he was worth. He had got his laughs. Indeed, he convulsed the audience, who were in hysterics. His reading of the famous letter was a sensation. There was Homeric laughter and cheers. But it was first-night success—and nothing else. The Press was good enough. The *Athenæum* said:

"Whether the character by itself [Lord Dundreary] would sustain any degree of interest we much doubt, but in the hands of Mr. Sothern, the gentleman who has been acting it for so many hundred nights over the water, it is certainly the funniest thing in the world.

"The part is abstractedly a vile caricature of an inane nobleman, intensely ignorant and extremely indolent. The notion once accepted by the audience that such an absurd animal could be the type of any class whatever, the actor was free to exaggerate to any extent the representation of the ridiculous. Mr. Sothern, in the quietest way, takes full advantage of his position, and effectually subdues the audience to his mood. Laughter, at all times irrepressible, finally culminates on a general convulsion, which, to our ears, seemed quite a peculiarity—it was so strange and yet so natural. The occasion was simply the reading of a letter from a brother in America, containing literally nothing more than that he feared a former letter must have miscarried from his having forgotten to direct it. This, with certain inane comments on its contents suffice to enable Mr. Sothern to produce the prodigious effect we have indicated. We are therefore disposed to believe that Mr. Sothern, as an eccentric actor, is a man of no ordinary genius, and reasonably desire his further acquaintance. The public, we have no doubt, will be of the same opinion. . . ."

But it did not seem that the public were of that opinion. Despite the Homeric laughter of the first night, and of each night—the volume lessened as the audiences grew smaller. It became apparent to Buckstone that *Our American Cousin* and Lord Dundreary was not what the public of London in general and of the Haymarket Theatre in particular really wanted to see. Business was shocking. The show had been produced on a Monday night. So hopeless did it seem that on the Thursday he "put up the notice" that it would be succeeded by *She Stoops to Conquer*.

But in the house that evening was that distinguished comedian and experienced man of the theatre, Charles J. Mathews. His practised eye appraised the thing and he believed in it. He went round to see Buckstone. He begged him to keep the show on. Buckstone demurred. He said it was no good. To his way of thinking, its success in the States was because they believed that Sothern was presenting a real English lord, and loved it. Over here, however, where we knew better, it was giving offence.

Mathews pooh-poohed this. Buckstone maintained that he was right, the part of Dundreary was giving offence to the "swells." Mathews laughed at him. "No such thing," he said. "It is just what they will adore. The English like to laugh at themselves. Have another go. Bill it, advertise it, push it. Give them a chance to know what they are missing. Get them to start to come and they will laugh and laugh and laugh. You will have a tremendous success. Give Sothern as free a hand as he likes. He knows what to do. You push it—all it needs is patience and push."

He convinced Buckstone. The manager advertised the show as no show had been advertised before. He asked the critics who had not yet attended to come and see it. He put out bills by the hundred. The critics came—and gave good notices. Henry Morley said:

"*Our American Cousin* is a piece of Transatlantic extravagance which will have a long run at the Haymarket, not only because it is well mounted and acted and presents Mr. Buckstone in a Yankee character, but more especially for the sake of a sketch new to our stage, given by an actor hitherto unknown in London, Mr. Sothern, with an eccentric and whimsical elaboration that is irresistibly amusing . . . shouts of laughter follow every look and gesture. He contrives, in the midst of all the extravagance, to maintain for his inane lord the air of a well-bred, good-natured gentleman, and shows an art in his absurdity that makes us curious to see what he can do in some other character. But it will be long before he has leave from the public to do anything but identify himself with Lord Dundreary. The piece is sure of a long run."

John Oxenford, in *The Times*, said that no character like Lord Dundreary had ever before appeared—"to test him by anything in the actual world would be to ignore his especial merit, which consists in giving a conventional notion the most novel and fantastic expression that can be imagined."

Then the public began to respond; the crowds grew. Lord Dundreary was talked of everywhere. Sothern had started with a small salary and percentage of profits, but when the show looked like being a failure he asked Buckstone to make it a straight salary. The manager agreed. Now Sothern repented and wanted to go back to the original idea. But Buckstone held fast to the alteration. He had taken the risk when the actor asked him, and now he would reap the reward. Business increased; Dundreary became the fashion. Men cultivated the Dundreary whiskers and wore Dundreary coats. There may be some who do not know what Dundreary whiskers were. They sprang from the side of the cheeks in luxuriant proliferation, and fell away at the sides as far as the shoulders, tapering to a point, leaving the cheeks themselves and the chin clean-shaven. Sothern also wore a heavy moustache, his hair was parted in the middle, and burst into long, frizzled curls over the temples, and of course, he wore a monocle. Such a run on the tailors did the new fashions cause that Sothern could have had as many free suits as he liked. Parcels from gentlemen's outfitters showered into his Haymarket dressing-room, containing shirts, collars, ties and the like, for the haberdashers knew that if he wore them on the stage they would sell out in the shops. Hatters almost buried him with hats and bootmakers sent footwear by the cartload. Dundreary photographs were everywhere. Epigrams *à la* Dundreary were coined by all. Little books about the non-existent lord were published by the hundred, all of them unauthorised. London, indeed England, was Dundreary-crazy. Not to have been to the Haymarket and seen Dundreary was a social solecism.

Cattle Show week—the theatre's big week of the year until the Motor Show eclipsed it—brought the country folk to see Dundreary and the Haymarket was besieged. It was a raging, roaring success and old Buckstone was jubilant. He would have smiled even more happily if he had not made arrangements for a pantomime—but he had. It was expected of him—practically every theatre had to do a pantomime; it was Christmas fare, like plum puddings. So *Our American Cousin* had to come off in the heyday of its success. Sothern was engaged to reappear after the pantomime, and Buckstone pulled his leg by saying, "Don't come back with that infernal Lord Dundreary."

The pantomime was produced, but it was not a success, and the infernal Lord Dundreary was back on January 27th. Again it went like wildfire. It provided one of those little dramas which happen in the theatre. A stopgap play is put on when managerial luck is low, a play of which little is hoped, almost, indeed, a bad play, with an unknown actor playing an extravagant part; it is brought in unheralded; it hangs fire—and then, with a little boosting—away it goes and makes a fortune just when money is sorely needed. It happens time and again, as it happened at the Haymarket in 1861. *Our American Cousin*, although most people have by now forgotten the title, made £30,000 for John Baldwin Buckstone. It set up the first really long run in theatrical history—400 nights—and it put a character into the English repertory of characters which many people believe was really flesh and blood. Lord Dundreary will never be forgotten. And he was born, so far as this country goes, at the Haymarket.

Buckstone, clever as he was and gifted as he was, had no money sense. Cash slipped through his fingers and he never knew where it went. The fine sum accruing from Lord Dundreary vanished into thin air.

And Buckstone was getting deaf. He could not hear what was going on. He would, when playing, watch the other actor's lips and when they ceased to move, would say his lines. Sothern used to hoax him. He would go on moving his lips long after he had finished a speech and Buckstone, to the astonishment of the audience, would stand silent, watching him intently.

Sothern became a power at the Haymarket. When *Our American Cousin* finished at last, he appeared in *Aunt's Advice*, which he adapted from the French. In March, 1863, he played in *The Little Treasure*, and a young actress was with him playing Gertrude to his Captain Maydenblush. That young actress was Ellen Terry, who scored a resounding success. She was only fifteen at the time. She did not like Sothern, however; he used to tease her, pull her hair and make her "dry up." But she admired his art, his wonderful eyes and hands. But she did not like being teased. She adored old Howe, who played her "father" in the show. They had a scene together in which she revelled—they both used to cry! "Oh, it was lovely!" exclaimed Ellen Terry.

She would, in after years, say that she regarded that Haymarket engagement as a lost opportunity. She was too young to realise it then, but afterwards she knew that she was surrounded by actors and actresses steeped in tradition and style, who understood the art of playing Old Comedy, almost lost to-day. Their deportment, their gestures, their bows, their curtsies, their grand manner bore the hall-mark of supreme art. But Ellen Terry leaves on record that the conversation in the green-room of the Haymarket was frank to a degree and that she recalled leaving it one night with a sweeping curtsy and saying, in the words of *The School for Scandal*, "Ladies and gentlemen, I leave my character behind me." It was whilst she was there that Tom Taylor introduced her to Watts, the famous painter, whom she was to marry. She played in *The Rivals*, and one night left out the tag of the play, so that the curtain did not come down. But she played with Buckstone, which, in Old Comedy, was a rich experience, and he taught her a lesson over that bit of forgetfulness she always remembered. During the same engagement she also played Hero in *Much Ado about Nothing*—the Beatrice was Louisa Angell. Ellen Terry wondered, in her girlish mind, if the time would ever come when she would play Beatrice herself. It came all right—and she was the finest Beatrice the stage has ever seen.

She also appeared with Mrs. Keeley, whom she adored. It was in a burlesque called *Buckstone at Home*. Ellen Terry played Britannia and came up a trap-door inside a huge pearl which opened to disclose her amid roars of applause. But her most cherished memory was the night when the young Prince of Wales—afterwards Edward VII—brought his bride to see the show. Wishing to remain unseen, they sat at the back of the box, their suite occupying the front places. That, however, would not do for the irresistible and daring Mrs. Keeley. She was playing a "principal boy" and had a song in which she introduced the heroes and heroines of the fairy tales. She improvised a verse and, pointing to the Royal Box, sang, "Here's another Prince at hand, but being invisible, you can't see him." The audience, however, caught the idea. They stamped and cheered and applauded, they stopped the show until the Prince and Princess came to the front of the box and bowed their thanks for the hearty if unwanted reception. What H.R.H. thought about the disregard of his wish to remain private is not recorded.

Sothern played in an extravaganza called *Bunkum Muller* in 1864 and then he made more Haymarket history, for on April 30th of that year he appeared in a play which to-day still holds the stage. It was the work of a then practically unknown playwright, who was glad to earn a pittance translating French dramas for Lacy, the theatrical bookseller, and who was delighted to receive the sum of £40 from Buckstone for the work in which Sothern appeared. The dramatist was Tom Robertson; the play *David Garrick*. It is only fair to say that when the play soared

*The Second in
Command*

Left
Mr. Cyril Maude as
Major Christopher
Bingham.

Right
Mr. Herbert Sleath
as Lieutenant Sir
Walter Mannering.

Miss Fanny Coleman as
Lady Harbugh.

Mr. Allan Aynesworth as
Lieut.-Colonel Miles
Anstruther, D.S.O.

Cyril Maude and Vivien Leigh in the special performance of *The School for Scandal* at the Haymarket in 1942 to celebrate Maude's 80th birthday.

into success Robertson received further payments, but the total sum he received would be scorned by any minor playwright to-day.

The part of David Garrick was the first that had really tested Sothern's powers since he had played Dundreary. The play had originally been inspired by a French version called *Sullivan*. Robertson had adapted and rewritten it and had sold it to the publisher for £10. It had lain amongst other unproduced plays for eight years before Sothern got hold of it. Then, before risking it at the Haymarket, he tried it out on tour at the Prince of Wales' Theatre, Birmingham. Sothern, a harsh critic of his own work, was dissatisfied, and wanted to put it aside, but was overruled. It did not get much praise from the local Press, but the public liked it. Finally, he determined to try it at the Haymarket. The result was a triumph. Sothern said that the performance of Nellie Moore as Ada Ingot made the play. That was over-generosity. His own performance was superb, especially in the "acted" drunken scene. Afterwards Sir Charles Wyndham made this play his own and the public never tired of him in it; but Sothern was the creator of the famous role and first produced the play.

Other plays of Sothern's at the Haymarket were *Lord Dundreary Married and Done For* (H. J. Byron); Watts Phillips's *The Woman in Mauve*, a great success; *Brother Sam*, by John Oxenford—in which he appeared as the extraordinary brother of Dundreary who wrote the letters; and Westland Marston's *The Favourite of Fortune*. In this latter he made a great hit as Frank Annerley. The play had a real Haymarket cast, including Buckstone, Chippendale, Kate Saville, Nellie Moore, Mrs. E. Fitzwilliam and Mrs. Chippendale. In 1866 he played in Tom Taylor's *A Lesson for Life*. In 1868 he had a play by Westland Marston called *A Hero of Romance*, which gave him an acrobatic chance. He had to leap from the top of a tower into an abyss (of unknown depth to the audience) dressed in strapped riding trousers. The public adored this sensational feat and rolled up in their thousands.

In 1869 he appeared in Tom Robertson's *Home* (its first production), Morton's *A Regular Fix*, and H. J. Byron's *An English Gentleman*. Then he went back to America, but returned in 1878 to the Haymarket to do a play by H. J. Byron called *The Crushed Tragedian*—in which his success rivalled Dundreary. He gave a performance of real genius as the old broken-down pro of the "laddie" school. He bade farewell in May, 1879, with a round of his favourite parts—especially Dundreary and Garrick.

Sothern was a grand actor who adorned nearly everything he touched. If he had done nothing else but Garrick and Dundreary, he would have earned his niche, but he looms very large in the temple of the Haymarket's great ones.

Buckstone was almost a cipher by this time. Sothern ruled the roost, but the old man did not mind. He was always in a mess, but always cheerful and always had a joke handy. Much else happened at the

U

Haymarket—besides Sothern. In 1864 Madame Beatrice had appeared there. And on Saturday, July 29th, a young lady had made her London professional debut there as Ophelia to the Hamlet of Walter Montgomery. He is almost forgotten now, but the young lady is not. She was Madge Robertson. She had been on the stage since she was a child. Bristol and Bath had known and acclaimed her and now she tested her fortune in London. As Ophelia she created a favourable impression. Then she played Desdemona to the Othello of Ira Aldridge, the Negro actor. Not so long ago there was a considerable discussion when a white actress played the same part to another negro's Othello. It caused no such excitement at the Haymarket when Madge Robertson did it. Aldridge is referred to always as "the great coloured tragedian," but appears to have been somewhat rough in his acting, although sincere and powerful.

Madge Robertson was at the Haymarket again in *A Hero of Romance* and was indeed the heroine on whose behalf Sothern performed that riding-trousered dive. She also played Hippolyta in Colley Cibber's old play, *She Would and She Would Not.*

In 1866 a young actor made a successful debut at the Haymarket in *A Dangerous Friend.* In 1867 he scored heavily as Orlando in *As You Like It.* His name was W. H. Kendal. He played in *She Would and She Would Not,* too, as did Madge Robertson. Before long, the two were to marry and as Mr. and Mrs. Kendal become one of the historic forces of the English stage. They both made their debut at the Haymarket, so far as London was concerned; they both started their climb to fame there and essentially they are a Haymarket couple, this happily married, most respectable pair of players. She was the greater of the two always and she was one of the finest actresses we have ever possessed. Old Buckstone himself, in those early days, picked her out as one of the best he had ever had with him.

Their name and fame are so familiar that they need no elaboration here, other than to establish them in the Haymarket history, to which they contributed so much. Madge Robertson was in *New Men and Old Sores* in 1869. It was a big success for her. Kendal appeared in 1868 in *Pietra* with Miss Bateman, and also with that actress in *Mary Warner.* But they both appeared in *The Rivals* and in a playlet, *Uncle's Will,* written especially for them by Mr. Theyre Smith. The Kendals were now the Haymarket's leading string.

And then came a playwright who was to give them some excellent vehicles and to make a name for himself as a straight dramatist— William Schwenk Gilbert. He also is of the Haymarket.

Madge Robertson was the sister of T. W. Robertson, whose *David Garrick* had won him fame at the Haymarket and who was destined as the playwright for the Bancrofts. He revolutionised the stage convention of the day, so far as comedies were concerned, and brought realism and credibility to the art of play-writing instead of the old fashioned fustian, bad construction and long-armed coincidence. As a writer of domestic comedy, Robertson was a pioneer and the best of his time. As players of domestic comedy in the highest form, his sister Madge and her husband, W. H. Kendal, were matchless.

The Kendals did much for the stage in general, but here there is space only for that part of their career which concerns the Haymarket. At that theatre they started their London careers, and there they fell in love. And in that theatre's company, appearing at the Theatre Royal, Manchester (for Buckstone sent his companies to that town between whiles and when other attractions held the Haymarket boards), they were married. Mr. Kendal played Orlando to his wife's Rosalind on their wedding day in 1869.

They lifted the status of the player still further, they were *persona grata* everywhere, and their reputation when they went into management was simply monumental. They did good plays, they eschewed vulgarity, they gave quality and they trained a generation of actors and actresses. And those twin pillars of the British stage were of the Haymarket.

Gilbert's plays there were successes for the Kendals, even if they were of no great dramatic value in themselves, but simply showing the shape of things to come. The most famous was *Pygmalion and Galatea* on December 9th, 1871; there was *The Palace of Truth* in 1870, which many years afterwards he turned into a comic opera; and *The Wicked World* in 1873. *Dan'l Bruce, Blacksmith*, another early "Gilbert," and a historical drama at that, got a fine notice from Joseph Knight in 1874, who records that the love scenes were finely presented by Marion Terry and Forbes Robertson, then quite young people. Herman Vezin, a grand actor, was in it and also the celebrated O'Dell. Gilbert's *Engaged* in 1877, in which there was not one sympathetic character, but in which satire ran riot, had Honey, Marion Terry, Miss Buckstone, Julia Stewart, Howe, Dewar and Kyrle in the cast.

Madame Janauschek made her first London appearance at the Haymarket in 1876. The public applauded, but the critics condemned.

Adelaide Neilson was there in 1876, too, in Tom Taylor's *Anne Boleyn*, *As You Like It* (she was a magnificent Rosalind), *Romeo and Juliet* (she was a wonderful Juliet, too). She played Julia in *The Hunchback* and made a tremendous success as Isabella in *Measure for Measure*, which had not been seen on the stage for twenty-five years. She was there again in 1878.

But by that time old Buckstone was no longer really in charge. He was old, he was ailing, and he was heavily, hopelessly in debt; the moneylenders had him fast. His years of success had not filled that ever-open pocket; he had taken no care, no forethought. Sothern had, during this time, practically controlled the theatre, but could not control Buckstone. Now John S. Clarke was really in charge and his name was on the bills. He was a first-rate comedian, born in America of English extraction. Trained for the law, he took to the stage, as did many other budding lawyers. He had a most successful career in America, and excelled as Major Wellington de Boots in a play by Stirling Coyne originally called *Everybody's Friend*, but later altered to *A Widow Hunt*. The part of the Major had originally been played by Buckstone. Clarke appeared in it for his London debut at the St. James's Theatre in 1867. He had played it all over America and it was to him what Dundreary was to Sothern. He had built it up. He went from America to England and back again and was a favourite in both countries. It was in 1878 that he really took control of the Haymarket and marked his accession to power by the production of *The Crisis*— in which he appeared with Charles Kelly, William Terris, Howe, Mrs. John Wood, Miss Westlake and Louise Moody.

He failed with W. G. Wills's *Ellen, or Love's Cunning*, and replaced it by *The Rivals*. Thereafter he presented other attractions, such as Adelaide Neilson—her last appearance in London—and many plays.

John Baldwin Buckstone was now only a name and a name which had no place on the bills. He had retired from active participation in 1878. He had held the Haymarket from 1853, twenty-four years of active work, and one year more of inactivity whilst Clarke took over from him. Those years had been packed with achievement and success for everyone but himself. True, his was the achievement, but he spent his money as it came. He gave Sothern £1,000 when the success of *Our American Cousin* was assured. That was the sort of man old Buckstone was. He had played every principal comedy part the stage had to offer. He had written innumerable dramas and farces, he was popular, he was beloved, he was a magnificent actor and a fine manager for everyone but himself. There are countless stories told of him. He was a great favourite with Queen Victoria, and knew it. She who overawed so many never scared him. He stood at the Royal entrance to receive her one night in the good old way, with two candles to "light her in." As the Queen approached a gust of wind blew out the lights. "There, just look at that now," was Buckstone's quiet remark, and the Queen laughed— she *was* amused that time. He made her laugh on the stage and he made her laugh off it. One night, in backing before her and the Prince Consort, he fell down two steps. She laughed again. And on another occasion, he had a great rush to get out of his stage clothes, take off his make-up and assumed his dress clothes to usher her out. Washing his face hurriedly, he got his eyes full of soap, which made them smart and water. He arrived before the Queen mopping them with a handkerchief. She complimented him on his performance. Deaf old Buckstone thought she was asking if he had a cold. "No, Ma'am, no," he said. "It's soap."

His deafness made things difficult for him; he could not hear his cues, so it was the prompter's job to give him a pat on the shoulder; then he knew he was to go on. One night, Lord Alfred Paget, a friend of his, went back stage. He saw Buckstone standing in the wings watching the playing of a love scene and awaiting his cue. His Lordship, not knowing what the prompter had to do, patted Buckstone's shoulder. Buckstone promptly walked on, to the horror of Sothern and the leading lady, who were engaged in a passionate stage kiss. The old actor realised what had happened. He put on a beaming smile and, shaking his finger at the two, said archly, "Aha, I saw you," and walked off to roars of laughter and applause.

The same thing happened when another unwitting friend tapped him on the shoulder. Again Sothern was holding the stage in a big scene and acting for all he was worth. Buckstone rushed on, in obedience to the pat, and shouted, "The sailors are here." Then he saw Sothern's expression. He paused. "At least," he added, "I thought they were. I'll go away and see." And off he toddled.

It is Sothern who leaves a tribute to Buckstone which sums him up:

"Buckstone must now be about seventy-five years of age, but old as he is he gets hold of his audience more rapidly than anyone I know. A simple 'Good morning' from him seems to set the house in a roar. His personal magnetism is simply wonderful. He acts as if he had string on all his fingers attached to the audience in front and plays with them and pulls them about just as he wants."

That is one actor's tribute to another.

J. S. Clarke organised a farewell benefit for Buckstone in August, 1879. The play was to be *Money*, and the old manager was to play The Old Member in the Club scene. But just before the event, the public learnt with sorrow that their favourite had been stricken down with paralysis. They had the benefits later, but the old man was not there. All the stars came, the place was packed for five performances—so great was the demand. Barry Sullivan played Benedict—everyone appeared.

But John Baldwin Buckstone had played his last part, cracked his last gag, faced his last audience. On October 31st, 1879, he departed this life.

But in leaving life, he did not leave the Haymarket Theatre, which he loved so dearly. He is there still. In a certain dressing-room, the room he always used, you can hear footsteps, you can sense a presence, you can see doors open and close without hands. There is nothing to worry about: it is only gentle, kindly, lovable Buckstone, still busy about the theatre he adored so much that he cannot leave it. Nobody minds, nobody cares. Buckstone's spirit and that of the Haymarket are one.

CHAPTER XXV

"ONLY THE HAYMARKET WILL TEMPT US"

WITH the death of Buckstone, another phase of the Haymarket ended. Many of its old favourites were passing away. Macready had died in 1873, at the age of eighty, old Farren had passed on in 1861, Charles Mayne Young in 1856, Charles Kemble in 1854, Madame Vestris in 1856, Vandenhoff in 1861, Charles Kean in 1868, and many another; Phelps passed away in 1870—the old ranks were thinning fast.

But there were, as always, others ready to step into the breach.

John S. Clarke was running the Haymarket by himself and not doing very well. He kept on the theatre because he, too, felt its charm and its grip upon the imagination, although he did little to add to its story or to give it fresh fame.

But there were people who had their eyes upon it, a man and a woman, husband and wife, who stood upon the crest of the wave, two people who did, in their time, more for the stage than anyone else and who rank in theatrical history amongst the most illustrious. They were Mr. and Mrs. Bancroft.

Those names are surely famous, yet it seems necessary that something must be said about them, because recently certain members of the staff of an organisation which provides entertainment for the whole nation confessed that they had never heard of the Bancrofts. There may be similar ignorance amongst the general public.

At the time when their story first comes into contact with the Haymarket Theatre, Mr. and Mrs. Bancroft (Marie Wilton before her marriage) had revolutionised the stage of this country. They did this at what had been an unlucky, derelict, out-of-the-way theatre, popularly alluded to as the "Dusthole," but really called, at that time, the Queen's. It had had, during its existence, very many names. It has another name now, for when last rebuilt it was called the Scala, and that handsome theatre is still very much on the active list. What is now the stage door was, in the Bancrofts' day, the front entrance, and the name it then had—Prince of Wales's—can be seen on the tessellated pavement inside the stage door. It had been originally a place for "Concerts of Ancient Music." Later it was the Regency Theatre of Varieties, the West London (there was another of that name), the Queen's, the Fitzroy and the Queen's again, when the Bancrofts took it over. It had never had much luck, it was little more than a "gaff." It stands outside theatreland proper, off the Tottenham Court Road, those few yards which make so much difference—much more then than in these days of adjacent Tubes and plentiful buses. But then it was of ill-repute. Many stars had tried to popularise it and failed, many people had found it a short cut to the Bankruptcy Court, but the Bancrofts were daring. Marie Wilton had decided on management, and when a determined woman makes up her mind, it often takes a great deal to stop her. She was not married to Bancroft then. He was to make his London debut under her management.

The management idea was hers alone. She wanted a theatre, and the only place available was the "Dusthole." Everyone tried to persuade her against it. But she borrowed £1,000 and she got the theatre. When it had been redecorated and put in proper repair, only £150 remained in the bank. But she chanced it, and opened.

Marie Wilton knew her business. She had been on the stage since childhood. H. J. Byron, the dramatist, was her associate, and she got the name of the unlucky playhouse altered to the Prince of Wales's by the Lord Chamberlain.

From the first, Bancroft was active adviser and a tower of strength to the brave little actress he was soon to marry. They opened with a mixed bill, but it was a success, despite the fact that a pile of shavings were found on fire beneath the pit and an orange woman's complaint of "If these are your haristocrats, give me the roughs. I've only took fourpence." They had trouble with the cabmen, who did not know the theatre under its new name. One would-be playgoer was driven to Marlborough House and when he expostulated, was told: "Well, you said to go to the Prince of Wales's, didn't you? 'E lives 'ere."

The management relied on burlesque to start with, but then came the playwright they were looking for—Tom Robertson, the author of *David Garrick*. He supplied the Bancrofts (who were married in 1867, when Bancroft became joint-manager with his wife), with that wonderful series of comedies which struck a new and modern note—*Caste, Society, Ours, Play, School, M.P.*, etc.—that wonderful series, each with a one-word title, which had swept away the worn-out old conventions and established a new form of play-writing. *Diplomacy* was a big success of the Bancrofts at the little bandbox of a theatre, *Sweethearts*, by W. S. Gilbert, Wilkie Collins's *Man and Wife*—many, many others drew all the town to see this new force in the theatre, and in a theatre which had been despised before. Here was another of those husband-and-wife adventures which have been so famous in the British theatre —and this was one of the greatest. Perfect understanding and affection existed between the two on and off the stage. They were respected by all and worshipped by playgoers and the time came when they knew that they must look for a bigger theatre. They had regrets at the necessity of leaving the little place they had made renowned and which had in turn made them famous too. But it was necessary.

They stood for quality now, the highest quality of their kind on the stage. Their shows were superbly mounted, perfectly cast and acted.

When the news got round that they wanted a new home, many play-houses were offered to them, but the Bancrofts replied, "No, the Hay-market only will tempt us." They had an offer of the St. James's Theatre, but it did not appeal to them. Bancroft's business mind played with the idea of pulling it down and erecting chambers—or flats—on the site.

The Haymarket was, at the moment, under John S. Clarke, not doing too well. The Bancrofts heard that Lord Kilmorey had bought the St. James's and that John Hare, who had been in so many of their plays, was to open there in management in partnership with the Kendals. Hare had been at the Court, which was even more remote. The idea of this new management coming nearer stung Bancroft to action. He must have the Haymarket, the theatre of their dreams, if it were humanly possible.

He went round there to see John S. Clarke. They had acted together, but did not know each other in private life at all. Bancroft sent in his name. Clarke saw him at once. Bancroft opened straight away without the slightest preamble:

"I have never had the pleasure of meeting you off the stage before, Mr. Clarke, but I will lay my cards on the table and say at once I want your theatre. How is it to be done?"

Clarke liked this direct approach and they promptly discussed several ideas and schemes. Bancroft left with the matter still in abeyance, but with high hopes. Weeks went by and he heard nothing from Clarke. Hope died in him. It seemed that the much-desired playhouse was not to be theirs. Reluctantly and sadly, they put it out of their minds. They must try elsewhere. Here was a place of distinction, of tradition, of atmosphere, just the place to mellow their new regimé. But it was beyond their reach. Then, quite suddenly, they heard from Clarke. He sent for Bancroft one morning and Bancroft rushed round to the Haymarket. The preliminaries were discussed and settled, and within a few days it was all agreed. Bancroft took over the remainder of Clarke's tenancy; the trustees of the property promised to get him a new lease and he, on his part, undertook to rebuild the interior. The Bancroft's dream had materialised.

In 1879 they said farewell to the Prince of Wales's. They were in the audience at the Haymarket when John S. Clarke announced that they were to take over. That was on September 30th, 1879, and that night the theatre closed. Next day the alterations began.

They had a busy time whilst the work was in progress. Bancroft was all over the place. He must have moved fairly quickly. J. S. Clarke called at the Haymarket to see him—and missed him. He wrote the incoming tenant a letter, on October 5th:

"DEAR BANCROFT," he said, "I called at the Haymarket yesterday to learn that Mr. Bancroft had just left by the stage door, and after-wards at the Prince of Wales's to be informed that Mr. Bancroft had just gone by the front door. A plague o' both your houses, thought I. I will try to look in at the stage door of the Prince of Wales's about 12.45 to-morrow, and take my chance of finding you. But if Mr. Bancroft shall have left by the window, I shall go on and take my chance at both doors of the Haymarket.

"Yours sincerely,
"J. S. CLARKE."

Whilst the first rough work of demolition was going on, Bancroft went to France to see Sardou, whose *Diplomacy* had been such a success for him and his wife, and who was writing a play for them. But he was soon back at the Haymarket. He would go to the theatre from his club, late at night (men worked at night in those days and did not mind it) to see masses of timber being hurled into the old pit, and decorations that had been so admired reduced to dust. The workmen complained about the fleas they disturbed. "They were as big as ponies." The auditorium was gutted. The work had a powerful attraction for Bancroft, for he was pledged to spend £10,000 on the theatre. He haunted the place, balancing himself on scaffold poles and walking along narrow planks like a tightrope performer. And it was whilst his old familiar surroundings were crumbling into dust that old Buckstone—Bucky as they called him—became dust himself. One last story of him. He was at a party at which a famous entertainer was also present giving his impressions of other famous people. Buckstone, deaf as a post, looked on with interest. He asked a man standing by who it was the artist was imitating. "Why, sir, it's you," the man shouted in his ear. "Oh, me, eh?" said the old man. "Oh, ah, devilish good, I dare say. But I could do it better myself."

Mr. and Mrs. Bancroft were now busy with their farewell production at their old theatre. They revived *Ours*, with a splendid cast—Arthur Cecil, Mr. Kemble, H. B. Conway, Forbes Robertson, Miss Le Thiere, Marion Terry and, of course, themselves. At the same time they were busy with their Haymarket plans. They wanted, very naturally, to make a splash and to have a magnificent company. But there were "casting" difficulties even then. The increase in the number of theatres had made it difficult to keep a company together—an easy matter in the old days. They discussed the opening play. They weighed the advantages of *As You Like It*, *The School for Scandal*, *Money*, *Masks and Faces* and *Old Heads and Young Hearts*. They found the latter play belonged to Webster, for Boucicault had let that excellent man have it and never worried what happened. But at length their choice was made —they would open their tenancy of the Haymarket with that genuine Haymarket play, *Money*. They had to make special terms about it— for under the law of copyright as it then stood the forty-two years of protection had nearly run out. Nearly, but not quite. The Bancrofts' revival of *Money* was the last one which brought money to the author, or, rather, his heirs.

They set about preparing a very elaborate production. Bancroft worked like a slave. He spent the day with architects, scene-painters, decorators, clerks of the works, stage carpenters, costumiers, upholsterers and the army of people which the rebuilding of a theatre and the preparation of a new production entails. He had vast masses of correspondence to deal with, and at night he had a long part to play. Bancroft was a man who had to do it all himself. His wife was a steadying influence and a loyal help. Her philosophy was that all would come right in the end.

There were to be two great novelties about the new Haymarket auditorium. The proscenium arch was to be in the form of a vast golden frame and there was to be no pit. Bancroft had decided to abolish that popular part of the house.

It was revolutionary, this pit destruction, but not altogether new. It had been tried at one or two other houses. But then the Haymarket was a "pit" house. Its pit was magnificent, and Webster, in his farewell speech, had backed it against all others in the world—and drawn cheers by so doing. Now Bancroft was going to abolish it. Mrs. Bancroft was against it. She scented trouble and pleaded for at least a tiny pit. But Bancroft, the business manager, was adamant. The pit must go.

When it came to policy and business, Bancroft was the undisputed leader of the pair. She, however, was by far the better performer. He was a good, sound, distinguished, but not great actor. Mrs. Bancroft had genius and in certain roles excelled all rivals.

The framelike proscenium arch, so familiar now, was a tremendous novelty then. Bancroft saw something like it at Frankfurt a little later, but he was much comforted to learn that it was derived from his idea, and that the Germans had not forestalled him. But he went further; he demanded hidden footlights, which, when the curtain was within a foot or so of them, would descend in their turn to avoid the heavy roller (which was the way all act-drops were made; tabs were not used). And the footlights must also ascend at the same time as the curtain, so that the stage should never be dark. This was completely revolutionary. But no one knew how to do it; not even Bancroft. But he was not to be put off by statements, always made in such a case, that because it had never been done before it could not be done now. He informed the builders it was their job to find out how to do it, and then do it. They did, too. Oliver Wales, the master carpenter of the Haymarket, found out a way and it worked perfectly.

Meanwhile, the reconstruction went on and the work pressed more heavily upon Bancroft. Naturally, they got behind, but the Italian workmen employed to lay the mosaic floorings worked all through the Christmas holidays. And at length the end was in sight. They were rehearsing *Money* at the Prince of Wales's because of the confuson and noise at the Haymarket, but they were able to fix the opening date. It was to be Saturday, January 31st, 1880.

They had found a tenant for the Prince of Wales's, of which they still held the lease, in Edgar Bruce, who took over directly they left—on January 29th, 1880. On that night their remarkable régime at the little playhouse ended. The last scene—showing the bitter winter of the Crimea (for "Ours" was a regiment)—matched the biting frost and cold outside the theatre. But the warmth of their reception, on what was a "farewell" and "hail" occasion, dispelled the cold. They received an immense ovation and every token of goodwill towards their new effort. Bancroft made a speech, thanking the public for its support during their nearly fifteen years at the Prince of Wales's and wishing the new tenant the same luck. He spoke of the Haymarket and asked for continued support. He got volumes of cheers.

Mrs. Bancroft was very overcome at leaving, and cried when it came to bidding farewell to her tiny dressing-room. It was a real wrench. In after years she frequently walked round the place to recall pleasant memories.

Despite the warmth of the audience, there were tokens of storm elsewhere. Bancroft's announcement of the abolition of the Haymarket pit had not been well received. There was rebellion and there were threats. That Haymarket pit was an institution. It was the best and most comfortable pit in London. It had regular patrons amongst the public who felt at home there—indeed, to many it was a club. They would not sit anywhere else. The Haymarket had always been a "pit" house. Its great secret was that the pit did not go underneath the circle, but was free and open, the circle being fixed to the back wall, and extending forward only very slightly. Bancroft knew his danger, but he knew his financial business, too.

In those days, it must be remembered, the pit occupied the entire ground floor. At the Haymarket the price was 3s. 6d. Orchestra stalls were only just creeping in, but they were advancing like a slow tide. Inch by inch, and row by row, the comfortable upholstered seats were pushing the bare pit benches further and further back, into the dark, low-ceilinged small space under the circle. But the pit—or, rather, the pittites—considered themselves the backbone of the theatre. They were, they maintained, the true playgoers, attending performances through enthusiasm and love for the theatre, and not as an after-dinner pastime, as was the case, they declared, of the occupants of the more expensive parts. They led the applause, said the pittites, they supplied the excitement and the enthusiasm all the time, not like the rich, undemonstrative folk in the circle and the boxes. What they said was true enough and is true to-day, when the pit is in danger of vanishing from every theatre. The pit had vanished at the St. James's and at the Opera Comique without protest, but the pit at the Haymarket was sacred to its habitues.

Bancroft knew and admitted all this, but he had to balance his budget. From his point of view, the applause of the pit did not make up for the loss of revenue in so comparatively small a theatre. He constructed a tier which he called the "second circle," especially for the patrons of the pit. The rumours and the threats grew, so, prior to his opening, he issued an advertisement which speaks for itself:

"As some disappointment may be felt at the abolition of the pit, Mr. and Mrs. Bancroft deem it necessary to explain the alteration. With the present expenses of a first-class theatre, it is impossible to give up the floor of the house—its most remunerative portion—to low-priced seats, and the management, being unwilling to place any part of the audience in close and confined space under the balcony, the only alternative was to allot to the frequenters of the pit the tier usually devoted to the upper boxes, and now called the second circle. In carrying out the structural alterations of the theatre, Mr. and Mrs. Bancroft have, they hope, specially attended to the comfort of visitors to those seats by raising the ceiling, building a new stone staircase, a refreshment-room, and by removing all obstacles to a clear view of the stage."

Mr. Bancroft thought that would mollify the pittites. He was wrong. It was perhaps a little tactless to tell them so much of his business and to admit that he was going to make money by depriving them of what they considered their rights. They did not want the second circle; it was nothing to them that the ceiling had been raised. The stone staircase left them cold and the refreshment-room did not thrill them. Even the promised clear view of the stage (a most unusual thing in the old theatres) did not placate them. They wanted the pit, with all its hard seats and its inconveniences. They were pittites and the pit was their realm. Bancroft knew all too soon that he must look out for squalls. The matter became one of general controversy. It had its champions for and against. But Bancroft faced the storm. He had taken his decision and nobody could move him.

They had a fine cast for *Money*. It included Forbes Robertson, Odell, Archer, Arthur Cecil, H. B. Conway, Mr. Kemble, Charles Brookfield, Mr. Vollaire (playing the Old Member), Linda Dietz, Marion Terry and the Bancrofts. She played Lady Franklin; he played Sir Frederick Blount, Bart. Now here is the actor-manager in his first venture at a practically new theatre, at a new phase in his career, who is not taking the leading part in the show. That was played by Conway, who had the role created by Macready. Nor was Mrs. Bancroft playing the part created by Helen Faucit. This is worthy of note by the modern people who decry the actor-manager.

All was clear inside the Haymarket for the opening. It was now a perfectly beautiful theatre—it still is. The Bancrofts had lavished money on it and, what was more important, had lavished taste as well. An unbiased expert said that, having seen most of the best theatres in Europe, there was nothing to equal the Haymarket in design, decoration, comfort or *tout ensemble*. The proscenium and drop scene were simply perfection. The delicate tints of the panels, the extreme finish of the paintings, the wealth of gilding, the general harmony in colouring displayed artistic merit of rare excellence. He said there was boldness in the distribution of the seats, and a liberality in apportioning the space which should be an example to others for all time. He admitted there might be more magnificent playhouses, such as the Scala, Milan, but as a home of comedy it had not a rival. The finishing touches were the ivory-coloured satin curtains designed by Mrs. Bancroft. The Prince and Princess of Wales were to have been present on the opening occasion, but were kept at Sandringham by fog. They came the third night and the Prince, who insisted on being taken all over the theatre, expressed great admiration.

That was all right for Bancroft. But he still had to face the displaced persons of the pit. Displaced persons, as is known all over the world to-day, are unhappy and troublesome. They have every right to be. And Bancroft was to hear from the people he had displaced.

The great day, January 31st, arrived, and the theatre was all ready for the opening. Outside, however, there was the worst fog for generations. It wrapped the city like a choking pall, and fogs in the eighteen-eighties have not their counterpart to-day. It was a real "pea-souper," a "London particular" as the inhabitants of the capital proudly called their devastating atmospheric murkiness. Bancroft and his wife went down early. They had plenty of cares on their minds, apart from the possibility of trouble about the pit, and did not want to cut it fine. Just as Bancroft was about to begin dressing there was a tap at the door. Henry Irving walked in. He had groped his way to the stage door, whilst going on foot to the Lyceum (he was not risking a hold-up in his carriage) to wish a rival actor-manager the best of luck. It was a great tribute. Bancroft, much touched, showed him round. Irving admired the curtain, the work of Daniel White and John O'Connor, the Shakespearean pictures in the panels by J. D. Watson and F. Smith, and found everything beautiful indeed. Bancroft suggested seeing his wife, but Irving thoughtfully would not have her disturbed. He knew all about first night nerves. The two stood in the balcony, a few moments before the public were admitted, and shook hands in friendship, whilst Irving wished the husband, wife and their lovely new theatre the very best of luck. That was how two rival Victorian actor-managers treated each other. Both were to receive the honour of knighthood in the not distant future. Irving then went off through the desperate fog to the Lyceum, and Bancroft proceeded to dress.

The house was packed. There was, despite the fog, a most distinguished audience who had got through the pea-souper somehow. And the new second circle was packed, too, with excited, somewhat feverish ex-pittites, prepared to do or die in a fight for their rights.

The curtain went up, the play began. And with it began the protest of the pit. There were hoots, boos, catcalls, whistles, and above all noise the strident shouts: 'Where's the pit?" Nothing could be heard above the continuous uproar. Useless for the rest of the house to "Sssh!" and demand silence in shocked tones. The pittites wanted an answer to their protests. Bancroft, never wanting in courage, walked on. He recognised the handicap of the funny make-up, the flaxen wig and the pink and white complexion to which the part of Blount condemned him. He knew he could not look impressive. But he went on and faced them. He spoke—or attempted to speak. He faced the storm, as had so many of the great ones before him—Garrick, Colley Cibber, Kean, Macready and even Mrs. Siddons. He was afraid for his wife. He did not want her upset, he did not want her boo-ed. He could look after himself. The decision was his. But she must be protected. So, standing in the centre of the Haymarket stage and looking out into the beautiful new auditorium he had created, he fought back at the angry crowd. The Haymarket was in riot again. It was like old times, the times of Foote, Dowton and the French players. This time it was not from motives of patriotism, anger at a deliberate hoax or the hurt feelings of the craft of tailors—it was a London audience demanding what it considered its rights—"the pit."

Bancroft tried to make himself heard, to take the blame.

"Ladies and gentlemen," he began, and was immediately drowned by cries of "Give us the pit, Bancroft." "Where's the pit?" He tried again.

"Ladies and gentlemen, will you first allow me to express my sincere regret" (cries of 'Where's the pit?') "my sincere regret at this disturbance, of which I fear I am alone the innocent cause." (Here he was again interrupted, but he kept on.) "If you will allow me to speak to you" (renewed cries of "Where's the pit?") "gentlemen, I am about to ask you a favour. I have never yet asked that of the public because I have no right to do so, but I am going to ask you to pay me a debt. As a theatrical manager for fifteen years you will at least admit that I am entitled to your respect." (Cheers and cries of "Where's the pit?") "I am quite unprepared to address you and in my agitated state you must take my words as they come." (Interruption.) "You ask me 'Where's the pit?' " (Cries of "Well, where is it?") "I am a business man and I dare say I am talking to many other business men. I can only tell you, with all respect, what I have told you in the newspapers. Remember that I don't take you by surprise. You have all known since July that there would not again be a pit in this theatre." (A voice: "We didn't want to know it.") "Gentlemen, I will tell you my reason in three or four words. I can't afford it. However anxious I may be to follow the example and tradition of those who have been here before me, I am not anxious to emulate them in one respect. Has any money ever been made in this theatre with the whole floor given up to the pit? A theatre, gentlemen, is a place of business. However inadequately I may express myself, I give you common-sense reasons. It is useless——" (Here he was interrupted by a loud shout of "Three cheers for Bancroft.") The cheers were heartily given. "Will you listen to the play?" he asked eagerly. From an overwhelming majority came an enthusiastic response. It was over. Bancroft had won. The pit had protested—it had lost—and it knew it had lost. Bancroft never restored the pit. The playgoers knew he had won—and besides, now they came to look around, it was not so bad upstairs after all. They could hear—they could see—and the play proceeded with immense success.

All this while Mrs. Bancroft had been in an agony of mind. She had a peephole in her dressing-room where she could see all that went on. As the row grew she was in a frenzy. She rushed downstairs, wringing her hands. She determined that she would go on and appeal to them for the sake of "Auld Lang Syne." Perhaps they would listen to her.

But her husband won the fight. She was still terrified that the demonstration would break out again when she made her entrance, but she need not have feared. The pittites would have lynched anyone who had dared to hoot their favourite. She walked on the stage cold with terror, to be received with such warmth and enthusiasm that her eyes filled with happy tears. All was well at the Haymarket.

That first-night uproar had valuable repercussions in publicity. The case for and against the pit was hotly debated in the newspapers and all over the place. John Hollingshead of the Gaiety, a first-class publicity man himself, cashed in on Bancroft's side. He was very outspoken:

"The only shadow of an excuse for this outbreak of theatrical protectionism was the comfortable character of the lost pit. In one of the worst constructed houses ever built, it was the one place where all those who were fortunate enough to get seats in it could see, hear and breathe. The pit visitors enjoyed this place for fifty years at too moderate a price whilst their wretched superiors were risking their necks in the dress circle or cramping their legs in the private boxes. Now the turn of the superiors has come, but who has any right to grumble?"

A typical Hollingshead manifesto, but designed, so far as his strictures on the Haymarket were concerned, to draw attention to what he considered to be the super-excellence of his own Gaiety. A manager in Liverpool gave his experience of a similar attempt to put the pit aloft, an attempt which failed. He drew attention, however, to the fact that there were no pits at the Opera Comique or the Charing Cross (afterwards Toole's Theatre), but admitted that Mr. Bancroft had a right to do as he liked. Sothern wrote saying that he had tried hard to make Buckstone do the same thing, and that, if he had, he would have made money. In view of this, it is interesting to note that the proceeds of that first Bancroftian performance of *Money* at the pitless Haymarket were given to Buckstone's widow.

Money—and the Bancrofts—succeeded. They began matinée performances at the Haymarket, an innovation which had been started at the Gaiety.

Before leaving that stormy, foggy first night, there are a couple of stories to tell. Dr. George Bird, a friend of Bancroft's, was present at the performance. He had a habit of always walking home from the play. It was not so easy that night. He lived in Welbeck Street. He found Oxford Street, crossed the road, and although he was certain he was somewhere near where he lived, he felt lost. So he groped his way along the railings feeling for a brass plate which would tell him a doctor lived there, and then he would make inquiries. Along the street he went, inch by inch, his hands groping for that medical symbol. At length his fingers touched a damp, smooth, shiny surface. He felt all round it. Yes, it was a doctor's plate all right. He struck a match and bent down eagerly to see the name—perhaps he might know it. It was his own name he saw. His homing instinct had been right.

A party of four started from Putney, where it was clear. But they soon got befogged and did not reach the theatre until everything was over. They started off home, found it impossible, and went to a friend's house in Bayswater, hoping to put the carriage and horse in the adjoining mews. It took them so long to get there that the mews was full up with the horses and carriages of other fogbound travellers. However, the friends took them in and must, indeed, have been good Samaritans. The carriage had to be left in the road, but the horse and driver sheltered for the night in the hall of the house itself!

The Bancrofts walked home, a servant going slightly ahead and carrying a white bouquet—one of the many showered upon Mrs. Bancroft—which acted as a sort of torch.

Mr. and Mrs. Bancroft stayed for five years at the Haymarket and then retired from actor-management. They made a few appearances as actor and actress elsewhere, but the Haymarket was their last managerial home. It was the culmination of their career. They had revived their old successes, always with magnificent casts and lovely settings, but the plays were never quite so good as in their smaller original frame at the Prince of Wales's. They did *School* and *The Vicarage*. They were going to do Burnand's *The Colonel*, but wisely staged it with Bruce at the Prince of Wales's, where it had a great success. They revived that old success of Webster's, *Masks and Faces*, with Bancroft and Arthur Cecil alternating as Triple and Colley Cibber. Mrs. Bancroft was a perfect Peg Woffington. With them also were H. B. Conway, Dacre, Teesdale, Kemble, Charles Brookfield, Kate Grattan, Stewart Dawson, Smedley, Dean, Marion Terry, Miss Wade, Mrs. Canninge and Mabel Grattan. Mr. Gladstone went to see it. He wrote to Bancroft: "For the capital acting of the chief parts I was prepared, but the whole cast, likewise, seemed to me excellent." They did *Society* and *Good for Nothing*. They produced *Plot and Passion*, but admitted themselves it was not a success. In the cast was A. W. Pinero. But the little farce by Burnand which followed, *A Lesson*, was very well received. *Plot and Passion* did not last. They were therefore quite glad to let the theatre for a matinée for a sensational event—the appearance of the celebrated Society beauty, Mrs. Langtry, on the stage.

Mrs. Langtry's name was in every mouth. She was mobbed whenever she appeared in public. People stood on chairs in the Park to catch a glimpse of her as she drove by in her carriage. Rumours about her simply increased her celebrity. She was the reigning beauty of the day. There had been talk of her becoming an actress—and now this talk crystallised at the Haymarket. Mrs. Labouchere had been coaching her—and Mrs. Labouchere was Henrietta Hodson, a well-known actress herself. She was to play Kate Hardcastle in a performance of *She Stoops to Conquer* at a matinée in aid of the Royal General Theatrical Fund. Excitement was at fever heat. The theatre was besieged. People fought for places and those who could not secure seats were loud in their wailings. Nobody believed that Mrs. Langtry could act, but they all wanted to see her try. Maybe plenty wanted to see her fail too!

The performance came. The Prince and Princess of Wales were in the Royal Box. Society packed the house and the Bancrofts sat as spectators in the stalls of their own theatre. Mrs. Langtry made her entrance to a very quiet reception. But as the play went on the audience warmed to her and applause grew and grew. They had expected nothing; they got quite a good performance. A cheque for £430 was handed to the Fund. And the Bancrofts engaged Mrs. Langtry. She was with them for three months. She appeared in *Ours* as Blanche Hay and in *She Stoops to Conquer*. Pinero, afterwards the great dramatist, made a hit in this as Diggory. And so high had Mr. Bancroft reached in public esteem that he was asked to dine with the Prince of Wales. He sat on the right hand of his host. His seventeen years of management had made him the doyen of the profession.

On Tuesday, April 25th, 1882, the Bancrofts presented a new play by Sardou called *Odette*. In the cast, besides their regular company (the Haymarket was almost a stock house in this respect), and, of course, themselves, was Madame Modjeska. The first act was a sensation and then it began to drag until it finished at an unduly late hour. Judicious cutting, however, turned it into a success.

They kept on with revivals, such as *The Overland Route*; Mrs. John Wood was with them in this. In 1883 they produced *Fedora*, by Sardou. With them in this was Mrs. Bernard Beere playing Bernhardt's part with triumph. They played a round of the Robertson comedies for the last time—the copyright was running out and they took farewell of them with a sigh, especially for *Caste*, in which Mrs. Bancroft had been so wonderful as Polly Eccles. In 1883-4, they resumed the run of

W

Fedora. They did a play by Pinero called *Lords and Commons*, but that did not succeed, nor did a curious revival of *The Rivals*. Yet in *Lords and Commons* they had a remarkable cast including Forbes Robertson, Charles Brookfield, Alfred Bishop, Mrs. Stirling, Mrs. Bernard Beere and themselves. They certainly gave it every chance.

But they were now considering retirement. Life seemed to have given them all it had to offer. They were famous and popular, they had made money and they had, as their last setting, the Haymarket Theatre, which they had always desired, and which they had made, more than ever, the home of English comedy.

In 1884-5 they announced their farewell season. They had been in management for twenty wonderful, successful years. They bade farewell in a round of their successes. *Diplomacy* was their opening. They could not get the original cast; so many now, like the Kendals, were in management themselves. Bancroft gave Orloff to Barrymore, the fine American actor, and played Henry Beauclerk. Forbes Robertson played Julian, Brookfield played Stein. Mrs. Bancroft played Lady Henry Fairfax, Mrs. Bernard Beere was Countess Zicka, and Miss Calhoun Dora. They played *Masks and Faces*, *Sweethearts*, *Good for Nothing*, and then came the night of their farewell. Irving expressed a wish to participate in this, and he spoke a speech of farewell to them, written by Clement Scott. J. L. Toole also made an appearance. But the chief fare of the evening was the first act of *Money* (with which they had opened their Haymarket venture), a scene from *London Assurance*, and the second and third acts of *Masks and Faces*. Two of those plays had been originally produced at the Haymarket when Webster was in command.

The Bancrofts' farewell to management, if not to the stage, took place on Monday, July 20th, 1885. The Prince and Princess of Wales were in the Royal Box; everyone who was anyone formed the rest of a wonderful audience. Even Robert Browning was there. The casts, those of *Money* and *London Assurance* (in which the Bancrofts did not appear) were composed entirely of stars who had been members of their company at some time. These included Alfred Bishop, Charles Wyndham, Arthur Cecil, David James, Coghlan, Charles Sugden, John Clayton, Mrs. Stirling, Ellen Terry, Mrs. Langtry, Mrs. John Wood, John Hare, William Terriss, Mr. Kendal, A. W. Pinero, Kyrle Bellew, Mrs. Kendal and Carlotta Addison. That will show the quality the Bancrofts had always given. In *Masks and Faces*, the last item on the bill, in which they themselves bade farewell, Bancroft as Triplet and Mrs. Bancroft as Peg Woffington, the cast was equally starry and comprised the company of their present season.

Bancroft cut a hole in the scenery to watch his wife's last entrance. Her reception was as moving as it was wonderful, and his own equalled it. At the end, to a perfectly marvellous ovation, he made a speech. It was a speech just as one might have expected, a little pompous in style, maybe, but sincere and from the heart. He paid a great tribute to his dear wife. He told the public that for the twenty-four years he had been before them he had never missed a performance for which he was billed to appear. Standing hand in hand with his wife amidst a bower of flowers and bouquets, he said farewell.

"We do so, ladies and gentlemen, with feelings of thankfulness, of great respect, and, if you will permit us to approach you so nearly, with feelings of deep affection." The curtain of the Haymarket fell on an epoch which had started in storm and ended in love and appreciation of two great people of our stage, a happy husband and wife, working together, understanding each other and giving the public (despite the pit) full value for money and that quality of acting and production of which even the Haymarket Theatre might be justly proud.

CHAPTER XXVI

"A PILGRIM AND A KING"

ALTHOUGH the Bancrofts left the Haymarket in 1885, it did not stand empty. The perfect theatre, the playhouse of perfection, has never done that. To be really alive, a theatre must always carry on, it must have continuity; just as its stage, when a play is toward, must never be left vacant, so must a good theatre always be open to its masters the public.

The Bancrofts said goodbye on July 20th, 1885. Crowds had waited all day to see that farewell performance; there was no boo-ing or trouble as there had been on the first night of their tenancy.

Those who want to know more of the Bancrofts at the Haymarket will find excellent stories about them in a book written by Charles Brookfield, one of their company, whose name appears in this history and whose *Random Reminiscences* is one of the best theatre books ever published. Charles Brookfield himself sometimes took the Haymarket for a summer season whilst the Bancrofts were on holiday, but he never had great luck. However, nothing could depress him. His wit triumphed over everything. His sense of humour was of the very best and never deserted him. Years afterwards, when he became Reader of Plays, censor under the Lord Chamberlain, he promptly licensed for public performance a play of his own which his predecessor had banned. You could never beat Charles Brookfield.

In the Haymarket box office, installed by Bancroft, was a lad who had come from the adjacent post office in Charles Street (now King Charles II Street), where he was learning the Morse Code to qualify as a telegraph operator. Whether Bancroft thought of having a telegraph fitted in his Haymarket box office (by arrangement with the Post Office, possibly) is not known, but he sent to the Charles Street branch to ask if they had a youth who understood the telegraph and would like a job in his box office. There was such a lad there. He liked the idea and took the job. He remained at the Haymarket, in that box office, for over fifty years, and for a very long time was in charge of it. His name was W. H. Leverton, known to his countless friends as "Bill." A tall, lean, well-preserved man, with a fresh complexion, clean-shaven, rather sharp of nose, and with a smile always in his eyes, he was, for generations of theatregoers, the outward and visible sign of the Haymarket Theatre. He never looked his age—he was, indeed, ageless—and he was always courtesy itself, for he came of a courteous generation. His hair, which kept its colour, was parted in the middle, and he wore always one of those high, stiff starched single collars known as "chokers." He never bowed to modernity in this respect; soft collars or double-fold collars were not for him. His attire was the formal, correct wear of the 'eighties, and matched his manners. Every playgoer in London knew him, and counted him a friend. He would even see the first nights of the shows, something a box office manager seldom succeeds in doing. There he would sit, at his window, looking across that rather small vestibule, and fitting his surroundings perfectly. He always had a smile for a customer; he was never ruffled, never surprised. Had you not known him, you might have guessed that he was a country solicitor, with well-filled black deed boxes. But he was part of the Haymarket Theatre for over half a century, and his passing left a gap. He never aged, any more than the Haymarket ever ages. He mellowed as that playhouse has mellowed and, when the time came, he just slipped into the shadows to rejoin his friends who had preceded him. The Haymarket has other records of long service, for nobody ever wants to leave it once they are there.

Henry Kemble, who enters during the Bancroft period, deserves more than a passing mention. This extraordinary and very good actor might have passed for a fine old crusted Tory squire. He was stout, solid, eminently conservative and a fine actor. A grandson of Charles Kemble and his wife, Miss De Camp, the stage and the Haymarket were in his blood. His nickname was "Beetle." He was noted for his sense of humour. Once he was out of the bill for a short while. He joined the queue at the Haymarket box office. On reaching the window he solemnly inquired of Leverton if Mr. Kemble was in the cast? Leverton, without batting an eyelid, replied, "No, sir, not in this play." "Oh," replied Kemble, disappointment in his voice. "You might inform the management that people are inquiring about it, will you?" He did this at intervals during the whole day. He had a curious, stuffy, high-pitched voice, but in his own line he was inimitable.

The Bancrofts vacated the theatre, but not the memories of their public. As long as they lived, they were popular. They became Sir Squire and Lady Bancroft. She died in 1921. He lived until 1926, when he was eighty-four years of age.

For years he was one of the sights of the West End. You might see him proceeding—to say strolling or walking was too undignified—towards the Garrick Club. He was always recognised. That silver hair, that darker moustache (he was always a moustached actor), that dignified gait, the perfect clothes, the grey top hat, the monocle with its broad silk ribbon, left nobody in doubt as to the wearer's identity. Sometimes his hands were clasped behind him, holding a gold-headed stick. He looked the gentleman of distinction and culture he so surely was. Passers-by would raise their hats by instinct, and he would respond courteously, whether he knew them or not. He was the epitome of the theatre of his time, leisurely, polished, painstaking and well-groomed, an aristocrat of entertainment. He died worth £174,535, for he was a man of the theatre who understood his job. And so he passes out of the story....

The Haymarket was taken over by Messrs. Russell and Bashford, the latter having been the Bancrofts' Manager there. They opened in September, 1885—it was usual to close down for the summer—with a play called *Dark Days* which lived up to its name, for it brought them no sunshine in the way of box-office returns. So they tried a sporting play called *Hard Hit*, and it hit them pretty hard too, despite a cast which included E. S. Willard and Marion Terry. The next venture was *Man and Wife*, a revival of a play which had succeeded at the Prince of Wales's, with Mrs. Brown-Potter and Kyrle Bellew in the leads. This, too, failed. The Haymarket was not being kind to the new management. Perhaps it knew that its right tenant—a man who had a curious link with the Bancrofts—was just round the corner.

One night in April, 1876, a tall, thin, fair-haired young man waited outside the pit entrance of the old Prince of Wales's Theatre in Tottenham Street, Tottenham Court Road, to see the first performance of the Bancrofts' production of *The Merchant of Venice*. With him were some other young men. Had the people around them known it, they were in distinguished company. For one of those youths was to become a famous dramatist, another a famous composer, and the third, the tall, fair one, one of the greatest actor-managers of all time, who was to wear the mantle of Sir Henry Irving. Little did that young man dream when he pushed his way in to see the Bancrofts that he would succeed them as actor-manager at the Haymarket—or did he even then hear his voices and see his visions, like a male St. Joan?

Anyhow, he said nothing about it at the time, for he was not even on the stage, although he was thinking very earnestly about acting, for he was an ardent amateur actor. His name was Herbert Draper Beerbohm; he was aged twenty-three and was in business with his father—a grain merchant. In 1878, two years after that Shakespearean evening *chez* Bancroft, he went on the stage, calling himself Herbert Beerbohm Tree. He had a meteoric career. During the first three or four years he played the Reverend Robert Spalding in *The Private Secretary* and Macari in *Called Back*, a part which put him on the ladder of fame. In 1882 he married Maud Holt. Only nine years after his entrance into the profession, he was famous enough and had a public following sufficient to enable him to risk actor-management. This shows his power and genius in a brilliant light. In April, 1887, he took the Comedy Theatre and produced *The Red Lamp*, a tremendous success, in which his own acting marked him as truly great. His performance as Demetrius was that of a supreme artist; it will never be forgotten by those privileged to see it. His catchword, "I wonder," swept all London. Herbert Beerbohm Tree was in the very front rank and amongst the leaders of his profession. It was obvious that the small Comedy Theatre could not retain his greatness for long.

He had already been at the Haymarket Theatre, engaged by Russell and Bashford for the ill-fated *Dark Days*. Poor as the play was, he had managed to make a success as Sir Mervyn Ferrand. He was there in another ill-fated venture with the new management. They presented a play called *Nadjesda*, in which a celebrated Austrian actress named Emily Rigl made her London debut. The first act contained what was then considered a "risky" situation—one which to-day would not raise an eyebrow. It was greeted with a storm of protest and hoots from the cheaper parts of the house—a scene recalling the riots of the Haymarket's earlier days and far more venomous and bitter than the first-night row of the Bancrofts. There was a counter-demonstration from the stalls, dress circle and boxes, but the upset sealed the fate of the play, for it never recovered. One man, however, rode the storm, and by a performance of consummate artistry Tree almost saved the situation. His performance as Prince Zabouroff almost pulled things through, and if the run of the play put little money into his pocket in salary, it nevertheless brought him public acclamation. It was a performance of perfect polish—such as he was always afterwards to give. It excelled his Macari—up to then his best part—and it showed what might be expected of him. But he played in another failure there as well, again as a villain and again making a personal success. Then came the preparations for the one success that management ever staged, *Jim the Penman*. The play was being cast and Tree expected with every confidence that he would get the title role. He had been so successful for Russell and Bashford that they could hardly overlook his claims; the leading role was surely his due. He did not get it; it was given to Arthur Dacre. Tree was cast for what was regarded as an inferior role, that of a German, Baron Harzfeld. This disappointment was one of the few which ever made Tree despondent, for he was a wonderful man whose work, spirit and whole life were filled with radiance. But the loss of Jim the Penman caused him to say, "My soul is dark." He accepted the other part, however. Perhaps his rebuff steeled him, perhaps his genius came upon him—perhaps it was a combination of both. For when that play was produced the performance of Herbert Beerbohm Tree as Baron Harzfeld was the only thing which mattered. He was the success of the play; he made the play's success. He was the talk of London— and he stepped straight into management at the Comedy.

But he wanted the Haymarket Theatre. He knew its worth, he knew the value of that perfect house, and he knew that once there he could have the proper setting, the correct atmosphere, the perfect blending of theatre and actor to enable him to achieve the ambitions he had in his active, imaginative, sensitive mind. He had not long to wait.

In the autumn of the same year that saw his managerial venture at the Comedy—1887—Russell and Bashford gave up the Haymarket and Tree took it over. He called it his "Great Adventure."

He transferred to the larger theatre his success, *The Red Lamp*, which he preceded by a little play called *The Ballad Monger*. He also appeared in this and the part of Gringoire was one of his masterpieces.

This was excellent showmanship, too, which illustrated his tremendous versatility. For the contrast between the fat, feline, ponderous but sinister Demetrius and the graceful, ragged, fervent poet, by turns pleading and passionate, was a real example of the player's genius. Marion Terry was his leading lady in both plays. His wife played in *The Red Lamp* too, for Maud Holt (Lady Tree) was a clever and gifted actress.

He began brilliantly, with a promise of what he was to achieve in the ten years of glory with which he filled the Haymarket Theatre. His was actor-management *in excelsis*. It was the peer in many ways of Irving's record at the Lyceum. If, at first, it was not so spectacular, that was because it was pitched in the Haymarket key as against the Lyceum's. But the public saw that here was the coming man—here was again quality, distinction and genius of acting and production.

Irving never liked Tree; he referred to him as a mummer, which delighted the younger man. For Tree *was* a mummer—he was theatre personified, and he gloried in it. That is not to say that he was blatant, "actory," or what is now described (so stupidly) as "Ham." Anyone more distinguished than Tree never trod the stage. Anyone with finer taste, a more poetic mind, a more delicate imagination never belonged to the theatrical profession. Throughout all his long career, the theatre came first, and finance a long way after. No matter how grim his failures—and he had his share—he always conceived the next thing to be done and to be made beautiful, and was always sure that success was waiting for him round the corner. And because he was true to his faith, success always was on hand. His great dictum was that the entire business of the stage was illusion. He lived up to that. He was, first and foremost, an actor—a mummer, if you like. And he was proud of it, and proud of his profession. He would rather have been a mummer than a marquis or even the Great Mogul himself.

Tree's second venture at the Haymarket was a play by Robert Buchanan called *Partners*. It should have been a success; it had everything—or so it seemed—that a success needed. But it did not bring the public into the Haymarket Theatre. Tree shrugged his shoulders and tried again. He did not worry about long runs at any time of his career. Indeed, he disliked them. They checked his artistic urge and frustrated his creative mind, which always wanted to be "getting on" and preparing something new. But he had certainly hoped for more. Marion Terry was again the leading lady. With *Partners* was a one-act play, *Cupid's Messenger*, by Alfred G. Gilmour. Tree, like all the actor-managers, gave full measure.

Partners was, in 1888, succeeded by *Pompadour*. This was an adaptation of Brachvogel's *Narcisse* by W. G. Wills and Sydney Grundy. Maud Holt played Pompadour. In the last act there was a scene in which Narcisse, played by Tree, had to hurl the Pompadour, whose proclivities he had discovered, down the steps of the Market Cross. He had to stand at the top of the steps while she clung round his neck, then tear himself free and hurl her headlong. At least, that was what Tree wanted to do. The Market Cross was a solid, well-built piece of scenery (as was everything Tree used) and there were a considerable number of steps. Mrs. Tree could not learn to fall down them without hurting herself. This reduced Tree to a frenzy. "Act, act," he shouted at her. "You can't be hurt if you will only *act*." However, Mrs. Tree could never "act" this scene sufficiently well to do that fall, and Tree had to compromise by simply pushing her away down the bottom step, which drove him to despair. But there you had the whole character of the man. What you had to do was to act—then everything would happen naturally; you had to lose yourself in your acting and you could not be hurt. That was really Tree's whole philosophy and his whole life. But it may have been that early difficulty with his wife which made him nervous himself on a "rostrum." For in later years he was always a little shaky on a "rostrum" and glad to get off it on to the flat stage. But if he had a big scene to portray, it did not matter where he was. For then he was acting.

Pompadour had charming scenery—the beauty of the production was highly praised. And there was a very pretty song which the Pompadour was singing when Narcisse first saw her sitting at a spinning wheel. Sydney Grundy wrote the words and George Henshel the music.

Despite the lack of the dramatic "back fall," *Pompadour* ran for over a 100 performances. It had as curtain raiser *A Compromising Case*. Whilst it was still being played, Tree's first big success at the Haymarket came on to the scene. Haddon Chambers, destined to be a lifelong friend, brought him a play which Tree liked.

They did not often take their plays into the country in those days to "try them on the dog," but Tree gave it a special matinée performance in June. The play was *Captain Swift*. It was a success at the trial performance, although certain critics condemned the last act. Tree did not care. He went away for a summer holiday and presented *Captain Swift* in September, 1888.

The play had come about as a result of the first meeting of the two men, actor-manager and playwright, in 1887. Chambers had only written one or two little pieces, but Tree, on being introduced, took a fancy to him. Tree ran into him outside the Comedy Theatre, before he went over to the Haymarket, and, to Chambers's surprise, said: "Have you ever thought of writing a play for me?" Chambers had not aspired to such heights, but promptly replied, "No, but I will." He went home to his lodging over a dairy in Bayswater, and set to work.

He brought the play, *Captain Swift: New and Original Play in Four Acts*, to Tree at the Haymarket, where the actor was by then installed. Tree let him read it to him, grew very tired of it, and before it was over departed for the Turkish baths. Chambers followed him there and caught him in the "hot room." There he read the last act to Tree, who finally accepted the play—indeed, there appeared to be no escape by any other means. Chambers had ridden after cattle in the bush and was a determined young man. He had put all he knew in this play, which was about a bushranger. Tree agreed to do it. But there were more snags ahead. Hastings, Tree's Stage Manager, had to pass it. His comment was: "Damned rot." There was Comyns Carr to be got over, who was Tree's friend and general adviser. Carr, with his leonine head and flowing beard, walked up and down the managerial room, criticising the play and destroying it with a cloud of words. Poor Haddon Chambers was writhing in agony. But he glanced at Tree, and found a sympathetic blue eye regarding him. Carr's back was to them. Chambers took a chance. He winked at Tree, who burst out laughing. Carr swung round and demanded the cause of the hilarity. "I laugh because I have an idea," replied Tree. "If Chambers does not object, we will give his play a trial matinée." Chambers, bursting with gratitude, did not object. Tree had made up his mind, despite his advisers. He was right. *Captain Swift* was an immense success. It was also a tremendous personal success for Tree. It showed what he could do with a "straight" part as against the strongly marked "character" parts in which he had scored so far. He never studied the part with the meticulous care he devoted to so many of his creations. He stepped straight inside it and "let the part play him"—which is real acting. He was Captain Swift, the ex-bushranger, now suddenly in the bosom of an English family— as English families were in those days—finding out for the first time what devotion to duty, home and decent living meant. Tree made a wonderful man of Swift, and the tragic end, when disclosure is upon him, was dramatic to a degree. The shot, the fall of the dead bushranger through the curtains was a real thrill. Produced at the Haymarket on September 1st, 1888, it ran 164 performances. Plays did not habitually run for three years in those days. Nor would Tree normally have allowed it. But profits accrued from his Haymarket venture for the first time.

In the same year, 1888, there was a revival of that old Haymarket stand-by, *Masks and Faces*, and *The Duchess of Bayswater*.

But Tree was preparing for his essay into Shakespeare, for the first of those series of productions which have made his greatness in the theatre endure for ever. That Shakespeare was reputed to be "box-office poison" and that Buckstone had barred it, did not worry him. Irving had succeeded, and the "Mummer" could succeed as well. That a broken manager had moaned, "Shakespeare spells ruin and Byron bankruptcy," only a short time before, weighed nothing with him. He wanted to do Shakespeare, and above all he wanted to play Falstaff. There had been a remarkable Falstaff at the Haymarket before in Henderson. Perhaps there would be a remarkable one again. There was. For Tree was the finest Falstaff of them all. There have been others since, acclaimed as magnificent, but those who saw Tree knew that the newcomers, good as they are, never quite touched those heights. It was not their faults, their performances were excellent, were technically superb, but they lacked that quality of Tree's which made his Falstaff such a gem—how one wished Shakespeare himself could have seen it—they lacked that quality of radiance which Tree always possessed and which lit up the character of the fat knight as with a bright light within. For he revelled in the part. He made it fat, he made it "lard the earth," and with it all he was a gentleman. He might consort with scum, he might drink the night through in low taverns with lower company, but always he was Sir John. Tree was at heart a comedian, a superb comedian, and he brought his great gift to bear upon this immensely comic role. He who loved a joke, who would create a joke at every opportunity, knew all about Falstaff. His *Merry Wives of Windsor*, produced in 1889, set a standard for production. It was with this play that he started that true repertory idea which he was to develop to its zenith at His Majesty's, for he was still playing *Captain Swift* when he staged this magnificent full-sized production for a series of matinées. Other managements gasped. Critics wondered, the public applauded and flocked in. His scenes of authentic Tudor settings, his wonderful glimpses of Windsor Forest, with their fairy motif, and the imaginative if humorous end, when the gigantic Falstaff finds himself alone and confronted by the tiniest elf of them all, showed his genius as a producer.

Yet he did this all at matinées to begin with, as he had done *Masks and Faces*. In that he had played Triplet, and even old Benjamin Webster had played it no better. Mrs. Bernard Beere was Peg Woffington and Mrs. Tree was Lucy Vane. His matinées were dusted with stars. He gave matinées on Wednesdays of his regular productions as well as Saturdays (the usual day), and his wife always asserted that he invented the mid-week matinée. To Tree a theatre was a place to be used, and an actor a person to create things for its use. His theatres never grew rusty. His *Merry Wives* had himself as Falstaff, Mrs. Tree as Ann Page, Rose Leclerq, a superb actress, as one of the Wives, Henry Kemble as Dr. Caius (a memorable performance), Charles Brookfield, and little E. M. Robson, the finest Sir Hugh Evans that the stage ever saw. He used the music of Nicolai and of Sullivan. His *Merry Wives* was a gay, triumphant frolic, lit up by his own radiance. And his Falstaff one of the greatest performances of the British theatre.

In 1889, *The Merry Wives* went into the evening bill and Shakespeare did not spell ruin that time.

The same year saw a production of *Wealth*, by Henry Arthur Jones.

The next play that Tree produced at the Haymarket was another big success. It was a version of *Roger la Honte*, adapted by Robert Buchanan. Here Tree had one of those things beloved by the actors of his day—and before his day—a "double" part to play. His creation of the two roles of Luversan and Laroque was magnificent—rivalling Irving's feat in *The Lyons Mail*. The one part was that of a good man, wrongly condemned, the other a drink-sodden, desperate villain. The playing of these parts alone would have filled the house, but the play was a good one. Minnie Terry, a mite of eight years old, played the child whose line, "I saw nothing—I heard nothing," condemned her innocent father—until the last act, of course. There was an actress in this play who had recently joined his company. He had seen her in a tiny part in an ill-fated play produced by Rutland Barrington at the St. James's, *Brantingham Hall*. He picked her out and engaged her, sent her on tour to give her experience and gave her a chance in London at the Haymarket in *A Man's Shadow*. It was not a large part—she was the "bad woman" of the play, but she had a good scene with Tree. She made a success and her name was—and is—Julia Neilson. It was the beginning of that wonderful career which was to achieve so much and which truly began at the Haymarket where this lovely woman and equally lovely actress was to make many successes.

The cast of *A Man's Shadow* included Tree in the two roles, James Fernandez, a magnificent actor, Leith, Charles Allan, E. M. Robson, Hargreaves, Henry Kemble, Tapping, Robb Harwood, Warden, Montagu, Mrs. Tree, Minnie Terry, Rose Norreys (so recently dead under such tragic circumstances in an asylum) and Julia Neilson. Charles Allan is worthy of note. He was a very sound actor, as well as a charming man, a wit and also a man of taste and judgment in food and wines. He had, however, a knack of saying the wrong thing. Once when, after dining with Tree, his hostess apologised for the somewhat indifferent dinner (as hostesses do, for it was actually a fine repast), he replied with a smile, "Oh, thank you, Mrs. Tree, it does one good to underfeed sometimes." And when Tree refilled Allan's glass with a rich vintage claret, he leant forward and said to his host, "Talking of cheap claret, I know a man who has a bargain in this class of wine. . . ." But the Trees adored him.

A Man's Shadow contained a court scene as its climax, and Tree lavished all his care as a producer on it and obtained fine effects. *A Man's Shadow* was a great success and ran for 204 performances. This was, of course, too long for Tree to be doing nothing new. A triple bill which Tree produced consisted of *Rachel*, by Clo Graves, *Comedy and Tragedy*, by W. S. Gilbert, and *Called Back*, by H. Conway and Comyns Carr.

That series is chiefly remarkable for Julia Neilson's performance as Clarice in *Comedy and Tragedy* and her delivery of the famous speech descriptive of an actor. She made a sensation in this. Also, to play opposite her, as she was very tall, Tree engaged a very tall actor. He told her, "Oh, I've engaged Fred Terry to play lover to you, because he's tall." Tree was here a *deus ex machina*. For the couple fell in love in that play and very shortly afterwards got married—to make theatre history themselves.

Mr. Gladstone came, with his wife, to see *A Man's Shadow* on its last night, in April, 1890. He sat in a box and approved the show. Afterwards he went on the stage and chatted (if such a phrase can be applied to the Grand Old Man) with Tree. He asked, amongst other things, what were the politics of the theatrical world? "Oh," said Tree, airily, "Conservative on the whole"—and saw the statesman's face cloud over, so added: "But the scene-shifters are Radical to a man." Gladstone cheered up and they parted friends.

Tree's next full-sized production, *A Village Priest*, was produced on April 3rd, 1890, and ran for 124 performances. It was a beautiful production, and the Abbé's garden was a thing of joy—how Tree loved to stage a garden. There was an apple tree in full bloom—one was persuaded it was a real one, so perfectly was it copied from the design of Alfred Parsons; and there was Tree, as the old priest, seated below it, surrounded by his flowers and his mellow garden walls. His performance matched the setting as a thing of delicate beauty. The play caused great controversy, for the plot hinged round a violation of the secret of the Confessional, and this caused anger amongst Roman Catholics. Letters by the score appeared in the Press and Tree joined in the dispute with a will. But the *Catholic Times* gave him absolution, and added: "We acquit the dramatist at once of any intention to attack the Roman Catholic priesthood. He has erred in ignorance and his error is also false in art. A noble drama could have been made of the subject if the Abbé had been kept faithful under all trials to his duty." The dramatist was Sydney Grundy, who adapted it from *Le Secret de la Terreuse*. He was not concerned with religious and doctrinal differences—he was out to make a good play, and he made it.

It was a success. And to see this play came the great Henry Irving. In the cast was Charles Allan, who managed to make himself felt, although, as a gendarme, he appeared only in the last act to speak one line, "Allons, Marche." Irving came back stage and Tree, with his wife, waited for praise of production and acting from the great actor. Tree felt he deserved it, for the part of the Abbé du Bois was one of his masterpieces. Irving shook hands. Said he, "Good night. Allan excellent. God bless you." And departed. One recalls Garrick's remark after Henderson's triumph as Shylock: "I thought the actor who played Tubal was excellent." The reason was probably the same.

Comedy and Tragedy went into the bill as a prelude to *A Village Priest*. The idea of repertory was filling Tree's mind. He simply would not worry about long runs, and with the utmost difficulty was made to keep plays on and therefore earn money for himself and the running of the theatre. He got his own way by a compromise. He decided on devoting certain Monday evenings to the production of new plays. These were called "Special Monday Nights." Many years later an idea of this kind was put up as a novelty. Tree had done it first. It was at his first "Special Monday Night" that he presented, in 1890, *Beau Austin*, by W. E. Henley and Robert Louis Stevenson. This was an exquisite play by a couple of geniuses about an exquisite, and it received exquisite production and playing from Tree. He took the same care as if it was being put up for a run—he always did this, nothing less than the very best ever suited him. No wonder he had become actor-manager of the playhouse of perfection. In his curtain speech, Tree said that it had been stated that he proposed to do a new play every Monday night. Nothing would please him better, personally, but it was considered physically impossible and conducive to strikes by the company. The play was produced on Monday, November 3rd, 1890, and revived later at His Majesty's.

In 1890 he also presented *The Waif*, by Cotsford Dick, and *Peril*, by Saville Rowe and B. C. Stephenson.

But the big event forthcoming was his production of Henry Arthur Jones's play *The Dancing Girl*, which was to give Julia Neilson her first real leading part. This was an outstanding success. It was so determined a success that it broke up the idea of the Special Mondays and drew from Tree the remark: "When is a repertory not a repertory? When it's a success." Not even Tree dared interfere with *The Dancing Girl*.

This play was the story of a girl from the Scilly Isles, of humble stock, who became a dancer and the mistress of a Duke, casting off her fisherman lover, John Christison. It was a gripping, swift-moving drama, with big scenes—notably that between the humble lover and the dancing girl, when, despite his knowledge of her frailty, he almost remains faithful, but finally takes the right course, for he ranked his soul above her beauty, and that of the arrival of her old father at a reception of the Duke's, where he denounces his daughter—and the Duke—in front of all the smart guests.

There were scenes set in the Scilly Isles and a wonderful ducal house interior with a "grand staircase." Julia Neilson played Drusilla Ives, the dancing girl, James Fernandez her father, Fred Terry the fisherman-lover (who, like the dancing girl's family, were Quakers), Rose Leclerq (the best exponent of Society women of her day and the great *grande dame* of the stage), Lady Bawtry, Rose Norreys, a cripple girl, Sybil Crake, the good angel of the play, and Tree the Duke of Guisebury. Also in the cast were Fred Kerr, Charles Allan, Mr. Batson, Robb Harwood, Charles Hudson, Adelaide Gunn, Blanche Horlock, Mrs. E. H. Brooke and Miss Hethcote. Produced on January 15th, 1891, it ran for 310 performances, an enormous run then—especially for Tree. There was also a bulldog in the cast—"Bully Boy"—who became very popular. Tree, as the fascinating Duke, was in danger of becoming a matinée idol. Julia Neilson swept all hearts and Fred Terry thrilled everyone.

During the very first week, Tree was taken ill. He had acute bronchitis. But he insisted on playing. He was taken from his home to the theatre in his brougham attended by a nurse and a doctor. He was swathed in blankets and had a rug wrapped round his head. He could not resist, ill as he was, getting a laugh by wearing his tall hat on top of it. After each performance he was taken to Garland's Hotel, which adjoined the Haymarket stage door, and kept in bed until the next performance. It was his only illness. He did not surrender.

Even the critics, never too kind to him, raved about his Duke:

"Mr. Beerbohm Tree achieves by touches fine, as well as touches broad, a marvellously lifelike portrait of the genial, generous, courageous rake, cynically bent on his own destruction. He is a delightful creature, this ducal defier of *les convenances*, as he chats to his dog, Bully Boy, as he dissembles on the eve of his intended suicide and as he prepares to wind up his life as a game he has played and lost."

Another said:

"Mr. Tree's performance is perfect. The third act places Mr. Tree (where he has not hitherto stood) on a level with our very best stage managers. No social picture on so large a scale has ever been so successfully presented. It was Du Maurier in action."

That was hardly fair to Tree. He stood in the very front rank of producers already, but the shadow of Irving hid the sun.

There had been considerable trouble with the author at rehearsals. He kept on foreseeing dangers in his script and wanting to alter it. It was, for its time, very daring, with its frequent exclamations of "My God!" and its open suggestion by Drusilla that she should "give herself" to John Christison. That part, superbly played by Fred Terry, was really a most trying one. He opened the play, and it was an ordeal. The opening speech was a test for any actor. Standing on the seashore, gazing through the window of a cottage (in which lived his beloved Drusilla) he had to say: "Thou miracle of grace and beauty. Thou one desire of my soul. No." (Turning from window, removing hat and gazing aloft.) "Grant me this, that loving her so much, I may for ever love Thee more. Grant that she may never come between my soul and Thee." To have to deliver such a speech to an audience hardly settled in their seats, without any warning and before their attention had been riveted was an ordeal indeed. The writer of this book knows, for he played the part afterwards. But Fred Terry the Magnificent held his house spellbound from the opening line. He and Julia Neilson roused a frenzy of applause in their big scene, when John casts off the woman he has so well and truly loved and who had so basely deceived him. Drusilla dies in the end; the Duke, about to commit suicide, is saved— and probably reformed—by the cripple girl; and John Christison finds consolation, and starts a family, with Drusilla's Quaker sister, Faith. Julia Neilson stepped right into the ranks of great actresses. *The Dancing Girl* was just the sort of thing playgoers of the 'nineties loved. They flocked to the Haymarket to see it, and the audiences there at that time were the smartest in the land.

CHAPTER XXVII

THE TRIUMPH OF *TRILBY*

UNDER Tree, the Haymarket became the smartest theatre in London in every sense of the word. It was not only the so-called "Smart Set" who went there, for the theatre became the centre of the social world of London, in so far as any theatre can, and remained so until Tree opened His Majesty's. His audiences were as brilliant as his plays. A Cochran first night in this generation may glitter—indeed, does glitter—with celebrities; but there was more to it at a Tree first night. He counted amongst his supporters all the great ones of the land. The front rank of art, literature, science, the law, medicine and politics, even the Church itself, all came to a Tree première—only he never called it that. No cameras flashed, no gossip-writers strained their eyes and ears. The event was enough in itself. There was no ostentation, no attending for the purpose of being seen. The people went to something which they had to see, and wanted to see. There was dignity, wealth, solidarity and substance—true quality everywhere. There were silks, satins and jewels; there were lovely women and gallant men. There was no pushing and shoving, but good manners and deference to the ladies; no cloud of cigarette smoke, no shrill laughter, but genuine interest and real applause. Great people came to see a great man in a great production. The theatre was an aristocrat, and the audiences of the Haymarket, under Tree, were aristocratic playgoers from the gallery downwards. It is something which will never again be seen.

Despite the—to Tree—grim success of *The Dancing Girl*, his active mind was off to fresh woods and pastures new. He was considering, as all serious actors must consider, the one great test part—Hamlet.

Tree, after a London success, would take the whole production to Manchester for a fortnight and there put the finishing touches to his plans. Henschel went there to play him the special music he had been commissioned to compose. It was in Manchester that Tree first played Hamlet and his wife played Ophelia. Incidentally, it should be mentioned that he did regular provincial tours.

On January 21st, 1892, Tree played Hamlet at the Haymarket. Again he brought Shakespeare to that stage. And he aroused violent controversy. His Hamlet was debated. Some people loathed it, some adored it. He wore a flaxen wig, and much fun was made of him. One wit said that his Hamlet was "funny without being vulgar"; others found great poetic beauty in it. On the whole, the Press were against him, but the public rolled up to see him. One girl, an artist, stood in the wings every night for a hundred nights to draw him in the character. She filled a book with remarkable studies. Rose Leclerq, Henry Kemble (Polonius), James Fernandez (the Ghost), Fred Terry (Laertes) and Arthur Dacre (Horatio)—the same man who had been cast over Tree's head in Jim the Penman—were members of a brilliant cast, and the scenic production drew universal praise. Tree himself adored playing Hamlet, whatever was said about him, and was never so happy. Whatever question there was of his rendering, there was nothing but praise for Mrs. Tree's Ophelia. It was Hamlet more than anything else which caused the two schools of thought to arise about Tree. Thereafter, he was either idolised or made fun of. There was constant war between his supporters and his detractors. But all united over certain parts he played —always strong character roles—and all agreed on his supremacy in these. Nor was there any discord over his wonderful stage productions. Such a man was bound to cause controversy. His almost overwhelming personality, his vitality, his insistence on his point of view, his wit and his often Quixotic behaviour were always a challenge. But as to his greatness and his stage power—those were never in doubt or questioned.

He followed *Hamlet* with *Hypatia*, a dramatisation of the Kingsley novel, by Stuart Ogilvie. Alma Tadema designed the scenery and costumes and Sir Hubert Parry wrote the music. That was how Tree worked. It was a very beautiful production, only surpassed perhaps by his later production of *Julius Cæsar*. Rehearsals were long and hard, but he found time to start an idea which came into concrete form later as his Royal Academy of Dramatic Art.

There were seven scenes in *Hypatia*, each of them a dream of beauty. Charles Kingsley's novel leapt to life on the stage under the master hand. Everything was correct and blended into a perfect whole. Tree was already pursuing his policy of surrounding himself with the very best, not only of art experts, but of performers as well. He never had an inferior company. He had all-star casts which shone the brighter for the fine setting. He was the perfect producer. He never bullied, never tried to impose restrictions; he let his actors and actresses have their heads in their conceptions, but he guided them with his expert eye and brain. He would invent business for them, but he would insist that they worked until the best had been obtained from them. What a cast that play had. James Welch, Henry Kemble, Olga Brandon, Lewis Waller, Fred Terry, Julia Neilson and Tree himself. He played Issachar, a Jew, a part which is not in the novel. It had been intended that he should play Philammon, but he gave the part to Fred Terry and took the character role, in which he gave his usual remarkable performance. Julia Neilson played Hypatia, and had a "back-fall" down a staircase. She pleased Tree with the way she did it better than his wife had done in *Pompadour*. Julia Neilson and Fred Terry, now husband and wife, added to their laurels as the lovers in this play. *Hypatia* was produced in 1893. It ran for 104 nights.

x

Oscar Wilde had brought along the scenario of Tree's next success, *A Woman of No Importance*. Here was modern light comedy as against classical tragedy. But it was just as perfect in production and acting. Mrs. Bernard Beere, Julia Neilson and Fred Terry, Tree and his wife, were in the cast.

Julia Neilson tells a good story of Oscar Wilde during rehearsals in her delightful book, *This for Remembrance*. The author did not see eye to eye with Fred Terry over the way certain scenes were being played and went to lunch with them to talk it over. The conversation turned on Dickens, however, for whom Terry was an enthusiast. Wilde delivered a long and marvellous eulogy on the great author and Fred Terry warmed to him as a brother Dickensian. Time went by so quickly that there was hardly a moment for the discussion of the disputed scenes, but to Wilde's ideas of this Terry quickly agreed. Dickens had done it. As Wilde was leaving, Fred Terry shook him warmly by the hand. "Well, Wilde," he said, "it's been a great pleasure to me to find another person who is fond of Dickens." "Oh, my dear boy," said Wilde, "I've never read a word of him in my life."

A Woman of No Importance was a big success and ran for 112 nights in 1893. It came off only because Tree had undertaken to produce Henry Arthur Jones's *The Tempter. A Woman of No Importance* was produced when the scandal about Wilde was at its height. He took a call and was badly "boo-ed." He beat a retreat. Tree came on and turned the hoots into cheers.

The Tempter was a costume play of the time of Henry IV. Its treatment was not unlike that of *Faust*. It was written partly in prose and partly in verse. It was a jumble. Tree went to Harrogate before the production. He said he did so "to drink pure sulphur and study the Devil." He had to make his first entrance from the flies. As the Devil, he had to hover over a doomed ship, which was wrecked before the eyes of the audience. There was a back-stage fire on the first night, too, which was extinguished without the audience knowing anything about it.

Julia Neilson and Fred Terry again played the lovers and had one beautiful scene which almost saved the play—but not quite. It dragged on until after midnight and finished to a half-empty house. Not a Tree or a Haymarket success. But playing a small part was a very young actress, later to become a very great one—Irene Vanbrugh.

Other productions at the Haymarket were *An Enemy of the People*, by the then much discussed Ibsen, and *Six Persons*, by Israel Zangwill. Tree revived *Captain Swift* whilst he got ready Robert Buchanan's play, *The Charlatan*. In this there was a part after his own heart—a part which only he or Irving could have played—a weird compound of eeriness, villain and hero in one. But the part was not greater than the whole. *The Charlatan* failed to attract. It ran only three months.

Tree now did a play which was before its time. His imagination was ahead of that of the public. Louis Napoleon Parker, now a distinguished dramatist—he had been one of that small party of youths in 1876 who went to see the Bancrofts at the Prince of Wales's—wrote a version of Anderson's *The Emperor's New Clothes*. Tree christened it *Once Upon a Time*, fell in love with it, and of course, produced it. He miscast himself—a thing he was to do often in later life—playing the Emperor instead of the Musician. It was beautifully done. Julia Neilson, Lionel Brough, E. Holman Clark, Tree and Mrs. Tree played in it. It ran for only a few weeks. It was a failure, but a glorious failure. It was the public's failure more than Tree's. That was in 1894.

He got ready *A Bunch of Violets*—founded on Octave Feuillet's *Mountjoye*. In this were Tree and Lily Hanbury, Lionel Brough, Holman Clark, and Mrs. Tree, who made a great success, as did her husband in the part of Sir Philip Marchant.

Tree had reached the heights and the Haymarket stood higher in public esteem and prestige than ever before. The actor-manager was socially courted; he was the associate of the great ones and of Royalty; he addressed learned societies, he was deferred to, he was a real celebrity. But this never prevented him from being an actor; it never deflected his thoughts from the theatre; it never damped for one moment that vivid sense of humour, that delight in jokes—in practical jokes too—that desire to "get a laugh" which was so much a part of his radiance. He was great and the Haymarket was great with him. He was giving great "theatre" in a great theatre—and he was happy. He did not want wealth; great riches never appealed to him; but he valued achievement and succeeded in all he did. He was, as his daughter wrote after his death, "a Pilgrim and a King."

A Bunch of Violets atoned for the failures. Produced on April 25th, 1894, it ran for 117 performances. These short but successful runs of Tree's Haymarket productions show the difference between conditions then and now, inside the theatre and out. It was possible in the 'nineties to lavish money on a production, to give it a magnificent cast and make money out of only 100 performances.

In 1895 Tree was summoned to Balmoral to give a Command Performance before Queen Victoria. This was during one of his summer tours, when he was in Edinburgh.

He had been to America in 1895. And during his absence overseas, Lewis Waller took over the Haymarket and produced *An Ideal Husband* —another Oscar Wilde success. Waller, too, gave it a real Haymarket cast, including himself and his wife (Florence West), Charles Hawtrey, Fanny Brough, and Julia Neilson. The play was a success *qua* play, but the Wilde scandal killed it, for people would not go to see his work. Lewis Waller, the *beau ideal* of the romantic school, was not so happy in this modern kind of work, but he could never fail to be impressive and gripping.

As a romantic or heroic actor, our stage has not his equal. Handsome and compelling, he was golden-voiced. His voice, masculinity itself, yet at the same time possessed of tenderness and charm, could ring like a blast of trumpets or chime like a peal of bells.

He left a gap never filled—unfilled to-day.

As soon as Tree got back from America he started work at once. But in his brain was now another idea. Those blue eyes had looked into the future, had visualised a theatre of his own—something which was to be of his own creation and something which was to be as beautiful as this lover of beauty could make it. Something he could call—and did call—his beautiful theatre. In 1892 Her Majesty's Opera House, standing opposite the Haymarket on the site of Vanbrugh's old theatre built in 1705, had breathed its last. It had been theatre at first, but opera house for centuries. Now it had fallen into disrepute and was demolished. Yet, apart from the land on which stands Drury Lane, that site was the most continuously theatrical in London. No wonder it caught the fancy of the chief man of the theatre. Tree had made up his mind to build his own beautiful theatre where Vanbrugh had built his. He loved the Haymarket Theatre, which he had filled—and still was to fill—with glory; but he wanted a home of his own. His maturity was reached. For the time being, however, he produced a revival of the Bancroft success, *Fedora*, with himself as Ispanoff, Mrs. Patrick Campbell as Fedora and—to everyone's great excitement—Lady Bancroft as the Princess. So that delightful lady came back to play again on the stage where she and her husband had said farewell to management and where they had done such fine work. Mrs. Patrick Campbell, the beautiful, the mysterious, unpredictable, the woman of wondrous grace—and the most tempestuous actress the theatre has ever known—had in Fedora a part which fitted her like a glove. She was then at the very height of her powers. Her performance and the return of the loved Lady Bancroft filled the Haymarket to overflowing. But alas! Mrs. Pat lost her voice, and had to leave. Mrs. Tree undertook the part at the shortest possible notice, but the magic was gone.

Mrs. Patrick Campbell had been with Tree at the Haymarket in another play, *John-a-Dreams*, a delightful comedy. Tree had also done *A Modern Eve*, by Malcolm A. Salaman, both in that full year of 1894.

But two things now absorbed him. He had decided on his new theatre on the site across the way. He was to leave the Haymarket Theatre, but not the Haymarket itself. Plans were being drawn up as the old building vanished before the housebreakers. He was also excited at having secured *Trilby*, which had been dramatised by Paul M. Potter from Du Maurier's world-famous novel. Tree was really thrilled. He saw himself as Svengali, the ugly, dirty, villainous, fascinating mesmerist bent on re-creating *Il Bel Canto*. It was a part after his own heart; he foresaw a triumph. He was right, for it was perhaps his best characterisation—certainly his most compelling and best remembered. He saw everything as a complete and wonderful whole, with one gap only— a most difficult and wide gap—who could play Trilby herself? She had to be right, for everyone knew Trilby. It was a complex problem and a complex part—not so much in the playing, perhaps, but in finding an actress who could not only play Trilby but be the Trilby of everyone's imagination. Tree and Du Maurier scoured the whole resources of theatreland. The public joined in the chase, so great was the interest in this production on the stage of the beloved novel.

It seemed that the perfect Trilby—even the possible Trilby—could not be found. She had to realise the pictures—for the drawings of Du Maurier were known to all. A false step, a slight error of mis-casting—and when Trilby came upon the stage, there would be a gasp of disappointment and the whole thing would fail. Think what was wanted. The sought-for woman must be very tall, have a perfect head and proportions and of course a perfect foot; she must glow with youth and vivacity, she must have brown hair, blue eyes; and she must have the ability to create in flesh and blood the figure which Du Maurier had created on paper by means of words and drawing. They tried, they tried and they tried, but it seemed in vain. Then they heard of a girl, quite unknown to London or to fame, who was only eighteen years old, and who had had a little experience in dear old Ben Greet's Shakespearean Company, with whom she had played Viola, Beatrice and Hermione.

But experience, however short, with Ben Greet, was worth years of experience elsewhere. For this grand old man of the theatre was a trainer of stars, a discoverer of genius. Never a really good actor himself, he could impart the power of acting to others. He knew all there was to know. He taught, he drove, he worked, and he got perfection from his youthful companies. He kept the banner of Shakespeare flying throughout the length and breadth of the land. He would play anywhere, in garden, park, village hall or theatre and also in schoolrooms. His pastoral plays—when the weather was fine—were delights. People watching them saw unknowingly the stars of to-morrow. When the Open Air Theatre in Regent's Park was hailed with delight as a novelty, old-timers smiled. They remembered Ben Greet, as did that experienced man of the theatre, Sydney W. Carroll, who gave London the joy of the Open Air Theatre. He never claimed originality, but he gave London what Ben Greet had given the whole kingdom, and a debt of gratitude is owed to him.

The Ben Greet Players were never as spectacular as the Benson Company, but they did just as splendid work and produced as splendid people. This was recognised in the end and Greet died—Sir Philip Ben Greet—Master of the Greensward in that Open Air London Theatre which carried on his old pioneer work.

Tree and Du Maurier went to see this young actress—hoping for the best, fearing the worst. They burst in upon her and found her lying full length on a couch, books all around her, studying the part of Desdemona. They gazed and they gasped. Here was Trilby—here was the very embodiment of Du Maurier's creation—if she could play it. Tree decided he could make her, even if she lacked the experience. He saw the intelligence on that lovely brow, that blue eye and that charming smile. They offered her the part, their hearts dancing. She accepted. In a week she was rehearsing.

They gathered a wonderful cast. There was Lionel Brough as the Laird, and that actor's rich gift of comedy and character made the part live; Edmund Maurice, every inch and in every way the magnicent Taffy; whilst the gifts and charm of H. V. Esmond brought Little Billee to actual reality. Rosina Filipi was Madame Vinard (although Annie Hughes played it in Manchester, where the play was "tried out"); Zou-Zou had a young actor to represent him who was destined for actor-management himself, for he was Gerald Du Maurier, the son of the author; and Dodor was played by Herbert Ross. Every part was perfectly cast. Manchester went mad about the play—and then it came to Town.

It had been awaited eagerly, with news from Manchester to whet the appetite of playgoers and put the London critics on their guard. Would *Trilby* on the stage disappoint the countless lovers of Trilby in the book? Was it really possible to dramatise the bohemian charm of Du Maurier's writing? They were soon to see.

The curtain at the Haymarket went up on *Trilby* on the evening of October 30th, 1895. From the start it gripped. The moment came for Trilby's entrance—and when she stepped on to the stage, there was a gasp, but not of disappointment—of wonder, of appreciation, of joy. That young actress was the incarnation of Trilby—she stepped right into fame that night. Her name, of course, was Dorothea Baird, one of the most delightful actresses and women our stage ever had. On and off the stage she was beloved. That night as Trilby she was acclaimed. Such a perfect realisation of stage personality had seldom been seen. Trilby conquered.

But what of Tree? For him it was a double triumph, that of producer and of actor. For his Svengali was a revelation of the actor's art. All that he had done before, splendid though it was, paled before what he did with that creation of Du Maurier's brain. If Dorothea Baird was Trilby, Tree was also Svengali, the real man alive, stepped out of those pages just as everyone had seen him, but bringing to life the written word. Here was everything an author could wish for, and more. Tree brought his own genius to bear on the part; he knew things about Svengali his creator had not seen. Here was the greatest stage sensation since Irving had played *The Bells*. Even those who thought it the correct thing to criticise him in everything he did were now loud and lavish in his praise. His every word, his every look, his every gesture—the dirt, the vileness, the villainy, all were there. So was the unspeakable tragedy of the man who had *Il Bel Canto* in his soul, but could not give it expression, and found the way to do so through that perfect instrument—Trilby. The subtle change which success brought to him, the vainglory of the fur-coated figure of Svengali, the impresario and conductor for *La Grande* Trilby, was wonderfully shown; while the final death scene made the whole house catch its breath and shiver, with its eyes riveted on the genius who held the Haymarket stage. A night of triumph, a night of achievement indeed for the "Mummer"! And almost his farewell to the Haymarket Theatre. But, as his farewell, he gave it his finest work so far and filled it with huge, enthusiastic audiences, so that it was proud of what it had gained by his hand. *Trilby* was the fashion; the theatre was besieged. Money poured in, the Trees were rich, Dorothea Baird was famous—and the Haymarket Theatre wound up ten years of glory.

Across the road the walls of the new theatre were setting their roots in the earth. Mrs. Tree was asked by a heavily-jewelled lady what her husband had given her as a token of *Trilby's* success. She replied proudly, "Her Majesty's Theatre, but I am not wearing it to-night."

But even with this vast success and a new theatre on his hands, Tree still felt the urge to create further. He loved playing Svengali —he felt it worth while; but still he must do more, he must do something new. Directly the freshness of a play had worn off, his immense enthusiasm drove him to that something new to think about and plan for. He had loved Falstaff in *The Merry Wives*; he would do Falstaff again, but in *Henry IV, Part I*. In the daytime, he worked on the ideas for Her Majesty's, as his new playhouse was to be called—it carried on the succession on that time-honoured site; in the evenings, he played Svengali to wondering crowds. And the critics had been unanimous: "Svengali—marvellous Svengali—a weird, spectral, Satanic figure— he literally took away our breath," wrote one of the keenest of them. But Tree had now got back his breath. And in his spare time, and at matinées only, he staged a full-sized and magnificent production of *Henry IV, Part I*. He played Falstaff. Lewis Waller played Hotspur. It had been in Tree's mind to alternate these two parts himself. But the public clamoured again for his Sir John and Waller was so perfect as Hotspur that he did not, at that time, make the change-over, although later he actually achieved his ambition. This amazing amount of work illustrates how great was his love for the theatre and what he could accomplish. He had no vast office staff, no gigantic organisation—only himself and his few lieutenants. But he knew what he wanted, he was of the theatre, and his assistants were practical experts as well. His love for his work, his belief in it, his radiance, made everything possible to him. This "Mummer" was magnificent.

At length came the summer of 1896. Tree said his farewell to the Haymarket. He loved the theatre, he knew its perfection. He had been its moving spirit for ten wonderful years. He had given it greater glory than anyone else—and for nearly two centuries it had been ascending. When he played Svengali for the last time, it was his last appearance as actor-manager of the Haymarket. The curtain descended and he said his farewell to the audience who acclaimed him with a catch in his voice. Tree's curtain speeches were events. They were not the hurried acknowledgments, the self-effacing references to the strength and value of his company, the scrambling sentiments so often heard. They were speeches worth listening to, well phrased and perfectly delivered. For he was a superb maker of phrases. His praise was bestowed justly and generously and in a manner which made the audience aware of his worth. His thanks were properly set forth, and his remarks always memorable. When he made a speech, he always had something to say and said it supremely well.

He had a catch in his throat indeed when he finally bowed himself off, because he knew it was the end of the Haymarket Theatre for him. He loved the place; it had become his home, and it suited him as he suited it. He was a worthy representative of that time-honoured playhouse, just as it was a worthy setting for him. Perhaps he would never have left it all his life but for that urgent desire to move on, to do something even better, to have a larger canvas, to create—yes, that was it, to create a playhouse for himself. And that playhouse was rising, brick by brick, just across the road. He knew that it would not have the tradition of the place he was leaving, but he hoped and believed he could give it a soul—that he could put his own soul into it—and surely enough he did.

Herbert Beerbohm's ten years at the Haymarket were ten years of glory. He offered excellent plays, sumptuous productions, supreme taste, full value and superb acting. His name glows in Haymarket tradition like a rich jewel. No matter how great were the others who made that story, his name is probably the greatest. For his personality endures after his deeply deplored and untimely death in 1917, endures in the history of his profession, in the hearts of all those who saw him and his work, in the stones of the beautiful theatre he built, and, indeed, in the very fabric of the playhouse of perfection—the Haymarket Theatre. He gave perfection to perfection whilst he was there—a decade of distinction and diamond brightness.

Herbert Beerbohm Tree—to become Sir Herbert Tree (and never was knighthood better merited)—was a very great man. Some thought him a poseur, some thought that odd vagueness, that elusiveness, that odd characteristic of faraway thought and visionary mind, was a pose. It was no pose; it was Tree. It was his charm, his true manner. For he was a mummer in the highest sense of the word. To him, life itself was illusion and the theatre real. To him, real life had to receive the illusion of the footlights before it really mattered. But he was wholly aware of the world. He had a beautiful mind and an imagination of shining intensity. He gathered beauty round him; he lived joyously with the best of people for his companions. A dreamer who did nothing by halves, he was a man of action who made his dreams realities. A man who loved laughter, who was at once a tragedian and a comedian, he was unique in his profession which has held so many strange and wonderful people in its service.

It is a trite saying that the line between comedy and tragedy is a hair's breadth in width. But he was the living example of it, for in his art comedy and tragedy mingled. He was a great comedian who could be a fine tragedian. His comedy was better than his tragedy because it was closer to his own mind. But when he had to bring imagination to bear upon a part, then the searchlight of his mind and the force of his intellect shone on that role. His brain worked with lightning rapidity; he moulded the character he was portraying with his artistic faculty as an artist would his clay—and made masterpieces.

They called him "Chief"—and chief he was. He inspired loyalty and he gave loyalty in return. He was to leave the Haymarket Theatre to become its neighbour. But he was a great and kindly neighbour to the home in which he had spent ten busy, creative, self-rewarding years. His greater fame lay ahead of him, but the foundation on which it rested had been built, as had the foundation of so many great careers, in the Haymarket Theatre. Tree never forgot that, and the Haymarket Theatre will never forget him. He leaves the story now—save for one incursion—to work at his own beautiful theatre, and the saga of the Haymarket goes on.

There is yet a word or two to say about those who served under him at the Haymarket, and have received so far merely a mention. There was Rose Leclerq, the supreme *grande dame* of the theatre, whom everyone loved, an actress who was respected and liked by every member of her profession. She had been born in Liverpool, and was daughter of Charles Leclerq, a very celebrated pantomimist, ballet-master and stage manager. She was sister to Charlotte Leclerq, a most distinguished actress who had acted with Charles Kean, Samuel Phelps and Fechter amongst others. She herself had made her first appearance at the Princess's, London, in 1861. She had been both at the Adelphi and at Drury Lane, where she had made an outstanding success as the heroine of *The Shaughraun*. She was distinguished and she was clever, and in her line one of the best actresses our stage has ever known.

James Fernandez was actually born in St. Petersburg (as it then was) in Russia, in 1835. He began his career in this country at Hull in 1853. He toured the provinces and made his first London appearance at the Queen's Theatre in the same year, afterwards playing at the Bower (a very tough blood-tub), the Surrey and the Grecian Theatres. He won fame at the Surrey under the management of Shepherd and Creswick and was there for six years. When the Surrey was burned down, he went to Astley's and then to the Lyceum. He starred in the provinces afterwards, and returned to Town in 1871 at the Adelphi, where he remained for three seasons. It was during this engagement that he made such an outstanding success in *Notre Dame* and *Claude Frolic*. He was also at Drury Lane with Chatterton and the Lyceum with Irving. A magnificently powerful actor, very popular, he died in 1915 at the age of eighty.

Lionel Brough, a name ranking high amongst character comedians of the British stage, had been born in Pontypool, Monmouthshire, in 1836. He came of a family of authors. He had started life in the office of John Timbs, when that man was Editor of *The Illustrated London News*. He was at one time assistant publisher for the *Daily Telegraph* and claimed to have originated the system of selling newspapers in the streets. He made his first appearance on the stage under the management of Vestris and Mathews at the Lyceum in 1854 in an extravaganza written by his brother, William Brough. He left the stage for some time, but returned to the Lyceum under Falconer. He left the stage again to join the staff of the *Morning Star*, remaining there for five years. He then began to give entertainments in London, also at the Polytechnic and on tour. He had a "Ghost" show which was very popular. In 1864 he went back to the stage, chiefly in the provinces, and in 1867 was back in Town. He was in the company which opened the Queen's Theatre, in Long Acre, where in the following year he made his first big success in *Dearer than Life*. He toured again, in the same company with Henry Irving, under J. L. Toole's direction. Later he became a star of burlesque and *opera bouffé*. He was, when he went to the Haymarket, a celebrated and mellowed comedian, and a most finished actor, whose memory is still treasured by the middle-aged playgoers who saw him. His niece, Fanny Brough, was also at the Haymarket and had a long and distinguished career. His son, Sydney Brough, was an excellent actor and tens of thousands of playgoers loved his daughter, Mary Brough, who in her later years was a pillar of the Aldwych farces, under Tom Walls's management.

All these and many more were of Tree's Haymarket period, which was now ended, and one of those little ironies not uncommon in the world of the theatre manifested itself.

When the Little Theatre in the Hay was first built it cowered in the shadow of the mighty playhouse built by Sir John Vanbrugh. That playhouse, through periods of alteration and rebuilding—and changes of name—had become Her Majesty's Theatre, the opera house of London. It fell into decay and became the prey of the housebreakers, and in its place Tree was now building his new theatre, on the same site and with the same title, Her Majesty's Theatre, for Queen Victoria was still on the throne. He was recreating Her Majesty's from the Haymarket Theatre, which now called itself Theatre Royal. Thus did the original little unlicensed playhouse outlive its rival and become the means, to a great extent, of giving it a new and more glorious lease of life.

The news that the Haymarket was to become vacant went round theatrical circles like wildfire. Two young men were looking for a

theatre in which to commence management. They had been treating for
the Garrick Theatre, but the Haymarket was a glittering prize. They
seized it. Their names were Frederick Harrison and Cyril Maude. The
managerial decision had been taken by Cyril Maude and his wife, the
lovely Winifred Emery—descendant of that Emery who had shone at
the Haymarket before, and a very great actress indeed. Frederick
Harrison was managing for Forbes Robertson at the time; he had also
been with Tree at the Haymarket, which probably explains how he
heard the news. He told Maude, who jumped at the chance—who would
not? They joined hands—they took over the theatre. And there they
remained together for nine years—nine years in which the Haymarket
became more than ever the theatre of distinctive perfection, a very
salon of a theatre, where only good taste and refinement reigned, where
the quality was of the very best, where the atmosphere was that of
old china, beautiful period furniture; indeed, that of the real homes
of England at a time when England really had homes—places pleasant to
live in and of which one could be proud. It was the day of the golden
sovereign, and under the Maude-Harrison régime the Haymarket was
as golden as the coin, and of the same indisputably high value.

It became truly the home of English comedy. It always gave the
same class of goods—it was the very spirit of the West End—and
always it wore a smile. That smile came to it from the charm of Cyril
Maude and the beauty of his wife—from their own art as players, and
from the courtesy and skilful management of Harrison. It was a place
of breeding and of good manners. It remains so to-day.

Both partners were men of good family and of good education.
Harrison was a graduate of Cambridge. The Church had been his
destiny, but he preferred the theatre—and that was the theatre's good
fortune. He had been with the famous Benson Company and was a good
actor. His régime at the Haymarket outlasted the partnership with
Maude—and he would have been a Haymarket knight had he lived a
little longer.

Cyril Maude—for some reason, known only to the powers that be,
still without a title to his name, for he so richly deserves one—traces
his descent back to one of the knights who killed Thomas à Becket.
Surely that cannot be held against him? He is of soldier stock, and there
was a V.C. in the family. He is a Londoner and it is delightful to know
that whilst these lines are being written he is still as active as ever,
despite the eighty odd years that trail so lightly behind him. His school
was Charterhouse. His own ambition lay between the Church and the
stage. The stage won. His people wanted a military career for him, but
he chose the equally dangerous battlefield of the theatre—and no
military Maude of them all ever won more decisive victories in the field
of warfare than he has won on the pitched battlefield of the stage.

They entered into the Haymarket in 1896, redecorated it, and each
undertook their appointed tasks. Harrison controlled the business side

and Maude the stage. Their business manager was Horace Watson. He, too, had been with Tree. Horace Watson was a real man of the theatre who understood exactly what the Haymarket wanted. Firm, yet courteous, never flurried, he had that touch of superiority which the Haymarket required. He remained there all his life, and when Harrison died, he assumed control and ran it in the same style, with the same golden glow and the same standard of quality until he, too, passed on. His son reigns in his stead and the Haymarket remains as it always has been, the theatre of atmosphere, charm and high quality. The Haymarket has no touch of vulgarity, nothing of the clamant age. It is serene and sure of itself. It knows its value and does not need to flaunt it, for quality always stands out clearly without advertisement. The Haymarket's quality will always be maintained whilst there is a Watson at the helm. May the day never come when there is not.

Tree wanted Leverton to go to the new theatre over the way. But the Haymarket was Leverton's home and he stayed on there.

Under the régime of Maude and Harrison one always knew the fare at the Haymarket; one expected the best of comedy—Comedy with a capital C—the best of stage production and the very best comedy acting to be seen anywhere. One went certain of a welcome, for the friendliness of Maude and his wife and the personality of Harrison and his staff filled their theatre with a happy atmosphere. It was a place where you could relax and enjoy yourself and feel the better for having visited. In that nine years these two men produced twenty-three plays. To-day, when London has swollen beyond control, when transport moves through the internal combustion engine and not by the legs of horses or men, that seems a great number and a low average in length of run. But it was not so then. For in those times expenses were small, living was cheap and 100 nights showed a nice profit. So one had success and not staleness; change and still stability. The Maude-Harrison era at the Haymarket was a golden one in every sense of the word.

CHAPTER XXVIII

REAL ACTOR-MANAGEMENT

THESE two new controllers of the destinies of the Haymarket started operations there as soon as Tree vacated it. His last action was one worthy of his spaciousness and generosity. As soon as the curtain had fallen on the night of July 15th, 1896, and the house was clear of the public, Tree gave four supper parties simultaneously. On the stage he entertained the company; in the auditorium, the stalls being cleared away, he entertained the stage staff; in the foyer he entertained the attendants, and in the refreshment saloon the orchestra. Nobody was forgotten. And he had another party for over 100 friends of his and his wife's at the Savoy Hotel.

One last thing is left to chronicle about Tree at the Haymarket. He installed electric light in the theatre. It had been the last to have gas laid on, and Tree brought electricity—he believed in light.

Maude and Harrison, in the home of English comedy, began with what was really a drama, a costume play, *Under the Red Robe*, adapted by Edward Ross from the famous novel by Stanley Weyman. But they were to find that the path of actor-management is by no means easy to tread. That argus-eyed guardian of public safety, the London County Council, demanded sweeping reforms back stage. They were, of course, quite right, as they always are, but it means loads of worry—and expense—for theatre people. So, instead of being able to rehearse on their own stage, they had to have a kind of tour of rehearsals borrowing stages of other theatres as and where they could.

They had got a magnificent cast, they were giving it a magnficent production, but for the moment everything was upset by the workmen. Nor was Maude set at ease by a message that H.R.H. the Prince of Wales desired to occupy the Royal Box for the opening night. Poor Maude doubted if it would be ready. But Harrison saw it through.

They were only just able, by the skin of their teeth, to get open on the date they had announced—October 17th, 1896. Cyril Maude suffered agonies of nerves on that occasion. He had his nerves as an actor, his nerves as an actor-manager with much at stake, and the knowledge that he had to live up to Haymarket traditions. He need not have worried, he was the right man in the right place.

Under the Red Robe was a triumphant success. Maude, the actor-manager, had not cast himself for the role of the hero, but played almost a minor character with a comedy trend, and, of course, played it beautifully. Herbert Waring was the duellist-hero, Gil de Berault, E. Holman Clark made an outstanding success as Clon, the dumb man, and Winifred Emery was the leading lady. What a lovely actress she was; her grace and her beauty were equalled by her talents. On and off the stage, she was gracious and charming. As an actress she was second to none. We look in vain for her equal to-day, for she could, and did, play anything.

Despite all their preliminary troubles, the play was a real success. It ran for 256 nights. It placed the new management firmly in the Haymarket saddle and showed London that a real actor-manager had come to Town. New names came along, too, to establish themselves. In that opening play were Sydney Valentine, playing Richelieu—a grand actor whose limp was hardly noticed by the audience, such was his command and power; Granville Barker played a small part, and there was young and pretty Eva Moore.

It was evident to all that Maude and Harrison were going to do things well. They followed with *A Marriage of Convenience*, adapted from the French by Sydney Grundy. William Terriss was in the cast, so were Sydney Valentine and Holman Clark. Those two men were acting together, many years afterwards, when poor Valentine died. He wore himself out working to bring about what is now British Actors' Equity; striving to prepare a contract which would be fair to both manager and actor. He succeeded, and "The Valentine" contract was accepted by both sides. It was the basis of Equity. But he was not a robust man and the toil and worry were too much for him. The play in which he and Clark were then appearing was *The Cinderella Man* at the Queen's Theatre. They were with another actor-manager, Owen Nares. All three have passed over now.

The Prince of Wales (Edward VII) came to see *The Marriage of Convenience*, and he sent for Terriss, Winifred Emery and Maude to express his pleasure. Maude was very nervous; so was his wife. Terriss put everyone at their ease by hoping that the Prince's horse would win the Gold Cup at Ascot the next day. That horse was the famous Persimmon. The Prince was delighted and there was a friendly chat.

Winifred Emery gave a beautiful performance in that play, so did Terriss, and, for the matter of that, so did Maude—for he had a better part than his previous one. Produced on June 5th, 1897, Diamond Jubilee Year—it ran for 113 performances.

Then came a play which must rank very highly in Haymarket history. They brought to the stage that famous novel of J. M. Barrie's (he was not knighted then), *The Little Minister*. Barrie dramatised it himself. He came to all the rehearsals, and once he nearly got killed. Maude had a little platform built out from the stage over the orchestra pit, as do most producers (or they did then) so that he could watch the action and be able to step straight on to the stage and make his alterations and suggestions. Barrie sat with him on this. Barrie liked to sit back in his chair and tilt it about. He leaned it against the railing and lolled back. The rail broke, and author and chair disappeared into the orchestra pit. No great depth, but a nasty fall and a nastier shock to a man never very strong. Barrie was stunned, but soon recovered, and the rehearsals went on; Barrie made light of it all, but it might have been very serious indeed.

Maude gives much of the credit for the success of *The Little Minister* to his wife's performance as Babbie. He is justified, but the whole thing was superbly played and superbly produced. Winifred Emery, as Babbie, had a part which called for every emotion an actress could show, and she had command of them all. That performance ranks high in the annals of Haymarket acting. Maude surrounded her with the very best available. W. G. Elliott played the Earl of Rintoul; C. M. Hallard, Captain Halliwell; Sydney Valentine, now a Haymarket stalwart, was Rob Dow, and was splendid; Sydney Fairbrother was Micah, a delightful actress playing a boy; Mrs. E. H. Brooke, an old Haymarket hand, played Nancy Webster. The Elders, in the skilled hands of Brandon Thomas, Mark Kinghorne, W. H. Tyler and E. Holman Clark, might have stepped straight out of the pages of the novel. And the Little Minister—the Reverend Gavin Dishart—himself? That was Cyril Maude. Some of his admirers—and he had multitudes—were a little dubious about this when it was announced. They looked upon Maude as a comedian, a character performer; they had forgotten he was also a first-class actor in every sense of the word. He gave a performance equal to that of his wife. It was full of grace, charm, wistfulness and had all the firmness and romance required. *The Little Minister* was a typical Haymarket triumph, a distinguished piece of work by a distinguished management. Everything about it was right. The music was composed by Sir Alexander Mackenzie, then the Principal of the Royal Academy of Music and our most distinguished musician. He would take no fee. But Maude and Harrison would not hear of this and gave him a vast silver bowl as a token of their gratitude.

In the days of Maude and Harrison a fine reserved seat at the Haymarket in that upper circle to which the Bancrofts had banished the pit could be had for 2s. Theatre-going was joyous then. And the Haymarket, always delightful, was never more so than when Maude and Harrison were in control, with the wise Horace Watson in front, and Maude and his wife—the perfect couple on and off the stage—to play the leads. This was their home—and it is equally delightful to remember that they first met at the Haymarket, where they were introduced by friends in a box one night.

The Little Minister, produced on November 6th, 1897, ran for 320 performances. Now more than ever before was the Haymarket the home of English comedy. Taste, charm and good acting—and wise play-picking—set this management on a pinnacle. Names were on the programme which were later destined for more prominent type; they were earning their experience and winning their spurs at the Haymarket—people like Bernard Gould, Dawson Milward.

J. L. Mackay, Annie Saker, Clarence Blakiston, and Cosmo Hamilton
(afterwards a popular novelist and playwright).

A strange interlude enters the story here. There was a new dramatist
who had come over the horizon with a considerable stir. Two years
previously, Maude, very daring, had asked him for a play. The man,
red-bearded and outspoken, said he would write one for him. According
to Cyril Maude, the dramatist then engaged a chair in Regent's Park for
the whole season and, seated thereon, wrote the play. This man was
new, he was unconventional, he was iconoclastic. He delivered his
manuscript in 1897. It was called *You Never can Tell*. The author was
Bernard Shaw. The Harrison-Maude management read it, and it seemed
to them that the title was appropriate. They could not tell at all. It was
utterly different to anything they had so far seen or tackled. But they
went into rehearsal. Maude wanted to do the play because the character
he was to play in it—William, the waiter—attracted him enormously.
But they found they had bought a bundle of trouble. The cast rebelled.
J. H. Barnes and Miss Coleman resigned. Harrison had never wanted
to do the play—it was Maude who insisted. Allan Aynesworth, that
distinguished actor who graced everything he touched and is still
to-day the embodiment of Edwardian charm and dignity, fought with
the author, who became despotic at rehearsals. Aynesworth thought the
speeches too long. The author, armed with an enormous blue pencil,
struck out about seventeen of them. Such drastic slaughter suited
nobody. There was general chaos, with Winifred Emery trying
to keep the peace and Cyril Maude hoping against hope that he
would play William. Kate Bishop was called in to play the part
surrendered by Miss Coleman; Sydney Valentine took up that of
J. H. Barnes.

Harrison, now roused, took a hand in the matter. There would
be no production—and there was not. The author took away his play—
and so Maude never played the part which he had so adored. He hopes
to play it yet and there are those who desire to help him to do so, for
that part would give him a chance of the best performance of his many
acting masterpieces. *You Never can Tell* did not make active Haymarket
history—although it wrote a chapter back stage. It is now a classic, and
still Maude hopes.

A whole volume could be written of the Harrison-Maude régime
at the Haymarket. It was the perfect mirror of its time—the grand,
spacious days of peace, plenty, golden sovereigns, leisure, quality and
security. And nowhere better than at the Haymarket was all this displayed. The gracious theatre itself, the acting of Winifred Emery and
Cyril Maude and their distinguished casts, the judgment and control of
Harrison, the sheen and gloss of it all, makes those who remember it
sigh for yesterday. Those well-dressed audiences, those happy people,
those nights when one knew that to-morrow would be as to-day—
when London was a gleaming city of fresh paint and window boxes, and

Miss Marie Löhr.

Mrs. Patrick Campbell.

Mrs. Brown Potter.

Miss Billie Burke.

taxation was a thing which worried the very few—a world which crumbled into dust in 1914, never to return.

In 1898, instead of Shaw, they staged a play by Henry Arthur Jones, called *The Manœuvres of Jane*. This gave Maude a splendid comedy part as Lord Bapchild, in which he truly revelled. So did his audiences. He had a rough time with the author. Maude got laughs by the hundred and naturally always wanted more. So he gagged, and gagged well. Henry Arthur Jones took a very poor view of this, and deluged him with complaints. He pursued Maude everywhere he went. When that actor took his ride in Rotten Row, as he loved to do in the mornings, he would hear hoofbeats pounding up behind him. Then he would hear Jones calling him, accusing him of his gags, deriding him. Maude would break into a canter, so would the author, Maude would make his horse gallop: the author did likewise. Round they would go in a mad chase and above the thudding of the hooves Maude could still hear the jeremiad of Jones. But Maude stuck to his guns. He kept the gags in—and added to them.

Produced on October 29th, 1898, the play ran for 281 performances. The gags were justified, but the royalties which accrued never appeased Henry Arthur Jones.

A Golden Wedding and *The Black Tulip* did not run very long. So there was a revival of *She Stoops to Conquer* in 1900, which was old English comedy played in the old English home of comedy just as it should be played and presented.

But the Boer War had come, and that early succession of disasters had fallen upon the Kingdom, to shake the people's belief, for the moment, in the military might of their chosen commanders, and to plunge many families into mourning and more into economic straits.

At the Haymarket they never lost faith. They had especial faith in at least one man who was commanding on the British side. For he had played on the stage of that theatre, he was therefore one of themselves. Cyril Maude, an Old Carthusian, had organised some matinées in aid of the Charterhouse mission. The cast had been partly professional, partly amateur. But one of the undoubted stars of that performance was an amateur actor and professional soldier, whose name was Colonel R. S. S. Baden-Powell. The bill consisted of a scene from *The School for Scandal, Gringoire, A Queen's Messenger*, a one-act play by Hartley Manners (afterwards to earn fame as author of *Peg o' My Heart*) and a special burlesque of Charterhouse flavour and topicalities, in which B.-P. played lead. As an actor he worked just as hard and enthusiastically as he did as a soldier or, in after years, as Chief Scout. At one rehearsal he appeared in his full cavalry uniform, which he had to wear as he was going straight from rehearsal to a function. He made a great hit in that show. In it he had to address a succession of Charterhouse "ghosts," the last being the spirit of the great soldier, Havelock. A few days later he himself was off to Mafeking, to write a page in the

Y

history of Britain at war which will never be forgotten, and to put a word into the English language, to say nothing of giving the world the magnificent Boy Scout movement. And he played at the Haymarket.

Not many theatres can claim great soldiers in their history, although General Burgoyne wrote a successful play for Drury Lane and Lord Kitchener supervised a battle scene for a Drury Lane drama—and joined the Drury Lane Lodge, to which he presented one of his swords of honour. The Haymarket, however, has B.-P., and a more suitable man for that theatre could not have been found.

Is it surprising that, with such inspiration, the Haymarket went all military and by so doing produced one of its best comedies and gave to Cyril Maude one of his best parts? The play was *The Second in Command*, by Captain Robert Marshall, produced there on November 27th, 1900, to run for 378 performances. It was the perfect comedy of its period—a period when the Army was a "professional" one, the officers thereof men of good family and social position. They were very gallant gentlemen who fought nobly and died bravely in their country's cause. The only pity was that so many of them died needlessly, because of the hide-bound tradition of those days. It was with these men that the play dealt. It was when "spit and polish" ruled, when khaki was new and somewhat deplored as drab, dull, not to say vulgar; of the days when a uniform mattered; when a soldier in full dress represented the romance and glory of war undimmed by items like high explosives, aeroplanes, flame-throwers, poison gas, tanks and atomic bombs; when a man could still keep his own head and possibly deprive the other fellow of his—although the war with which it dealt had precious little glory and much long-range death about it. Still, however, the martial romance clung, and *The Second in Command* had its full share.

Maude produced the play beautifully; he got every ounce out of it. The uniforms were correctly made by the finest firm of military tailors, but at a dress rehearsal a young subaltern was thrown into despair because he claimed that the trouser stripe on the orderly's overalls was too wide. Such things mattered terribly. Again there was a fine cast. Herbert Sleath, Allan Aynesworth, Wilfred Forster, Sybil Carlisle, A. Vane Tempest, Fanny Coleman (she approved this play more than she had done *You Never can Tell*), and Muriel Beaumont. Winifred Emery was not in it—a happy event was pending which subsequently provided the English Bar with a distinguished figure. Cyril Maude played Major Christopher Bingham of the Dragoons. His performance was a masterpiece. He was "The Second in Command," the gentleman, the lovable figure of a good-natured, rather thick-headed, well-intentioned soldier, brave as a lion but modest as a violet, always good form, because that he could not help, and always most sympathetic and lovable. In the end he got the V.C., to his own complete astonishment, and the only thing about the play with which the audience disagreed was his murmured, self-conscious and very confused remark: "I wish—

I wish—I was worth it." *The Second in Command* as a period play
should rank as a classic in stage repertoires. It was of its time a gem of
perfection, a reflex of current thought, taste and manners. It was a
tribute to that little British Army which went a damn long way and
always managed to win in the end, largely because of men like "Major
Christopher Bingham." To say that Maude was perfect in the part is
not to overstate. He was unforgettable. It was real Haymarket.

This play was followed by a revival of Robertson's *Caste*, with Maude
as the ideal Eccles. His wife was back again, and it was a triumph for
both. And before the production of *The Second in Command* they had
presented *The School for Scandal*, showing Maude as the ideal Sir
Peter and his wife the equally ideal Lady Teazel; also *The Rivals*,
with Winifred Emery as Lydia and Maude as Bob Acres—a delightful
Bob Acres.

Those old English comedies shone with brilliance in their perfect
settings. And in 1900 they had also produced *Frocks and Frills*, a
play about a dress shop. Maude, whose standard was accuracy, paid
visits to real dress shops and was very embarrassed amongst the
glamorous mannequins. And the experts called in—leading costumiers
—all judged the play solely from the point of view of the dresses and
how they were worn, like the subaltern critic of *The Second in Command*.
Frocks and Frills, produced in January, 1902, ran for 113 performances,
and Maude made a personal success.

Then came *There's Many a Slip* in 1902, and *The Unforeseen* in
the same year, neither of much account. So Maude fell back again on
old English comedy and presented *The Clandestine Marriage*, an
essentially Haymarket play, for its authors were George Colman the
Elder, a Haymarket manager, and David Garrick. Maude played Lord
Ogleby. However good King may have been as its creator—Garrick
had refused it, and always regretted doing so—he can never have
transcended Maude.

The picture of gallant senility—always a gentleman with a young
heart despite the ravages of the years—which Maude gave, was a *tour
de force*. His famous scene when he makes his toilet, or, rather, has
his toilet made for him, was wonderful. And, of course, there was an
ideal cast.

There was Mrs. Charles Calvert as Mrs. Heidelberg, A. E. Matthews
as Brush, the valet, Eric Lewis as Canton (and what an actor), Allan
Aynesworth as Sir John Melville (and perfect), Albert Bernard, George
Trollope, Vivian Robins, Jessie Bateman, Maidie Hope and Violet
Darrell, and many others. An enormous success for all.

From old comedy they went to modern comedy, presenting *Cousin
Kate*, by Hubert Henry Davies. Here Maude was his own sprightly self
again, all senility gone, but replaced by his particular charm and art.
He was partnered by that magnificent actress, Ellis Jeffreys, and between
them they gave Haymarket audiences a splendid time in this slight but

very amusing and well-made play. Beatrice Ferrar, who became a Haymarket pillar of strength, Rudge Harding and Pamela Gaythorne were also in the cast. Produced on June 18th, 1903, it ran for 242 performances. In the October of that year, Maude gave it a curtain raiser, and played in it as well. This was W. W. Jacobs' grim super-thriller, *The Monkey's Paw*. The sense of paralysing fear that Maude evoked in that cameo (which he made a standby) contrasted with the gaiety of the light-hearted Irishman he played in the main play.

On October 6th, 1903, *Joseph Entangled* was produced, with Maude as Sir Joseph Lacy. They were all entangled on the first night of this, for there was a fire back stage unsuspected by the audience and then the electric light failed. But the show ran for 127 performances, largely on Maude's performance. He had his following—all the actor-managers had their faithful adherents who came to see them, no matter how badly the critics had treated the play. And how right those followers were: they always saw something worth remembering. After the production of *Lady Flirt*, the Haymarket had to be redecorated, and Maude went to the New Theatre to do a play which he was to bring to the Haymarket in due course.

Mention of *The Monkey's Paw* brings up the question of curtain-raisers, those often delightful and always welcome little one-act plays whereby the actor-managers gave full value to the clients of the cheaper parts of their house, and also chances to understudies and rising players. The Haymarket was a stronghold of them. There were *The Shades of Night*, *The Ghost of Jerry Bundler* (another Jacobs drama), *Compromising Martha*, *Charley the Sport*, *The Nelson Touch* and a host of others. There certainly was value for money at the Haymarket in Edwardian days.

The play which Maude produced at the New and then took back to the redecorated Haymarket Theatre in 1905 was *Beauty and the Barge*. This was a W. W. Jacobs' full-length play and it was of Haymarket vintage. Cyril Maude played Captain Barley, the old amorous, light-hearted bargemaster. He made it one of his many masterpieces. In the cast were Kenneth Douglas, Edmund Maurice, Frederick Volpe, Mary Brough, Lennox Pawle, E. M. Robson, Jessie Bateman, Marsh Allen, and other fine players. The scene on the riverside with the sailing-barge moored alongside, and the scene in the inn with buxom flaxen-haired Mary Brough, in a satin blouse of violent blue, as the landlady, little E. M. Robson as the tiny but valiant chucker-out and Lennox Pawle as the burly Mate were joys. But the greatest joy was the Captain Barley of Cyril Maude—whose watchword, explaining all his peccadilloes and interferences, was "Affability, that's what it is with me. No harm. Too much affability." *Beauty and the Barge* was a high spot at the Haymarket.

Maude and Harrison then presented *Everybody's Secret*. There was, however, another and unfortunate secret which was leaking out. All was not well at the Haymarket. There were differences of opinion

between the two partners. That association which had put on so many
plays, added such lustre to the Haymarket in particular, and the
English theatre in general, was drawing towards its end. The rights
and wrongs of that ever-to-be-regretted difference or its whys and
wherefores are no concern of this story—a story which has to do with the
history of the theatre and not the private business of those directing it.
The split must be chronicled because it affects the destiny of the
Haymarket, and that is all. But there was still a little longer of this two-
handed glory. Maude appeared as Napoleon Buonaparte in *The Creole*
in May, 1905, and as Joseph Lebanon, the pushful, interfering Jew, in a
revival of Pinero's *The Cabinet Minister* in June, 1905.

Then the partnership came to an end. Frederick Harrison and
Cyril Maude, who had between them done so much for the continued
fame of the Haymarket Theatre, who had presented plays with perfect
casts, exquisite stagings and flawless acting for nine years, dissolved
their association. The public received the news with dismay. They knew
Maude the actor better than they knew Harrison. But they were also
aware of the teamwork that existed.

Cyril Maude, who was perhaps the most typical of all Haymarket
actors, left that perfect setting for his art and went into management
at the Playhouse Theatre—the old Avenue, upon which Charing Cross
Station fell. It nearly ruined him, but he won through and gave a fresh
and brilliant chapter of history to that riverside theatre which was for
so many more years his own home.

When one thinks of the Haymarket one thinks instinctively of
Cyril Maude—they are synonymous.

In 1900, when Maude went on tour for a while, he let the theatre to
that couple of old Haymarketians, Julia Neilson and Fred Terry. They
wanted to produce a play about Nell Gwynne. Indeed, they were in
something of a hurry, for Marie Tempest, also in management, had a
play on the same subject. It was a race between them. Their play was
Sweet Nell of Old Drury; Marie Tempest's play was *English Nell*,
written by Paul Kester. The rehearsals of both *English Nell* and *Sweet
Nell of Old Drury* started much about the same time, but the Terrys
had some of the usual troubles with production—more than their share
this time—and Marie Tempest won the race and got her play on first
at the Prince of Wales's Theatre on August 21st, 1900. The Terrys
produced on August 30th, 1900, nine days later.

Would London stand two plays about Nell Gwynne, with two of the
most popular actresses opposed in the part? The answer was that they
would. *English Nell* ran for 161 performances. *Sweet Nell of Old Drury*
never stopped running whilst that wonderful couple held the stage
together. They took it to the Globe (the old Globe) when Maude
returned to the Haymarket, and it still ran on; it was revived, it was
toured, it was played with Phyllis Neilson Terry in her mother's part
—altogether it was a glorious success. That Julia Neilson was not a bit

like Mistress Nellie mattered not a whit. Everyone loved her—as they loved the original of her part—and she gave a beautiful performance. Fred Terry's study of Charles II was a perfect and unforgettable portrait.

In the original cast, with the Terrys, were Louis Calvert, C. M. Hallard, Arthur Royston, Sydney Brough, Lionel Brough, Loring Fernie, Malcolm Cherry, Fred Volpe, E. V. Rae, Arthur Applin, Leon M. Lion, Fred Sargent, Clito Clifford, Constance Collier, Lilian Jefferys, Lilian Braithwaite and Mary Mackenzie. What a galaxy; stars of the day, old Haymarket names, and stars to come. *Sweet Nell of Old Drury* is a Haymarket play and a Haymarket success.

On another occasion when Maude went on tour—he did this regularly and showed his good sense—the theatre was let to Mrs. Langtry. She, it will be remembered, had made her debut there. She came back in 1898 as actress-manageress to produce *The Degenerates*. There was a wild rumour that this play by Sydney Grundy was founded on her own life. Not a word of truth in it; but it was fine publicity all the same. The regular Haymarket audiences who turned up found themselves in strange company. For Mrs. Langtry was now a Queen of the Turf, and the loyal sporting fraternity came along to support her theatrical venture. Jockeys, trainers, bookmakers, and racegoers thronged the sedate, stately theatre, odd conversations concerning running and prices were heard, tips were given and taken and the bars did the record trade of the theatre's history. There is a rumour that one Sunday afternoon a cockfight was held there—but this has never been proved. Mrs. Langtry did other seasons there. She had become a good actress, despite those who decried her, and she was, besides being a very beautiful, a very clever woman indeed.

Charles Hawtrey was her leading man in *The Degenerates*, but he had to leave for another engagement, and Fred Kerr took his place.

There was a stage-door keeper then called Horsford, who had been there with Tree. He would report to Tree his opinion of the company for each new play as they assembled for the first rehearsal. "I've seen the company, Mr. Tree, sir," he would say; "it's a fine body of men." The old Army sergeant judged in the old Army way. He was a loyal servant, but not perhaps always a tactful one, although he always meant well and what he said came from his heart. After a first night he informed Tree, with delight in his countenance, "You've had a great success to-night, sir. I see two gents comin' out of the pit circle and as they was passing one said to the other that there weren't ten or a dozen actors wot could have took your bit better." But Tree understood him and adored it all.

When, in 1905, Cyril Maude left the Haymarket, Frederick Harrison carried on by himself. He also was the embodiment of the Haymarket tradition from the managerial point of view. He was never so much in the limelight as Maude, although he had been an actor. He kept with him Horace Watson as his right-hand man—Horace Watson the wise, who knew as much about the Haymarket as did Harrison. He also kept Leverton in the box office—and the Haymarket box office would have seemed strange indeed without him. A jewel had gone from the Haymarket string, never to be properly replaced, but the chain was intact. Harrison knew his public, he knew his audiences, he knew the taste of his people, and above all he had that quality the theatre required.

His reign extended right down to modern times; it was long, distinguished and it was most prosperous. It is quite impossible, because of limitations of space (for this history is written at a time of austerity when paper is scarce), to give a record of every play produced at the Haymarket right down to the time of writing. Highlights must therefore be studied in as much detail as possible and many deserving cases passed over with a mere mention; some must be omitted altogether.

To say that Harrison had given up acting during the Harrison-Maude régime is not quite correct. He had made a few appearances for the grease paint is hard to get out of the mental pores of a man of the theatre. He had wanted to appear in *Under the Red Robe*, but Maude had dissuaded him. He had, however, played William of Orange in *The Black Tulip*, the Comte de Candale in *A Marriage of Convenience* and Falkland in *The Rivals*, and had given a good account of himself. He ruled the Haymarket wisely and well for thirty years, nine of them in association with Maude and the rest by himself, from 1896 to 1926, when he died.

His record of success and production was remarkable. He was like a dealer in precious stones, the gems being the plays. Some of them were of pure water, some almost priceless, some of lesser lustre, and there were quite a few which were flawed and almost worthless. It must be the course of this history, therefore, to pick out the gems which are worthiest and leave the rest. Some plays were his own ventures, in some he shared with others, sometimes he let the theatre. But he never did a play which in his judgment was unworthy; he never allowed any play to come into this theatre which was not, to his mind, worth-while, nor a management to have the privilege of occupying the Haymarket Theatre unless he considered they were of sufficient calibre. His staff were his to a man—and a woman. They were as loyal to him as he was to them. All of his period is of the best time of the theatre, when theatrical management in the West End of London was a business for experts only and adventurers were not permitted—certainly never permitted at the Haymarket.

When he died, this handsome, distinguished man, a playgoer thought he had discovered a new Haymarket ghost. There, sitting in a box, his eyes told him, was what must be the ghost of Frederick Harrison, loth, like Buckstone, to quit his beloved home. But it was not a ghost; it was a living man—John Galsworthy. The problem was solved by Hannen Swaffer, the famous journalist and critic, who was in the theatre and to whom the worried playgoer appealed. As usual, Swaffer was right.

When Cyril Maude left, Frederick Harrison got another famous actor-manager to join him. This was Charles Hawtrey, the prince of light comedians, a different type from Cyril Maude, but of the Haymarket quality all the same. Hawtrey was a great character and a superb actor. His was the art which concealed art. He never appeared to be acting. He was absolutely natural to the inexpert eye, but acting full steam nevertheless. For years he had been famous as the greatest "liar" on the stage. There was nobody like him, in farce or comedy, to lie his way into and out of a difficult situation, with such ease, assurance, and aplomb. The public always wanted him to be the same; they wanted that bland stare, that calm exterior, that easy manner, and they wanted that impeccable moustache. Once he shaved it off to play in a costume part. It was unpopular. So he grew his moustache again, became the good-natured, untruthful philanderer with a heart of gold, and filled the theatre. Hawtrey was really a great actor who was never allowed to be so. He was, for quality and style, the right choice for Harrison. But those associated with Hawtrey in business usually found after a time that he lacked any financial sense—and was always in monetary difficulties. There was no bad intent, no desire for gain; he just could not help it. And nobody liked him any the less or admired him any the less either.

Harrison joined hands with him in 1906. They staged *The Indecision of Mr. Kingsbury*, a revival of that great Hawtrey success, *The Man from Blankley's*, by F. Anstey; *Lady Huntworth's Experiment*, a delightful comedy written by R. C. Carton. Miss Compton was in the lead, and there were good parts for Hawtrey and for Weedon Grossmith. And then *Her Grace the Reformer*, by Mrs. Henry de la Pasture, saw the end of the Hawtrey period in 1907. The Haymarket was not having luck.

But it is one of the axioms of the theatre that better luck is always round the corner. It is less of a gamble running the Haymarket than it is with any other theatre. It attracts the best by its own prestige. Its management is able to take its pick of offerings, of dramatists and very largely of actors.

The plays which filled the Haymarket stage from 1907 until 1947 and have left a mark will be duly chronicled as the history of the Haymarket draws to its present close—a close only so far as this book is concerned. May the day be far off when it closes altogether.

CHAPTER XXIX

A PAGEANT OF PLAYS

THERE were some plays after the Hawtrey régime which linger in the memory of Haymarket playgoers, some successful, some not so successful, some downright failures and a cause for what is known in the theatre as the "Bird." Sometimes the "bird," even at this stately theatre, almost reached the proportions of a good, old-fashioned Haymarket riot. But those occasions have been few in this perfect playhouse in more recent years. The Haymarket went on, as it goes on to-day, making new names, giving young players a chance to make good in its ideal surroundings, giving them the breath of tradition to strengthen their inexperience and immaturity. As an instance, on May 28th, 1907, a young Australian actress, who had played only minor parts in London, stepped into a leading role in a comedy called *My Wife*. Her name was Marie Lohr, and she was seventeen. Of true theatrical stock, she was born in Sydney, New South Wales. Her mother was that fine actress, Kate Bishop, her father Lewis J. Lohr, of the Opera House, Melbourne. She had played as a child in Australia; she had come over here and played, also as a child, at the Garrick in 1901. Then she toured with the Kendals, afterwards playing tiny parts in Town. She had rejoined the Kendals, and then Tree had given her a chance, of which she took full advantage, as Rosie Mackenzie in *The Newcomes* at His Majesty's. She went back with the Kendals again and then— she came to the Haymarket. As Beatrix Dupré in *My Wife*, the lightest of light comedies, she made an immediate success. It marked her for stardom. It was a charmingly young, fresh and natural performance —all of which attributes this lovely actress retains to-day. C. Aubrey Smith (now so justly knighted), Fred Lewis and that eternally young and eternally excellent actor, A. E. Matthews, were also in the cast. Matthews made a big success in his scene where, as a very smart and particular young man, he turned up a complete wreck as a result of travelling half across Europe in a third-class non-sleeper. It was a gem of comedy acting.

Eva Moore gave a delightful performance in 1907, in a beautifully mounted costume play called *Sweet Kitty Bellairs*. It was a dramatised version of a popular novel by Alice and Egerton Castle. Here was all the romance, colour and stateliness of the eighteenth century, and Eva Moore was the very embodiment of the fascinating, lovely and re-sourceful young widow, Kitty Bellairs.

And in the same year, 1907, there came to the Haymarket a very stubborn success which had at first been turned down by that theatre's play-readers. It eventually got produced elsewhere and it went from West End theatre to West End theatre on a kind of tour of the town. It made the reputation of its author, Somerset Maugham, and it put the seal of greatness in straight plays (she was already a star of musical comedy) upon its leading lady—Ethel Irving. The play was *Lady Frederick*. The scene in which Lady Frederick damns the calf-love of her young admirer by admitting him to her toilette secrets (considered very daring then), and the finished acting of Ethel Irving and C. M. Lowne had a fitting setting at the Haymarket. Indeed, Ethel Irving became the Haymarket's leading lady, remaining on there to play in *Dolly Reforming Herself* in 1908, which ran for 120 performances. She also appeared as Kate Hardcastle in a very beautiful revival of *She Stoops to Conquer*, which had a limited season, but which was of the highest quality. Holman Clark played Old Hardcastle and Robert Loraine was young Marlow, with the best possible Tony Lumpkin in George Giddens.

There was a sad story in 1909. Billie Burke, who had become very popular in this country before going back to America, returned with a comedy which had been a success for her in New York. She brought it to the Haymarket, and London was prepared to welcome this pretty auburn-haired actress who was so fascinating and alluring. But the play, *Love Watches*, was more than even the well-bred Haymarket audience could stand. That play got the "bird" well and truly. The patrons wanted to be kind to Billie Burke, but they would not have *Love Watches* at any price whatever.

Better days and better plays were in store. Herbert Trench came to the Haymarket Theatre and an era of glory ensued. Trench, a man of great taste and distinction, a man who believed in quality—in fact, a man with the true Haymarket spirit, wrote a glowing page in the history of that theatre.

He began operations with a production of *King Lear*. This alone was exciting. It had not been seen in the West End since Irving had produced it in 1881 at the Lyceum, twenty-eight years previously. To launch this tragedy—with its so-called unactable part of the mad King —as the beginning of a policy was a bold and arresting stroke. But Trench never lacked courage. He believed in the theatre. He presented *King Lear* on September 8th, 1909. Norman McKinnel was Lear, and Ellen O'Malley Cordelia. Marie Polini (afterwards Mrs. Owen Nares, and always a fine actress) was Regan, Charles Quartermaine a grand Edgar, Dawson Milward a handsome and villainous Edmund, James Hearn Gloucester, C. V. France Kent, Fisher White Cornwall, whilst H. R. Hignett was a very excellent Fool. The production fitted the play —it was simple, Druidical and stern. It was, here and there, impression-istic; it used a form of lighting for cloud and storm effects which was then novel, but it never stepped out of the period. One believed in the blasted heath, one believed in the savagery—it was of the iron age—it owed nothing to whimsy or children's picture books. The Heath, the Cliff, the Hovel, and Lear's Throne of monoliths were all true to the play—and the fight between Edgar and Edmund one of the best-staged battles ever seen. It's only weak spot was the Lear of Norman McKinnel. He gave, as always, a sound and earnest performance. He was powerful, he was everything—except Lear. He never quite got inside the pathos of the old man. His rages were not terrifying, nor were his curses. But it was, nevertheless, the best Lear the stage could show in 1909, when tragedy was at a discount. McKinnel was a fine actor, but Lear is a monumental part requiring almost divine inspiration. McKinnel was not inspired. It was a memorable production and was well received. But it did not bring the public of 1909 into the Haymarket Theatre.

Trench then staged a comedy, by Rudolf Besier, called *Don*. This was a typical Haymarket production written by an expert dramatist with something to say, produced with perfection and acted as it deserved. It is indeed as nearly perfect a comedy as can be found. It even preserved the "unities," for when the curtain fell on an act, the action of the next scene started from that situation. Trench had got together what was to all intents and purposes a stock company. It was the days of the old Haymarket of Webster and Buckstone returned. *Don* had realism, wit, characterisation and drama of the highest order. Charles Quartermaine, in the title role, gave one of the most finished performances the Haymarket has ever seen. And the rest were on that level too. What a cast it was. Besides Quartermaine, there was Dawson Milward, James Hearn, Ellen O'Malley, Charlotte Granville, Christine Silver, Frances Ivor and Norman McKinnel. Here Norman McKinnel had a part which fitted him like a glove. He did not enter until the last act, but his presence hung over the play like a menace all through. He was a stern, religious fanatic, prepared to kill in his zeal and ardour, ready to take life to prevent or punish sin. The scene between him and Quartermaine, where McKinnel held the unconventional young man at the pistol's mouth, was one of the strongest ever seen in a theatre. *Don* very justly ran for 208 performances.

On December 8th, 1909, Herbert Trench made another experiment. He staged Maeterlinck's *Blue Bird*. This was a large, expensive and very lavish production—lavish in size, but exquisite in colour, beauty and taste. It was as daring in its way as *King Lear*. Sophisticated London might easily have laughed at the phantasy of the poem—for poem it was. Tree had failed with *The Emperor's New Clothes*. Trench risked failure with this.

But the London of 1909 was sophisticated in a different way from the London of 1947. It was not so tired, it did not live so fast, it was always younger at heart and much more sentimental and simple. Also, it had not forgotten leisure; it had time to think and time to linger over beauty. Still, there were many who had their doubts. There was a huge cast and many elaborate scenes. Two children played the leading roles. People sensed it as a Christmas show—a species of pantomime. There were characters called Sugar, Fire, Bread; there was a cat and a dog. The wise folk nodded their heads and said, "Oh yes, nice for the kiddies, a pleasant change from the Drury Lane panto." Few had read the play. Fewer knew anything about it at all. But the Haymarket was packed with a smart audience when the night came. They watched those two children, Tyltyl and Myltyl search for the Blue Bird of Happiness. There was a superior, condescending smile on many faces. But that soon went. The sheer beauty of the whole thing began to grip that smart, satiny, starched-shirt audience. Eyes began to grow moist, throats began to contract, not so much with sadness as with the joy of beholding a lovely thing. Norman O'Neill's perfect music stole over their senses. The Dog of Ernest Hendrie, a perfectly marvellous performance, honest, rough, upright, intelligent and always the friend of man—the only friend—in the animal world, was balanced by the sleek, sinister, velvet Cat of Norman Page, impassive, cunning and stealthy. Fisher White was as rugged as the Oak he represented, and C. V. France was Time. The voices of the unborn, raised in triumphant song as they got ready to enter the world, the majestic beauty of their kingdom, was breathtaking—but when a graveyard filled the stage, the audience winced. Could Death ever be beautiful? had it any place in this thing of grandeur and joy? Yet there were the children amid the graves, calling upon the Dead! The audience almost closed its eyes in dread. And then came Tyltyl's triumphant cry: "There are no dead"— and all those humble but mournful mounds of earth sprang to life in radiant lilies. Stout, well-fed stockbrokers blew their noses and wiped their eyes, smart women cried unashamedly—and the whole house cheered the production to the echo. It was a first night such as the theatre—even the Haymarket—seldom sees. It was quite unforgettable. *The Blue Bird* ran for 274 performances and was revived the following year. Then the forest scene was omitted and another played instead. The only criticism was that it showed man as the enemy of all creation —animal, vegetable and mineral. Only the dog was man's friend—and at the same time, his slave. But most likely it is true. *The Blue Bird* is one of the brightest pages of the Haymarket story.

In 1910 another new name came to the old theatre. It belonged to the daughter of a man and woman who had both earned great fame there, Fred Terry and Julia Neilson. The daughter was lovely Phyllis Neilson-Terry, bearing both their names, and bearing them worthily. She had already appeared in her parents' company as Phillida Terson. She had understudied her mother and played for her. She had made a great success as Viola at His Majesty's, her father playing Sebastian, and now she crossed the road to the Haymarket to play her first leading part in comedy. The play was *Priscilla Runs Away*, and it was produced on June 28th, 1910. She was only eighteen, and as lovely as a young beech tree.

The play was a charming, romantic story of a mid-European court.

Phyllis Neilson-Terry made a big success, and with her in the cast were Lyall Swete, Charles Maude, C. V. France, Donald Calthrop and others. It ran for 192 performances.

The play which followed—*All that Matters*—was indeed another matter. It gave poor Phyl Terry a taste of an irritated audience. It was a long-drawn-out affair of the English countryside, with wise old labourers, a sort of domestic feud, a love affair which did not run smoothly—but nothing that mattered at all. Everything was too long, including the lingerie of one of the actresses, which trailed below her skirt and caused the audience, already bored, to snigger. They never got serious again. The clever and brilliant cast battled manfully, but it was useless. Such people as Norman Trevor, C. V. France, Lyall Swete, Helen Haye, Charles Maude, Fisher White, and Miss Terry herself, did their best —a grand best—but all to no purpose. A scene representing a seaside cave with waves dashing over the mouth of it, moved the gallery to derision. They wanted to know whether it was *Aladdin* or *The Forty Thieves*. In the last scene, Fisher White fought a pitched battle with the unruly house. He, as a wise (and somewhat annoying) old countryman, with a catchword, "Thank the Lord," had a very long speech to put over. There had been many long speeches and the "gods" were not in the mood for more. But so well did he play that scene, so well did he speak that speech, that his courage, skill and technique restored tranquillity. He drew towards the end. He paused, turned upstage, reached the door and again faced round. "One last word," he cried— and from the gallery a voice replied, "Thank the Lord!"

It was a bad night for the Haymarket, but there was no ill-feeling about it. The audience gave the players their meed of applause, despite the booing of the play.

There were happier times in 1911, when *Lady Patricia*, by Rudolf Besier, gave Mrs. Patrick Campbell a part which she played with such perfection that the audience purred with pleasure. It was an artificial comedy of manners, and its heroine was a woman of pure affectation and unreality—a poseur whose poses had become part of herself— yet attractive and charming and triumphant all the time. What a joy Mrs. Pat was in that play. And there was a lesson in the art of acting from C. V. France, as Baldwin, an almost entirely silent gardener, who held the whole house spellbound in a scene where he lit Chinese lanterns in a tree, repeating the same phrase over and over again. It sounds incredible, but it was a triumph. Athene Seyler, fresh from the Royal Academy of Dramatic Art, now one of our leading actresses, made her debut in *Lady Patricia*. Much of the action passed on a platform in the branches of a great tree. It was altogether delightful.

An extraordinary thing happened at the Haymarket in 1911. It was one of those occurrences which do happen in a theatre when all the rules are broken and yet trumps turn up all along the line. Trench took a chance—a very daring chance. He brought to the smart,

distinguished Haymarket Theatre a play and company of players which
had been playing in small towns and never expected to come to London
at all, let alone to the Haymarket. The play was a Scots comedy, the
players all Scots. It was all in dialect, and concerned Lowland Scots of
humble birth and degree. It did not seem the thing at all. Nobody had
heard of anyone in the cast. They were almost a big family; many of
them, indeed, did belong to the same family by birth or marriage. One
of them had written the play and took the leading part; the leading lady
was his daughter. The play was called *Bunty Pulls the Strings*. The
author was Graham Moffatt, and the Moffatt clan, male and female,
figured largely in the play. It was produced one lovely summer night,
July 11th, 1911. An almost unwilling audience attended. The stalls and
circle expected to be bored, while the cheaper gentry anticipated having
to register disapproval. For plays in the Scottish vernacular and plays
about Scottish life were not popular as a rule. Even the romantic
Highlands did not get across the footlights too well, and this was an
affair of parlours and kirkyards.

There was doubt and trepidation. But that play succeeded. It had
its audience standing up and cheering. Such real life, such observation,
such situations, such pungent and homely wit, so well told a story
and so well played it swept into success. Once again a genuine article
triumphed, for when a thing is real and sincere, it nearly always wins
out in the theatre. The author became famous, the cast stars overnight.
It did not thrill them overmuch. They were all troupers, used to
travelling about the country. The West End to them was just a "date"
like any other town. But it was a date they played for 617 performances,
leaving an ineffaceable memory when at last they went away.

If Herbert Trench had done nothing else at the Haymarket, *Bunty
Pulls the Strings* would have been sufficient. But that man, that poet
born at Avencore, Co. Cork, did much more than that. He wrote a
glorious page of Haymarket history. Educated at Haileybury and Oxford,
he was a Fellow of All Souls, and for years was Examiner for the Board
of Education. This absolutely untheatrical background was no handicap
to success. Theatre Guild of New York has discovered that. Trench's
season at the Haymarket has much the same stamp and distinction as the
work of the American Guild.

A triple bill followed *Bunty*—two one-act plays and a shortish
full-sized one. The one-act-ers were *The Joyous Adventure of Aristide
Pujol*, written by William J. Locke, with Leon M. Lion in the title role,
and *The Golden Doom*, an Assyrian or Babylonian play by Lord Dunsany,
with Allan Jeayes and Lyall Swete in the cast. There were a number of
curiously made up characters denominated as "Spies." They spoke no
word. One of them was Claude Rains.

The long play was *The Younger Generation*, by Stanley Houghton,
the brilliant young Manchester playwright whose early death robbed
our stage of one who would have enriched it. *The Younger Generation*

was an excellent domestic comedy. That triple bill was produced on November 19th, 1912. It ran for 114 performances.

On April 2nd, 1913, Laurence Irving came to the Haymarket. He did first a remarkable production of *The Pretenders* and then a play called *Typhoon*. This was a story of a Japanese who loved a French-woman. His Japanese friends disapproved, but love proved too strong. Then the woman did an unforgivable thing; she insulted a picture of the Mikado. Promptly her Jap lover killed her. At his trial for murder, his wily associates threw dust in the eyes of a stupid and bewildered French judge (wonderfully played by Arthur Whitby), and the prisoner got off. But he had broken the rules. His compatriots told him he must atone by committing *hari-kari*. So whilst they feasted in a room, behind the screen the Japanese who had loved too well and betrayed his trust "changed his world" in the approved Japanese way. A bare recital of the outline of this play conveys little of its frightening intensity. It revealed the menace of Japan at a time when this country was allied to her. Many who saw it discovered a side of the Japanese character of which they had been ignorant. The chief role was stupendously acted by Laurence Irving—there is no other word. It was one of the great performances of the British stage, and he was ably seconded by his wife, Mabel Hackney, and by Leon Quartermaine. Laurence Irving touched the heights his father had reached, and those lucky enough to have seen that performance hold the memory dear. But *Typhoon* did not catch the public taste immediately; it was transferred elsewhere before it met with success. It had to make room for a melodrama called *Within the Law*, a super-crook play. We have seen many such since, but this one was the first of its kind—slick, fast moving and novel. It was produced by Sir Herbert Tree, and in it Mabel Russell, hitherto a star of musical comedy and pantomime, made an outstanding dramatic success. *Within the Law* ran for 477 performances, and saw the great change fall upon our country when the war of 1914-18 darkened the skies and altered life for ever.

The Haymarket met the war with a revival of a play which its erstwhile actor-manager, Cyril Maude, had produced at the Playhouse after leaving the Haymarket. It was *The Flag Lieutenant*—one of Maude's best productions and performances. At the Haymarket his part was played by Godfrey Tearle, who was indeed a handsome naval officer. *The Flag Lieutenant* was the best naval play ever written.

But the Haymarket deserted the war theme and went back to comedy in April, 1915, with a big success called *Quinney's*, by Horace Annesley Vachell. This gave Henry Ainley one of his great parts, and as the blunt, bluff, plain-spoken dealer in antiques and curios he gave one of the finest of his gallery of wonderful portraits. Of its kind, *Quinney's* is a classic, but it owed much to Ainley, then at the top of his form, before the tragedy overcame him, blurring that genius and dimming that shining light of histrionic talent.

War looked in again, but in a very light and amusing manner, in 1917, with *General Post*, in which lovable George Tully made a great hit (it ran for 532 performances), and again in 1918 with *The Freedom of the Seas*, by Walter Hackett, with fine acting from Sydney Valentine and Marion Lorne (Mrs. Walter Hackett). In 1919 that almost legendary theatrical impresario, J. L. Sacks, the South African, brought a success to the Haymarket in the form of *Uncle Sam*.

Space runs short and there are yet so many jewels in the casket of the Haymarket. One, however, shines with such brilliance as to demand attention. Its production is a milestone in the theatre's record. The date is April 22nd, 1920; in the play *Mary Rose*. This masterpiece of Barrie's became an immortal. Its almost intangible magic captured the first audience who saw it as it has succeeding ones. But never since that first production has it had so perfect a cast. Beautiful Fay Compton, with that voice of music and that strange fey personality, was Barrie's heroine come to life. She gave a performance of transcendent, inspired artistry that lives whenever the play is recalled. She herself was under a spell. She says in her own book, of this part:

> "During rehearsals we all felt the spell of her; she weaved an enchantment of forgetfulness, brushing away from our minds the world of to-day, taking us back to the 'seventies, to her orchard and her pretty home, not allowing us to remember the streets and traffic of the nineteen-twenties or the reality of a stage, an auditorium or an audience."

What Fay Compton says of the part can be truly said of her own performance—a masterpiece of beauty, of stage technique, of complete and utter understanding. She took that audience with her to Fairyland when she went herself. This lovely play, a truly fitting play for the Haymarket, had a cast worthy of it, for besides Fay Compton, there were Leon Quartermaine, Mary Jerrold, Arthur Whitby, Norman Forbes and Ernest Thesiger, all perfect players for a perfect play. Norman O'Neill's music was so wonderful, it seemed to have grown naturally out of the play.

The stagecraft in the way of lighting and effects contrived by Charles La Trobe was also magnificent, adding to the wonderful whole. But then Charles La Trobe is part of the Haymarket, the stage director *par excellence*, who knows his theatre, its traditions, and the stage of the past and the present, who, like the Haymarket, keeps the grandeur of the older times, with the efficiency and speed of the present day— and who has served the Haymarket nobly for thirty years and more.

In *Mary Rose*, Barrie gave the world and the Haymarket one more classic play, a thing of perfection in a playhouse of perfection, and Fay Compton gave a performance which will live in history. She has given many such, she will give many more, but this was and will be outstanding. She became, very naturally, the Haymarket's leading lady.

Miss Ellen Terry
in her Lady
Macbeth Costume

~~Miss Ellen Terry.~~
Constance Collier
as cleopatra in
Beerbohm Tree's
production of
Anthony & Cleopatra
in 1906.

Mr. Henry Ainley.

THE MODERN TOUCH: Noel Coward and Moira Lister in a scene from
Present Laughter at the Haymarket Theatre, 1947.

She played in *The Circle* by Somerset Maugham, a fine play with a fine cast, including Allan Aynesworth, Holman Clark, Ernest Thesiger, Leon Quartermaine, Lottie Venne, Tonie Edgar Bruce, W. W. Palmer and Cecil Trouncer. There was trouble at the first night over inaudibility. Why, heaven only knows, with a cast like that. She appeared, too, with Leon Quartermaine—the two were married during the run, in 1921—in a revival of *Quality Street*; in *The Prisoner of Zenda* in 1923; in that lovely play *The Man with a Load of Mischief*, in 1925. She was also in *Ariadne*, by A. A. Milne (1925), *The White Witch* (1926), a revival of *Mary Rose*, and then she played Ophelia—a magnificent Ophelia—to the equally magnificent Hamlet of John Barrymore at the Haymarket in 1925. One thing Barrymore could not stand, was the British habit of serving teas in the auditorium during matinées. It is on record that he suddenly broke off in a soliloquy, leapt in the air in rage, shouted "Tea, tea, tea"—and having expressed himself, resumed his part. He has many sincere sympathisers.

Fay Compton also played *This Woman Business* at the Haymarket in 1926.

Other outstanding Haymarket successes at that time were *The Dover Road*, 1922, with Henry Ainley; *Havoc*, the splendid war play, in 1924, in which Richard Bird made a big success. In 1926 came another long-running play *Yellow Sands*, a Devonshire comedy by Eden Phillpotts, outstanding in which were Cedric Hardwicke, Ralph Richardson (now both knighted) and Frank Vosper. The year 1928 saw *The Fourth Wall*, a success, and at Christmas time a production of *Pickwick*, staged by Basil Dean, with Charles Laughton as Mr. Pickwick. Fine actor as Mr. Laughton is, he was not too happily cast as Pickwick, for his talents do not run along the lines of smiling benevolence; his personality is too strong for that gentle, simple-minded soul. The production was a thing of beauty, but it was not Dickens—because it was not Pickwick.

In 1929 a play was produced at the Haymarket which was fraught with drama of a personal nature, quite apart from its theatrical value. And its theatrical value was great, for it was by St. John Ervine, one of our very best dramatists, in his very best manner. The title was *The First Mrs. Fraser* and the leading lady was Dame Marie Tempest, on top of her form. The leading man was Henry Ainley and that was where the drama came in. Ainley had scored triumphs at the Haymarket, notably in *Quinney's*. Then he was missed from the stage. This magnificent actor, this fine, handsome man, this good fellow with a big heart and a voice of gold had a great failing. Others of his profession had suffered in the same way: Gustavus Brooke and, the greatest of them all, Edmund Kean. The latter had played at the Haymarket when his enemy drink robbed him of his fire and his immense power—a shadow of his former self. Ainley was suffering in the same way. He had put up a fight, he had struggled hard. He believed he had won. It had not been possible to employ him on the stage; he had gone away to wrestle with his fate.

Z

Now he came back; he was to try again. He stood upright, he looked his foe in the eye. And the Haymarket opened its doors to him. The first-night audience gathered and wondered. They wanted Ainley to succeed, they loved him, they admired him. He had not an enemy in the world, everyone wished him well. But what he had to do, he must do alone. So here he was, in the arena again, playing lead at the Haymarket. What were they to see? Was it to be a painful repetition of what they had seen before or was it to be the old Ainley in new endeavour? They need not have worried. Ainley had won. He was himself again—older maybe, but that was natural; a bit more rugged and showing his scars, but all the handsomer and stronger for that. It was the Ainley of *Quinney's* and pre-*Quinney's* whom the Haymarket audience cheered that night, back in his old form, as fine an actor as ever trod the Haymarket—or any other —boards. It was a night of triumph for Ainley, Marie Tempest, the whole cast, the author and the theatre, and the applause had a deeper and more sonorous note because one of the princes of the stage had come back again. That play ran from its first night, July 2nd, 1929, for 632 performances. And it was announced that Henry Ainley would play Hamlet for a series of matinées. He had never played this great part and expectation ran high. He studied it hard, he gave his whole mind to it, a mind now unclouded by the memory of his old foe. Perhaps he worked too hard, perhaps he was not yet strong enough for such an endeavour when he showed the Haymarket audience his Hamlet in April, 1930. It was a Hamlet played with speed, a Hamlet apt to run past himself, whose judgment could not keep pace with his anxious thoughts, a Hamlet of action but indecision. His unmatched voice spoke the lines with the music he could command as could few other people. It may not have been a great Hamlet, but it was a notable one. Alas! it was almost his swan song. It was his last classic role. A friend persuaded him to enter social life again, to partake of its pleasures and the old weakness reasserted itself, the old wound was reopened. Ainley played only a few more parts—no more at the Haymarket. The actor's foundation stone—his memory—failed him. The younger generation knew him only as a wonderful voice over the radio—where he could read his script—a great actor had gone from us—such a one as we seldom see to-day. He is in the Haymarket Valhalla, where he won his last great victory.

Other Haymarket memories are *Ten Minute Alibi*, a crime play of a novel kind, written by Barre Lyndon, which ran for the amazing number of 878 performances from its production in 1933; and in 1934 *Touch Wood*, by Dodie Smith, beautifully produced by Basil Dean. This authoress had not then discarded her *nom-de-plume* of C. L. Anthony. Flora Robson, Dennis Arundell, Stafford Hilliard, Eric Cowley, Marie Ney, Elliot Mason, Oriel Ross, Frank Pettingell and Dorothy Hyson were in the cast. There was *The Phantom Light*, by Evadne Price, a play which took place in a lighthouse, with fine performances by Gordon Harker and Edna Best, in which Harker ate the sausages and emulated Munden; there were two brilliant comedies by Ivor Novello, *Comedienne* and *Full House*, both starring that grand actress, Dame Lilian Braithwaite; and many others.

During the Second World War the Haymarket suffered from blast, but fortunately escaped serious damage. In a welter of wartime entertainment, it kept up its tradition and prestige. Its quality never varied, with H. M. Tennent's productions such as *The Doctor's Dilemma*, starring Vivien Leigh, with Peter Glenville, Frank Allenby, Morland Graham, George Ralph (that actor of quality and understanding) and Austen Trevor.

The same firm was also responsible for *No Time for Comedy*, by S. R. Behrman, with Diana Wynyard, Rex Harrison, Elisabeth Welch, Lili Palmer, Arthur Macrae and Walter Fitzgerald, also *Design for Living*, the Noel Coward play, with Diana Wynyard, Rex Harrison and Anton Walbrook. Noel Coward also did *This Happy Breed* and *Present Laughter*. There was a delightful *Love for Love*, there was *A Midsummer Night's Dream* done as a Carolian masque, a revival of *Hamlet* and of *The Duchess of Malfi*, all things of value and directed by John Gielgud —who played as well. There was also a revival of *Lady Windermere's Fan*. That is the sort of quality the Haymarket housed during the Second World War.

And last on the list, a new star, Eileen Herlie, young in years and experience, but a fitting leading lady for the perfect theatre.

To list all the plays, all the successes and also the occasional failures would need more space than post-war restrictions can grant. And this history is not for scholars; this is not a book of reference, but an attempt to tell the life-story of a theatre—and of those who gave it life—so as to interest those who do not approach the drama as students, or who may not even be playgoers.

One more highlight remains. On a spring afternoon in 1942 a young man of eighty came back to the Haymarket to celebrate his birthday. He had, in his day, contributed his full share to its greatness; he had been its actor-manager and had given it years of success. He had not changed, nor had the theatre to which he returned—alas! for one afternoon only. It was Cyril Maude come to show the Haymarket Theatre that at fourscore years he was as young as the theatre at two hundred and twenty-two. Surrounded by the stars of to-day, who did him homage, he showed them what Haymarket acting was like in Edwardian days, and he showed them too that he had lost none of his skill, his charm or his power to attract. At that matinée, when the house was filled, not only with the young people of the War, but with his old followers who had flocked there to see him, he played Sir Peter Teazle and a one-act play just as he had played them in the early days of the century. Nothing had gone, nothing had left him. He and the Haymarket were the same in agelessness and in quality. That day he *was* the

Haymarket again as once he had been for nine glorious years. It was another memory to cherish. It was something which proved that the past can live with the present and show no wear and tear, no loss of value. He was acclaimed; he was cheered and he raised a magnificent sum for the R.A.F. Benevolent Fund. It was, to some people there, more than a marvellous occasion, more than the momentary return of a figure of the Haymarket. It was almost a rebirth of the theatre, a reunion of its great —all of them seemed to be there, not only Maude, not only the shade of Buckstone, but the great shadows of the past, Fielding, Macklin, Henderson, Elliston, Edwin, Buckstone, Shuter, Palmer, Liston, Macready, the two Colmans, Phelps, Creswick, the Kendals, Gilbert, Vestris, Dibdin, Kean, Sothern, Webster, the Bancrofts, Tree, even old John Potter and that strange man, Johnson of Chester, all seemed to have come to celebrate this continued fame of their old playhouse—even "Romeo" Coates might have been welcome—to applaud the man who at eighty still stood upright, smiling, confident, a master of his art, the exemplar of what Haymarket, and English comedy acting really meant. And the history of the Haymarket stood around him and bowed. Times had changed, much had happened, life itself was different, but the Haymarket and its true sons and daughters remained as they were—standing for the quiet greatness of their country, for a time when quality mattered more than almost anything else. It was a wonderful Haymarket occasion, almost unparalleled in theatrical history, and not to be lightly forgotten.

And on that scene which joined the past of the Haymarket with its present, by an actual living link, the curtain must fall upon the story of this unique and beautiful playhouse. Omissions there are, but the framework is here, in proper sequence and in order. The Haymarket began, the Haymarket goes on—the end is not yet.

All that remains is, to follow the fashion of the Haymarket's own youth and to speak its epilogue . . . no, not an epilogue, for that comes at the end of a story—and the end of the Haymarket's story is far away; all that can be marked is an interval.

CHAPTER XXX

INTERVAL MUSIC

Now comes an interval in the story of the Haymarket Theatre. Two hundred and twenty-seven years have passed since that story began; it is devoutly to be hoped that an even longer period will pass before that stately playhouse disappears from the London it has graced for so long. For over two and a quarter centuries it has watched London change, watched many things come and go, watched the methods of living alter with the clothes of London's inhabitants, watched life quicken from a measured tread to fever heat. Two world wars have come and gone, but still the Haymarket stands, unmoved and untroubled. It is so English, so tenacious, so very sure of itself. It has, indeed, few fears. So far it has not altered its methods or control; it remains individual whilst so many of its companions are becoming mere cogs in a wheel. It has kept its personality through all that time. That is not surprising, for only two other theatres in London have anything like its antiquity. Theatre Royal, Drury Lane, is its senior by fifty-seven years, the Royal Opera House, Covent Garden (once Theatre Royal, Covent Garden) is its junior by twelve years. All three are Theatres Royal, even if the Haymarket's actual Charter died with Samuel Foote. It stands on royal soil, however; it is a Crown lease, so it is secure and can still be regarded as a royal theatre. Old Drury stands where it has always stood, but it has altered its outward semblance four times and its interior many times. Covent Garden has changed out of all recognition from the theatre which Rich built, although it still stands where it did. The Haymarket has changed its exterior once only—and shifted its position a few yards from its original site, so slight a change as to be disregarded. It, too, has often changed its interior. But every change there has made it nobler, more beautiful, more of the aristocrat. It maintains the past whilst accepting the present. It was the last theatre to change from candles to gas, it was late with electricity, for it likes the old ways, although it does not refuse the new. And the new ways, in some strange manner, melt into it, so that the change is not noticeable. The Haymarket might still be candle-lit, so complete is its atmosphere. It is to-day a beautiful modern theatre, perfectly equipped with all a modern theatre needs. Yet it remains the same place as it was when Fielding fought for freedom, when Theophilus Cibber used it to defy Drury Lane, when Foote flouted the law of the land, when the Colmans worked there, when Liston made them laugh, when Macready wore the wonderful waistcoat, when "Romeo" Coates made a fool of himself, when Buckstone and Sothern drew all London and put

Dundreary whiskers on the cheeks of the "swells," when the Bancrofts retired, when Tree did *Trilby* . . . it is a microcosm of England, which takes all alterations, absorbs all shocks, and still remains the same at heart. For the Haymarket insists on being itself, and indeed can do no better. It eschews the froth of progress, the spume of chromium and metal, of barbaric architecture calling itself modernity, of the braying of microphonic amplification, the conquest by machinery. It takes only what seems best to it. Like an old English inn, it gives comfort and service with dignity and quietude. It does not shout, it relies upon its reputation.

But it keeps abreast of the needs of its patrons. It gives them space which accords with its dignity. It knows that even Haymarket audiences contain a large proportion of people to whom a play is simply a series of intervals between drinks. So it provides for them too. It could not go sideways, or upwards, so it went down. Stuart Watson, who guides it, delved below that lovely auditorium so that Haymarket patrons might be refreshed in comfort. He gave them no, not bars, but a salon—large, spacious, airy and dignified, decorated in perfect taste, where there is no pushing and confusion, but where English people could have their English drinks, their tea, or their coffee or their more potent liquids, in the same atmosphere as that which they had just left and to which they would return. There is no suggestion of a public-house, no suggestion of a cocktail bar at a night club or a restaurant. It has the drawing-room atmosphere, or, more correctly, the air of the salon—not the saloon. And there is such a difference.

Nobody shouts at the Haymarket, nobody rushes about, the staff are quiet, courtly, and unobtrusive. They are like the well-trained servants in the old-time English mansion. And like those old-time people, they are proud to be there.

Most people, when they go to a theatre, never look to the right or the left. Many arrive late and hurry to their seats. Most of them talk all the time. They believe that, in a theatre, all there is to see is the play. How wrong such people are. They cross the Rotunda at Drury Lane oblivious of the fact that they are breathing history; they crowd into Covent Garden unaware of the mid-Victorian charm, and they go to the Haymarket as if they were entering a cinema.

Perhaps it is not their fault, for to-day people are so accustomed to machine aid, to the twirling of knobs, to the pressing of buttons, to the touching of switches—so accustomed to having most things done for them, so accustomed to seeing everything look just the same wherever they go that, when they are face to face with individuality, they pay no heed. When next the Haymarket is visited, look around you.

You enter from the street under a portico of noble pillars and at once the years drop away. You have stepped back in time, a thing which it is easy to do in London, if only you are conscious of it. You are in a vestibule, still small, as is the Haymarket tradition, but unlike the vestibule of any other playhouse. It has rich woods in its panels and pillars, and its box office has a large window (which invites you to buy), not those odd little half-secret orifices common to so many theatres. There, in that box office sits Miss Mary Flynn, who went there a very young girl thirty years ago, as Mr. Leverton's assistant and now carries on the efficient courtliness and grace of the Haymarket. All the attendants are quiet-voiced and polite. If you want to go to the dress circle you go upstairs, through doors which shut out the draughts and noise of the outer world, and you will notice that the walls are covered, not with paint or distemper or modern stuff, but with rich wallpaper which strikes exactly the right note. The dress circle is partitioned off at the back with glass screens, shutting out the undesirable noises and making the place warm and draughtless.

Perhaps you want to see the Manager, Mr. Stuart Watson. You go down a corridor and find white, gleaming doors. You enter the managerial suite. You are in an office—but something which is totally unlike an office. It is a lovely panelled room, and it leads to an equally delightful inner apartment. You seem to be in a real old English country house, or the Town mansion of the eighteenth century. There is no suggestion of modern office equipment, so terrifyingly efficient and yet so useless after all. For Mr. Watson, who runs the Haymarket so efficiently, is, you see, at home.

The walls are adorned with exquisite prints—mostly of the Haymarket and of people who have played there. History is in the air and on those walls, too. If you are lucky, Mr. Watson will take you round and Charles La Trobe will accompany you. They will show you that stage, which is on the street level, and still has windows opening on to the street— a thing unique in theatres. Indeed, you step from the street on to the stage almost at once. They will point out the old beams above the stage, and the old grid, too. And you will notice that it is all as spick and span as a battleship. A bomb missed them by a few feet and destroyed Garlands Hotel, which adjoins that stage door. A paving stone, hurled high in the air, fell through the stage skylight, but did no other harm, save to a few fittings. Five times the Haymarket was hit by incendiaries, but the staff put them out. The Haymarket endures.

You go to the front of the stage and look from there at the auditorium. There is the theatre of perfection spread out before you. It is quiet and it is regal. Its lovely tones of marble, old gold, its mellowed panels of timber, all harmonise into a perfect whole. It has two tiers nowadays —there used to be three. There were three in the Bancroft reconstruction and the third was done away with in 1905—which is the auditorium you see to-day. You look at the ceiling with its paintings like those of an Old Master. That ceiling was painted by Joseph Harker, the great theatre artist. And, having got himself up there, he refused to come down until he had finished the job. His sons took his food up to him.

The sweep of the circles is majestic, the lighting and its placing is ideal. Romaine Walker, who did the job in 1905, and Joseph Harker, who designed and painted those ceiling pictures and murals, made it all new and still retained the traditional atmosphere. It might never have been touched since 1720; if they told you so, you would believe it.

The reason is that this English theatre only uses the best of everything and therefore shows value all the time. Leaving the stage, a long-carpeted and wall-papered corridor takes you to the Royal Box. You go into the Royal Room first. Now, all royal boxes have royal retiring rooms behind them. That at the Haymarket is an eighteenth-century drawing-room, with a marble fireplace above which stands a beautiful mirror with a carved, gilded frame. It is genuine period, so is every piece of furniture in the room. Here you have the best of the past around you. The Royal Box itself is spacious and comfortable and on the stalls level.

You notice the carpet, blue, with a gold "H" surmounted by a crown, and that the seats match the carpet—blue, gold, blue-white and lovely wood panels everywhere. All the colours are quiet, nothing clashes, nothing glitters. It has the rich maturity of old wine. And Mr. Watson and Charles La Trobe gaze at it lovingly. Then again into that Queen Anne salon, to hear how it was dug out of the sand which is below the theatre until the London blue clay was reached. How it has fifteen-feet thick walls with concrete about them and steel sheeting inside. But you see the delicate Queen Anne tints, the beautiful mouldings, the work of John Murray, and you are grateful again for the preservation of atmosphere. It might have been so different. During the excavation— which the beginning of World War II interfered with—they found only a couple of old pennies, an ancient wooden waterpipe and an old sword, eaten away with rust. Nobody knows where that sword came from. Some say it was a "property" sword, but what would it be doing there, so deep down and so far from the stage? One likes to think—and to believe—that it was lost during one of those old Haymarket riots (when the Little Theatre in the Hay stood next door), perhaps during that riot against the French players, perhaps during the fine old row over Foote's Bottle Conjuror. It might even be the sword the Duke of Cumberland lost and advertised for. Or perhaps, even, it was flourished by one of those vengeful tailors clamouring for the blood of sturdy old Devonshire Dowton. Anyway, it is a Haymarket sword.

Everywhere there is charm, peace, soft colouring, perfect matching and harmony. There is that indefinable atmosphere which holds you and grips you. Almost all its staff, from Mr. Watson downwards, have spent their lives there. Charlotte Pitcher, still alert and in her eighties, was the Haymarket's housekeeper for fifty odd years and kept the theatre as it should be kept. Chippendale, who died only a year or so ago, was there when the Haymarket was lit by gas, and he supervised the introduction of electricity by Tree—he spent a lifetime there. It was not his fault either when the new electric lights caused an unrehearsed effect.

Tree spoke of how gently the evening was falling. The staff, new to the electric lights, switched them down, and down they went—with a crash. That evening fell heavily. It only happened once. That lovely crown-decked carpet has a story too. It was extended by Frederick Harrison to cover the pit. Tree came to see this wonder. "A carpet in the pit," he said. "But they'll spit on it." "Not in the Haymarket," came the quiet reply.

Upstairs, downstairs, wherever you go, is the same air of peace and changelessness, the same feeling of well being.

Stand at last in the vestibule and look out at modern London flowing by. You hear no sound because of those well-fitted doors, yet you are flush with the pavement and almost on it. Perhaps in your ears is the sound of a distant minuet. There goes London of to-day past the Haymarket of to-day, which is also the Haymarket Theatre of yesterday, the day before and many years on top of that. The building has changed once, the interior several times, yet it is still the Haymarket of old, the Haymarket of Georgian London. And that London which rolls by, although it wears different clothes, and travels in a different way, is still the same old London that the older Haymarket Theatre knew. Beneath that asphalt roadway, those paving stones, still lies the earth which knew the roll of the hay-wains, felt the prod of the horses hooves and somewhere too in that earth lies the roots of the old hedgerows, and many seeds now dormant which would, if those stones were cleared away, bloom again in the sun and the rain. But the Haymarket Theatre, the finest flower of the old Hay Market, of that erstwhile country lane, still stands and blooms, its roots down with those hedgerows and old trees. Sun may scorch it, snow drape its pediment, rain beat upon its roof and its walls, but it stands foursquare, laughing at time and laughing at the bombs which scarred its neighbours, a part of that London which never changes inwardly, wearing its crown, holding to its title—a King's house on King's land—a landmark of London for centuries past and, please heaven, for centuries to come. May war, time or town-planner never interfere with that precious part of London—of England itself, held within the Little Theatre in the Hay, that playhouse of perfection.

LONDON
  May 22nd, 1947.

LIST OF PLAYS

INDEX

The Performance to commence at SEVEN with Mr. CHARLES MATHEWS's revived Comidetta THE

WOLF & THE LAMB.

General Dragonfeld		Mr. CHIPPENDALE.
Colonel Breeze	Mr. HOWE.	Mr. W. FARREN.
Henrietta	Miss LINDLEY.	Rhu Honeycomb · Mr. M. OLIVER.
		Mary Miss WEEKYS.

After which, at a Quarter to Eight, (7th, 8th, 9th, 10th, 11th, & 12th Time) a New and Original Comedy in Three Acts, entitled

OUR AMERICAN COUSIN

The Dresses by Mr. BARRETT & Miss CHEERY.   Properties by Mr. FOSTER.   Machinery by Mr. OLIVER WALES.
" THE ENGRAVINGS BY

Messrs. O'CONNOR & HOBBIS.